Dr. Jerry McElroy

Urbanization, Planning and Development in the Caribbean

edited by
Robert B. Potter

MANSELL

LONDON AND NEW YORK

First published 1989 by
Mansell Publishing Limited, *A Cassell Imprint*
Artillery House, Artillery Row, London SW1P 1RT, England
125 East 23rd Street, Suite 300, New York 10010, USA

British Library Cataloguing in Publication Data
Urbanization, planning and development in the Caribbean.
　　1. Caribbean region, Urbanization
　　I. Potter, Robert B.
　　307.7′6′091821

　　ISBN 0-7201-2012-8

Library of Congress Cataloging-in-Publication Data
Urbanization, planning, and development in the Caribbean / edited by
　Robert B. Potter.
　　　p.　　cm.
　　Includes index.
　　ISBN 0-7201-2012-8: $54.00
　　1. Urbanization—Caribbean Area.　2. Regional planning—Caribbean
　Area.　3. Caribbean Area—Economic policy.　4. Caribbean Area—Social
　policy.　I. Potter, Robert B.
　　HT384.C37U73　1989
　　307.76′09729—dc20　　　　　　　　　　　　　　　　　89-31618
　　　　　　　　　　　　　　　　　　　　　　　　　　　　　CIP

This book has been printed and bound in Great Britain. Typeset in
Compugraphic Paladium by Colset (Private) Ltd., Singapore, and printed and
bound by Biddles Ltd., Guildford, on Onslow Book Wove paper.

Contents

for Katherine

Preface

This book stems from the general lack of readily accessible material on urban, planning and development issues in the Caribbean region. Often, even quite basic background materials are hard if not impossible to come by; for instance, those summarizing existing housing conditions within principal cities, or overviews of the local housing market, the structure of employment or the history of national settlement policies. If the need is for a source which covers all of these issues together with other cognate ones for a particular country or group of territories, the task is harder still. Those who seek comparative data and accompanying interpretative essays covering the countries of the Caribbean as a whole will find little to aid them.

Perhaps this situation is not so surprising given the history of the Caribbean region and its foundations in plantations and agriculture. But fundamental though these agrarian and rural influences remain today, nonetheless, contemporary Caribbean societies are also strongly urban in character, a feature which poses a series of challenges. More specifically, the balance between rural and urban imperatives is a crucial ingredient in the development debate. Further, approaches that play down the salience of the interrelations and interactions that exist between rural and urban areas in the contemporary Caribbean are not likely to be greatly beneficial to any serious consideration of Caribbean development paths.

It would, of course, have been nice if a single author had been able to address these themes across the entire Caribbean region. But the reality is different. Although it is not too difficult to identify common elements in the urban histories of Caribbean countries, such as those of rapidly growing cities and towns, shortages of adequate housing, underemployment, unemployment and misemployment, and uneven patterns of national development, the variations and contrasts that characterize these countries are just as intriguing, and presumably are of far greater importance to those whose job it is to formulate policies. The region is so complex and diverse that clearly a whole team of authors was required. In the end, the list of contributors covers academics, public servants and planners. They presently reside in the Caribbean, United States, United Kingdom and Australia, and in disciplinary terms cover the fields of geography, planning, economics, political science and sociology. It is regretted that the chapter commissioned on the Dominican Republic and Haiti was not received for publication.

I was fortunate to find a publisher enthusiastic about the project from the outset. In particular, I must single out Penelope Beck for her positive and patient support, advice and encouragement. Over and above their written contributions to the book, Dennis Conway, Brian Hudson, Colin Clarke and Klaus de Albuquerque provided valued assistance at the start; as also did Hugh Clout and Jean Soumange. Within the Department of Geography at Royal Holloway and Bedford New College, University of London, Kathy Roberts assisted with some retyping, and Erica Milwain and Ron Halfhide drew several of the figures. The editing was completed during sabbatical leave provided by the College, for which I am extremely grateful. Virginia provided invaluable help with proofing and indexing.

Robert B. Potter
Englefield Green

Contributors

Thomas D. Boswell, Professor of Geography, University of Miami.

James E. Biggs, Graduate Student, Department of Geography, University of Miami.

Colin Clarke, Lecturer in Geography, University of Oxford and Fellow of Jesus College.

Dennis Conway, Associate Professor of Geography at Indiana University.

Klaus de Albuquerque, Professor of Sociology at the College of Charleston, South Carolina.

Peter Furley, Senior Lecturer in Geography, University of Edinburgh.

Albert Gastmann, Professor of Political Science, Trinity College, Hartford, Connecticut.

Derek Hall, Principal Lecturer in Geography, Sunderland Polytechnic.

Brian Hudson, Senior Lecturer in Urban and Regional Planning, Queensland University of Technology.

Scott MacDonald, International Economic Adviser, Office of the Comptroller of Currency, Washington, DC.

Jerome McElroy, Professor of Economics at St Mary's College, Indiana.

Robert B. Potter, Reader in Geography, Royal Holloway and Bedford New College, University of London.

Guy Robinson, Lecturer in Geography, University of Edinburgh.

Mike Samson, Social Geographer and Demographer of the Government of Curaçao.

Alan Strachan, Lecturer in Geography, University of Leicester.

Mark Wilson, Geography Teacher at Queen's College, Barbados, and formerly Housing Planner with the Ministry of Housing and Lands, Barbados.

[1]

Urbanization, Planning and Development in the Caribbean: An Introduction

Robert B. Potter

urban Δ = total Δ

In common with the other nations making up what is referred to as the Third World, colonialism and dependent development are critical to an understanding of the Caribbean. In fact, colonial status and dependency can be said to represent the whole history of the Caribbean region (Lowenthal, 1972). The legacy of colonial settlement and subsequent orientation to West European economies is witnessed in a large number of shared socio-economic characteristics, foremost among which are open economies with strong agricultural orientations and a marked tendency toward monoculture. But these forces are just as apparent in the form of dependent urbanization, the realities of which are vividly expressed in the highly skewed and spatially uneven urban settlement patterns that are to be found throughout the Caribbean region. The small size of Caribbean countries adds a further dimension to these socio-spatial characteristics. Post-war trends toward the development of tourism and manufacturing industry as generators of economic change are held by some to be generally promoting increasing levels of what may be referred to as 'urban bias' in development.

Overview

The aim of the present volume is to provide a comprehensive overview of both historical and contemporary facets of urbanization, economic change and planning in the Caribbean region taken as a whole. Although traditionally seen as falling within the hegemony of the United States, in the post-war independence period, variant paths to economic development and territorial planning have been followed in the region. These have ranged from state socialist approaches in Cuba, and at specific junctures and to varying degrees in Grenada, Guyana and

1

Jamaica, through to mixed economies of an avowedly capitalist persuasion.

Presently, there is no text covering in a detailed, comprehensive and comparative manner the related issues of urbanization, territorial planning and development paths in this strategic world region. The volume published by Cross (1979) some 10 years ago still represents the principal work concerning urbanization in the Caribbean. Although this remains a useful and interesting text, its scope is strongly sociological and theoretical, and the overall approach thematic, covering theories of urbanization and dependence, the economic order, population structure, social organization, race, class, education and politics. Specifics of planning and detailed consideration of particular territories are not included. A more recently produced monograph by Hope (1986), although supposedly discussing the entire Commonwealth Caribbean, deals specifically only with the four nations of Barbados, Guyana, Jamaica and Trinidad. This book has been specifically designed to fill this gap in the literature on this important region of the developing world.

The examination of the complex issues surrounding urbanization, development and planning in the Caribbean, as well as being of concern to those working in and on the region itself, should assume wider relevance by providing insights for those concerned with other regions. Perhaps no other area of comparable size within the developing world shows such heterogeneity in its political composition, country size, resource base and overall levels of development, ranging from More Developed Countries (MDCs) such as Trinidad and Tobago, Jamaica, Barbados and Guyana, to Less Developed Countries (LDCs) like Dominica, Haiti, St Vincent and St Lucia. The book thereby also stresses a vital, but sometimes neglected theme in geographical development studies, namely that the Third World and its problems are far from homogeneous. Thus, it also emphasizes that current planning and development issues – such as development from below, agropolitan development, selective closure, aided self-help housing imperatives and the economic role of the informal sector of the economy – all need examining afresh in different political, socio-economic and cultural settings. Perhaps, nowhere provides such an 'island microcosm' better than the Caribbean Basin.

Accordingly, this volume presents commissioned chapters on urbanization, planning and development in all the major countries of the Caribbean with the exception of Haiti and the Dominican Republic. A chapter covering these countries under the heading Hispaniola was commissioned but not received in time to be included. As is often emphasized, the Caribbean is a sea and not a land mass. The myriad islands of the Caribbean chain extend over a distance of d it

Table 1.1. Basic data for the Caribbean territories.

Territory	Population ('000s) ca. 1985	Area (1,000 km^2)	Population density (per km^2)	Percentage growth of population p.a., 1970–83
Trinidad and Tobago	1,166	5.1	229	0.5
Jamaica	2,301	11.0	209	1.5
Cuba	9,992	115.0	87	1.1
Barbados	252	0.43	586	0.5
Guyana	936	215.0	4	ND
Eastern Caribbean				
St Lucia	128	0.62	206	1.9
St Vincent	138	0.39	269	2.6
Dominica	92	0.75	100	1.3
Grenada	120	0.34	326	0.9
Montserrat	12	0.098	122	−0.2
Antigua and Barbuda	80	0.44	182	1.5
St Kitts and Nevis	44	0.26	169	0.7
Anguilla	7	0.16	44	0.1
British Virgin Islands	13	0.15	ND	ND
French West Indies				
Martinique	327	1.1	297	−0.7
Guadeloupe	331	1.8	184	−0.4
Belize	159	23.0	7	3.0
Hispaniola				
Dominican Republic	6,102	49.0	125	3.0
Haiti	5,185	28.0	185	1.7
Bahamas	226	14.0	16	2.7
Puerto Rico and the US Virgin Islands				
Puerto Rico	3,398	8.9	382	2.4
US Virgin Islands	105	0.34	309	6.9
Netherlands Antilles	261	0.96	272	1.6

> what does it mean?

ND, no data available.

Sources: *New Geographical Digest* (1986), Fraser (1985).

approximately 4,000 kilometres (Blume, 1974). The countries and groups of countries identified for inclusion in this book are listed in Table 1.1. The aim was to include the experiences of all the principal territories of the region, thereby reflecting its full socio-cultural, political and economic diversity. Accordingly, 12 main groupings of territories have been recognized, covering a total of 23 principal units (Table 1.1). Separate chapters are devoted to the larger territories, such as Cuba, Trinidad and Tobago, Jamaica, Guyana, Bahamas, Netherlands Antilles and Barbados. The large number of territories making up the Eastern Caribbean are covered together in one account, as are Martinique and Guadeloupe under the heading the French

West Indies. Finally, although comprising part of the mainlands of Central and South America respectively, Belize and Guyana are customarily regarded as being part of the Caribbean, and this is true of the present volume.

Viewed at the world scale, the territories of the Caribbean are distinguished by their small size, but the marked variation that characterizes both their territorial extent and population totals is attested by the background statistics given in Table 1.1. These data are provided as a comparative introductory guide and may show minor variations from those included by the authors of the specific country related chapters. As well as the age-old problems surrounding the definition of urban areas, the contributors may have used marginally different data sources and/or time periods. The islands vary in terms of population size, from Cuba with close on 10 million inhabitants to tiny Anguilla with only 7,000. Guyana, on the other hand, has a relatively small population, but is by far and away the largest territory. A further notable general characteristic is the high population densities of Caribbean territories, and in the case of a quite substantial number, levels standing between 200 and over 500 persons per square kilometre are recorded.

Urbanization in the Caribbean

In common with other regions of the developing world, rapid urbanization in the Caribbean is a product of the post-1945 period. This is so despite the establishment of urban centres in the region as points of administrative and commercial control at the outset of the colonial period in the fifteenth and sixteenth centuries (Clarke, 1974). But the large-scale movement of rural populations to urban centres, which has thereby also served to swell rates of natural increase in urban populations, has largely occurred since the late 1940s and 1950s. The twin 'push' of rural poverty and the 'pull' of socio-economic opportunities in the urban arena – both real and perceived – have been effective. Caribbean towns and cities have through time had very little to do with manufacturing activities, but where jobs in the formal sector do exist they are better paid. The existence of enhanced facilities, both in the public and private sectors, has further acted as a spur to cityward migration.

Interestingly, data published by the United Nations (1980) show that the Caribbean region is at present not only considerably more highly urbanized than the Third World in aggregate, but is more highly urbanized than the world as a whole (Table 1.2). This was as true in 1960, when somewhat in excess of a third of the total population of the Caribbean region were living in towns, as it is of the projected

Table 1.2. Total population living in towns and cities and level of urbanization in the Caribbean, 1960–2000.

Date	Total population of the Caribbean living in towns and cities	Percentage of total population living in urban areas	
		Caribbean	World
1960	7.7	38.2	33.9
1970	11.1	45.1	37.5
1980	15.7	52.2	41.3
1990	21.6	58.7	45.9
2000	28.8	64.6	51.3

Source: United Nations (1980).

urbanization level of 64.6 per cent in the year 2000. Currently, it would appear that over half of all Caribbean denizens reside in towns and cities (Table 1.2).

The impact of cities on the socio-economic landscape of the Caribbean region has been dramatic. West and Augelli (1976) note that in 1950, the region had only seven cities with a population over 100,000, three of these being in Cuba. By 1970, the number had risen to at least 12. Table 1.3, which has been compiled by the present author using data derived from the *New Geographical Digest* (1986), shows the population size of capital cities and all those with over 100,000 inhabitants at the latest available date for which data are available. This indicates that in the early to mid-1980s, there were at least 24 urban places which had reached the 100,000 population level. Indeed, three located in the Hispanic Caribbean, Havana, Santo Domingo and San Juan, had well and truly passed the million mark.

Data concerning current levels of urbanization and aspects of economic structure collected by the present author for the groups of territories included in this volume are shown mapped in Figures 1.1 and 1.2. In Figure 1.1, levels of overall urbanization and of urban primacy – the percentage share of national population living in the largest city or town – have been mapped. The pattern revealed reinforces that noted at the regional scale (Table 1.3). The general impression is one of relatively high overall levels of urbanization. The highest total is recorded by Cuba, at 68 per cent, but levels of well over half apply to Puerto Rico, Trinidad and Tobago, Martinique, the Dominican Republic, Bahamas and the Netherlands Antilles. The fact that high levels of urban primacy are common within the region is also clearly attested, and often well over 30 per cent of the total population of territories live in the largest settlement. This is true, for instance, in the cases of Trinidad, Jamaica, St Lucia and Martinique.

Table 1.3. Population of the principal towns and cities of the Caribbean.

Territory	Urban area	Population ('000s)	Date
Trinidad and Tobago	Port of Spain*	250	1982
Jamaica	Kingston*	671	1980
Cuba	Havana*	1,924	1982
	Santiago de Cuba	349	
	Camagüey	251	
	Holguín	190	
	Santa Clara	174	
	Guantánamo	170	
	Cíenfuegos	105	
	Bayamo	109	
	Matanzas	101	
Barbados	Bridgetown*	88	1976
Guyana	Georgetown*	188	1983
Eastern Caribbean			
St Lucia	Castries*	45	1980
St Vincent	Kingstown*	33	1980
Dominica	Roseau*	20	1981
Grenada	St George's*	31	1978
Montserrat	Plymouth*	3	1980
Antigua and Barbuda	St John City*	24	1975
St Kitts and Nevis	Basse-Terre*	15	1980
Anguilla	The Valley*	2	1976
British Virgin Islands	Road Town*	4	1980
French West Indies			
Martinique	Fort-de-France*	100	1982
Guadeloupe	Basse-Terre*	15	1979
Belize	Belmopan*	3	1980
	Belize City	55	1980
Hispaniola			
Dominican Republic	Santo Domingo*	1,313	1981
	Santiago de Los Caballeros	279	
Haiti	Port-au-Prince*	888	1982
Bahamas	Nassau*	130	1977
Puerto Rico and US Virgin Islands			
Puerto Rico	San Juan	1,086	1980
	Ponce	253	
	Bayamón	209	
	Caguas	174	
	Carolina	148	
	Mayagüez	133	
US Virgin Islands	Charlotte Amalie	12	1980
Netherlands Antilles	Willemstad*	146	1971

* Capital city.

Source: *New Geographical Digest* (1986).

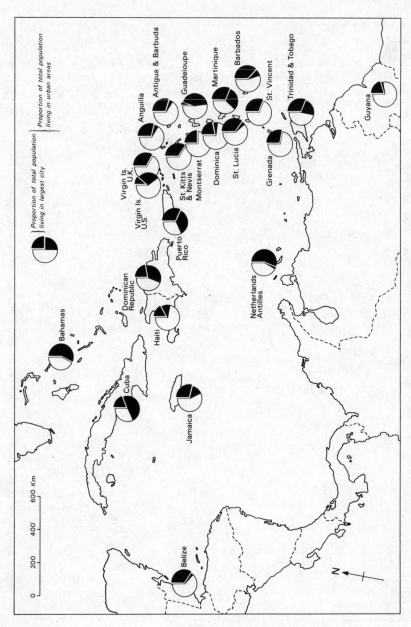

Figure 1.1. Levels of urbanization and urban primacy in the Caribbean.

8

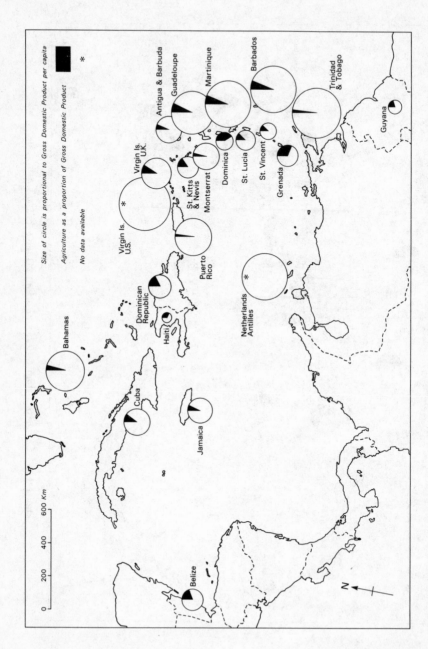

Figure 1.2. Gross Domestic Product per capita and contribution of agriculture to GDP in the Caribbean.

Aspects of current economic structure are summarized in Figure 1.2. Levels of Gross Domestic Product (GDP) per capita are shown, along with the percentage of GDP which is accounted for by agriculture. The figure serves to stress the marked variations in levels of development that pertain in the Caribbean region at the present time, ranging from middle-income countries such as Trinidad (US$5,670), Barbados (US$4,580), Martinique (4,820), Guadeloupe (4,340), Bahamas (3,620), Puerto Rico (3,350), the United States Virgin Islands (7,010) and the Netherlands Antilles (4,540), to the impoverished nations of Haiti (199), Guyana (436), St Vincent (630), and Dominica (750). The interrelationships existing between urban development and economic structure are of some salience. While as anticipated there is a reasonably strong relationship between overall levels of urbanization and of Gross Domestic Product per capita ($r = +0.53$), there is little in the way of an association between urban primacy and GDP ($r = +0.09$). On the other hand, the size of territories as measured by their areal extent is negatively associated with levels of urban primacy ($r = -0.25$).

The fact that the majority of Caribbean nations show high levels of urban primacy is clearly attested by Figure 1.1, and as noted, generally, the major town includes around one-third of the total population of the entire nation. The major growth of primate cities is stressed by West and Augelli (1976) and they note that, generally, the primate urban centre has a population greater than the combined total of the next three largest centres. The pressures on housing, jobs, social services and all manner of facilities that are the outcome of urbanization over and above industrialization were commented on by West and Augelli (1976: 120), in the following terms:

> The disproportionate concentration of a territory's wealth, political power, and social services in the chief urban center inevitably shortchanges the small cities and towns. Whether it be government allocations for new schools, roads, and public housing, or the location of new industry or attracting tourists, the smaller urban communities get far less than their share.

The early gateway origins of urban centres within the Caribbean have not only resulted in strong spatial skew at the national level, but also congestion at the intra-urban scale. West and Augelli (1976: 120) note how the chief consideration in the origin of most Caribbean cities was their function as sheltered maritime ports which could be defended with relative ease. Hence, the typical urban site 'was on the shore of an embayment protected at the land-ward side by commanding hills on which forts overlooking the sea approaches were built'. It is these strategic origins which give many Caribbean capitals their somewhat cramped and huddled character today, with high-density narrow streets which are poorly suited to cars, buses and other commercial vehicles. These commonalities at the intra-urban level are, of course, modified by the prevalent cultural imprint, varying from the grid iron or rectilinear pattern of Spanish colonial towns to the geometrically more varied and *ad hoc* urban form which is more typical of British colonial urban places.

Development Planning in the Caribbean

The big town – small town and developed region – underdeveloped region contrasts have given rise to a near universal social and spatial polarity which has set the overall contemporary agenda for planning and development in the Caribbean region. It can be argued that the problems involved are rendered particularly acute in small dependent nations such as those found in the Caribbean.

The newly independent formerly colonial territories, perhaps inevitably in seeking to develop, came to equate the state of development with the processes of urbanization and industrialization. Having been colonial producers of agricultural staples for so long, when decolonization afforded political independence, it was perhaps inevitable that it should serve to enhance the desire for a measure of economic independence to go with it (Potter, 1985). The movement toward industry as the 'royal road to catching up' (Friedmann and Weaver, 1979: 91) was closely associated with a process of industrialization by import substitution. Such an approach had, of course, an immediate appeal for countries that had traditionally imported most of their manufactures in return for the export of primary products such as sugar. The call for industry as the mechanism for economic development found currency in the West Indies via the arguments of Arthur Lewis (1950), who maintained that an array of industrial activities was possible in the Caribbean. Thus started an era of industrialization by invitation, which boiled down to the attraction of enclave industries – often branch plants established by leading multinationals (Kowalewski, 1982) – by means of affording fiscal incentives, tax-free holidays and infrastructural provision. Such foreign plants frequently produced goods for the overseas home market, manufacturing such items as ice hockey equipment, for instance. This policy was successfully pioneered in Puerto Rico, with its 'Operation Bootstrap', and was soon followed elsewhere in the Caribbean region.

The relative merits and disadvantages of industrialization by invitation have been discussed on many occasions, but the arguments are particularly polarized in the case of territories the size of those in the

Caribbean. While jobs are created both directly, and indirectly through the operation of income multipliers, there are many problems that are associated with such developments. The size and financial might of many First World corporations have undoubtedly meant that they have been able to exact favourable terms in their negotiations with Third World governments. At the extreme, they have, for example, been able to threaten during negotiations, that if their terms are not met, they will, quite simply, go elsewhere. Equally, even when established, some stay only while the going remains good, leaving during hard times, or when the tax-free period expires. Similar arguments apply with respect to that other great component of post-war economic change in the Caribbean, tourism (Bryden, 1973). In this instance, it is accepted that there are massive leakages of the revenues that are brought in. The dependency theory school, following the seminal writings of Frank (1969), and locally in the Caribbean those of George Beckford (1972, 1975), maintain that by these mechanisms, the dependent relations of the pre-colonial era have merely been replaced by equally pervasive forms of neo-colonialism (see Clarke, 1986). This is all the more alarming for those who see a geographical corollary in deepening spatial concentration on the primate city/coastal zone, bolstering the kinds of spatial contrasts alluded to previously.

In a recent essay, the present author has attempted to provide an examination of the special relevance of these arguments in small dependent nations such as those found in the Southern Caribbean (Potter, 1989a). This discussion culminated in the presentation of a model pointing to the difficulties confronting such nations, and this is reproduced here as Figure 1.3. The exogenous realities for Caribbean territories consist, on the one hand, of the extraction of social surplus value, both by the export of agricultural staples and raw material resources at minimal market prices, and investment and expenditure abroad by élite groups. In the other direction, flows of imported foods, manufactured goods, tourists, enclave industrialization, new technology, aid and consumerism are characteristic. The geographical pull of accessible and previously well-developed sites with good infrastructural facilities for industry, and of safe and scenic beaches with regard to tourism have served to skew recent developments to those very same leeward coastal tracts that centuries earlier had first attracted mercantile capital (Potter, 1989a). The channelling of new developments into the 'relative economic oases' might be said by some to have left an 'economic desert'. The socio-economic contrasts between the two are real and affect the daily lives of citizens, but are based on strong urban–rural flows which involve unequal exchange. This may be in the form of low procurement prices for agricultural products or low wages in the tourist and domestic sectors. The disadvantageous terms of trade

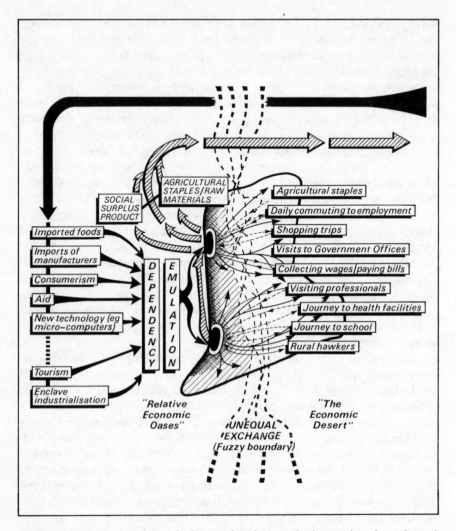

Figure 1.3. A simplified model of internal and external relations for a hypothetical Caribbean country. (Source: Potter, 1989a:271).

that affect Third World countries at the global scale are thereby matched by harsh urban–rural terms within countries. This is revealed in long journeys to shops, places of education, health centres, government offices and all manner of other facilities. But the twist in the case of island micro-states is that small territorial size and the historical legacy of concentrated infrastructural provision may well be used as a justification for maintaining or even enhancing a highly polarized pattern of spatial development. The model is a greatly simplified one, and light will no doubt be cast on its appropriateness in different Caribbean settings by the various contributors to this book. Clearly, the model will be modified by territorial size, by culture and, most significantly, by the precise paths to development that countries have pursued over the past 20 year period.

The model of capitalist, centre-out, 'top-down' economic development planning which was applied as an article of faith in the 1960s and 1970s, has been questioned as an invariant path to progress. In its place, ideas for periphery-in and 'bottom-up', collectivist and socialist systems of change and development have been articulated more recently. If countries of the Third World have been held up rather than pushed forward by their close involvement in the past with the First World, it is logical to posit that they must cut themselves off to some degree if they are to reduce the shackles of their dependency (Potter, 1989b). In the Caribbean, such an approach is, of course, well exemplified by the case of Cuba in the post-1959 revolutionary era (see, for example, Hall, 1981; Susman, 1974, 1987). In Cuba, the main thrusts of planning and development have all involved strenuous efforts to urbanize the countryside and to ruralize the town so as to reduce rural–urban differences in both consumption and production (Acosta and Hardoy, 1973; Gugler, 1980; Slater, 1986).

It is an important theme of this book that policies which affect urban development are inextricably bound up with overall strategies of economic development and thus by extension to societal and political goals in general: 'In particular, these wider aims involve fundamental ideological and political choices concerning the economic efficacy and social morality of personal and territorial welfare differences, and the overarching concepts of social justice and equity' (Potter, 1989b: 323).

It is precisely these arguments which have underlined the drift of other countries to the socialist model of economic structure within the Caribbean (see Jameson, 1981). In the 1970s, Forbes Burnham and his People's National Congress government declared Guyana a Co-operative Socialist Republic (Payne, 1984). Burnham saw the path that he was taking as somewhat different to that of pure communism, but the approach did, nevertheless, involve state nationalization of the bauxite and sugar industries. At about the same time, Michael Manley came to power in Jamaica and his People's National Party Government stressed equality as the touchstone of its vision of democratic socialism.

But perhaps the most incisive development of the 1970s was the coup led by Maurice Bishop and the New Jewel Movement in Grenada in 1979 (Henfrey, 1984). This brought to power the People's Revolutionary Government after a period of very repressive rule associated with Eric Gairy. As a result of the revolutionary government's concern with nationalism, participatory democracy and its establishment of close links with Cuba, Payne (1984: 20) has eloquently described the Eastern Caribbean in the wake of these changes as a potential 'Sea of Splashing Dominoes', as other countries showed some signs of drifting toward the left. The struggle between left and right was well and truly once again in Uncle Sam's backyard and would lead to the eventual overthrow and death of Maurice Bishop, and militarily to the US invasion of Grenada. Not that this brief account of these battles of left and right in the Commonwealth Caribbean represents anything other than a cursory summary of the political economy of development in the region, as the final overthrow of dictators such as Rafael Trujillo in 1961 and Baby Doc Duvalier in 1986 in the Dominican Republic and Haiti respectively bear ample witness (see Payne, 1984; Vendovato, 1986; Potter and Binns, 1988).

Planning the balance which is to be established between urban and rural initiatives and investments is central to the whole issue of development planning. At whatever resolution, planning involves a degree of state control over pure market forces, focusing particularly on the balance that is struck between the autonomy of the individual and the collective responsibility of the state (Conyers, 1982; Cooke, 1983; Potter, 1985). The goals and aims of physical development or spatial land use planning must conform with those of systematic branches of the corporate planning exercise, such as economic and social planning. It is the issues that surround urban change and development which form the focus of the individual contributions to the present volume.

Structure and Content of Chapters

The book aims to cover the contemporary and past implications of these factors, thereby providing the first-ever comparative account of urbanization and development planning in this diverse region. The country-by-country essays have been written by academics who have undertaken intensive research in the countries concerned. Given the diversity of urban and developmental experiences of Caribbean territories, the contributors were invited at the outset to consider the salience of a number of themes in structuring and preparing their chapters on specific countries or groups of countries. Each and every writer was, of course, free to organize and develop their arguments as they saw fit, and thereby to vary the emphasis, adding to, modifying or even deleting entirely the themes initially suggested for consideration. In the event, most of the authors have made at least skeletal use of the suggested framework. Hopefully, this has enhanced the comparative utility of the volume, and helped to negate the customary complaint that

edited books lack coherence. Specifically, it was suggested that the
authors might consider five broad topics:

1   *The historical circumstances of urban development*: a summary
    from initial colonization to the present, with particular emphasis
    being placed on the era of mercantilism, primary production, social
    structure, dependency theory, and the degree of skew of population,
    settlement and economic activity.

2   *An overview of the present rate and pattern of urbanization*:
    focusing on the national scale and between major administrative
    areas, charting the contemporary circumstances of rural-to-urban
    migration, natural increase and the like, using the latest census data
    and/or research, and assessing their significance.

3   *A broad overview of the links existing between current and past
    urbanization and patterns of economic development*: that is,
    defining economic development in the sense of change, whether this
    is judged to be positive or negative (Brookfield, 1975). In this
    regard, possible topics for consideration included the degree to
    which an explicit urban-industrial path to development has been
    followed, the effects on agriculture, the influence of tourism, socio-
    cultural traditions, size of country, multinational companies, aid
    and trade, and perceptions of society and space. Commentaries on
    both spatial and social inequalities are germane here, along with
    an assessment of the degree to which patterns of territorial deve-
    lopment can adequately be explained by internationalist and
    nationalist factors respectively.

4   *The internal structure of the leading urban settlements or zones*:
    with particular reference to social structure (class, race, ethnicity),
    housing conditions, employment and the provision of goods and
    welfare services, the roles of the informal and formal sectors, and
    the extent of their interrelation.

5   *Planning and politics*: as expressed at all spatial scales and from
    physical development (land use) to social and economic planning.
    The historical development of the national planning system might
    profitably be chronicled, together with its philosophy (top-down,
    bottom-up, élitist, participatory, industrial, agropolitan, basic
    needs and selective closure, secondary cities, decentralization), and
    the treatment of housing issues (self-help, state provision, and aided
    self-help) might all receive attention.

Final Comments

A great deal of popular concern and interest surround the idea that places around the globe are gradually becoming more and more alike. Indeed, superficially there seems to be more than a grain of truth to this observation. Cities and towns, whether they are located in the developed or developing regions of the world, contain the same types of large stores and high-rise apartment blocks and are increasingly oriented to, if not dominated by, the motor car. Likewise, the consumption of essentially the same range of fast foods, soft drinks, cigarettes and cars, generally manufactured by multinational companies, is as prevalent in Kingston or San Juan as it is in London or New York.

In more academic terms, writers on urban development and the global economy, such as Armstrong and McGee (1985), have emphasized what they see as the increasing *convergence* or similarity that is occurring between countries with regard to patterns of consumption, as mediated through the dominant capitalist economic system. It might be added that this applies particularly to high-income groups in developing countries who in many circumstances lead lives virtually identical to those of their counterparts to be found in cities in the developed world. But viewed at the world scale, the reverse seems to be true of patterns of production, with respect to which increasing *divergence* or dissimilarity appears to be characterizing countries around the world. This is related to the international division of labour, whereby some countries are regarded as industrial strongholds and others as primary producers.

The role of cities and the nature of the relationships established and maintained between urban and rural areas is crucial in this regard (Potter and Unwin, 1989). Some maintain that cities are the spatial points at which new forms of production and consumption are introduced, gradually to be spread beneficially to the rural peripheral areas. Others refute this essentially modernizationist argument, pointing to what they see as the role of the city in diffusing patterns of consumption, while production, incomes, wealth and power are ever more concentrated in major urban-industrial nodes, generally those of the metropoles.

The 'divergence of production and convergence of consumption' thesis is extremely interesting, for it provides at least a broad framework for understanding why it is that at the global level, in certain respects urban form and urban life are increasingly homogeneous, while in other respects, wide differences, as exemplified by shanty towns and massive participation rates in the informal sector, for example, point to differences if not of kind, then certainly of degree. How have states assessed and responded to the balance between processes of convergence and divergence, and how have they reacted in their programmes of economic, social and physical development planning, so as to affect the balance existing between urban and rural portions of the national territory? To what extent has the emphasis been placed on increasing domestic production, particularly in the spheres of agriculture and import-substitution industrialization as opposed to allowing consumption norms to converge on those of the west? These issues assume a special relevance in small-island micro-states such as those which are to be found in the Caribbean region.

Surprisingly, however, the rise of systematic environmental planning has been relatively slow in the Caribbean (Clarke, 1974). There is an argument that it is the small size, relative insularity and parochialism of West Indian societies that mean that policy makers and politicians rarely think in spatial, geographical and locational terms. Further, this is also reflected in a relative dearth of material on urbanization and planning issues in the Caribbean, despite one or two interesting essays written on the topic early on (see, for instance, Broom, 1953; Stevens, 1957). Indeed, as Franklin (1979) has noted, with respect to the Third World in general, spatial land use planning is seen by many as far less important than economic development planning, with some effectively regarding it if not as an irrelevance, then certainly as a luxury. Hudson (1986) has stressed the importance of physical planning in the Caribbean region, pointing in particular to the fragile nature of their ecosystems. The Caribbean is a zone which faces a considerable array of physical environmental hazards, as witnessed by the devastation suffered in Jamaica as a result of Hurricane Gilbert. In addition, the region is associated with periodic economic, political and social upheavals, as demonstrated by events in Grenada and more recently, Haiti.

It is the comparative basis of this volume, set in an essentially heterogeneous context that is important. For example, while all of these territories share colonialism as a key historical trait, the involvement of the Spanish, French, Dutch and British, among others, means that the islands are indelibly stamped by contrasting socio-cultural imprints. First and foremost, the chapters presented in this book represent first-hand empirical reports and critiques of past developments and current policies from the active battlefront of a zone where stark environmental, cultural, social, political and ideological contasts are to be witnessed. In such circumstances, planning – literally foreseeing and guiding change in all spheres of social and economic life – not only involves the widest possible remit, but stands as a particularly tall order. The planning process itself and the kinds of applied research which are needed to support it can only benefit from detailed scrutiny of the urban planning and developmental experiences – both shared and contrasting – of the various territories which comprise the region.

ACKNOWLEDGEMENTS

Thanks are due to Brian Hudson, Derek Hall and Colin Clarke for their comments on this chapter.

REFERENCES

Acosta, M. and Hardoy, J. (1973) *Urban Reform in Revolutionary Cuba*, Occasional Paper No. 1, New Haven, Connecticut: Antilles Research Program: Yale University.

Armstrong, W. and McGee, T.G. (1985) *Theatres of Accumulation: Studies in Asian and Latin American Urbanization*, London: Methuen.

Beckford, G.L. (1972) *Persistent Poverty: Underdevelopment in Plantation Economies of the Third World*, New York: Oxford University Press.

Beckford, G.L. (1975) 'Caribbean rural economy', in: Beckford, G.L. (ed.) *Caribbean Economy: Dependence and Backwardness*, Mona, Jamaica: Institute of Social and Economic Research.

Blume, H. (1974) *The Caribbean Islands*, London: Longman.

Brookfield, H. (1975) *Interdependent Development*, London: Methuen.

Broom, L. (1953) 'Urban research in the British Caribbean: a prospectus', *Social and Economic Research*, 1, 113–19.

Bryden, J. (1973) *Tourism and Development: A Case Study of the Commonwealth Caribbean*, New York: Cambridge University Press.

Clarke, C. (1974) 'Urbanization in the Caribbean', *Geography*, 59, 223–32.

Clarke, C. (1986) 'Sovereignty, dependency and social change in the Caribbean', in: *South America and the Caribbean*, London: Europa Publications.

Conyers, D. (1982) *An Introduction to Social Planning in the Third World*, Chichester: Wiley.

Cooke, P. (1983) *Theories of Planning and Spatial Development*, London: Hutchinson.

Cross, M. (1979) *Urbanization and Urban Growth in the Caribbean: An Essay on Social Change in Dependent Societies*, London: Cambridge University Press.

Frank, A.G. (1969) *Capitalism and Underdevelopment in Latin America*, New York: Monthly Review Press.

Franklin, G.H. (1979) 'Physical development planning and the Third World', *Third World Planning Review*, 1, 7–22.

Fraser, P.D. (1985) *Caribbean Economic Handbook*, London: Euromonitor Publications.

Friedmann, J. and Weaver, C. (1979) *Territory and Function: The Evolution of Regional Planning*, London: Arnold.

Gugler, J. (1980) 'A minimum of urbanism and a maximum of ruralism: the Cuban experience', *International Journal of Urban and Regional Research*, 4, 516–35.

Hall, D. (1981) 'Town and country planning in Cuba', *Town and Country Planning*, 50, 81–3.

Henfrey, C. (1984) 'Between populism and Leninism: the Grenadian experience', *Latin American Perspectives*, 11, 15–36.

Hope, K.R. (1986) *Urbanization in the Commonwealth Caribbean*, Boulder, Colorado: Westview Press.

Hudson, B. (1986) 'Landscape as resource for national development: a Caribbean view', *Geography*, 71, 116–21.

Jameson, K.P. (1981) 'Socialist Cuba and the intermediate regimes of Jamaica and Guyana', *World Development*, 9, 871–88.

Kowalewski, D. (1982) *Transnational Corporations and the Caribbean*, New York: Praeger.

Lewis, W.A. (1950) 'The industrialisation of the British West Indies', *Caribbean Economic Review*, 2, 1–61.

Lowenthal, D. (1972) *West Indian Societies*, London: Oxford University Press.

New Geographical Digest (1986) (First edition), London: George Philip.

Payne, A. (1984) *The International Crisis in the Caribbean*, London: Croom Helm.

Potter, R.B. (1985) *Urbanisation and Planning in the Third World: Spatial Perceptions and Public Participation*, London and New York: Croom Helm and St Martin's Press.

Potter, R.B. (1989a) 'Rural–urban interaction in Barbados and the Southern Caribbean: patterns and processes of dependent development in small countries', ch 9, in: Potter, R.B. and Unwin, T. (eds) *The Geography of Urban–Rural Interaction in Developing Countries*, London and New York: Routledge, 257–93.

Potter, R.B. (1989b) 'Urban–rural interaction, spatial polarisation and development planning', ch 11, in: Potter, R.B. and Unwin, T. (eds) op. cit., 323–33.

Potter, R.B. and Binns, J.A. (1988) 'Power, politics and society', ch 7, in: Pacione, M. (ed.) *The Geography of the Third World: Progress and Prospects*, London and New York: Routledge, 271–310.

Potter, R.B. and Unwin, T. (eds) (1989) *The Geography of Urban–Rural Interaction in Developing Countries*, London and New York: Routledge.

Slater, D. (1986) 'Socialism, democracy and the territorial imperative: elements for a comparison of the Cuban and Nicaraguan experiences', *Antipode*, 18, 155–85.

Stevens, P.H.M. (1957) 'Planning in the West Indies', *Town and Country Planning*, 25, 503–8.

Susman, P. (1974) 'Cuban development: from dualism to integration', *Antipode*, 6, 10–29.

Susman, P. (1987) 'Spatial equality and socialist transformation in Cuba', ch 9, in: Forbes, D. and Thrift, N. (eds) *The Socialist Third World: Urban Development and Territorial Planning*, Oxford: Blackwell, 250–81.

United Nations (1980) *Patterns of Urban and Rural Population Growth*, New
    York: United Nations.
Vendovato, C. (1986) *Politics, Foreign Trade and Economic Development: A
    Study of the Dominican Republic*, London: Croom Helm.
West, R.C. and Augelli, J.P. (1976) *Middle America: its Land and Peoples*,
    Englewood Cliffs, New Jersey: Prentice-Hall.

[2]
Jamaica
Colin Clarke

Introduction

In developed countries, industrialization has created urbanization: indeed, the emergence of urban Britain during the nineteenth century was predicated upon its becoming the 'workshop of the world', a status it achieved via imperialism. The objective of urban and regional planning in Britain and the rest of Western Europe has been to guide and direct capitalistic development: it has been largely a post-World War II phenomenon, and has played an important part in West European democracies, where the role of the state has been to curb unbridled accumulation in the interest of environmental preservation and to grant wider social access to items of collective consumption, notably housing.

In the Third World, in contrast, and especially in those Caribbean states, like Jamaica, which were once colonies of Britain, the same assumption cannot be made about the response of urbanization to the process of capital accumulation. In the Caribbean, capital accumulation was originally a rural phenomenon, based upon the production of sugar by the slave plantation: accumulation and reinvestment were sited in Britain, not within the islands. Historically, therefore, towns were trading nodes, usually ports, and imposed by the imperatives of mercantilism, not industrial capitalism. The consequence has been that Caribbean urbanization has responded more to internal demographic pressures towards non-rural dwelling than to the economic drive of an indigenous manufacturing – or servicing – base. In short, Caribbean cities share with their Latin American, African and Asian counterparts the characteristic of urbanization without industrialization and the over-inflation of their labour markets.

It follows that planning in the Caribbean, which is also a post-World War II development and, like the towns themselves, has been implanted by imperialism, has had to contend with an urban and

21

regional scene where the growth assumptions of the West European and North American economies are not being fulfilled; where 'unemployment' in various guises is endemic; where neither the individual nor the state has sufficient resources to construct urban housing of the quality regarded as essential in the mixed economies of Western Europe; and where deficiencies recorded in housing and employment are being rapidly compounded by population growth, including cityward migration.

Caribbean urbanization is on a divergent path from that of the developed world, and planning must comprehend the mainsprings of these differences if it is to have the hoped-for impact on town and country (Hope, 1986). Crucial to any such understanding is a grasp of Caribbean dependency, its roots in British mercantilism, its historical impact upon the social structure via slavery, and its implications for the distinctive urban system and the spatial structuring of towns. It is to the historical roots of urban development in the specific context of Jamaica that this chapter turns first.

Historical Aspects of Urban Development

Jamaica, in common with other Caribbean societies, has been moulded by three institutions – colonialism, the sugar plantation, and slavery – and so too has its urban system. Colonialism implies that Jamaican cities were not indigenous creations, but transplanted from Europe; the sugar plantation indicates that the economic base was not urban-located manufacturing industry; slavery has left a legacy of racial hierarchy, cultural pluralism and social inequality, which, in the absence of economic growth, has been only slowly transformed since independence in 1962. Lack of local urban roots and of a dynamic urban economy would be more manageable today if Jamaican towns were small and stable in size. However, Kingston, the capital, now records approximately 750,000 inhabitants, and Spanish Town and Montego Bay, the second and third towns, approach 100,000. While Kingston's growth rate has slackened, many of the smaller towns have recently increased by at least 4 per cent per annum – a figure twice the national average growth rate.

Post-World War II optimism in Jamaica about rapid economic 'take-off' has given way to a more pessimistic and realistic appreciation of the Caribbean's continuing dependence (Clarke, 1983). Development and underdevelopment are no longer construed as parallel, unrelated circumstances, but as organically linked conditions. Third World countries like Jamaica lack an autonomous capacity for change and growth, and are subordinate to the advanced countries which monopolize capital and technology and benefit from the terms of trade which are constructed to the disadvantage of primary producers, especially those exporting tropical products. Jamaica's towns lack the substantial manufacturing base of the European Victorian city, yet most have experienced several decades of a Victorian type of demographic explosion. Attempts to attract scarce (foreign) capital investment to Jamaican towns have been pathetically inadequate compared to the needs for labour absorption in formal sector jobs. Jamaica's political leaders in independence have had to rediscover what colonial officials merely assumed: that the key positions in the world economy were taken up long ago by Western Europe and North America, and that Japan's rise to economic prominence was not a harbinger of wholesale Third World development.

Dependency was inherent in British imperialism and its economic cornerstone – mercantilism, the objective of which was to stimulate British manufacturing and overseas trade through the monopolistic system of the triangular run. Kingston, in particular, was a vital contributor to this commerce, exporting sugar, importing West African slaves, and receiving capital goods and consumer items from Britain. Kingston's fortune hinged on Jamaica's heavily protected sugar exports; sugar accounted for 90 per cent of the value of Jamaican output and it was the largest producer in the world by the end of the eighteenth century, but the price it paid for its prosperity was the abnegation of an industrial role, which was reserved for British towns. By no means all Jamaica's exports were channelled through Kingston: outports such as Montego Bay, Savanna-la-Mar, Lucea, St Ann's Bay, Morant Bay, Port Antonio and, later, Falmouth, expanded with the sugar trade (Figure 2.1), and for a while their combined traffic equalled 88 per cent that of Kingston's (Clarke, 1975a: 13).

The seriousness of the dearth of manufacturing in Kingston, the outports and Spanish Town – the capital until 1872 – became evident only during the nineteenth century with the abolition of the slave trade in 1808, closure of the free ports (in Kingston, Montego Bay, Savanna-la-Mar and Lucea) in 1822, and the equalization of the sugar duties after 1850. Jamaica's urban economies went into a steep decline, and by 1877 it was reported that there was not enough employment 'for one quarter of the honest and industrious poor in Kingston who would be willing to work. The idle boys and men of Kingston were supported by their mothers, aunts or grannies, who worked as servants or in other domestic and feminine occupations, or by their women who worked on the wharves, in coaling, or in loading bananas' (Olivier, 1936: 206). More than a century later and with a population 10 times as large, the labour market in Kingston has scarcely changed, so far as the poor are concerned.

24

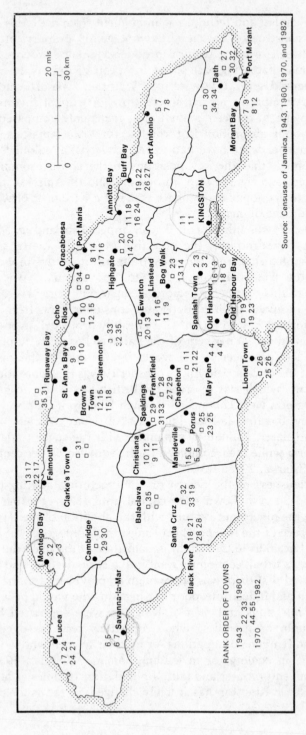

Source: Censuses of Jamaica, 1943, 1960, 1970, and 1982

Figure 2.1. Urban hierarchy of Jamaica 1943–82.

While imperialism slotted Kingston and the other ports into a specific niche in the North Atlantic system of mercantilism and determined their non-industrial nature, slavery fitted each racial category of the population into a hierarchy of legal estates which was even more exploitative and rigid than most class structures of the eighteenth or nineteenth centuries. Urban society was stratified along white, brown and black lines into citizens, freemen and slaves: these legal estates coincided with cultural distinctions based on family, religion and education, and produced three major cultural strata (modified European, hybridized Jamaican and creolized 'African'), in rank order of prestige and power (Smith, 1984). Each legal-cultural stratum was further subdivided by colour and/or class, but, generally, whites owned property and blacks provided labour in a pre-capitalist urban economy that was monetarized via mercantile links to Britain. A major change in the social order took place in 1834 when slaves were emancipated and the majority of the urban and rural population was no longer owned by the minority. Yet white domination persisted until the eve of World War II, undisrupted by the capitalist basis of post-emancipation labour relations and the emergence of a peasantry. This unchanging social framework in which the majority were freemen but not citizens was based upon imperialism and white racism, and was reinforced by a restrictive property franchise and the pauperization of many of the ex-slaves and their descendants (Clarke, 1984).

During the eighteenth century, slave plantations had been coastal and had exported sugar, rum and molasses through Kingston and the outports; inland centres remained of minimal importance and traded in slave-produced goods which were sold or bartered in the Negro, or Sunday, Markets. But after emancipation the sugar ports declined, internal marketing expanded, and an additional set of central places – Christiana, Balaclava, Clark's Town and Brown's Town – emerged to serve the peasant communities which 'burrowed into the interior' (Figure 2.1). The net consequence of the driving force of the plantation and the peasant modes of production is that, mountain fast-nesses in the interior excepted, rural Jamaica is evenly and densely popu-lated. Yet the 10 largest towns in 1970, Kingston, Montego Bay, Spanish Town, May Pen, Mandeville, Savanna-la-Mar, Port Antonio, Morant Bay, St Ann's Bay and Ocho Rios, were split 3 to 7 as between inland and coastal locations, a clear indication of the persistence of a colonial 'gateway' pattern of urbanization (Clarke, 1974).

Post-World War II economic diversification via industrialization, tourism and bauxite mining, processing and shipping has reinforced the urban–port relationship. It is not surprising, therefore, that while Jamaica's population increased by 15 per cent between 1960 and 1970 – a decade of heavy emigration – the 10 largest towns housed 88 per cent of this growth, and by the later date accounted for just over one-third of all Jamaicans. More spectacular still was the growth of Kingston by 30 per cent in the 1960s, so that by 1970 its population of 506,200 was equivalent to more than 25 per cent of all Jamaicans. Clearly, diversification based on foreign capital merely intensified the process and pattern of dependent development during three centuries of British colonialism.

Urban Population Concentration and Growth

Without massive economic growth there was little prospect that Jamaica would be able to complete the demographic transition to low fertility and low mortality in the generation following independence – even with the assistance of family planning programmes. Admittedly the crude birth rate has fallen from 40.6 per 1,000 in 1962 to 22.6 per 1,000 in 1986, but it has a long way to go before it gets under 10, the level the crude death rate reached before independence, and it now stands at 5.5 per 1,000. In 1986, the natural increase was 17.1 per 1,000, but the rate of growth is brought down to 9 by outmigration to the US and Canada, which is currently running at about 20,000 persons per year (The Statistical Institute of Jamaica, 1987a).

Dependency has frustrated the demographic transition: it has also created a specific type of urban growth in which over-concentration of population in the first-ranked settlement or 'hypercephalism' is the norm, and the increase in population in the entire urban system is generated by massive migration flows. In fact, the hypercephalic gap between Kingston (524,638 population in 1982) and Spanish Town (89,097) and Montego Bay (70,265) closed during the 1970s, just as it did when Montego Bay displaced Spanish Town as the second-ranking town in the 1950s. This provides at least prima facie evidence that urban demographic growth has been a more widespread phenomenon since independence, though Spanish Town's proximity to Kingston also suggests that agglomeration around the capital city may be occurring.

The urban hierarchy is still dominated by Kingston, which had 24 per cent of the Jamaican population living in it in 1982: it had six times the population of Spanish Town and 7.5 times the population of Montego Bay, though in 1970 it had been 12 times as large as each (Table 2.1). A major factor has been the growth not only of Spanish Town (7.1 per cent per annum) and Montego Bay (4.1 per cent), but also of May Pen (4.1 per cent) and Mandeville (8 per cent), and indeed of virtually all small towns in the system – all have more than 2,000 population, except Claremont. Whereas the tenth-ranking town in 1970 (Ocho Rios) had 6,000 inhabitants, its counterpart in 1982 (St Ann's

Table 2.1. Population of Jamaica's major towns 1943–82, ranked by the 1982 census figures.

Towns	1943	1960	1970	1982
Kingston				
Metropolitan Area	202,900	376,500	506,000	524,600
Spanish Town	12,000	14,700	39,200	89,100
Montego Bay	11,500	23,600	43,500	70,300
May Pen	6,000	14,100	25,400	41,000
Mandeville	2,100	8,400	13,700	34,500
Old Harbour	1,925	4,200	5,100	15,100
Savanna-la-mar	4,000	9,800	11,600	14,900
Port Antonio	5,500	7,800	10,400	12,300
Linstead	2,300	3,800	6,000	9,200
St Ann's Bay	3,100	5,100	7,100	9,100
Christiana	2,800	4,400	7,300	8,900
Morant Bay	3,700	5,100	7,300	8,800
Ewarton	–	–	4,200	8,800
Bog Walk	–	2,800	5,600	8,500
Ocho Rios	–	4,600	5,900	7,800
Port Maria	3,200	4,000	5,400	7,500
Falmouth	2,600	3,700	3,900	6,700
Brown's Town	2,700	3,900	5,500	6,400
Santa Cruz	–	1,400	2,100	6,000
Highgate	–	3,300	5,600	6,000
Lucea	1,800	2,800	3,600	5,700
Chapelton	–	4,400	4,200	5,300
Old Harbour Bay	–	3,400	4,400	5,300
Annotto Bay	2,800	3,600	5,500	5,200
Porus	–	2,700	3,800	4,900
Lionel Town	–	2,700	3,300	4,700
Buff Bay	1,300	2,800	3,300	3,700
Black River	1,300	3,100	2,700	3,600
Frankfield	–	2,100	3,000	3,100
Cambridge	–	–	2,400	2,900
Runaway Bay	–	–	1,100	2,900
Port Morant	–	2,300	2,200	2,900
Spaldings	–	2,000	2,200	2,500
Bath	–	2,000	1,600	2,300
Claremont	–	1,400	2,200	2,000

Sources: Censuses of Jamaica 1943, 1960, 1970 and 1982.

Notes: 1. Portmore, which had 5,100 residents in 1970 and 73,400 in 1982, has been excluded from this analysis.
2. The 1982 figures are the final census count.
3. All figures are rounded to the nearest 100.

Bay) recorded 9,000 (The Statistical Institute of Jamaica, 1987a). The whittling down of Kingston's primacy (which has been going on since 1960) has been due not only to competitive growth among other towns, but to the small size of the Kingston Metropolitan Area's absolute increase between 1970 and 1982 of 18,000 (Table 2.1). This was only a small fraction of the capital's intercensal increase between 1960 and 1970 of 130,000 and could not have been foreseen.

Two patterns of urban concentration emerge: coastal and inland (Figure 2.1). Sixteen out of the 35 towns are coastal, but only five of the top 10 in 1982 compared to seven in 1970. There is evidence for strong urban growth in the second, fourth, fifth, sixth and ninth towns (Spanish Town, May Pen, Mandeville, Old Harbour and Linstead), all of which are located inland, on crucial east–west or north–south routes leading to Kingston – for there is an enormous amount of daily commuting to the capital. The first four listed towns form the core of a key zone of urbanization and rapid intercommunication which extends westwards from Kingston via Spanish Town, Old Harbour, May Pen, Porus, Mandeville and Santa Cruz, a very rapidly growing settlement, to Black River, which is declining in significance. A secondary chain of small towns, which runs inland from May Pen, linking Chapelton, Frankfield, Spaldings and Christiana, is becoming a comparative backwater, while Bog Walk, Linstead and Ewarton are increasingly important.

Heavy in-migration characterizes the most rapidly expanding towns, and Spanish Town, Montego Bay, Mandeville and May Pen have annual rates of increase many times the national rate of increase – which Kingston (0.85 per cent per annum) does not. Whereas between 1943 and 1970 the principal migratory stream was directed to Kingston, and 43 per cent of all island movers were living in the capital in 1960 (Hewitt, 1974), step-wise migration along the south coast has become truncated in the 1970s and has focused sharply on Spanish Town, Old Harbour, May Pen and Mandeville. The reasons for Kingston's lack of pulling power will be discussed later, though it is noteworthy that it retains one of the lowest sex ratios in the island at 867 males per 1,000 females, a major hallmark of Caribbean urbanization, and itself a reflection of sex selectivity in cityward migration. In the case of the other major towns, including Montego Bay on the north coast, migration can be put down to economic development. Spanish Town has about 80 modern factories; Montego Bay is the centre for tourism and has manufacturing and a free port; Old Harbour, May Pen and Mandeville – together with the smaller towns of Bog Walk, Linstead and Ewarton – are associated with the bauxite industry. Interestingly, Spanish Town (915 males per 1,000 females), Montego Bay (910), May Pen (939), Mandeville (924) and Old Harbour (932) have more balanced sex ratios than Kingston, implying greater male in-migration and the existence of superior employment opportunities.

Almost 900,000 Jamaicans now live in settlements of more than 2,000 inhabitants; and 760,000 are urban according to the internationally accepted definition of a town, set at a threshold of 20,000 population. Using the first definition, 41 per cent of Jamaicans were urban in 1982, while even the more stringent yardstick produced a figure of 35 per cent. This has come about largely through the propensity of rural Jamaicans to migrate. High rates of natural increase (though lower now than previously), especially in the mountainous interior, the extremes of large plantations which deny access to land and small plots which are uneconomic to work, together with rural underemployment and seasonal unemployment conspire to promote cityward migration. Furthermore, agricultural work is poorly paid and generally held in low repute. For decades, rural Jamaican parents have wanted their children to have urban, white collar jobs, which are seen as easier, more secure and better paid; and the educational system has reinforced these values.

It would be quite wrong, however, to assume the rapid and easy absorption of the migrant population into the urban labour market. As long ago as the 1930s, a colonial official described unemployment as Jamaica's principal problem, and emphasized the seriousness of the situation among school leavers who constituted the principal urban migrants (Orde Brown, 1939). According to the 1960 census, 12.6 per cent of the Jamaican labour force was unemployed, rising to 18.4 per cent in Kingston, where 60 per cent of the entire island unemployed were concentrated (Clarke, 1974; 1975a).

Has this had a direct bearing on Kingston's lack of dynamism? Only indirectly! The main cause of the lack of population increase in Kingston between 1970 and 1982 has been the excessive violence generated by armed gangs affiliated to the Jamaica Labour Party (JLP) and the People's National Party (PNP) (the government from 1972 to 1980). Murder and mayhem split the West Kingston ghetto into two mutually hostile camps and led to arson on a grand scale. Eyre (1984; 1986) estimates that 21,400 people were made homeless in one small area of 200 hectares, and that another 130,000 quit the inner districts of Lower Kingston in the late 1970s and established a 'refugee' movement to the more peaceful outer suburbs of the capital and to adjacent towns such as Spanish Town and May Pen (Eyre, 1979a).

A further factor must also be taken into account, namely the spilling over of Kingston into new settlements beyond the confines of the Kingston Metropolitan Area at Bull Bay to the east and at Portmore to the west (Clarke, 1983). Portmore, a new town constructed by private contractors and reached from West Kingston via a causeway across Hunts Bay, had a population of 73,200 whose source of employment and servicing is Kingston. The inclusion of these two settlements in the 1982 calculation for Greater Kingston produces a population approaching 600,000, a figure which fits more squarely with past censuses and forward projections, even taking into account reduced in-migration and enhanced out-migration since 1970.

The incomplete demographic transition, adjustments to resources real and perceived via cityward migration, and continued (but reduced) hypercephalism can all be laid at the door of dependency. But what in detail has been the nature and success of economic development in Jamaica? What economic landscape has been constructed, especially since World War II, and how does the urban scene fit into it?

Urbanization and Economic Development

Jamaica is Greater Antillean in the size of its territory (11,396 km^2) and population (2,190,375 at the 1982 census), as well as in its location in the Caribbean: unlike the Windwards and Leewards, Jamaica is large, with a complex and substantial system of towns, and a long history of production of internationally significant crops – by the early nineteenth century it was the world's largest supplier of sugar and coffee. Historically, however, Jamaica's economic strength has been rural and agricultural and not urban-industrial – and its towns have been ports, markets and administrative centres but not places for commodity transformation or manufacturing.

Three economic trends have influenced, or been influenced by, urbanization since World War II: (1) diversification into tourism and bauxite has created pockets of development that have stimulated some of the larger towns, except Kingston which is influenced by neither; (2) incentive industrialization has been an important but totally inadequate stimulus to job creation in Kingston; (3) the emphasis on diversification has led to the recent neglect of the plantation and peasant farming systems, to the exent that Jamaica cannot fulfil its export quotas for most crops and the value of food imports exceeds that of food exports (Clarke, 1974). Each point deserves further elaboration.

Tourism
The tourist industry is heavily concentrated on the north coast of Jamaica and clusters around the international airport at Montego Bay, and most visitors are from the USA. Like other sectors of the economy, it is only slowly recovering – if at all – from the deep depression into which Jamaica plunged during the late 1970s, when the PNP's socialist policy scared the US government and the US press and led to massive Jamaican middle-class emigration and capital outflow. In terms of its

urban impact, tourism has provided a focus for the substantial refurbishing of the central sections of Montego Bay and Ocho Rios; otherwise the industry remains very much as it always has been – an enclave, both economically and spatially, in the larger national economy, and with low labour requirements.

Bauxite Mining

Bauxite mining and the chemical transformation of the red earth into alumina (a half-way stage towards the production of aluminium) has contracted economically and spatially since the mid-1970s, when the nationalization of Kaiser stimulated other forms of disinvestment. The six North American-based multinationals that were operating in the early 1970s have now been cut to one foreign firm, but Alcan's Kirvine and Ewarton alumina kilns, together with Clarendon Alumina Production (CAP) and the Kaiser bauxite plant ensure that bauxite and alumina still account for over half the value of Jamaica's exports. Despite the contraction of the industry, which is also an enclave, it has provided great stimulus to the growth of Mandeville (Alpart), Linstead (Alcan), May Pen and Old Harbour (CAP), though, as in the case of tourism, bauxite is not a large generator of jobs.

Incentive Industrialization

From the point of view of its economic base, the least dynamic of the large Jamaican settlements is Kingston, though government employment, and general commercial, servicing and port activities do provide a degree of diversification and security lacking in Montego Bay. It was largely to stimulate modern manufacturing in Kingston – the city has a long tradition of manufacturing tobacco (cigars), beer, aerated beverages, bread, leather goods and clothing–with a view to mopping up labour surplus that an Industrial Development Corporation (IDC) was set up in 1952. A variety of tax incentives (eventually extended to 10 years) were offered to local and foreign manufacturers to encourage their investment, and import duties on steel, iron, non-ferrous metals, crude rubber and leather were reduced. By 1970, 200 'footloose' enterprises were operating in Jamaica under these schemes, 147 in Kingston and 24 in Spanish Town: about half were in Jamaican ownership. In the period 1960–70, firms associated with the Jamaican IDC provided 10,000 jobs out of the 15,000 added in all factories. But the yearly increase in the labour force was 10,000, a figure far in excess of industrial job creation (Clarke, 1974).

Since the economic decline of the late 1970s, which involved an element of deliberate destabilization by the USA, all the import incentives established during the 1960s' industrialization programme have been revoked, and special contracts have been introduced together with Public Sector Free Zones, the latter producing clothing for the US market with preferential tariffs offered through the Caribbean Basin Initiative. In 1986, there were 19 companies operating in the Free Zone in Kingston and two in Montego Bay, with a total labour force of 7,800 (Planning Institute of Jamaica, 1987). Not only is the total labour employed small in number, but it is mostly female, un-unionized and almost certainly underpaid.

Plantation and Farming Systems
Whatever the labour absorptive capacity of the urban centres – and it is clearly limited, both structurally and dynamically, the secular decline in agriculture in the last 20 years has greatly compounded labour problems. The total quantity of sugar produced in 1986 was less than half the amount milled in 1966; banana exports by volume were reduced to one-tenth in the same period, while coffee exports fell to less than one-third their previous level. This decline affected plantation and peasant sectors alike, and resulted in a drop in the proportion of the labour force employed in agriculture from 38 to 33 per cent (The Statistical Institute of Jamaica, 1986). This sad state of affairs is to be explained by government inattention to agriculture, crop failures, nationalization of most sugar estates, inefficiency in agricultural management, and the general unpopularity of agricultural work.

In the light of the economic problems detected across the spectrum of the economy, it is not surprising that Jamaicans have emigrated in their thousands or that for many, cityward migration has been a substitute for emigration. The nationalization of sugar, bauxite and, more temporarily, tourism in the 1970s, undoubtedly led to a great deal of dislocation in the production process: taming the multinationals in all three sectors was achieved at a high price and caused a major decline in employment.

Jamaica remains, as it always has been, an open economy whose urban system is geared to the onward movement of primary products – bauxite, sugar, bananas and coffee – to overseas markets or to the supply of services (bureaucratic for locals and touristic for foreign visitors). The various economic sectors are spatially concentrated into speciality regions which are outward-orientated enclaves and lack internal linkage.

This is least true for Kingston, which imports consumer durables and fuel for the whole country as well as being a supplier of public and private services on a large scale. However, it is in Kingston that population build-up has created massive supplies of surplus labour. Hence, Kingston is a symbol of urban sophistication and modernity (a transplanted European town now being remodelled as an American city) and a lure to potential immigrants; and it is also a trap into which the powerless, the indigent, the sick, and the young soon fall and accumulate. Against this, it must be said that the 1970s gang warfare has tarnished the capital's image, and many of the most impoverished Jamaicans are now spread more widely *outside* Kingston than for many decades (Eyre, 1979a).

Internal Structure of the Leading Urban Settlements

Traditionally, the Jamaican élite – during colonialism white or pass-as-white – resided on rural estates or in the capital, Spanish Town to 1872, Kingston thereafter. It has been in the towns, particularly in Kingston, that race, culture and class distinctions have been most explicit and most clearly expressed spatially (Clarke, 1975b; Knight and Davis, 1978). If dependent urbanization in Jamaica had its roots in the long history of British imperialism, it is not surprising that the relationship between superordinate and subordinate was determined, politically as well as economically, using racial and cultural as well as class criteria. Differential access to power and resources under imperialism cut across different modes of production during the nineteenth century (plantation and peasant), and produced a hierarchy of whites, browns and blacks, based upon distinctions of colour, which was simultaneously a hierarchy of cultures ranked in an imperially determined order from most to least European (Clarke, 1984). Class utilized these non-class differences, reinforcing the boundaries of the three strata while providing finer grained occupational differentiation within them.

The polarization of whites and blacks in Kingston is expressed in social and spatial dimensions. Whites are confined to the low-density élite suburbs; blacks are concentrated at high density in West Kingston and East Kingston; people of mixed race are located socially and geographically between blacks and whites and merge with each (Figure 2.2). Since independence, but especially since the economic decline and gang warfare of the late 1970s, whites and Chinese have been decimated by emigration. As the non-negroid population has declined, so the social stratification has been simplified and values have been reorganized around an enhanced evaluation of blackness. Moreover, the once denigrated traits of low-status blacks – consensual cohabitation, membership of cults and sects, and Creole speech – have become increasingly embraced as facets of national culture.

Changes in employment structure in Kingston since independence have been less significant in remodelling the social structure of the capital than the erosion of the white élite – though there has certainly been an enormous growth in jobs in public and private services. In 1960, approximately two-fifths of the labour force was employed in public

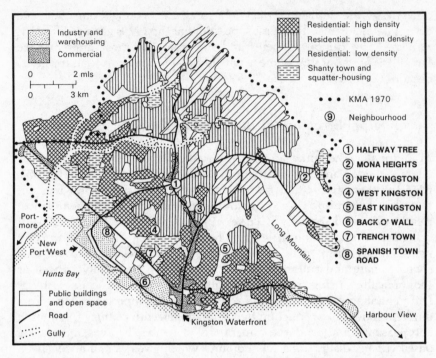

Figure 2.2. Kingston, Jamaica, 1970: neighbourhoods and land use.

service and more than 10 per cent in the construction industry, yet the proportion engaged in manufacturing was not only low (24 per cent) but scarcely larger than the personal service section (21 per cent) (Francis, 1963). Moreover, the 1960 census figure showing that 38,700 persons were in manufacturing gave an inflated picture of factory employment. Industrial concerns with 10 or more workers, or smaller if using substantial motive power, employed only 17,000 people in 1960, and probably no more than 10 per cent of Kingston's classified labour force worked in factories at that time, even when account is taken of enterprises established through the IDC. Over half the people described by the census as employed in manufacturing were undoubtedly in small-scale enterprises, working as carpenters, seamstresses, shoemakers and repairers or as other self-employed workers. A similar system of petty activities is revealed by other data in the 1960 occupational tables: over 40 per cent of Kingstonians were in manual and service occupations, notably, labouring, car cleaning, gardening and car 'watching' for men, and domestic service and market selling for women (Clarke, 1966).

Post-independence evidence from the Factory Inspectorate confirms the slow growth of manufacturing employment during the years when incentives to local and foreign capitalists were reasonably attractive, but even so, the numbers employed had reached only 29,400 by 1970. Since then, the bitter experiences of the 1970s have led to factory closures and a general loss of jobs, especially during the late 1970s when the IMF imposed stringent cut-backs on the economy in return for loans: by 1985, factory employment was no more than 27,800 persons, but in a city with almost double the population recorded in 1960.

Failure to achieve labour absorption through industrialization resulted in the increase in the rate of unemployment in Kingston from 15.5 per cent in 1943 to 18.4 per cent in 1960, 22.6 per cent in 1970 and 29.6 per cent in 1980, a proportion which has been maintained into the mid-1980s (The Statistical Institute of Jamaica, 1987b). These long-run statistics for unemployment in Kingston are useful for charting secular increases in 'informal sector' employment (Maunder, 1960): but they are not to be taken as indicators of idleness; nor are they an adequate summary of employment stress under dependent development. These last two points require further elaboration.

No system of social security exists in Jamaica and the unemployed cannot remain idle indefinitely. There has therefore developed a sub-culture of 'scuffling' or scraping a living from socially denigrated or outright illegal activities, such as selling or recycling scrap and salvaging food jettisoned on the city's dump or 'dungle', begging, stealing, pimping and prostitution. These activities proliferate wherever 'unemployment' is a permanent and prominent feature of neighbour-hood life, as it clearly is in the lower half of Kingston and on the out-skirts of Spanish Town and Montego Bay.

What then is the 'formal sector'? The formal sector entails large-scale activity, heavy capital investment, permanency of employment, regulated pay and hours of work, and sometimes the provision of pension and other social security rights: manufacturing firms, national and local government bureaucracies, retail outlets and wholesalers, banks and insurance companies meet these criteria. In contrast, the informal sector lacks these features and is characterized by casual labour, small-scale enterprise, and self-employment. It is easy to enter informal occupations, most of which are unskilled and require little if any capital outlay, but a distinction can be made between respectable petty manufacturing and servicing and the scavenging and illicit activities which many pass off as unemployment (Hart, 1973).

The high and rising rate of unemployment in Kingston during the last 50 years is a measure of undeclared employment in the informal sector. During the last two decades, a major development has been the expansion of the ganja or marijuana trade in Jamaica, and the emergence of West Kingston not simply as a major place of consumption – the Ras Tafari have been using it as a 'sacred weed' for more than half a century (Smith, Augier and Nettleford, 1960) – but as nexus for peddling and smuggling. Indeed, as unemployment soared to over 50 per cent in many districts in the late 1970s (Grose, 1979), ganja became entangled with guns, gangs and politics in a quintessentially West Kingstonian version of informal sector activity, which – for several years – brutalized daily life to a degree unknown in most other Jamaican towns or Caribbean capitals.

Throughout the colonial period and the first quarter century of independence, the employment structure of Kingston and the other Jamaican towns has been split into two sectors or circuits. This urban dichotomy has been a microscale expression of a global situation in which formal sector employment – especially in manufacturing and sophisticated servicing – has largely been pre-empted by the developed world, leaving Third World cities largely dependent on the labour-absorptive capacity of small-scale employment (Santos, 1979). The basic distinction between the sectors or circuits in Kingston, Spanish Town and Montego Bay is essentially the same as in other Third World cities and can be reduced to finance and industrial capitalism versus penny capitalism.

In the early 1970s, it was usual to treat the two sectors of Third World urban economies as though they were separate and to focus on the absorptive capacity of the informal sector whose employees subsisted largely by earning from one another or, on a casual basis, from the formal sector. In this way the urban poor were able to make ends meet by stringing together a number of ill-paid jobs. Most social scientists now accept the morphological difference between formal and informal sector activities but argue that both are motivated by profit and dominated by finance and industrial capital. The two sectors often relate in complex ways, the lower circuit selling cheap labour and transformed or recycled goods to the upper circuit and purchasing from it certain consumer items which are sold in very small quantities (Santos, 1979). Linkage of manufacturing via outworking systems seems to be less prevalent in Jamaica than in other countries, perhaps because urban industrialism in Kingston is less dynamic than in neighbouring Latin American countries and much modern manufacturing is of a privileged enclave type. On the other hand, domestic service, which is the largest employer of female labour in Kingston, depends heavily on wages channelled directly from formal sector employment, often provided by the government (Clarke, 1975a).

Dependent urbanization and the creation of insufficient formal employment with secure wages has condemned many Jamaican urban dwellers to poor quality, high density housing. This is especially true of Kingston, where the worst housing is located adjacent to the harbour on either side of the central business district, but especially in West Kingston. Here the decades-long problem has been compounded by lack

of government funds for home subsidies, by inflated land prices boosted
by housing shortages and speculation, and by real estate profiteering
(Clarke, 1975a; 1975b).

House ownership in Kingston at the end of the colonial period was
confined to the élite sections of suburban Kingston; renting was the
norm elsewhere, even for the suburban middle class. Among the
capital's urban poor, rented accommodation took three forms: rooms
in single-storey tenements, often with several tenements of variable
quality per plot; ground spots, on which individuals constructed single-
room, wooden houses for their own occupation or to sub-let; rooms for
rent or small apartments in government housing schemes (Brodber,
1975). As Kingston's population increased after 1960, private tenements
were further subdivided in the belt wrapped around the central business
district, while new single-storey buildings were crammed into the
already overcrowded rent yards (Clarke, 1975b).

Between 1960 and 1970, the majority of new houses were provided in 26 government-underwritten but privately built mortgage-
insurance schemes, which, like the earliest ones at Mona Heights and
Harbour View (Figure 2.2), drew most of their residents from the more
densely populated middle-class areas rather than from the West
Kingston slums. Clearly, the Jamaican Labour Party, which led Jamaica
into independence, found it easier to underwrite the loans of other
agencies than to supply the funds required for low-income housing.
Kingston's poor are quite unable to make reliable repayments for long-
term loans.

The housing situation for the middle stratum improved as Portmore
was developed in the 1970s, but as the economy later contracted and
confidence in the government of the People's National Party waned, the
house-building programme faltered. In 1977 almost 7,000 units in public
and private sectors were completed throughout Jamaica, but the number
dropped to 4,400 in 1978 and 1,400 in 1980. The result was a leap in
unemployment in the construction sector and the entry of even more
labour into the informal sector. Simultaneously, the burning of blocks
of tenements in inner West Kingston reduced the housing stock available
to the urban poor and created the exodus to Spanish Town and the
subsequent construction of rent yards and squatter camps (Eyre, 1983).

For the poorest of the poor who are unable to pay regular rent,
the cheapest housing solution, for decades, has been squatting. Three
thousand squatters were enumerated in Kingston and St Andrew in the
1960 census, but the police estimated 20,000 squatters in 1961. In that
year, squatter settlements were located on vacant land on the fringe of
the tenement area in West Kingston and on the outskirts of the built-up
area of the city, mostly on government-owned land. Dwellings consisted
of one-room huts constructed from packing cases, fish barrels,

cardboard and polythene (Clarke, 1975a). The morphology of many of
the older squatter settlements resembled that of the rent yards in West
Kingston (where properly carpentered buildings and glazed windows
were common) (Hanson, 1975), but neither displayed the development
trajectory frequently associated with squatting in Latin America, since
both lacked the sense of security bestowed by ownership of land or its
promise (Clarke and Ward, 1980).

Squatter settlements and rent yards are distinguished by tenure not
by fabric. Both can be combined and described as shanty towns because
they involve poor fabric, are static and lack sewerage and piped water
(Eyre, 1972). Ann Norton (1978), who analysed Sanitary Survey Data
for 1968, calculated that 80,400 Kingstonians, or 23 per cent of the
population in her study, lived in shanty towns (Figure 2.2). For Montego
Bay, Eyre (1979b) estimated the shanty towns (then mostly rent yards)
housed 67 per cent of the urban population in 1978, and it would be
surprising if a similar proportion was not recorded in Spanish Town
post-1980.

As Jamaica's largest towns have grown, most of the new
employment has been created by informal (often illegal) means, and self-
employment has been married to self-help housing in the form of rent
yards and squatter settlements to create do-it-yourself urbanization.
Evidence from Kingston, Spanish Town and Montego Bay shows that
informal housing (squatting and precarious renting) is growing and not
declining; it is fundamentally related to dependent capitalism (which
lacks investment surpluses for mass housing) and helps to sustain it by
keeping wages low.

Planning and Politics

Planning in Jamaica is in a weak position to confront the urban
problems created by dependent development, now intensified by the
experience of 10 years of economic decline or stagnation. From the time
of the introduction of urban planning to Jamaica in 1947, when a
Government Town Planner was appointed, it was conceived as physical
planning and its theory and practice was that of British planning, based
upon a century of British urban experience. At that time, almost nothing
had been written about Caribbean – or Third World – urbanization,
and Jamaican towns, of which only Kingston was of any significance,
were treated as if they were transplanted European settlements, which is
literally true in a way of Kingston, founded and planned in 1692
(Clarke, 1966).

Jamaica created a Town Planning Department in 1950, but its
activity was confined to advising on the design of houses and the siting

and layout of housing schemes, most of which were earmarked for victims of the 1951 hurricane. The government enacted the first Town and Country Planning law in 1958, enabling Provisional Development Orders to be placed on any area in the island: wherever these development orders were applied, planning permission had to be obtained for certain types of development. In 1958, also, the Government Town Planner was appointed the authority for interpreting Jamaica's first 10 year plan, so far as physical planning was concerned. Maps were prepared showing the distribution of population, roads, water supplies, schools, hotels and medical and health centres in Jamaica.

So far as urban areas were concerned, the Town Planning Department was directed to prepare a plan, not for Kingston, which contained almost a quarter of the Jamaican population and the largest slum, but for the area adjoining the tourist resort of Ocho Rios, on the north coast. Nevertheless, a rudimentary land-use map of Kingston was produced in 1947, followed by further maps of increasing sophistication and detail in 1952 and 1960 (Clarke, 1975a). In 1960–62, a crisis in West Kingston stimulated by Jamaica's impending independence, by the referendum about whether Jamaica should withdraw from the West Indies Federation, and by the disaffection of the 'back to Africa' Ras Tafari movement from the goals of Jamaican society, necessitated attention being given to urban social problems. Using 1960 small area census data and information provided by national and local government departments, the Town Planning Department began for the first time to analyse housing and public health issues in the capital. Monitoring of the detailed internal problems of Kingston came to an end soon after independence. In 1968 a land-use zoning system for Kingston was published, and since then much of the work of the Town Planning Department – now with Jamaican senior staff – has been to vet applications for changes in land use in the light of that schema, though a certain amount of land use and socio-economic analysis is carried out for the larger towns.

Major problems for urban planning in Jamaica are that physical planning has a very low status *vis-à-vis* sectoral planning – the six planning regions based on Montego Bay, Black River, St Ann's Bay, Mandeville, Kingston and Port Antonio are scarcely used, in practice; and development monitoring and enforcement powers have resided with the rural parishes and the Kingston and St Andrew Corporation – which are inefficient if not, in some cases, venal. Subversion by offices, retailers and wholesalers of the residential zoning requirements around suburban Half Way Tree in Kingston has become a national scandal, and development control in the capital has recently (1987) been returned to the professional planners.

It would be wrong, however, to imply that Jamaica has not been assiduous in the assembly of material to facilitate physical planning, even if it has not formulated a regional policy on that basis. In 1971, *A National Physical Plan for Jamaica* was published, accompanied by a *National Atlas of Jamaica*. These involved the co-operation of the Town Planning Department and the Ministry of Finance and Planning, with substantial assistance for the atlas from the United Nations Development Programme, and were intended to lay down physical planning guidelines for the period 1970–90. Since then, the national physical plan has been revised for the period 1978–98, and the National Planning Agency (formerly the Central Planning Unit) has produced an *Urban Growth and Management Study* (1978) – largely devoted to Kingston and Spanish Town. What has been the burden of these reports?

Five major goals have been identified: (1) to relieve population pressure and urban growth in Kingston; (2) provide better urban facilities and public housing; (3) develop alternative employment opportunities outside Kingston; (4) encourage integrated regional development; and (5) provide guidance on the rational use of public and private funds for urban development (Fanger, 1978). It is not clear, however, who was to implement these worthy objectives or whether, once adumbrated, they were to be left to market forces. That many of these objectives were not actively pursued may be inferred from a recently held seminar of the Town and Country Planning Association of Jamaica, which argued that settlements are central to economic development; that it is crucial to link physical planning strategies into national planning for economic development; and that the conception of a national settlement system can be useful for planning only if it is integrated into national economic development planning.

Three additional criticisms can be made of urban planning in Jamaica. Firstly, there seems to be very little awareness of the peculiar nature of dependent urbanization, of the importance of the informal sector for employment (PREALC, 1976), and of the capacity of peripheral capitalism to transform the urban scene to its own ends: for example, the development by local financiers, since independence, of New Port West in West Kingston and of New Kingston, a large commercial complex located in suburban St Andrew and rival to the central business district. Secondly, there is no conception of the need to create a high-powered administration for the capital city to replace the ramshackle Kingston and St Andrew Corporation (KSAC) (Figure 2.1) or to bring the 'many Kingstons' into one coherent framework. Although the 1960 census recognized an urban-demographic unit called the Kingston Metropolitan Area (KMA) (Figure 2.2), it has no functional role. The Kingston Development Area approximates to the KSAC and is larger than the KMA of 1960 vintage, but exists solely for purposes of planning. However, since 1970 the KMA has been extended to include Portmore, and so it once more closely approximates to the built-up area of Kingston. In addition, there is the Kingston Metropolital Region (KMR), embracing the KMA post-1970, Spanish Town and various spillover settlements adjacent to each (National Planning Agency 1978). Surely, the KMA or KMR ought to supersede the KSAC and be given enhanced organizational and planning powers. Thirdly, perhaps because of its British heritage, Jamaican urban planning seems to be unnecessarily subordinate to economic planning and passive to the point of being innocuous.

In saying this one has to be aware that some of the more positive, creative, planning functions since 1968 have been vested in the Urban Development Corporation (UDC) whose remit is to carry out and/or secure the laying out and development of designated areas, and, since 1983, in the Kingston Restoration Company Limited, which is engaged in fabric refurbishment and community projects in downtown Kingston. UDC projects have been carried out in the coastal resorts – Montego Bay, Ocho Rios, Negril and Oracabessa, in some of the small towns (Comprehensive Rural Township Development Programme), and in and around Kingston – the Kingston Waterfront (to redevelop through offices, shops, hotels, apartments and public buildings the derelict and abandoned port area); the West Kingston Development Project (to refurbish the area burnt out in the late 1970s); and Portmore (to provide a commercial and administrative centre for what has been essentially a non-serviced new town). The UDC has also been active in housing provision, and it is to the issue of government involvement in housing that attention is now directed (Urban Development Corporation, 1985).

In 1960, when the Town Planning Department first gave its detailed attention to Kingston, it estimated that 120,000 people were living in inadequate accommodation, 80,000 of whom were at densities of more than two persons per habitable room or more than eight persons to each hygienic water closet – measures deemed to represent overcrowding according to the criteria of British planning (Clarke, 1966). In short, more than one quarter of Kingstonians required rehousing. Of course, the Jamaican government had been involved in housing schemes for the poor since the 1930s and had accommodated 40,000 people between 1946 and 1959 (no one knows, however, how much of this housing was urban or where it was located). But to house the overcrowded 80,000 and to accommodate the projected population increase to 1970 of 184,500 was estimated to cost £50 million, a sum then almost equivalent to the national annual budget – an impossible task (Clarke, 1966).

Intensification of the housing problem in Kingston between 1960 and 1970 is easy to explain. To provide adequate accommodation for Kingston's 130,000 new residents (the estimate of 184,500 was not reached, largely because of heavy emigration to Britain, Canada and the USA) 35,500 new housing units were required: and even if this rate of building had been achieved, it would have made no impact on the pre-existing deficit. The year 1965, which was the central point in the post-independence economic boom, was quite the best for new construction, but fewer than 2,500 units were completed in government and private schemes taken together. In most years in the decade, the output of all types of government financed units barely exceeded 1,000, even when government-underwritten mortgage schemes are included (Clarke, 1975b).

It is not surprising that the housing problem in Kingston intensified. Data from the Sanitary Survey of Kingston and St Andrew, show that even more people, many of them recent migrants, concentrated in the slum areas of West and East Kingston in the years after independence. Between 1960 and 1967, almost 50 per cent of the city's total population growth was absorbed in West Kingston neighbourhoods adjoining the Spanish Town Road, the population in all the zones of dilapidation increasing from 120,000 to 164,000 (Clarke, 1975a).

Assuming the KMA's population (including Portmore) grew by 100,000 during the 1970s, 25,000 units would have been needed just to keep pace with new household formation: by 1982, 16,000 households had been accommodated at Portmore alone by West Indies Home Constructors. Moreover, governments of both the JLP (1962–72 and 1980–89) and PNP (1972–80) have involved themselves ever more deeply in the housing issue, and have focused their activities not on the tenements and rent yards but upon the squatter settlements of West Kingston. Two policies have evolved: clearance followed by rebuilding, and upgrading.

During the 1960s, the squatter settlements at Trench Town and Back O'Wall (Tivoli Gardens) were cleared and new housing schemes constructed containing 450 and 800 units respectively. Despite oral promises to the contrary, the new housing was not allocated to the original squatters, but to backers of the political party in power, the JLP. During the late 1960s and 1970s the overt dissatisfaction of West Kingstonians with the inequalities of the urban system was institutionalized and harnessed by the two political parties. Provision of homes and jobs became a major political exercise carried out for the benefit of supporters of the victorious party. Paradoxically, the struggle in West Kingston was not for structural change, but to secure power for one's party, and through it, to obtain resources that were in chronically short supply (Clarke, 1975b).

Under the JLP administration 1967–72 patronage networks were carefully extended by the Minister of Finance, Edward Seaga, who completed the redevelopment of Tivoli Gardens in his West Kingston constituency. During that period, 1,523 units were constructed for the poor, mostly in West Kingston. The PNP in government responded by redeveloping its constituencies overlapping the Trench Town squatter areas, but thereby placed its supporters in territory adjacent to ancient JLP bailywicks (Jamaica Department of Statistics, 1978). By 1980, about 3,500 units – mostly apartments – had been constructed, housing at least 14,000 persons. Taking into account private building at Portmore and other places, it is likely that Kingston went a long way during the 1970s not only to redevelop the worst sections of the capital but to house its population increase.

The consequences of these developments were not entirely positive, however. West Kingston's housing projects became the battleground of the two increasingly opposed political parties as the JLP tried to make Jamaica ungovernable: gangs with guns were put at the disposal of both parties (Eyre, 1983). Moreover, in the late 1970s, there was upper-middle class flight, occasioned by Manley's socialism and the perpetual violence, which reduced property values in many areas to about one-quarter their previous value but simultaneously released some pressure on property.

Nonetheless, it would be unfair to dismiss the PNP's involvement in Kingston's housing problems as entirely a matter of establishing platforms – based on the National Housing Corporation (1974) and the National Housing Trust (1976) – from which to confront the JLP strongholds. In keeping with its socialist orientation, the PNP also recognized the importance of giving security to squatters and of providing infrastructure and amenities. By 1980, 19 squatter sites were being upgraded by the government in collaboration with the United States and the Netherlands. In the same year the World Bank completed 5,500 core units under its site and services programme, the object being to provide essential infrastructure prior to, rather than after, self-help housing had taken place (National Planning Agency, 1981).

The statistics are borne out by field observation: housing conditions in Kingston have improved, especially since 1970, even if it has been at the expense of political party competition and what Alan Eyre (1983) has called the ghettoization of West Kingston. The sewerage system has been extended to virtually the whole of Kingston (in 1960 it was confined to the built-up city as of 1900), and 87 per cent of households in 1982 had both piped water and toilet facilities. Nonetheless, the government (1987) recognizes in its *National Shelter Sector Strategy Report* that there remains a substantial housing deficit in Kingston, the origins of which go back into the late colonial and early independence periods. Forty per cent of the dwellings in the KMA (76,000 units) require replacement (8 per cent) or upgrading (32 per cent); approximately 60,000 people still need complete rehousing, and another 240,000 require substantial house improvements. These figures show how marginal the improvements have been in Kingston since 1962 – the first quarter-century of independence.

In addition, it is clear that some of the growth strains endured by Kingston in the 1950s and 1960s have appeared elsewhere in the urban system, notably in Spanish Town and Montego Bay. Sixty-one per cent of all smaller town dwellings require replacement (4 per cent) or upgrading (57 per cent), though the magnitude of the problem is less than in Kingston, which has two-thirds of Jamaican urban houses. In the face of this enduring problem, the government intends to mobilize the funds of the National Housing Trust and Jamaica Mortgage Bank to provide improvement grants for the poor, in addition to supporting new housing for middle-income groups, many of whom can also secure funding from banks, building societies or insurance companies. Moreover, renewed emphasis will be given to self-help projects.

Conclusion

Neither late colonial nor post-independence economic growth has underpinned Jamaican urbanization: more accurately, dependent development did so to a limited extent until the mid-1970s, when a sharp decline set in. Lower circuit, or informal, activity has clearly remained the employer of about half the labour force in Kingston since 1960, with the balance in that circuit shifting towards the illegal sector since 1975. Some of the other towns, notably Spanish Town, Montego Bay, Mandeville, May Pen and Old Harbour have stronger economies than Kingston, being based on manufacturing, bauxite and tourism, and formal sector employment here is more vigorous than it was in 1960, with the consequence that the urban hierarchy is now more smoothly graded.

Since independence the urban situation has not worsened as sharply as was envisaged, because of emigration. Moreover, many of the symptoms of stress that in 1960 and 1970 were so obviously focused on Kingston have been displaced to Spanish Town – directly by refugee migration from Kingston and indirectly by its receiving cityward migrants who might otherwise have gone to Kingston – and Montego Bay.

The role of the state, which has been weak with regard to employment generation – modern manufacturing is capital not labour intensive – has been more active in resolving housing problems, largely because it has accepted the economic non-viability of occupants of state housing schemes, many of whom are undoubtedly hopelessly in arrears with their payments. This has been one small but important contribution to Jamaica's indebtedness, which has forced it into IMF hands since the late 1970s. Jamaica now has the highest debt per capita of any country in the world.

State intervention in housing – especially for the poor – has been predicated upon the determination of both political parties to use housing to patronize its supporters. As each party itself is a multi-stratum coalition, the entire social hierarchy has been bifurcated and potential inter-strata antagonism has been deflected into inter-stratum tension and violence among the poor, with collective consumption – housing – as the bone of contention. The state has also collaborated with private capital not only to redevelop the Kingston Waterfront and New Kingston, but in the underwriting of middle-income housing schemes.

Planning has thereby been left with a weak, reactive role. Many of its potential functions have been hived off to the UDC: moreover, the political parties have played to their followers over the heads of the planners. Political conflict has been crucial to the development of the old squatter sections of West Kingston, leaving the tenements and rent yards set in an intractable matrix of rented property. Yet political conflict has not been of a spontaneous, grass roots kind, à la Castells, but has been directed by each political party at the other, with West Kingstonians as the gladiators and housing as the reward for combat.

Anyone flying into Kingston airport and looking inland across the harbour cannot fail to be impressed by the housing schemes which cluster to north and south of the Spanish Town Road, where Back O'Wall and Trench Town were once squatted. It is clear that political rivalry and competitive patronage networks have motivated urban renewal; they have also led to refugee flight, in the wake of arson, of many of the inner city, tenement-dwelling poor, who have subsequently settled in Spanish Town and other destinations.

It is ironic that while the PNP has, since 1975, embraced democratic socialism and the JLP is avowedly pro-capital, their ideological differences, though loudly proclaimed and the basis for mutual antipathy, have not given rise to divergent policies towards housing. Ideological difference has fuelled their competitiveness; and it has been that competitiveness which has drawn them into the arena of the KMA – traditionally a PNP bastion – where almost a quarter of the Jamaican constituencies are located.

ACKNOWLEDGEMENT

I am indebted to Dr Alan Eyre of the Department of Geography, University of the West Indies, Jamaica, for his very helpful comments on an earlier draft of this chapter, and to Jesus College, Oxford, for a grant which enabled me to undertake a period of urban field work in Jamaica in 1987.

POSTSCRIPT

Since this chapter was written, Jamaica has been devastated by Hurricane Gilbert, which traversed the length of the island on 12 September 1988, destroying 20 per cent of the housing stock and damaging a further 50 per cent. By a miracle only 45 people were killed. This disaster, the first major hurricane to strike the island since 1951, has completely changed the housing scene in urban and rural Jamaica, and has obliterated many of the gains recorded since independence. It is a reminder of the fragility of Jamaica's environment – natural and man-made; for the 1692 earthquake destroyed Port Royal (and led to the founding of Kingston), while the 1907 earthquake caused destruction comparable to Hurricane Gilbert. Rebuilding Kingston and the other settlements to standards fit for independent Jamaica will be a major challenge to people, politicians and planners alike. At least it will provide work.

REFERENCES

Brodber, E. (1975) 'A study of yards in the city of Kingston', Kingston: Institute of Social and Economic Research, University of the West Indies, Working Paper No. 9.

Clarke, C.G. (1966) 'Problemas de planeación urbana en Kingston, Jamaica', in: *La Geografía y los Problemas de Población*, Union Geográfica Internacional, Conferencía Regional Latinoamericana, Tomo 1, México, Sociedad Mexicana de Geografía y Estadística, 411–31.

Clarke, C.G. (1974) *Jamaica in Maps*, London: University of London Press.

Clarke, C.G. (1975a) *Kingston Jamaica: Urban Development and Social Change*, Berkeley, Los Angeles and London: University of California Press.

Clarke, C.G. (1975b) 'Ecological aspects of population growth in Kingston, Jamaica', in: Momsen, R.P. Jr (ed.) *Geographical Analysis for Development in Latin America and the Caribbean*, Chapel Hill, North Carolina: CLAG Publications.

Clarke, C.G. and Ward, P.M. (1980) 'Stasis in makeshift housing: perspectives from Mexico and the Caribbean', *Comparative Urban Research*, 8, 117–27.

Clarke, C.G. (1983) 'Dependency and marginality in Kingston, Jamaica', *Journal of Geography*, 82, 227–35.

Clarke, C.G. (1984) 'Pluralism and plural societies: Caribbean perspectives', in: Clarke, C., Ley, D. and Peach, C. (eds) *Geography and Ethnic Pluralism*, London: Allen and Unwin, 51–86.

Eyre, L.A. (1972) 'The shanty towns of Montego Bay, Jamaica', *Geographical Review* 62, 394–413.

Eyre, L.A. (1979a) 'Quasi-urban melange settlements', *Caribbean Review* 8 (2), 32–5.

Eyre, L.A. (1979b) 'Growth in squatter and informal areas in Montego Bay: 1958–78', Kingston: Ministry of Housing.

Eyre, L.A. (1983) 'The ghettoization of an island paradise', *Journal of Geography*, 82, 236–39.

Eyre, L.A. (1984) 'Political violence and urban geography in Kingston, Jamaica', *Geographical Review* 74, 24–37.

Eyre, L.A. (1986) 'Party political violence and the struggle for residential space in Jamaica', in: Kleinpenning, J.M.G. (ed.) *Competition for Rural and Urban Space in Latin America: Its Consequences for Low Income Groups*, Amsterdam-Nijmegen: Netherlands Geographical Studies, No. 25.

Fanger, U. 1978) 'Urban policy implementation in the Dominican Republic, Jamaica, and Puerto Rico', *Ekistics*, 45, 20–9.

Francis, O.C. (1963) *The People of Modern Jamaica*, Kingston: Department of Statistics.

Government of Jamaica (1987) *National Shelter Sector Strategy Report*, Kenya: International year of shelter for the homeless.

Grose, R.N. (1979) 'Squatting and the geography of class conflict: limits to housing autonomy in Jamaica', Ithaca, New York: Programme on International Studies in Planning, Cornell University.

Hanson, G. (1975) 'Shantytown stage development: the case of Kingston, Jamaica', Louisiana State University, unpublished PhD dissertation.

Hart, K. (1973) 'Informal income opportunities and urban employment in Ghana', *Journal of Modern African Studies*, 11, 61–81.

Hewitt, L. (1974) 'Internal migration and urban growth', in: *Recent Population Movement in Jamaica*, Paris: CICRED, 24–55.

Hope, K.R. (1986) *Urbanization in the Commonwealth Caribbean*, Boulder and London: Westview Press.

Jamaica Department of Statistics (1978) *Abstract of Building and Construction Statistics*, Kingston.

Knight, P. and Davies, Omar (1978) 'An analysis of residential location patterns in the Kingston metropolitan area', *Social and Economic Studies*, 27, 403–33.

Maunder, W.F. (1960) *Employment in an Underdeveloped Area: A Sample Survey of Kingston, Jamaica*, New Haven: Yale University Press.

Ministry of Mining and Natural Resources (1971) *A National Physical Plan for Jamaica* and *National Atlas of Jamaica*, Kingston.

National Planning Agency (1978) *Urban Growth and Management Study*, Kingston.

National Planning Agency (1981) *Economic and Social Survey of Jamaica 1980*, Kingston.

Norton, A. (1978) 'Shanties and skyscrapers: growth and structure of modern

Kingston', Kingston: Institute of Social and Economic Research, University of the West Indies, Working Paper No. 13.

Olivier, S. (1936) *Jamaica the Blessed Isle*, London: Faber and Faber.

Orde Brown, G. St J. (1939) *Labour Conditions in the West Indies*. London: HMSO.

Planning Institute of Jamaica (1987) *Economic and Social Survey of Jamaica*, Kingston.

PREALC (Programa regional del empleo para América Latina y el Caribe) (1976) 'Guidelines for action in the informal sector of central Kingston', Geneva: International Labour Organization.

Santos, M. (1979) *The Shared Space*, London: Methuen.

Smith, M.G. (1984) *Culture, Class and Race in the Commonwealth Caribbean*, Kingston: Department of Extra-mural Studies, University of the West Indies.

Smith, M.G., Augier, R. and Nettleford, R. (1960) *The Ras Tafari Movement in Kingston, Jamaica*, Kingston: Institute of Social and Economic Research, University College of the West Indies.

The Statistical Institute of Jamaica (1986) *Statistical Yearbook of Jamaica 1986*, Kingston.

The Statistical Institute of Jamaica (1987a) *Demographic Statistics 1986*, Kingston.

The Statistical Institute of Jamaica (1987b) *The Labour Force 1986*, Kingston.

Urban Development Corporation (1985) *Annual Report 1983–84*, Kingston: UDC.

[3]
Trinidad and Tobago
Dennis Conway

Introduction

As one of the largest territories in the southern Caribbean in terms of areal extent – 1,980 square miles (5,128 square kilometres); in terms of population – 1.25 million persons in 1986; and in terms of natural resources, Trinidad, and to a lesser extent its ward island Tobago, has always been viewed as a Caribbean country with considerable potential. First a Spanish colony, Trinidad was ceded to the British in 1802, thus ending two hundred years of indeterminate Spanish administration in which French, Venezuelan and Dutch influences prevailed as much as Spanish. At various points in its history Tobago was held by the Dutch, the French and the British, but in 1815 it too was ceded to Britain and in 1888 was merged with Trinidad to form one colony of the British Empire.

As a plantation economy, its colonial fortunes fluctuated. Then, in the early twentieth century, Trinidad experienced some prosperity during phases of oil exploitation. Considerable reserves were found and extracted by the British, Dutch, and US companies in the south around Point Fortin and San Fernando. Texaco built a large refinery north of San Fernando at Point-à-Pierre in 1956, and when the United States built and manned bases at Chaguaramas and Waller Field, Trinidad's destiny as a More Developed Country was apparently assured.

From 1958 until 1962, Trinidad and Tobago was a member of the Federation of the West Indies and this ill-fated experiment of the Colonial Office to divest itself of its colonies in the Caribbean was quartered in Port of Spain. However, when Jamaica seceded from this unworkable political arrangement in 1961, Trinidad's Prime Minister Eric Williams remarked that 'one from ten leaves none' and duly led Trinidad and Tobago into independence in 1962. Later, in August 1976, the country adopted a new Constitution, under which it became a

49

Republic within the British Commonwealth. In 1980, a Tobago House of Assembly was formed with certain powers over that island's finances, economic development and social services. This last concession to Trinidad's ward island came in the face of disquiet and dissatisfaction with Tobago's inadequate receipt of her share of the petro-dollar fortunes and mutterings among her radical spokesmen of 'secession' and independence (Niddrie, 1980).

The early 1980s, however, witnessed a rather dramatic change in fortunes for the twin-island nation. There was no insulation against the softening oil markets, the petro-dollar boom was too short-lived, and the citizens of Trinidad and Tobago had acquired consumption habits that could no longer be sustained: 'T'ings get hard!' (Worrell, 1987). Dr Williams' successor, George Chambers and his People's National Movement (PNM) government were voted out of office in 1986 and A.N.R. Robinson, a Tobagonian, heads a government of 'reconstruction'. There is an imperative to plan for adjustments in Trinidad and Tobago's development strategies (Demas et al., 1984). The petro-dollar bonanza of the late 1970s has not generated sustainable economic growth, and a restructuring of priorities and reliance on the resilience of the people to withstand 'hard times' is now the order of the day. Interwoven with this uneven trajectory of the nation's contemporary fortunes is the accumulation of problems accompanying uncontrolled urbanization.

Immigration, demographic heterogeneity, uneven economic growth, the colonial and post-colonial experience of Trinidad and Tobago, have all engendered an urbanization process that has its structure and trajectories rooted in the socio-historical past, but in contemporary times has accelerated its pace to become a major phenomenon, influencing all facets of both the public and private domains. Trinidadian urbanization is one of the most significant processes complicating the nation's attempts to move forward, but its many dimensions still remain uncharted and only vaguely understood by her body politic. True, there is recognition of its magnitude, its accelerating rates of growth, even some of its accompanying consequences such as housing shortages, road congestion, inadequate infrastructure, services and the like (Hope, 1986). However, a comprehensive accounting of urban growth and urbanization in Trinidad and Tobago and the roles planning and urban management have played in the evolution of an urban process that has been anything but 'controlled', remains to be undertaken. This chapter attempts such an accounting.

The remainder of the chapter develops the argument that a lack of understanding of the consequences of uncontrolled urbanization has led to an intolerable situation in Trinidad in general, and the Capital Region in particular. First, the historical process of urban growth and colonial settlement is outlined. Then the twentieth-century record of internal and international migration and ensuing patterns of growth and redistribution of Trinidad's population are documented. A third section elaborates on the evolution of the internal structure of the nation's major urban centres, Port of Spain and San Fernando. Next, the economic policies and the uneven performance of Trinidad and Tobago's economy during the era of state capitalism, from the mid-1960s onwards is outlined. Finally, the role of planning and its inability to influence urban processes in general and the Capital Region's multiplicity of problems in particular are discussed. This latter account illustrates how migration and settlement into and within the region have, together with specific financial, legislative and land tenure conditions, effectively frustrated the planning process in contemporary urban Trinidad.

Historical Processes of Urbanization and Colonial Settlement

Although Trinidad had been claimed as a Spanish colony as early as 1592, for the next two hundred years or so, the Spanish empire's urban model did not develop as it did elsewhere in New Spain. St Joseph, the colony's initial capital, was always a token administrative hub; rural missions and *encomiendas* were the centres of control of the Indian populations, and with the commercial development of cocoa collapsing in 1725, Trinidad stagnated. By 1765, Trinidad's population of Spanish and Christianized Indians was estimated to be only 2,503 persons (Brereton, 1981). St Joseph had actually been abandoned by its Spanish settlers when, in 1757, a new Spanish governor arrived and relocated his residence to Port of Spain (see Figure 3.1).

At that time, Port of Spain was a fishing village and a port of call for ships trading in tobacco. Her population stood at a mere 300–400 inhabitants; Spaniards, free-coloureds, foreigners, traders, fishermen, farmers and rum distillers. It was not until after 1783, when the Cedula of Population decreed generous terms for French planters and their slaves to settle and develop Trinidad's plantation economy, that Port of Spain assumed its central administrative and commercial position. The city's population had increased to more than 1,000 inhabitants by 1784, over half being 'new colonists'. By 1797, its population was over 4,000 persons and the city was one of the busiest in the Caribbean, accommodating French settlers and British merchants as well as the Spanish administrators and *Cabildo* (municipal council). The 'new' post-1783 Trinidadian society was soon to be Afro-French with French

52

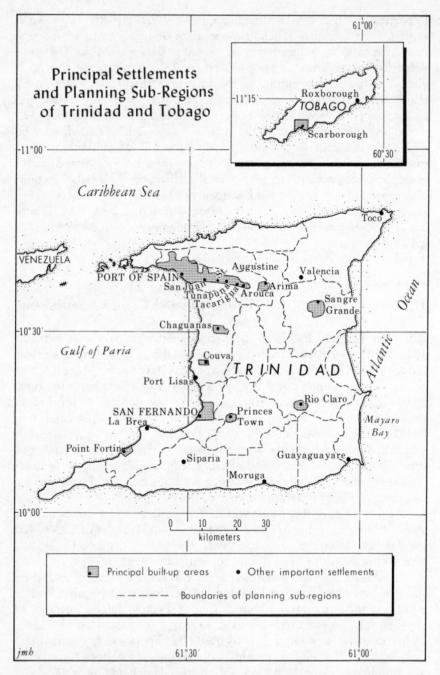

Figure 3.1. Principal settlements and planning sub-regions of Trinidad and Tobago.

planters, French free-coloureds and African slaves replacing the Spanish and Indian populations of the early colonial period.

Topography and ecology influenced the regional concentration of the country's plantations and estates: sugar cane on the flat alluvial plains of present-day St George and Caroni counties, cocoa and coffee in the mountain valleys of the Northern Range and in the east where there was heavier precipitation and suitable sheltered aspects. The plantocracy lived in their large wooden country houses on their estates and, if they could afford it, they also maintained a residence in Port of Spain, thus forming a distinctive urban strata in these early days. By 1797, free coloureds already outnumbered the members of this 'white' élite, and constituted an artisan intermediate class of smallholders and urban dwellers. Both were soon eclipsed in numbers by African slave labour, most of whom were patois-speaking, of Francophone Caribbean origin, thus beginning the next demographic transition of Trinidad, toward an Afro-Caribbean heritage. Then, the turbulent era of the French Revolution and its republican reverberations throughout the Caribbean sealed the fate of Trinidad. With Spain allied to republican France, the British capture of Trinidad was deemed an essential stratagem. Accordingly, Spanish Trinidad succumbed to a British expedition in early 1797, and under British control the French plantocracy and British commercial interests enjoyed a thriving commercial partnership.

Tobago's early colonial history was quite different from Trinidad's. The island's strategic location and fertile soil attracted several European appetites. The seventeenth century saw the island changing hands between the Dutch, the Courlanders and the French at least 10 times and, in addition, was twice settled and abandoned by dissident Barbadian planters (Niddrie, 1980). By 1815, when the Congress of Vienna finally confirmed British sovereignty of Tobago, the island had changed hands a few more times, but the resident plantocracy, English and French, had begun to demonstrate its potential as a cotton and sugar producer. From 1809 to 1827, Tobago's economy was monocultural, its sugar plantations yielding economic prosperity to the planter élite and bringing Tobago's Afro-Caribbean population as slaves. After Emancipation in 1834, the removal of protective tariffs on sugar in England in the 1840s, and the devastating 1847 hurricane, Tobago's fortunes dimmed. The collapse of the West Indies Bank of London in 1848 left Tobago's planters without any financial life-line, and the remainder of the century saw estates abandoned, many reverting to the Crown and remaining under forest. Some land settlement attempts were initiated to encourage small islanders to colonize Tobago as proprietary farmers, but by the 1880s, Tobago's economy had deteriorated considerably. After attempts to link Tobago with other small islands in the British Caribbean, she was finally made a charge of neighbouring Trinidad in 1888/9 (Niddrie, 1980). Thus, a predominantly African/Protestant rural Tobago, with virtually no urban centres of any size or importance, was to be linked with an urbanized and richer multi-cultural colony, where Port of Spain, San Fernando and Arima already represented sizeable towns of commercial and administrative significance.

Trinidad after Emancipation in 1834 had indeed undergone another demographic switch as fortunes took a turn for the better. The British 'Crown Colony' administrative aversion to republicanism, cemented an allegiance between authoritarian governors and the French-creole plantocracy at the expense of the urban-based free-coloured intermediate class. The planter's needs for more labour to replace the slaves, who had 'voted with their feet' and left the sugar estates, were met by administrative efforts to recruit small islanders, then Madeirans and finally, and successfully, to recruit indentured labour from China and India. Between 1845 and 1917, a total of 143,939 Indians came to Trinidad, of whom only 33,294 eventually returned to India (Clarke, 1986). The terms of indenture initially included a return at the expiration of contract, but soon land acquisition in lieu of return became common practice. The Crown Colony's decision to release land for small farming in 1869 – denied to ex-slaves after Emancipation (Blouet, 1976) – prompted the settlement of East Indians in the west and south. Natural increase, helped by continued immigration of landless and debt-burdened peasants from Uttar Pradesh, consolidated the rural East Indian presence in southern Trinidad (Clarke, 1986). By 1895, East Indians constituted 87 per cent of the sugar estate labour, almost half still indentured, but most of the free East Indians also remained in agriculture, cultivating padi rice (Brereton, 1979). By 1901, East Indians made up one-third of Trinidad's total population (Ramesar, 1976). However, they remained outside Trinidad's urban realms and thereby peripheral to the political and economic changes which were to gradually mould populist sentiment among the Afro-creole intermediate class in the last half of the nineteenth century (MacDonald, 1986).

Trinidad's multi-cultural society not only received demographic infusions from Asia during this time: ex-slaves fleeing from their plantations in the Windward and Leeward Islands were encouraged to settle in Trinidad (Conway, 1986). With cocoa surpassing sugar as a profitable export staple in the 1870s, many of these small islanders and indigent French-creoles prospered, while the sugar industry underwent a series of crises and 'restructing' during the 1880s and 1890s. In addition, the colonial government's aversion to accommodating the Trinidadian Afro-French creoles led to the recruitment of a large number of Barbadians to staff her civil service and police force. Grenadians and

Barbadians, who were better assimilated to the British ways, spoke king's English, and were Protestant and loyal, gained preference in the Trinidadian professions and came to constitute an important urban-based Afro-creole group (MacDonald, 1986).

Urban Trinidad in the late nineteenth and early twentieth century was a crucible of societal change and political economic realignments. Improved educational faculties, Catholic and Protestant, catering for the French- and English-creoles had fostered European cultural values. In Port of Spain, St Mary's College and Queen's Royal College initially served the offspring of the white élites, but island scholarships and enfranchisement of 'coloured' deserving children enlarged the range of educational opportunities for the intermediate Afro-creole groups. Tobago, on the other hand, had a smaller number of schools and although Protestant churches provided elementary education, the public education of Tobagonians suffered in comparison to urban Trinidad. Relatively better educated West Indian immigrants, from Barbados in particular, also augmented a growing middle-class of urban Afro-creoles, and it was not long before the mobilization of popular support, encouraged by a persistent high degree of freedom of speech, translated itself into social protest and political consciousness-raising. The first decade of the twentieth century and the disturbing experiences of Trinidad's involvement in Britain's World War I, heralded the growth of black intellectualism, radicalism and opposition to Crown Colony government and a nationalistic rejection of white supremacist ideology (Brereton, 1981; MacDonald, 1986).

Then, the discovery and exploration of oil in the south of Trinidad began a new sequence of economic prosperity, urbanization and regional development for the main island after 1910. Meanwhile Tobago stagnated in its ward status, her population and economic fortunes suffering hardship brought on by the crisis in sugar; the mainland beckoned and Tobagonians responded. San Fernando (Figure 3.1) experienced its second phase of rapid population increase from 1911 through to 1946. West Indian small islanders fleeing the hard times in their declining plantation economies sought opportunities in the oil industry and its related service industries in Trinidad's second city 'in south'. East Indians, who had already begun to move in to dry-goods commerce in the city by the 1870s, took advantage of more opportunities in the urban service sector and, along with Syrians and Chinese minorities, established themselves in San Fernando during these first three decades. By 1931, however, East Indians accounted for only 17 per cent of San Fernando's population. The city was still the preserve of the French- and English-creoles (3 per cent), West Indians (22 per cent), and Afro-creoles (58 per cent) (Clarke, 1986).

Port of Spain, still the primary city of the rejuvenated Trinidad, did not relinquish its central position in spite of the south's economic uplift. As if reflecting the emerging dominance of their two major cities, 'South' and 'North' were to maintain their separate identities as the twentieth century witnessed increased population growth, increased rates of population redistribution and further economic fluctuations in the two-island nation.

Twentieth Century Population Redistribution

Data from the censuses taken in Trinidad and Tobago since merger, enable us to record accurately the considerable population growth that has occurred. From a modest total population of 171,179 in 1881, Trinidad and Tobago's 1986 population was estimated to be 1.25 million.

Since 1901, four phases of growth are apparent: (1) the first decade 1901–11, with very high rates of birth, death and net immigration and a resultant high rate of total population growth; (2) the next two decades 1911–31, in which birth and death rates dropped steadily, but in concert so that the rate of natural increase remained constant, accompanied by a considerable decline in net immigration, which led to a reduction in the annual rates of population growth; (3) the period 1931–60, in which birth rates rose slowly at first, then dramatically during 1946–60 and death rates continued to decline, while net immigration increased early, but then declined in the 1950s, so that its positive influence on total population growth was less marked than during the decade 1901–11 (Harewood, 1967); and (4) the decades 1960–80 which have experienced decreases in birth rates, a continued decline in death rates and a reduced effect of net immigration on total population growth, but the annual rate of growth is still high enough to be of significant economic and societal consequence to Trinidad and Tobago's future. When the patterns of international and internal migration are included in this growth scenario, the differential impacts of growth via uncontrolled urbanization and regional differences in settlement concentration and dispersion pose even greater consequences.

The significant contribution of international immigration from India and the neighbouring British West Indies in the first decade of the twentieth century was, in fact, the tail end of a mass influx started in the mid-nineteenth century which for several decades contributed to over 40 per cent of the overall growth. After indentured East Indian immigration finally came to a close in 1917, and other opportunities opened up for small islanders in Panama and later in Aruba and Curaçao, immigration to Trinidad made very little contribution to total growth in the next two inter-censal periods (1911–31). It was not until the opening of the

US bases in Trinidad that large-scale immigration from the British West Indies again made an impact (Harewood, 1967). The 1950s was a decade of considerable emigration from both islands to Britain, but unlike other West Indian diasporas to the 'mother country', this outflow did not reach dramatic proportions (Segal, 1975).

The final two decades (1960–80) have witnessed certain qualitative as well as quantitative shifts in the role of immigration. Although undocumented, during the second half of the 1970s to the present, Trinidad seems to have experienced an increased influx of Grenadians and Vincentians, who are being absorbed into the urban black underclasses of Greater Port of Spain and the East Main Road Conurbation, but who have also found informal sector opportunities in the oil industry service sector 'in South'. The emigration of Trinidadian professional classes in the late 1970s and early 1980s, both to Canada and the United States, was met somewhat by immigration from elsewhere in the Caribbean, but a significant inflow of expatriate (British), Canadian and United States professionals also matched this 'brain drain' of nationals. Indeed, emigration and immigration are occurring simultaneously, and together with substantial international circulation volumes, this international mobility is influencing Trinidad's urban experience in distinctive qualitative ways, in excess of the quantitative effects. In general, the contemporary period evidences a modest quantitative impact of international immigration on the nation's population growth.

The internal redistribution of these international flows, the 'internal' migration of Tobagonians and the internal migration of Trinidadians, particularly rural-to-urban flows, have been and continue to be considerable. When added to relatively high rates of natural increase of the urban population in the latest decades, it becomes clear that the pace of urbanization is quickening via both of these demographic processes. During 1970–75, natural increase contributed 57.9 per cent and rural-to-urban migration 42.1 per cent to urban growth (Hope, 1986). With fertility rates generally declining, it can be anticipated that by the mid-1980s, migration's share will have increased.

Census data for the period 1921 to 1980 show that there have been considerably different patterns of growth of the 'South' and 'North' urbanized areas (Table 3.1). The 1911 oil boom prompted urban growth in the south in San Fernando and St Patrick, but it was matched by rural increases in Victoria due to the development and settlement of Crown lands. Similarly, in the north, rural population increases occurred in St Andrew and Mayaro as undeveloped Crown land was settled there in the first two decades of the century. However, by 1921 there was evidence of rural-to-urban movement as well as immigration to the major towns Port of Spain and San Fernando, and to minor towns along

Table 3.1. Population of Trinidad and Tobago, 1921–80

Administrative areas	Population (000's)					
	1921	1931	1946	1960	1970	1980
Port of Spain	61.6	70.3	92.8	93.9	62.7	54.9
St George	75.8	91.5	146.4	267.5	323.7	400.1
Caroni	50.6	51.2	61.7	90.5	115.3	140.2
St Andrew/St David	30.3	29.0	28.3	38.6	45.1	50.0
Nariva/Mayaro	9.3	14.8	16.0	23.3	28.4	31.1
San Fernando	10.6	14.4	28.8	39.9	36.9	33.5
Victoria	67.1	69.3	87.4	132.7	163.2	186.9
St Patrick	34.1	46.8	69.2	108.2	117.2	123.5
Tobago	23.4	25.4	27.2	33.3	38.8	39.5
Trinidad and Tobago	365.9	412.8	558.0	828.0	931.1	1,060.0

Sources: Central Statistical Office Censuses (CSO: Post of Spain, Trinidad and Tobago).

the Port of Spain–Sangre Grande railway. By 1931, the pace of urban growth had quickened, but internal movement had not yet reached its maximum proportions. While San Fernando continued to experience growth in the 1931–46 inter-censal period, Greater Port of Spain was already extending its boundaries via rural-to-urban and urban-to-suburban relocations. Tobago lost population to mainland urban centres like Arima and Toco. Already the East Main Road conurbation was beginning to fill in (Simpson, 1973). But, natural increase contributed most to urban growth prior to the onset of World War II.

Between 1946 and 1960, approximately 90 per cent of Port of Spain's loss of residential population was absorbed in the immediately adjacent suburban wards of St George county, Diego Martin in the west, and St Ann's and Tacarigua in the east. However, replacements from elsewhere compensated for this suburbanization. St George, and more particularly townships along the East Main Road, also showed gains from other counties during 1946–60, especially St Andrew, Caroni and Tobago. Only St Patrick in the south experienced gains through in-migration, as all other counties outside the Capital Region and San Fernando netted losses (Simpson, 1973).

More detailed estimates of internal migration patterns in Trinidad and Tobago for the period after 1960 are possible, due to improvements in the 1970 and 1980 census enumeration schedules and the availability of migration data from the Continuous Sample Survey of Population (CSSP) conducted by the Central Statistical Office for the years 1971, 1974, 1977 (Hunte, 1975).

Census estimates of internal migration between 1960 and 1965 indicate that Port of Spain began to lose population more rapidly than replacement could compensate and 50 per cent of St George's in-migrants came from the capital city. Also, Victoria, the county surrounding San Fernando, received a suburbanizing population from that city as well as an inflow from nearby St Patrick. The volume of this southern pattern was, however, only a third that of the interchange into and within the Capital Region. The during the next five years, 1965–70, absolute numbers of migrants doubled. St George county received approximately 36,000 persons, still 50 per cent coming from Port of Spain, but appreciable proportions (8–9 per cent) were now moving into the region from all over Trinidad, San Fernando, St Andrew, St Patrick, Caroni and Tobago included. Port of Spain, on the other hand, lost 32,700 persons, most through suburbanization, and suffered a dramatic net loss of residential population by 1970 of 31,200 persons.

CSSP data for the five-year period 1969–74 show an even greater amount of internal migration in Trinidad and Tobago than was evident during the 1965–70 period. Again, Port of Spain was the source of the majority (44 per cent) of St George's increment of 45,900 persons, with Caroni, St Andrew and Victoria being other significant contributors. Victoria, continuing the earlier trend of suburbanization, was the recipient of 4,700 residents from San Fernando and, together with Caroni, received over 10,000 in-migrants during the five-year period 1969–74. Port of Spain, although experiencing a net loss of over 16,000 persons, received approximately two-thirds of its 7,800 in-migrants from nearby St George. Since survey research undertaken at the same time (Conway, 1976) had suggested this type of move as the culmination of a step-wise transition, this additional CSSP evidence of such moves into the city from the conurbations in St George appears to be further confirmation (Conway, 1981, 1984). Elsewhere, net losses were the common trend throughout rural Trinidad and even the major cities, so that by 1974, the Capital Region was *the* major destination for internal (and international) migrants.

CSSP data for the next five-year period 1972–77 evidenced a 15 per cent reduction in absolute volume of movement and a 4 per cent reduction of in-migration into St George county. In essence, the period was one of continued attraction to the Capital Region but now appreciable proportions were also moving to other regions, Caroni and Victoria especially. Port of Spain also continued to receive some migrants from St George, again a maintenance of the step-wise pattern noted earlier, but still lost more residents (12,100 persons) in the interchange of in-migrants for suburbanites. San Fernando also continued to lose population to nearby Victoria but also to the northern conurbation in St George.

Interestingly, throughout the 1970s, there appears to have been little interchange of residents between Trinidad's two major cities, Port of Spain and San Fernando. Also, retaining a separation which is part cultural, part geographical and part economic, 'South' and 'North' seem to have experienced different patterns of migration and urbanization. What inter-regional transfers occurred between the two regions have been generally one-way from south to north into the St George conurbation, into Diego Martin in west St George, and east into St Ann's, Tacarigua and Arima wards, but rarely directly into Port of Spain. Only a counter-stream to Victoria partially balances this uneven exchange.

In sum, the twentieth-century pattern was one of increased urban primacy up to 1946, with Greater Port of Spain and San Fernando accounting for approximately 22 per cent of the national population at that time. Then, rapid suburbanization within the conurbation occurred from 1946 through to 1960, with St George county, surrounding Port of Spain to the west and east, acquiring a dominance which it has never relinquished. Also by 1960, both Port of Spain and San Fernando had reached their highest populations to date, 94,000 and 40,000 respectively, and from that time onwards they started to lose residential population. The decade 1960 to 1970 witnessed the continued rapid growth of St George, but in the oil belt a smaller but significant suburbanization movement was also contributing to the growth of Victoria and St Patrick counties. Most recently, in the 1970–80 decade, there has been continued infilling and suburbanization in St George, growth in Caroni county, where the government's Port Lisas project and other industrialization adventures attracted labour and attendant services, and further suburbanization in the oil belt counties of St Patrick and Victoria. By 1980, the dominance of the urbanized county of St George was pronounced with an estimated 43 per cent of the national population residing in this Capital Region – approximately 460,000 persons, and an undisclosed number who commute daily across county boundaries into the region – possibly as many as 15,000 from Caroni, 5,000 from St Andrew and even 4,000 from Victoria (Hunte, 1975; Hunte and Pujadas, 1983).

The Evolving Internal Structures of Port of Spain and San Fernando

Nineteenth-century Port of Spain was a flourishing commercial centre. As a port with a fine roadstead and with its location making it suitable for British mercantilist efforts in the Americas, the city prospered. By 1838, the city population had grown to 11,701, of which 'coloureds' made up approximately 60 per cent, while 'blacks' and 'whites' comprised the remaining 25 and 16 per cent respectively (Brereton, 1981). Although 60 per cent of the early buildings were destroyed in the Great Fire of 1808, the physical form of the city's central core was established. The wharf district was the commercial heart and streets were paved establishing a north/south grid pattern that remains as the present Central Business District (CBD). Adjacent to the CBD, east of the markets and shops on George, Nelson, and Duncan Streets, poorer urbanites crowded into the available accommodation. With black small island immigration swelling their numbers, high density 'barracks' and 'yards' were constructed in 'Corbeaux Town' and east of the city centre in East Dry River and Laventille.

Demand for residential land soon led to areal expansion beyond this core, however. Sugar estates on the adjacent periphery were bought up and better-off citizenry began a suburban expansion to the northwest. Two landscaped areas, Victoria and Harris Squares, gave this early residential development a neighbourhood identity which was to survive future expansion and engulfment. Farther west, a satellite community of Woodbrook was developed for upper-class suburbanites.

During the period 1838–1900, technological advances in services and improved transportation hastened residential decentralization of the upper white and coloured classes. By 1885, the city boasted a mule-drawn tramway, a telephone system and horse-drawn cab services (Ottley, 1970). Continued immigration of black small islanders, Chinese, Madeirans, Syrians and cityward movements of Afro-creoles 'off the plantations' swelled densities in eastern districts of the inner city. The resultant pressure initiated a suburban sectoral expansion of this low-income area into the Laventille hills during this growth period of the nineteenth century. This more haphazard eastward encroachment was partly a result of the anarchic land market conditions at the time, with a mosaic of relatively small coffee and cocoa estates, many of which were abandoned, providing plenty of opportunity for uncontrolled occupancy and settlement by the poor. On the other hand, the planned north-west and northern expansion of élite communities was more orderly, controlled and exclusionary (Goodenough, 1978).

Through the first decades of the twentieth century the separate directions of residential suburban expansion continued. Westward, more estates were developed for British and European families seeking to distance themselves from the now notorious and overcrowded city centre and area 'back of the bridge'. St Clair, an estate on the edge of town adjacent to the country club and racecourse (the Savanna), superseded Woodbrook as the premier 'status-address' district. There was one internal development, however, that did alter the city's nineteenth-century sectoral growth pattern (Figure 3.2). By the 1920s,

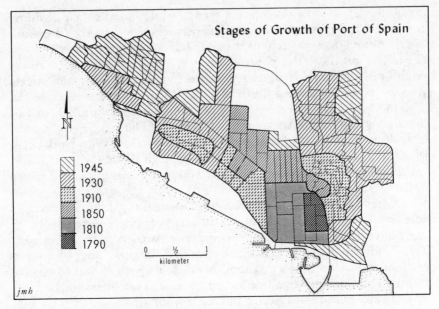

Figure 3.2. Stages of growth of Port of Spain.

the Peru estate lying to the west of the high status areas of St Clair and Tranquility had become an East Indian enclave. Later developing as a separate community of St James, the presence of this ethnic village halted farther westward sectoral expansion of upper-status districts. Thereafter, élite residential development was diverted northward in the Maraval, St Ann's and Cascade Valleys (Conway, 1976).

Commensurate with the urbanization experience of the main island, Trinidad and the virtual absence of urban growth and change in Tobago, the two major cities, Port of Spain and San Fernando, are likely to have experienced internal transformations of their residential spaces. Port of Spain's morphological development, evolving urban ecological structure and areal expansion, can be documented because of the compatibility of the more recent censuses between 1931–70 (Conway, 1976; Goodenough, 1978). San Fernando's social-spatial structure, although amenable to ecological cross-sectional analysis for 1931 and 1960, is more difficult to assess because of the aggregation mismatch between sub-areal units and the smaller scale of its community associations (Clarke, 1986). Despite these methodological difficulties, it is instructive to examine the evolving internal structure of each of these cities to establish whether there is evidence in urban Trinidad of the reconstitution of social and spatial formations during the country's transition from a racially denominated societal ordering

(Braithwaite, 1953; Clarke, 1973; Goodenough, 1978) to a more contemporary 'modernizing' stratification, where socio-economic and family status differentials selectively divide urban space (Briggs and Conway, 1975; Conway, 1986).

Using the census materials mentioned above, the present author has carried out multivariate analyses to examine urban residential change in Port of Spain (Conway, 1976, 1987). Although there were changes in variable definitions between censuses, there appeared to be considerable similarity in the urban ecological dimensions which emerged for 1931 and 1960. Ethnic–religious variation was a dominant feature of residential differentiation in both periods. There was little evidence of much reordering of residential patterns in Port of Spain during the period 1930 to 1960, continuing a trend of ethnic, racial and religious divisions of urban structure which has persisted since the nineteenth century (Goodenough, 1978).

In the 1960 to 1970 longitudinal analysis – a more extensive urban area – a smaller scale of enumeration districts and a larger number of ecological variables were used than in the 1931–60 comparison. Continuity was evident in the dominance of ethnic-racial differentiation both in 1960 and 1970, but some change by 1970 was also evident. East Indian and 'white' spatial segregation continued, but family status and socio-economic status characters of the urban population were beginning to discriminate residential areas. By 1970, there was the beginning of a reordering of the urban ecology of Port of Spain. A distinct socio-economic status dimension of residential differentiation had emerged as a major construct and, with the exception of East Indian separation, there was a selective decline in significance of ethnic/racial status differentiation (Conway, 1976, 1987).

Ecological studies of San Fernando's social-spatial structure since 1931 note the transition of the city's social hierarchy from domination by white élites prior to World War I to a multi-racial élite, in which Afro-creoles and 'westernized' Presbyterian East Indians began to enter the upper ranks. At Independence in 1962, the old upper stratum of privileged white families had developed into a coloured Creole class, mixed with British expatriates and with creolized East Indian appendages. Then the petro-dollar fortunes of the 1970s provided material prosperity and the entry to southern élite circles of East Indians, and was accompanied by the movement of young East Indians into the professions. Thereby, the East Indian ascension to social acceptance in San Fernando society has been accomplished (Clarke, 1986).

Whereas spatial patterns of residential differentiation in Port of Spain reflect the ethnic, racial divisions of urban society in 1931 and 1960, in San Fernando there was less spatial divisiveness. In 1931 there were major concentrations of whites in the premier neighbourhoods, and East Indians dominated southern and western residential areas, but racial exclusiveness was nowhere perfect, and there was considerable heterogeneity (Clarke, 1986). A factorial ecology of San Fernando in 1960, conducted by Conway and Jacks, 1977, however, did find ethnic associations with socio-economic and family status common to those emerging in Port of Spain. In general, San Fernando's smaller overall size and the mismatch between level of data aggregation and apparent size of social/communal networks prevents urban ecological analysis from discerning the spatial mosaic of residential differentiation therein. Port of Spain's contemporary experience and the urbanization of the Capital Region, on the other hand, can be examined further.

The centralization of administration and decision-making power in Port of Spain which persisted throughout colonial times, continued after Independence in 1962. As a result, colonial and post-colonial regimes either deliberately encouraged, or at least did not discourage, concentration of a wide range of facilities in the Capital Region (see Figure 3.3).

Major social amenities such as schools and hospitals were mainly located in Port of Spain. In fact, prior to World War II, all secondary schools and all major hospitals were either in the capital or in San Fernando. Even the more basic amenities such as potable water, electricity and sewage disposal systems were concentrated in Port of Spain and the surrounding urbanized areas of St George. By the end of the 1970s, the whole urbanized corridor stretching from Carenage in west Diego Martin to Arima in east St George (Figure 3.3), including the valley settlements on the southern slopes of the Northern Range, was served by pipe-borne water. A sewerage system was extended from Point Cumana in the west to San Juan in the east and the Diego Martin Valley was linked to the main system.

Road development continued as Port of Spain's centrality in commercial, administrative and political affairs increased, so that by the mid-1970s, the Capital Region was served by approximately 56 miles of major rural roads – like the Beetham, Churchill–Roosevelt, Princess Margaret Highways, Southern Main Road and the Solomon Hochoy Highway – and 110 miles of major urban roads, including the major east-west arterial, the Western and Eastern Main Roads.

Since the petro-dollar bonanza, although there has been an attempt to improve all of Trinidad's road network, the Capital Region has enjoyed considerable road improvements and development. The Diego Martin valley roads have been widened and dual-carriageways link this major residential suburb to the Western Main Road. A completely new highway has been built across the Mucurapo swamp linking the Western Main Road to Wrightson Road downtown in order to bypass the

The Capital Region of Trinidad

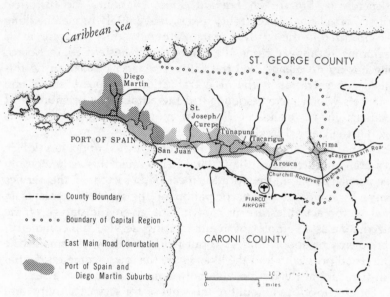

Figure 3.3. The Capital Region of Trinidad.

congested township of St James. The Churchill–Roosevelt highway has been widened and a dual carriageway will eventually extend to Arima. The old Eastern Main Road light railway right-of-way has been converted to a Priority Bus Route, thus easing travel to Port of Spain for commuters residing in the eastern segment of the Capital Region. Yet, in spite of the road improvement programmes, automobile ownership and the resultant overcrowding of roads, the Capital Region has more than kept pace. In 1970 there were 21 vehicles per kilometre of road length in Trinidad, but by 1980 there were 41 vehicles owned per kilometre of road length (Planning Division, 1975).

Not surprisingly, Port of Spain and the Capital Region developed as the primary locus of employment opportunities, particularly in the secondary and tertiary sectors of the national economy (the production and distribution of manufactured goods and of services). Today, downtown Port of Spain is the prime commercial centre, with concentrations of similar commercial activities in definable quarters of 'downtown' – wholesaling south of Independence Square, retailing centred on Frederick and Chacon Streets, banking on the north and south sides of Independence Square, financial services (insurance, discount and finance houses) on Abercromby and Chacon Streets, and government/legal services around the Red House on St Vincent Street. Recent government building of the new Halls of Justice just north of

Woodford Square and the twin towers of the Financial Centre just south of Independence Square on Edward Street continues the historical pattern of Port of Spain's centrality and primacy. Only branch banking has decentralized in the last few years. Although a few shopping malls are beginning to appear along the Western and Eastern Main Roads, retailing has by no means 'fled the City'. The recent exception to this continued concentration is the decentralization of grocery stores and supermarkets which have responded to the automobile orientation of Trinidadians in all walks of life and moved to accessible points throughout the Capital Region.

Sixty-one per cent of Trinidad's employment opportunities in services are concentrated in the Capital Region and this estimate only reflects participation in the formal (measured) sector of the service economy. Estimates of the participation of the region's residents in informal sector activities are unknown, but given the nature of the urbanized zone as a complex of manufacturing, service and commerce, there are plenty of opportunities for out-work, repair work, small-scale retailing, food provision and the like. Thus, the low-income residential areas in the Capital Region provide both a haven as well as a sizeable market for an enormous amount of informal sector service activity, and thereby contribute to the region's pre-eminence.

Uneven Economic Development under State Capitalism

From the time oil was discovered in 1907, Trinidad's fortunes have revolved on the development of its petroleum and asphalt resources and on how it was going to utilize this sector's production and revenue to diversify and develop its economy. The years of World War II (1939–45) provided one boost to the diversification thrust. The doubling of oil output between 1934 and 1938, construction activities associated with the establishment of US bases and the stimulation of food production resulting from the accompanying considerable increases in incomes, all increased domestic demand and led to the establishment of a large number of manufacturing and repair plants, making a variety of foods, beverages, and consumer goods for Trinidadian consumers.

However, it was St Lucian-born economist W. Arthur Lewis who supplied the first persuasive development model for Trinidad and the rest of the Commonwealth Caribbean, arguing that despite the region's small size and fragmentation, an impressive array of industries was indeed possible. Lewis concluded that the only solution to the pressing problems of Caribbean unemployment and poverty was to industrialize. Countries should adopt a strategy combining regional import sub-stitution and export promotion industrialization. The latter should be based on attracting foreign capital, technology and expertise by way of generous incentives, tax holidays, infrastructural support and region-wide promotion and co-ordination (Lewis, 1950).

Trinidad and Tobago's colonial administration remained somewhat lukewarm to Lewis's ideas, but on his assumption to power in 1956, Dr Williams set about implementing this strategy of 'industrialization by invitation'. With personal advice from Arthur Lewis and from members of the Puerto Rico Economic Development Administration, a development plan based on Puerto Rico's 'Operation Bootstrap' was adopted in the PNM's First Five Year Plan (1958-62) (Government of Trinidad and Tobago, 1957; Sebastien, 1982).

In order to provide for this industrialization programme's pre-requisites, the role of the country's public utilities was emphasized in the First Five Year Plan. Public sector revenues, which had always been sizeable, were drawn upon to improve the social and economic infrastructure. The Second Five Year Plan (1964-9) went further, advocating governmental control (take-over) of public utilities (Government of Trinidad and Tobago, 1963). With the implementation of these two investment thrusts and with increases in recurrent expenditures implicit in the public running of these utility companies, accumulated reserves were run down. At the same time, fiscal incentives to industry (especially large overseas investments) via the 'invitation package' were narrowing the tax base, so that by the end of the 1960s there was a financial squeeze in the making.

By the time of the Third Five Year Plan in 1969, it was fairly evident that 'industrialization by invitation' was not working. Job opportunities in the private sector had grown far too slowly to cope with population increase, yet expectations were rising – 'Black power consciousness', Caribbean independence, working-class consciousness coalesced in an undercurrent of popular pressure for government action.

Conscious of the demands pressing for a new invigorating direction for Trinidad, Dr Williams designed his Third Five Year Plan as a 'middle way', where government in partnership with industry would be expected to provide the necessary initiative(s) for prosperity and development (Government of Trinidad and Tobago, 1970; St Cyr, 1981). Foreign capital was to be an adjunct to national capital and the popular sectors, the co-operatives, the trade unions, the small businesses, small farmers and the handicraft industries were to be assisted to encourage self-reliance. Making a case for 'State Capitalism' and the expansion of the state sector so that it was actively involved in the running of the economy, the Third Five Year Plan noted 'innate deficiencies' in the performance to date of private enterprise in Trinidad and Tobago. Such agencies as the Development Finance Corporation, the Industrial Development Corporation and the National Petroleum Company were thus to promote joint ventures and public partnership ventures with private foreign or local capital.

By the end of 1972, the government owned shares in 32 companies representing an investment value amounting to almost TT60 million, this not including the dollar-equivalent of full ownership of the four public utility companies. Then the windfall of petro-dollars began in late 1973. With public revenues almost all gone by 1973, the resultant growth in net foreign assets and increases in government deposits with the Central Bank, came just in time to rescue Dr Williams' 'mixed economy', State Capitalism model of development.

From 1974 onwards, the question of economic development no longer centred on whether or not local or foreign financial resources could be mobilized, but rather how this huge petro-dollar financial surplus would be deployed so as to encourage a diversified and interdependent economy with long-term sustainable capacities sufficient to absorb and provide for Trinidadian and Tobagonian labour and their dependants.

Dr Williams, responding to Chamber of Commerce pressure, accelerated his government's path towards more State Capitalism. Huge investments were made in infrastructural development – roads, highways, port improvements, a natural gas pipeline and reservoir development. The Port Lisas industrial estate (Figure 3.1) was earmarked as the country's new 'growth pole'. Road links, water service, piped natural gas, a complex of gas turbines to provide electricity and a modern deepwater port facility with heavy gantry cranes were constructed to upgrade the industrial estates' infrastructure. Nearby Chaguanas received financial assistance to develop housing and social services as well as improving basic amenity provision in the area. Port Lisas became the headquarters of government's venture in capital goods production; the Iron and Steel Company of Trinidad and Tobago (ISCOTT) was one project, a joint venture fertilizer plant with AMOCO, Fertilizers of Trinidad and Tobago (FERTIN) another. Complaining that local professionals and firms had not performed to expectations, in 1979 Dr Williams promoted a bilateral (government-to-government) approach to the construction and implementation of Trinidad and Tobago's 40 or so projects (Ryan, 1984). By 1981, shortly before his death, the failure of this refinement of the State Capitalism model was apparent, in spite of the political rhetoric levelling blame at local professionalism, technical skills, and the arrogance of foreign governments and multinational corporations (Ballah Report, 1982).

Dr Williams' last modification of State Capitalism failed to generate sufficient output and economic vigour to enable the economy to withstand the downturn of world market fortunes which accompanied the US-led recession in 1981–83. There was a continuation of the problem of financing manufacturing and productive enterprises which had plagued Trinidad in the 1960s, despite the increased revenues. Foreign exchange problems emerged and there appeared to be an unwarranted 'flight of capital' out of Trinidad during the 'seven years of plenty' – 1973 to 1980. The absolute level of real output in agricultural production actually declined during the 1970s. Manufacturing output fluctuated during the period but was generally concentrated in demand-led assembly activity, so that when CARICOM (Caribbean Community) trade difficulties emerged in the early 1980s, and Guyana and Jamaica were unable to meet their financial commitments to their community creditors, manufacturing's fortunes waned (St Cyr, 1981). Equally critical was the inadequacy of incomes policies to intercede in wage and salary negotiations and external and internal inflationary pressures which contributed to high rates of wage and price inflation. Import prices escalated in the post-OPEC period, excessive expansion in the Trinidad and Tobago money supply occurred, production bottlenecks were commonplace and last, but by no means least, there was widespread institutional corruption.

Trinidad and Tobago in the 1980s is a country where the petrodollar influx has not brought solutions to the structural problems the country faced in the post-colonial period. Despite government's high level of involvement in running the economy, there has always been a distinct lack of centralized planning to regulate and co-ordinate the disparate activities of all the state enterprises (Sandoval, 1983). For various reasons, including the size and significance (in terms of political and economic clout) of the private commercial (importer) sector, bad management and planning, patronage and party – bureaucratic hiring practices, corruption and the like, as well as the depressed state of the world market and the global economy – many state enterprises have been running at a loss year-in, year-out. The national airline BWIA, ISCOTT, Caroni Ltd, National Fisheries and Trinidad Meat Processors are but a few in need of an annual subsidy. Lack of concern for any policies to curb or control the on-going process of urbanization were just other manifestations of government's inability to assume responsibility for planning and co-ordinating the country's development.

Planning and Politics

The genesis of national planning in the Commonwealth Caribbean is traceable to Lord Moyne's Royal West Indies Commission of 1938–9 and this commission's report (eventually published in 1945) on the planning and development of Britain's Caribbean colonies (HMSO, 1945). Town planning, or more correctly, the collusion of the colonial administration and municipal councils with the urban élites and plantocracy in the subdivision of residential estates, their exclusionary practices and the maintenance of services and infrastructure at the behest of the wealthy, had long been practised in Trinidad's cities; Port of Spain, San Fernando, and Arima (Ottley, 1970).

The Colonial Office's notion of a national plan for her individual charges was equally biased and short-sighted. Planning was to ensure that development assistance (loans and Treasury Grants) was efficiently formulated and implemented (Reid, 1987). Trinidad and Tobago, therefore, in anticipation of the Moyne Commission's visit in 1938, attempted to prepare local development plans, but their myopic focus was to anticipate and thereby successfully acquire resources from the Colonial Development and Welfare Fund (Nicolescu, 1958). In effect, this initiative, like its counterparts in other colonies, was interwoven with the territorial competitiveness engendered by the promotion of the West Indies Federation. As well as countering co-ordinated planning among the Commonwealth Caribbean, it spawned fragmentary schemes among internal departments in order to compete for Colonial Office funds. It also engendered distrust, or lack of interest, among national politicians. Lack of adequate data (except censuses which were efficiently managed), lack of planning expertise, lack of institutional resources and the scepticism of politicians, severely hampered this first colonial initiative, and it left no permanent legacy of institutional and managerial structures for national planning in the post-colonial era (Reid, 1987).

This paltry start notwithstanding, Trinidad's attainment of Independence heralded a new era for planning. Dr Williams and the PNM had to demonstrate they had control over the strategic sectors of the economy as a means of meeting the major social objectives of development - employment creation, reduction of income inequalities, wealth generation, infrastructural development, human resource development, and so on. Unfortunately, the plans were politically motivated symbols, eminently useful as mechanisms for demonstrating to potential aid donors that the PNM and Prime Minister Williams appeared to have control over Trinidad's economic trajectory, but less useful as operational blueprints communicating national objectives to the public and private sectors (Little, 1982).

Unfortunately, the economic sectoral planning embarked upon in the country's Third Five Year Plan in 1969 (Government of Trinidad and Tobago, 1970) and the Government White Papers on Public Participation in Industry in 1972 and 1975 (Government of Trinidad and Tobago, 1972, 1975), although accompanied by an apparent institutional concern for integration with regional planning objectives, was not seriously modified to accommodate spatial concerns. Indeed, government's implementation of physical planning strategies was quite delinquent. In retrospect, the record is nothing short of deplorable.

Although the Town and Country Planning Ordinance of 1960 had stipulated that the Minister responsible for Planning should direct his Town and Country Division to develop a national development plan for submission to Parliament for approval, such a regional economic master plan was not immediately forthcoming. In fact, the Town and Country Planning Division's efforts throughout the 1960s were very much focused on current day-to-day physical planning problems – building permits, access rights-of-way, land use disputes – and on problems involved in planning and promoting housing development schemes in and around Port of Spain (Laventile, Diamond Vale, Barataria and Morvant), in San Fernando, Tobago and elsewhere in Central Trinidad. Finally in 1974, the Town and Country Planning Division did produce a Draft Plan, a co-ordinating document entitled *The National Framework* and in 1975, a series of eight regional plans were published which incorporated the essential features of Trinidad and Tobago's National Framework. By 1977, this protracted effort was at the stage of an evaluation of alternative strategies and an Interim Draft Report complete with alternatives, their rationales and the Planning Division's recommendations was circulated for comment among several government and quasi-government agencies involved in the physical planning process. With this feedback incorporated into the document, two volumes of the *National Physical Development Plan of Trinidad and Tobago* were produced in 1978: Volume I consisted of a Survey and Analysis, and Volume II contained Development Strategies and Proposals (Planning Division, 1978). This planning document, which claimed to have 'had the benefit of over six years of conceptual thinking', was then submitted for Ministerial action. The responsible Ministry was that of Finance, a portfolio always held by Dr Williams and later by his PNM successor George Chambers. Suffice it to record that the Prime Minister's customary disinterest in spatial issues and planning was matched by a distinct lack of effort to promote this plan. For the next two years this regional economic planning blueprint only made it to a Public Inquiry. Then it was further revised in response to that input. Whether Dr Williams' death further delayed action, or whether his successor was too busy to concern himself with it, for another three years the plan languished in and among government ministries. Finally in April 1983, the *National Physical Development Plan* was introduced in Parliament and a short while after adopted (August 1984). At last, 23 years after the initial 1960 planning ordinance and 14 after the rhetorical recognition of the relevance of spatial issues in the Third Five Year Plan of 1969, regional planning guidelines were being established in Trinidad and Tobago. Although the

Demas Task Force, appointed by Cabinet in 1982 to formulate a multi-sectoral development plan for the Republic for 1983–6, recommended approval in its present form, members of the Force were by then concerned with its long gestation period.

In effect, present-day Trinidad and Tobago is a very different place to what it was in the early 1970s. Yet it was pre-1970 conditions which were analysed and which served as the basis for the Plan's advocacy of: (a) an overall national growth centre strategy; (b) the development of a functional hierarchy of urban settlements; (c) the implementation of strong land use controls in agriculture and conservation areas; (d) the institution of a comprehensive rural development programme in six selected depressed areas; (e) undertaking a massive housing and construction programme; (f) the phasing of major development undertakings; and (g) the implementation of physical, social and economic measures for the creation of fuller employment and structural change in the country (Planning Division, 1978). In short, by the mid-1980s, Greater Port of Spain is the dominant urbanized core, the central magnet for the twin-island nation's social, economic and political activities, yet it is overcrowded, unmanageable and problem-ridden.

The uninhibited sprawl of low-income housing in low-density settlements throughout the Capital Region which continued virtually unabated from the 1950s onwards, is now a major constraint on land supply. Whereas illegal squatting by the poor on Port of Spain's western and eastern peripheries during the 1960s was restricted to a few notorious locations such as John John and Waterhole, now squatting is very evident on the hillsides of Diego Martin, Carenage, Point Cumana and Cocorite. When the demand for land and housing in the Capital Region really took off in the 1970s, fuelled by the rapid growth of a wealthy middle-class, and matched by their adoption of metropolitan expectations concerning modern residential styles, the already dwindling supply of available land was doubly jeopardized. Such subdivision activity was given government stimulus after 1978, resulting in an even more rapid engulfment of the remaining (distant) space in the wards of Arima and Tacarigua.

However, a major constraint to the provision of housing in Trinidad and Tobago as a whole, but particularly in the Capital Region, is the uncoordinated structure and organization of government administration, which has never really came to grips with the idea that uncontrolled urbanization, housing and land development should be handled efficiently.

Not that there was not enough institutional involvement. Legal requirements to obtain approval for residential development were laid out in two ordinances: the *Public Health Ordinance of 1917* (revised in 1950) under which approval was granted for construction based essentially on environmental health considerations, lot drainage, disposal of solid waste and ventilation; and the *Town and Country Planning Ordinance of 1960*, under which approval was granted for land use, compatibility of use, nature of activities and servicing ability. Hence, the two representative statutory bodies administered residential development approval according to their mandates. But they were not the only agencies involved. Others had to give their stamp of approval before permission was granted. These included the Water and Sewerage Authority (WASA) under the *Water and Sewerage Act of 1965*, for all servicing of water; the Highways and Drainage Division of the Ministry of Works for advice on the subdivision of land; and the Ministry of Works, the Town Engineer's Department and the Chief Fire Officer for advice if multi-storey, commercial or any other non-residential activities were contemplated. Little wonder that this cumbersome system of building approval procedures could delay development plans and postpone implementation for up to three years. Indeed, a 1977 inquiry by the government-appointed Scoon Committee identified the following woeful list of shortcomings of this system of statutory bodies: (a) delays and loss of plans; (b) unnecessary movement of plans between authorities; (c) conflicting standards between agencies; (d) overlaps in areas of authorization and the unrealistic standards expected of plan details (Scoon Report, 1977).

This was not the sole administrative bottleneck, however. Since its inception in 1962, the National Housing Authority (NHA) has been unable to undertake successfully, or indeed even launch, a viable programme of housing development. The Scoon Report lamented the NHA's poor performance and its lack of effective co-ordination of housing plans with other statutory bodies. Difficulties involved in the management and operation of contractual tendering arrangements with the construction sector often led to high-cost overruns being passed on by the NHA. There was a continual lack of funds allocated to housing, and the release of such funds was often delayed. The NHA was plagued by lack of resources and skilled personnel, which inevitably inhibited proper planning, implementation and monitoring of projects it did undertake. Finally, the overall lack of a national physical planning strategy prevented the NHA from being able to integrate housing project development with other aspects of regional economic planning (Scoon Report, 1977). This last point is, of course, a recurrent theme in this chapter.

Conclusion

The inadequacies of administrative capabilities, the lack of recognition of the extent to which urbanization has proceeded out of control in contemporary Trinidad and the current problems of reconstruction and readjustment to the hard times of the late 1980s are realities to be faced. This chapter has focused on the nature and pace of uncontrolled urbanization and the incapacity of government planning to manage the process. Government planning has failed to acknowledge spatial variations in societal organization, regional economic structures and resource distribution, and has paid insufficient attention to the spatial adjustment and readjustment of settlement patterns. The latter have generally evolved in anarchic fashion, and planning has failed to incorporate concerns for regional strategies and their integration with the whole national system, such that balanced and controlled growth of the urban space economy can be achieved. A blinkered preoccupation with national economic development problems, concern with the performance of economic sectors, manpower productivity, fiscal solvency and the like, means that regional planning objectives have never been considered seriously as part of government planning strategies.

The tardy acceptance of the 1982 National Physical Development Plan for the twin-island nation in 1984 is a sad reflection on government's appreciation of the attendant problems of uncontrolled urbanization. Being recognized as the seventeenth long-term objective in the Demas Report on *The Imperatives of Adjustment: Draft Development Plan, 1983–1986* (Demas *et al.*, 1984) still puts spatial concerns too far down the list of priorities. All of Trinidad and Tobago's problems notwithstanding, urbanization remains, in effect, uncontrolled.

REFERENCES

Ballah Report (1982) *Report of the Committee Appointed by Cabinet to Review the Entire Programme of Government-to-Government Arrangements*, Port of Spain: Government Printing Office, 25 March 1982.
Blouet, B.W. (1976) 'Land policies in Trinidad, 1838–50,' *Journal of Caribbean History*, 9 43–59.
Braithwaite, L. (1953) 'Social stratification in Trinidad: a preliminary analysis', *Social and Economic Studies*, 2/3, 6–175.
Brereton, B. (1979) *Race Relations in Colonial Trinidad, 1870–1900*, New York: Cambridge University Press.
Brereton, B. (1981) *A History of Modern Trinidad, 1783–1962*, Kingston, Port of Spain, London: Heinemann.
Briggs, R. and Conway, D. (1975) 'The evolution of urban ecological structure: theory and a case study, Port of Spain, Trinidad', *Social Science Quarterly*, 55, 871–88.
Clarke, C.G. (1973) 'Pluralism and stratification in San Fernando, Trinidad',

Social Patterns in Cities, Institute of British Geographers, Special Publications, No. 5, 53–70.

Clarke, C.G. (1986) *East Indians in a West Indian Town: San Fernando, Trinidad, 1930–70,* London; Allen and Unwin.

Conway, D. (1976) Residential Area Change and Residential Relocation in Port of Spain, Trinidad, unpublished PhD dissertation, Austin, Texas: University of Texas.

Conway, D. (1981) 'Fact or opinion on uncontrolled peripheral settlement in Trinidad: or how different conclusions arise from the same data', *Ekistics* 286: 37–43.

Conway, D. (1984) 'The commuter zone as a relocation choice of low income migrants moving in a step-wise pattern to Port of Spain, Trinidad', *Caribbean Geography* 1: 89–106.

Conway, D. (1986) 'Caribbean migrants: opportunistic and individualistic sojourners', *Hanover, NH: UFSI Report,* No. 24, 15.

Conway, D. (1987) 'A spatial–temporal analysis of the residential system in Port of Spain, Trinidad, 1931–70', in: Yadar, C.S. (ed.) *Contemporary City Ecology,* Vol. 6, New Delhi: Concept Pubs, 19–61.

Conway, D. and Jacks, J.A. (1977) 'A re-evaluation of the societal scale concept: city size and residential differentiation in Trinidad', Paper presented to the SSRDG Meeting, Virginia Beach, Virginia, October.

Demas, W.G. *et al.* (1984) *The Imperatives of Adjustment: Draft Development Plan, 1983–1986,* Port of Spain: Government Printing Office.

Government of Trinidad and Tobago (1957) *Five Year Development Programme, 1958–62,* Port of Spain: Government Printery.

Government of Trinidad and Tobago (1963) *Second Five Year Plan, 1964–1968,* Port of Spain: Government Printery.

Government of Trinidad and Tobago (1970) *Third Five Year Plan, 1969–1973,* Port of Spain: Government Printery.

Government of Trinidad and Tobago (1983) *Accounting for the Petro-Dollar,* Port of Spain: Government Printing Office.

Goodenough, S. (1978) 'Race, status and urban ecology in Port of Spain, Trinidad', in: Clarke, C.G. (ed.) *Caribbean Social Relations,* Liverpool: University of Liverpool, Centre for Latin American Studies, No. 8, 17–43.

Harewood, R.J. (1967) 'Population growth of Trinidad and Tobago in the twentieth century', *CSO Research Paper,* No. 4, Trinidad and Tobago, Central Statistical Office, 69–94.

HMSO (1945) *West India. Royal Commission, 1938–39; Recommendations* Cmnd 6174.

Hope, K.R. (1986) *Urbanization in the Commonwealth Caribbean,* Boulder. Colorado, and London: Westview Press.

Hunte, D. (1975) *The Socio-Economic Implications of Internal Migration in Trinidad,* Port of Spain: Central Statistical Office, 35.

Hunte, D. and Pujadas, L. (1983) *1980 Population and Housing Census: Review of the Preliminary 1980 Census Count,* Port of Spain; Central Statistical Office, 12.

Lewis, W.A. (1950) 'The industrialization of the British West Indies', *Caribbean Economic Review* 2, 1–61.

Little, I.M.D. (1982) *Economic Development: Theory, Policy and International Relations*, New York: Basic Books.

MacDonald, S.B. (1986) *Trinidad and Tobago: Democracy and Development in the Caribbean*, New York: Praeger.

Nicolescu, B. (1958) *Colonial Planning: A Comparative Study*, London: Allen and Unwin.

Niddrie, D.L. (1980) *Tobago*, Midleton, Ireland: Litho Press Co.

Ottley, C.R. (1970) *The Story of Port of Spain*, Trinidad and Jamaica: Longman Caribbean.

Planning Division (1975) *Planning for Development: The Capital Region*, Port of Spain: Government Printing Office.

Planning Division (1978) *Planning for Development: National Physical Development Plan Volume 1 – Survey and Analysis*, Port of Spain, Government Printing Office.

Planning Division (1978) *Planning for Development: National Physical Development Plan Volume 2 – Strategies and Proposals*, Port of Spain, Government Printing Office.

Ramesar, M. (1976) 'The impact of the Indian immigrants on colonial Trinidadian society', *Caribbean Quarterly*, 22, 6–7.

Reid, G.L. (1987) 'National planning and the project cycle in the Commonwealth Caribbean', *Integración Latinoamericana*, Special English edition, 48–57.

Ryan, S. (1984) 'Administrative capability and choice of development strategy: the case of Trinidad and Tobago', *CISCLA Working Papers*, San German, Puerto Rico: Universidad Interamericana.

Sandoval, J.M. (1983) 'State capitalism in a petroleum-based economy: the case of Trinidad and Tobago', in: Ambursley, F. and Cohen, R. (eds) *Crisis in the Caribbean*, New York: Monthly Review Press, 247–68.

Sebastien, R. (1982) 'State sector development in Trinidad and Tobago', *Tribune*, 2(1), 42–82.

Scoon Report (1977) *Report of the Scoon Committee on Housing* Port of Spain: Government Printing Office.

Segal, A.L. (1975) *Population Policies in the Caribbean*, Lexington, Massachusetts: Lexington Books.

Simpson, J.M. (1973) *A Demographic Analysis of Internal Migration in Trinidad and Tobago*, Mona, Jamaica: University of the West Indies, Institute of Social and Economic Research.

St Cyr, E.B.A. (1981) *Industrial Development Strategies in Caribbean Countries: Trinidad and Tobago*, Economic Commission for Latin America and the Caribbean, Office of the Caribbean: Port of Spain, 59.

Williams, E. (1963) Speech on 'International perspectives for Trinidad and Tobago', *Freedomways*, delivered in August 1963.

Worrell, D. (1987) *Small Island Economies: Structure and Performance in the English-Speaking Caribbean since 1970*, New York: Praeger.

[4]
Cuba
Derek R. Hall

Historical Aspects of Urban Development

Introduction

After Cuba had been brutally conquered by the Spanish in the early sixteenth century, its estimated 200,000–300,000 indigenous Indians were soon eliminated, and the island was subsequently employed as a stepping stone for further Spanish conquests of Central and South America.

Eventually the process turned full circle, and by the middle of the nineteenth century Spain had lost all its colonies in the Americas except for Cuba and Puerto Rico. Severe military rule was employed to suppress the increasingly frequent violent anti-colonial protests and US-based expeditions. For American expansionists, following the Louisiana and Florida purchases, Cuba appeared ripe for US incorporation, an argument reinforced by the way in which the Florida peninsula pointed straight to the island's heart.

By the 1860s, Cuba was producing more than 30 per cent of the world's cane sugar. Much of the work was undertaken by African slaves, supplemented by indentured Chinese labourers, shipped in during the 1850s and 1860s. Some 600,000 slaves were brought to Cuba during the nineteenth century, until the Atlantic slave trade was ended in 1867. Slavery was not abolished in Cuba until 1886, 13 years after its demise in Puerto Rico.

In 1895, an invasion of the island by factions of the Cuban independence movement, unified under Jose Marti, provoked three years of deadlocked aggression between nationalists and colonists. This was broken in 1898. The United States, now with substantial economic interests in the island, and foreseeing Cuba's strategic location with the Panama Canal under construction, declared war against Spain, and destroyed the European power's fleets in a matter of weeks.

There followed four years of American military occupation. Although Cuban independence was proclaimed in 1902, its efficacy was constrained by the Platt Amendment, whereby the US maintained the right to intervene in Cuban affairs, as it did several times before the Amendment was repealed in 1934. Its lasting psychological effects provided a basis for the strong anti-American element of the 1959 revolution. Indeed, surviving from the Amendment, the United States to this day retains a naval base at Guantanamo, on the south-eastern extremity of the island, which it can only vacate by mutual agreement.

While the population of the island grew rapidly in the late eighteenth and the first half of the nineteenth century (Table 4.1), increasing turmoil, in the last decade of the nineteenth century, brought population decline. Little detailed indication is available as to the extent of urban development, until 'urban population' was employed as a Cuban census category in 1899. However, Morse (1971: 5a), attempting to assess urban primacy in Latin America, suggested that there was a 'primacy dip' around 1800 in Latin America due to war devastation, the colonization of new areas, economic reorganization and disruption of the primary export sector.

Post-colonial Urban Growth and Development

The definition of 'urban population' adopted for the first three post-colonial censuses comprised a locality containing a thousand or more inhabitants. The definition of the two subsequent censuses (1931 and 1943) was more wide-ranging, including settlements of fewer than a thousand inhabitants, particularly those with residents living in 'named streets'. The 1953 enumeration employed an even more liberal definition – citizens living in all agglomerations of more than 150 people where such facilities as electricity and medical services existed. The numerical significance of this last definitional change is indicated in Table 4.1.

For the half century following the end of Spanish colonialism, Cuba's level of urbanization gradually but steadily grew, witnessing a quadrupling of the island's urban population (Table 4.1). Following a moderate urban growth rate up to 1919, a very rapid increase of nearly 5 per cent per annum was recorded up to 1931, partly reflecting the growth of the sugar industry following heavy US investment, and the stimulus of World War I. A subsequent slowing down of urban growth was a response to the global economic depression, although Cuba's urban population continued to increase at a rate higher than that of its rural counterpart.

Table 4.1. Cuba: national population growth 1774–1981 and urban and rural populations 1899–1981.

Census	Total population ('000s)	Urban population Total ('000s)	Urban %	Urban av. annual % increase	Rural population Total ('000s)	Rural %	Rural av. annual % incr.
1774	171.6			–			
1792	272.3		19*	(2.5)**			
1817	572.4			(2.7)**			
1827	704.5		13*	(2.1)**			
1841	1007.6		12*	(2.6)**			
1861	1396.5		14*	(1.6)**			
1877	1509.3			(0.5)**			
1887	1631.7			(0.7)**			
1899	1572.8	741.3	47.1	(–0.3)**	831.5	52.9	–
1907	2049.0	899.7	43.9	2.67	1149.5	56.1	4.77
1919	2889.0	1291.0	44.7	3.62	1598.0	55.3	3.25
1931	3962.3	2035.0	51.4	4.80	1927.0	48.6	1.71
1943	4778.6	2607.5	54.6	2.34	2171.1	45.4	1.05
1953	5829.0	3324.6	57.0	2.75	2504.4	43.0	1.53
		(3283.3†)	(56.3†)	(2.59†)			
1970	8569.1	5187.8	60.5	3.30	3381.3	39.5	2.06
1981	9723.6	6712.0	69.0	2.67	3011.6	31.0	–0.99‡

* Percentages for Havana only, calculated by Morse (1971:5a).
** Average annual % increase of total national population.
† 1953 figures if using 1931/1943 'urban' definition.
‡ Partly the result of regrouping and reclassification of rural settlements as urban.

Sources: CEE (1983:4, 8); Dyer (1957:224); author's additional calculations.

The 1943–53 average annual urban growth rate of nearly 3 per cent reflected immediate post-war sugar prosperity, further industrial development, improved road transport links and the growth of tourism. By contrast, the growth rates of rural areas continued a decline which had been accelerating since 1899. Absolute rural growth was moderate, averaging 20,000–40,000 per annum: for the 1943–53 inter-censal period urban growth was double that figure.

Four major factors influenced the increasing level of urbanization (Dyer, 1957): (1) the pull exerted by metropolitan Havana; (2) the growth of manufacturing (especially the role of sugar mills in or near towns); (3) improving transport facilities; and (4) the higher standard and level of services and facilities available in urban areas compared to the countryside. Sugar cane was processed in about 160 mills scattered throughout the country, and urban development was stimulated particularly by Cuba's largest and newest mills in the east of the country (Pollitt, 1984). Some mills were located at or near ports, where urban growth represented a response to both industrial and export-related considerations.

By the end of the nineteenth century, however, most urban development had taken place in the west of the island, particularly in and around Havana. Otherwise, Cuba's pattern of urban settlement consisted of five cities within Santa Clara province in the centre of the island (Figure 4.1) – the largest being the port of Cienfuegos – and just three scattered cities in the east. By 1931, with completion of the railway network, but before a comprehensive high-grade road system could be established, urban development had proceeded in most areas of the country. Continued concentration of activities in the Havana region, however, saw the rise of Marianao as the country's third largest urban centre (after Santiago de Cuba).

Regional centres established themselves both to the south-east and south-west of the capital, and in Pinar del Rio, in the far west. The success of the Remedios tobacco region in north-eastern Santa Clara province, producing almost half of Cuba's crop, encouraged the growth of three urban centres, including the port of Caibarien, which served both the tobacco industry and the region's several small sugar mills. Eight new cities in eastern Cuba all reflected a rapid twentieth-century expansion of the sugar industry in this part of the country, complemented by a consolidation of the railway network. The interior of the country contained just 3 per cent of total population in 1899. But with subsequent rapid urban growth, the 1931 figure was 7 per cent and that for 1953, 12 per cent. By contrast, the relative positions of Havana and other port cities remained almost constant.

Between 1899 and 1931, 15 urban centres attained populations of 10,000 or more, to add to the existing 13 centres, and these were joined

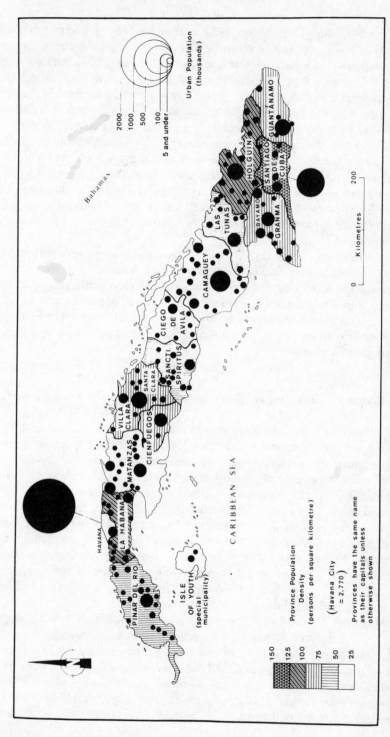

Figure 4.1. Cuba: urban populations and province population densities, 1985. (Source: *Cuba en Cifras* (1986); author's additional calculations).

by an additional 17 between 1931 and 1953. This pattern could be related to the expansion of metropolitan Havana and the emergence of seven cities to the south-west and south-east of the capital, such growth being the response to the development of motor transport using the Central Highway, as was that of two new cities in Central Matanzas Province. Continued growth in central Santa Clara Province (renamed Las Villas in 1940) saw the emergence of three urban centres located in or adjacent to the tobacco region. Extension of the Central Highway into eastern Cuba aided the diffusion of urban growth effects such that an almost uniform doubling of the population took place in Central Highway cities between 1931 and 1953, in contrast to much smaller increases in cities elsewhere. An exception to this was the doubling of population in Guantanamo, largely as a result of the adjacent presence of the United States Naval Base.

In summary, Dyer (1957) could argue that the pre-revolutionary growth of cities of 10,000 or more was closely related to developments in transport, often coupled with industrial development, and that this relationship was reflected in the successive growth of port cities, railway centres, and finally of highway towns. Where all three were brought together effectively, as in Havana and Santiago, large cities and rapid urban growth resulted.

The Economic Base: Sugar Monoculture and Industrial Dual Economy

Dependence on the production and export of a single commodity determined the structural characteristics of the Cuban space economy in a number of critical areas. Sugar companies directly owned or rented over 70 per cent of the country's arable land; 22 large sugar companies, 13 of them American, owned over 70 per cent of the land devoted to sugar, but they cultivated less than half of the 2.75 million hectares they possessed. Consequently, Cuban yields per unit of land were among the lowest of leading cane producing countries. By contrast, 20 per cent of the country's remaining agricultural land supported 85 per cent of all farms, while a quarter of the country's labour force was employed in sugar, including some half-a-million landless agricultural labourers.

Much of the railway system was a mere adjunct to the sugar industry, with over 60 per cent of private lines being owned by sugar mills, and 80 per cent of all railway freight monopolized by sugar cane and its products. Sugar accounted for over 80 per cent of the country's exports and a third of national income. The Cuban economy was therefore vulnerable to fluctuations in world prices. Monocultural dominance constrained production of fruit, vegetables, milk and dairy products, eggs, poultry and meat, much of which had to be imported. The sugar cane harvest – *zafra* – lasted just three to four months of each year, followed by the *tiempo muerto* – dead season; a similar pattern was imposed on most mills, railways and ports, reflecting the relative dependence on the sugar trade and its seasonality.

The internal economic levers operated by the United States were considerable: control of about 40 per cent of raw sugar production, and domination of the balance; ownership of 50 per cent of the public railway system and over 90 per cent of telephone and electric power industries; control of the country's two large nickel processing plants; with UK capital, joint ownership of the three main oil refineries and almost complete control of petroleum distribution; ownership or domination of the majority of key manufacturing plants and the largest chain of supermarkets, several large retail stores, and most major tourist facilities. About 25 per cent of all bank deposits were held by branches of American banks (Bellows, 1964: 14–17). The United States dominated Cuba's foreign trade, taking 70 per cent of Cuba's exports and providing 80 per cent of its imports. Trade with the rest of Latin America was limited except for petroleum imports from Venezuela, Aruba and Curaçao, which were largely US and UK controlled.

Substantial exports went to Asia and Western Europe, but imports were minimized by customs and fiscal barriers. The surpluses thus derived were used to finance the trade deficits experienced with the United States and Venezuela. United States pressure kept trade with socialist countries minimal, usually imports comprising such items as caviar and glassware, for the use of the Cuban élite. Cuba's exports were largely agricultural and mineral primary products, while the bulk of its imports was manufactures and semi-manufactures.

Foreign trade was largely oriented to the needs of the US-owned enterprises and the local economic élite: a quarter of the annual 750 million import bill was devoted to raw materials used in the foreign-owned factories. A further fifth was devoted to such luxury items as cars and their spare parts, consumer durables, alcohol and luxury food items. The privileged minority, concentrated mainly in Havana, enjoyed a pseudo-American life-style and preferred American-produced goods. Local industries were stunted by the general poverty of the domestic market: Cuban-owned factories were usually small, often little more than workshops, with basic equipment, traditional methods and low productivity.

Foreign plants, largely US-owned monopolies, dominated particular market sectors, from wheat flour to rubber products. Most were modern, geared to mass production, and were capital- rather than labour-intensive. Often the plants were located in Cuba merely to take advantage of the favourable tax climate, and while their output inflated

Cuban production statistics, they contributed little to the country's economic development.

Urban Primacy: the Concentration of Activities in Havana

Although manufacturing outside of sugar was relatively rudimentary, three-quarters was located in the capital, thus skewing spatially, as well as organizationally, Cuba's industrial development. The most notable feature of Cuban urban development was, and arguably still is, the dominance of the capital city. Havana is outstanding as a primate city and the Caribbean's largest urban centre. By 1953, 13 per cent of Cuba's total population lived in the city, and together with the populations of such adjacent urban areas as Marianao and Gunabacoa, the figure for Greater Havana rose to 1.2 million, or nearly 21 per cent of the country's total.

Havana's primacy resulted from the interactions of its long history as the centre of civil and military administration; and the ready availability of a deep, well-sheltered harbour. Some 80 per cent of all Cuban imports passed through the port of Havana, further reinforcing the city's economic pre-eminence within the country, and emphasizing its transmission role in the country's dependency relationship with the United States, geographically expressed by the city's proximity to the Florida peninsula. Alongside the economic, political and administrative dominance of the capital city, most of the country's cultural life, higher education and high-level medical facilities were also concentrated in Havana at the expense of the rest of Cuba.

Consequent Socio-economic Conditions

Considerable non-seasonal unemployment persisted, not just in the sugar industry but also in construction, shoe, textile and other industries: estimates of the national total varied in the mid-1950s from 20 per cent (US Department of Commerce, 1956) to 50 per cent (Bellows, 1964).

In 1953, over 90 per cent of all rural dwellings had no electric light, running water, bath, refrigeration, or inside toilet (Fernandez-Nunez, 1976), and over 50 per cent had no toilet facilities whatsoever. Four-fifths of such dwellings were *bohios*, wooden, single-storey family structures with thatch roofs and dirt floors. Urban housing was somewhat better, but still relatively poorly provisioned, with marked inequalities. In 1953, over 45 per cent of urban dwellings had no running water. While 95 per cent of Havana's dwellings received electricity, 6 per cent of the capital's population lived in squatter settlements. The uncertain rural employment situation in general, and the seasonality of the sugar harvest in particular, saw a peripatetic labour reserve establishing temporary accommodation in spontaneous settlements on the edge of a number of towns and cities. By 1959, between 650,000 and 750,000 dwelling units, out of the country's total of 1.4 million, were considered to be sub-standard (Hamberg, 1986).

It has also been argued, however (Packenham, 1986), that in comparison with other Latin American countries, before 1959 Cuba was both 'relatively well off' as measured by per capita income, and 'quite progressive' in terms of literacy, educational opportunity and per capita levels of energy consumption, daily newspaper circulation, radios, television sets and physicians being on a par with a number of European countries (Gonzalez, 1974).

Outline Response of the Revolution

The leaders of the successful ousting of the Batista regime were not initially communists but rather bourgeois nationalists. When victory was attained in 1959, the revolutionary struggle was aimed against the inequalities of Cuban society, and was not yet burdened with any particular dogma other than a strong sense of nationalism. However, the antagonistic attitude taken by the United States saw the Cubans increasingly pushed into the arms of the Soviet bloc.

The decentralization of population and economic activity, and the interaction of urban and rural areas were promoted as key spatial policies to complement overall ideals of social and economic equality and growth, particularly reacting against the previous concentration of activities and wealth in Havana. A regional development programme emphasizing the pivotal role of small- to medium-size urban settlements was balanced by positive discrimination against the capital, although the tenacity of this policy has somewhat fluctuated over the years.

Economically, the country has seen changing fortunes and policies which have impacted upon its overall spatial development. Following the US boycott, a debate ensued until the mid-1960s concerning economic strategy, one which closely resembled that concerning Soviet industrialization in the 1920s (Carciofi, 1983). The 1960s saw an emphasis upon mass labour mobilization and the idealism of moral incentives. But while this period witnessed a greater egalitarianism within the country, it was not successful economically. The failure to reach the planned 10 million tonne sugar harvest target in 1970 emphasized the systematic misallocation, waste and disorganization which had resulted from a decade of socialist idealism. The 1970s, and the first half of the 1980s, consequently saw a shift towards economic rationalization, with a recognition of the need for the country to exploit its comparative advantages rather than to pursue a too rapid policy of diversification.

With increasing economic pressures, however, since 1986, a re-emphasis has been placed upon moral incentives and mass mobilization within a 'rectification of errors' campaign. Somewhat paradoxically, the Party Congress of 1986 also saw the acceleration of a trend to replace revolutionary veterans with younger technocrats within the higher echelons of the Party, tied to a drive for greater economic efficiency and modernization. At the time of writing, however, the Cuban leadership was still referring to *perestroika* and *glasnost* as particular to the Soviet Union and having little relevance for the Cuban situation.

An assessment of some of these elements, as responses to the nature of the pre-revolutionary space economy, comprises most of the rest of this chapter, with, first, a discussion of the planning framework.

Planning and Politics

Before the revolution, a number of largely physical plans had been propounded, including from 1926 a regulatory plan for the city of Havana. In 1943, the National Economic Council was established to appraise the country's natural resources and make recommendations for economic production and urban planning, although both its purpose and name changed over the years (Schroeder, 1982). Regulatory plans for Havana (1958), Varadero, Cojimar and a number of other places were projected, but in the face of intense land speculation and increasing internal upheaval, were not effectively realized.

Economic Planning

Economic planning received high priority after 1959, but for the following 20 years the pendulum of development policy swung back and forth as a succession of economic problems were confronted (Schroeder, 1982: 487). Early idealism saw planners aiming to transform the economy rapidly from colonial-agrarian to an independent-industrial state.

A National Planning Council (JUCEPLAN – Junta Central de Planificación) was established in 1960, alongside centralized ministries, as the government agency responsible for formulating development policy. A Department of Physical Planning (DPF) in the Ministry of Construction was given the task of drawing up national and regional plans. In 1964, the DPF was transformed into the Institute of Physical Planning (IPF), with a greater authority and freedom of action, to provide a territorial dimension to the directives and sectoral plans of JUCEPLAN (Acosta and Hardoy, 1972, 1973).

JUCEPLAN is a relatively small organization with only about 200 professional staff, mostly economists, and is organized into departments responsible for three levels of analysis: the national economy as a whole; broad economic sectors, such as industry, foreign trade, agriculture, and transport; and, thirdly, branches within those sectors, such as textiles or sugar, each of which is in turn divided into sub-branches.

The early period of almost 'traditional' socialist planning soon came to an end. The 1962 plan, based on a Czechoslovak model, proved too rigid for Cuban conditions, as did a medium-term plan for 1962–5 using Polish advice. Any notion of medium- or long-term planning was abandoned. There followed a prolonged debate during the period 1963–6, reminiscent of that in the Soviet Union in the 1920s. Lacking professional statisticians, and feeling the bite both of the US embargo and adverse weather conditions, the Cubans then introduced a system heavily influenced by Che Guevara, and moved away from the Soviet-style centrally planned economy, a situation which was to persist from 1966 to 1970 (White, 1987: 154).

'Mini-plans' for priority sectors would now dominate, although not co-ordinated at a national level. Almost paradoxically, relations between state agencies and enterprises became highly centralized, to the extent that the financial autonomy of the latter virtually disappeared. A further complicating element was the fact that the political leadership assumed command of national economic planning, substantially constraining the role of JUCEPLAN, and lending an individualistic and sometimes eccentric dimension to development. The final ingredient for this period was the replacement of 'economic mechanisms' in macro-economic management by political mass mobilization (Roca, 1977).

But 10 years after the revolution, although considerable progress had been made towards balancing the provinces' population, area and economic activity (Susman, 1974), inequalities, economic organization and production problems persisted. If economic and political performance were to be improved, the population needed to be better incorporated within decision-making processes. Also, the country's leadership took personal blame for the failure to reach the 1970 sugar harvest target, as well as the high economic costs, resource dislocation, and loss of national pride which followed. For these reasons, comprehensive changes in the country's political and economic structure were brought about in the early to mid-1970s, the 'institutionalization' of the revolution. This was to place a heavy emphasis on the role of spatial organization in the planning process.

After a long period of gestation, the national Party's First Congress – itself a significant event, coming more than 15 years after the revolution – in 1975, sanctioned the reinstatement of a centrally co-ordinated economic administration – as the New System of Economic Management and Planning (Sistema de Dirección y Planificación de la Economía, or SDPE). This change resembled the marginal reforms brought to Soviet central planning in 1965 and provided local enterprises with greater responsibility and accountability within the framework of 'orthodox' five-year economic plans (starting with that for 1976–80) (Roca, 1986). A greater degree of local and popular participation in economic planning was also introduced through the local government system of 'organs of people's power' (OPP or Poder Popular), in 1975. As the spatial framework for the new economic-administrative systems, provincial and municipal boundaries, which had not changed since colonial days, were redrawn. This involved reducing the size and increasing the number of provinces from six to 14, to provide a pattern of more homogeneous and rational political and economic units. By contrast, the 407 municipalities were aggregated into 169 units with, excluding Havana City, an average urban population of 20,290. This had the effect of decentralizing to municipalities and provinces a number of administrative and economic responsibilities previously concentrated in Havana, and also of eliminating the intermediate 'regional' level of administration. Additionally, each provincial capital was established as the highest-order centre of a local central place hierarchy within an increasingly integrated urban – rural landscape. Subsequently, the 1980 Party Congress called for a further strengthening of provincial capitals by diversifying their occupational and industrial structures, and by broadening their service functions for the rest of their province. It also sought stronger population growth, particularly in the smaller municipal centres.

In summary, the redrawn territorial-administrative map of Cuba serves a number of important requirements: state direction, control, planning, and popular participation, trading off administrative centralization and economic management efficiency with the require-ment of local economic and geographical conditions to facilitate regional planning ideals of spatial equalization and the optimum use of resources (Barkin, 1980). However, none of these developments add up to any fundamental decentralization of the system.

Spatial Planning

The Institute of Physical Planning (IPF) was integrated with JUCEPLAN to produce a formal central co-ordinating agency for provincial and local level proposals. In all cases, the IPF is meant to work in conjunction with its own provincial offices and with the OPPs. It draws up annual, five-year and longer-term perspective plans, which are presented to the political leadership. The guidelines for physical planning set out in 1978 emphasized its role for providing long-term plans of 25 to 30 years duration, acting as the spatial expression of socio-economic changes, and as the link with long- and medium-term economic plans.

The preparation and maintenance of the national plan represents an intimate state involvement in the whole economy and a centralization of each sector's control. Plan preparation involves IPF technical staff working with the staff of a number of key ministries (Edwards, 1979). The main empirical device for implementing these grand strategies is a series of territorial plans, each of which covers an area of a few hundred square kilometres. Most have been prepared for agricultural areas, for the purposes of establishing state farms and producer co-operatives. Urban plans, thirdly, are essentially structure plans detailing existing and future planned land uses for all towns with a population of more than 20,000. These are expressed at a scale of 1: 10,000.

The IPF of JUCEPLAN determines the guidelines of the national plan, prepares blueprints for nationally important regional plans, establishes the macro-level of investment location (i.e. the specific province or town), and directs the methodological parameters to be employed in the lower-level plans. More generally, it is also concerned with studies of the country's political-administrative divisions and projections of national urbanization processes.

Provincial physical planning offices of the OPPs undertake the production of those lower level plans: for less important regional plans, town and village, intra-urban details and the localization of investment decisions.

During the mid-1980s, numerous urban and regional plans at differing scales were being executed and revised, and a plan for the distribution of productive forces for the year 2000 was nearing completion. Studies were also being undertaken on the employment of new methodological techniques, on information systems, and on the very future of physical planning itself (Fernandez-Nunez, 1985).

Revolutionary Responses

In response to pre-revolutionary patterns of development and urbanization, two fundamental planning goals aimed at reducing inequalities in access to goods and services received the revolutionary leadership's attention: an integration of town and country, in social, economic, and political terms, and at different spatial scales – local, provincial and national; and a reduction in social and economic disparities between Havana and the rest of the country.

Integration of Town and Country

Foreshadowed by Castro's 1953 'History will absolve me' speech, redistributive and developmental policies were aimed at raising rural living standards, improving the overall spatial balance of population and activities, and emphasizing agriculture's prime role in the economy. This took two forms: 'urbanizing' the countryside, and 'ruralizing' the urban population (Gugler, 1980: 520). Within five months of coming to power, an agrarian reform law was implemented to expropriate all large estates, eliminate rents for small tenant farmers, and encourage the establishment of agricultural co-operatives. Networks of rural 'popular stores' and medical outposts were developed to provide basic foodstuffs and other items at low prices, medicines and primary health care, while the number of rural schools was doubled in two years. Both of these were policies which had been initiated by the guerrillas in liberated areas during the revolutionary struggle.

A policy of full employment eliminated seasonal unemployment among agricultural workers and actually had the effect of producing labour shortages at harvest time – a problem which required 'revolutionary' responses, as detailed below. Minimum monthly wages were established in 1963, and by 1968, the rural minimum wage had been raised sufficiently to bring it on a par with the urban minimum.

The embodiment of 'urbanizing' the countryside lay in the government's rural new towns – comunidad – policy which, from 1959, saw a gradual concentration of rural dwellers in new centres equipped with basic urban services. The purpose was essentially four-fold: to achieve an overall nucleation of rural settlement, and a provision, particularly for previously poorly served regions, of urban-type facilities, to stabilize the workforce, and to reduce rural-to-urban migration. It was argued that education and health services, water, and power, could all be provided much more efficiently in clustered settlements. Each comunidad was meant to be developed in relation to specific notional population thresholds for food and clothes shops, cafes, day nurseries, primary schools, small clinics, social centres, bookshops, Party offices and (with minimum populations of 280) cinemas (Edwards, 1979).

By 1964, there were some 150 new towns, containing 26,000 housing units, and ranging in size from as few as 20 houses, up to centres of several thousand units each, such as Ciudad Sandino. But the 1960s were times of economic instability, and many new towns were hastily put up and poorly planned. Of the 246 built between 1959 and 1971, many comprised single-family detached dwellings which were soon considered both too costly and ideologically unsound. From the early 1970s, therefore, new towns were increased in size, to be composed of several hundred families, and characterized by four- or five-storey walk-up apartment blocks often made of pre-fabricated materials.

Most rural new towns are related to a specific element of economic development: about a third having been established and located in relation to sugar cane production, a quarter for livestock development, with about a sixth based in multi-purpose schemes (Barkin, 1980: 35).

By 1976, 335 new towns had been created, housing a total population of about 135,000 (Gugler, 1980). These had increased to 360 by 1982, housing about 4.5 per cent of the 'rural' population (Susman, 1987b). But when a programme was launched in 1977 to encourage small private farmers to form producer co-operatives, it was argued that it would take the state 30 years to provide all the required basic infrastructure and services to private farmers through the new towns programme. From then on, an emphasis was placed on self-build housing, with land remaining in the ownership of the farmers, and government loans being made available for construction materials. This programme appears to have been relatively successful, especially in the underpopulated central provinces, where it has been employed to attract and hold the population.

As a result of full employment policies, and the elimination of seasonal unemployment, seasonal labour shortages for planting and harvesting began to be experienced. In keeping with the early revolutionary ethos, to tackle this problem, major mobilization campaigns were embarked upon, a policy which was to characterize much of the 1960s. During April 1968, for example, half-a-million residents of Havana were mobilized, at the rate of 125,000 per week, to help develop the capital's green belt and other rural works (Garnier, 1973). Some 58,000 mostly urban volunteers aided the 1965 sugar harvest, a figure which rose to 170,000 for the 1970 effort, but which thereafter fell off dramatically – to just over 20,000 for 1974 – with the reappraisal that followed. Since that time, two very explicitly spatial policies have maintained the 'ruralizing' policy dimension: green belts, and 'schools in the countryside.'

As an explicit link between economic and physical planning strategies, the development of green belts has provided an important element of Cuba's urban 'ruralization' process, and a significant contribution to urban food supplies (Barkin, 1978).

When national programmes of agricultural diversification were introduced, they were just adequate to support the ration programme which was meant to guarantee an acceptable minimum basic diet for every citizen. Ironically, the income redistribution process dramatically increased national demand for basic foodstuffs, but inadequate supplies and transport bottlenecks confounded the new aspirations. It was soon obvious that substantial effort was required to meet the needs of large metropolitan areas. Two further approaches were therefore pursued. Around each new urban centre, a substantial area was set aside for state farm livestock production, and a green belt programme was put into effect, partly to permit the growing of tubers, vegetables and coffee in areas where volunteer workers and schoolchildren from nearby accessible areas could be mobilized for cultivation and harvesting.

In addition to the mass mobilization of urban dwellers, green belts were also introduced as an integral part of urban 'ruralization' to provide recreational facilities for nearby urban populations and also to enhance environmental protection efforts. This was particularly important for the two largest cities – Havana and Santiago – since little effort had previously been put into a rational land use policy for urban fringe areas. The largest and best known example of the programme – the 745 hectare Lenin Park in the south-west Havana green belt – employs the irrigation facilities of adjacent state farms for boating lakes, a zoo, aquarium, amusement park and some 50 other recreational facilities within a green belt park setting. In 1980, 2.8 million visitors used the Park (Agencia de Información Nacional, 1983).

The education system has very self-consciously provided opportunities for the under-served rural population, and has acted as a vehicle to aid the integration of urban and rural dwellers. The literacy campaign launched in 1961 employed 240,000 volunteers, mostly urban teachers and students, for an estimated one million, largely rural illiterate, adults. The process of mobilizing schoolchildren to assist sugar cane cutting or to cultivate gardens was also initiated in the 1960s, and was incorporated into school curricula as part of the changing conception of education, helping to overcome traditional barriers between town and country. It had the additional bonus of ameliorating situations of (however induced) labour shortage.

This urban–rural interaction was taken a stage further in 1971 when a programme to locate secondary schools in the countryside was inaugurated. In the policy's first year, seven (1.5 per cent) out of 478 secondary schools were located in rural areas, but by 1979, this figure had risen to 533 (40.4 per cent) out of 1,318 (Leiner, 1985). Such schools possess full boarding facilities for around 500 students and staff, with the cultivated agricultural lands located adjacent to the school buildings and sports facilities. Goals are established for agricultural production and finance, and are integrated into national and regional plans. The crops most commonly cultivated are citrus fruits, coffee, pineapples, and vegetables. The schools are usually located close to a village from which workers performing supervisory and specialist roles for the school's agrarian activities are drawn.

During the summer vacations, the students' parents and other relatives are invited to stay at the schools and work a nominal three hours a day for their subsistence, providing a double function of relieving pressure on hotels and other holiday accommodation at recognized resorts, and adding to productive labour.

The education system thus incorporates strong spatial dimensions of rural–urban interaction, reinforcing social and physical planning ideals: a rustication of urban youths, and an improvement in accessibility to education for formerly under-provisioned rural dwellers.

Regional Equilibrium: Positive Discrimination against Havana, and Provincial Development

The revolutionary administration inherited a space economy whereby a concentration of wealth, services, and facilities in Havana was complemented by a general inadequacy in the rest of the country. In 1959, the capital's population amounted to 1.5 million – about a quarter of Cuba's total. It symbolized mis-shapen capitalist development by its very size, concentration of wealth, its parasitic economy, and very explicit inequalities. Over the next 15 or so years, several policies addressing the problem of the capital were to follow in fairly rapid succession, often reflecting the changing political and economic circumstances of the country as a whole.

As the capital was 'cleaned up' – of gambling, prostitution, large landlords, proprietors and foreign tourists, with former private beaches and exclusive clubs opened up and housing rendered financially much more accessible – increased in-migration took place for the first three or four years after the revolution. But in 1963, this was stopped, as Cuba began to implement more conventional socialist policies, such as developing state farms. In particular, there were to be no more developmental works or investments in the capital. Employment was not to increase, and any industrial renewal was to be relocated out of the city. The longer term consequences of such a policy were to be felt in the late 1970s and 1980s, by which time capital investment in housing and necessary infrastructures was critically necessary.

Coincidentally, in the early to mid-1960s, the first master plan for the city was prepared, in order to prevent further growth while aiming to resolve internal problems. But without resources, internal inequalities – between central and peripheral locations, for example – could not be satisfactorily addressed. Perhaps learning a little from the 'cadre schools' of the Chinese 'Cultural Revolution', 1967–8 saw an attack on bureaucracy, with the abolition of some government posts and the relocation of others to provincial centres. Closely intertwined with mass mobilization, green belt development and urban 'ruralization', many bureaucrats were put to work beautifying the city and transforming the province into the 'Garden of Havana'. The capital had always been poorly provided with parks and green spaces; now within two years, 40 million coffee bushes, four million fruit trees and two-and-a-half million ornamental trees were planted by mobilized urbanites.

However, with the phasing out of such 'heroic' approaches, the early 1970s saw the Havana Master Plan make provision for moderate growth and the location of new economic activities which could meet certain safeguards, acknowledging the infrastructural and employment economies of scale to be derived from such location. This was partly a response to the costly duplication of facilities being experienced in the provinces, and the inability of sufficient new provincial housing to act as counter-magnets to the capital.

The pattern of urban planning which followed appeared to be a mélange of unfortunately adopted models: Soviet industrial city design, aspects of Le Corbusier, and some already outdated western principles of transport planning. But only into the late 1970s were significant quantities of basic materials made available for the residents of the capital to begin to redress almost two decades of neglect, and restrictions have been maintained on new employment and housing (Anon, 1981).

By the early 1980s, the capital's population had crept up to 1.9 million, a fifth of the national total. The population of the 14 other major cities, which in 1959 barely reached one million, or about 16 per cent of the total, had increased to 1.8 million by 1980, or 18 per cent of the country's total. While this reverse initially appears to be relatively minor, Susman (1987b) points out that Havana's 1959–80 increase of 26 per cent reflected an average annual growth rate of just 1.1 per cent, whereas the figures for the other 14 cities were 80 per cent and 2.8 per cent respectively, considerably more than twice the capital's rate.

In the first five years after the revolution, nearly half of all government sponsored housing (55,000 units) was built in the countryside, in stark contrast to pre-1959 conditions when almost all new standard housing was urban, and much of that built in Havana. Together with 30,000 new dwellings built privately, the early post-revolutionary phase saw 17,000 new dwellings per year, compared to a 1945–58 average of 10,200.

The housing which became available in the capital during the 1960s was largely the result of emigration to the United States and elsewhere. New investment and growth were emphasized for other large and medium-sized cities, however, such that the contribution of migration to the annual rate of urban population growth steadily decreased, from about 1.4 per cent before the revolution to an average of about 0.6 per cent per annum for the 1959–70 period (Gugler, 1980).

The eastern Oriente province, traditionally agricultural but with substantial natural resources and demographic growth 50 per cent above the national rate, was selected for the most ambitious of the 1960s long-term development policies. From 1963, economic growth coupled with decentralization and urban–rural integration saw the encouragement of agricultural growth and diversification. From the 1970s, a second and more advanced stage of development saw a programme for the exploitation of substantial non-ferrous metal resources – with the establishment of Nicaro-Moa as the country's largest heavy industrial site – the redevelopment of the country's second city, Santiago, as a major industrial, educational and tourist centre, and an emphasis on the growth of small urban centres to support a fishing centre, tanning, textiles, rice cultivation, dairying, refrigeration and light metals industries.

Elsewhere, two important port-related development programmes took place in the 1960s. With the development of Cienfuegos as a south coast maritime centre, an oil refinery, power station and fertilizer plant were established. Later, the country's first nuclear power station was sited here. Tourism and an important sugar loading role are also critical for Cienfuegos' development plans. The latter activity dominates the second new port – Nuevitas – on the north Camagüey coast, although electrical engineering, cement and fertilizer plants, an abattoir and thermal power station have all been established here.

During this period, new plant was established for the production of such domestic appliances as washing machines and refrigerators in Santa Clara, and a number of agricultural processing plants, attempting to emphasize horizontal integration of industrial and agrarian activities, were set up in several smaller urban centres where specific programmes of agricultural development were meant to add impetus to decentralizing processes.

Housing

The perennial problem – housing policy – as in other spheres, has
tended to change, often dramatically, both in its spatial and ideological
contexts. Pre-revolutionary shortcomings had been experienced in
housing quantity, quality, infrastructural support, and rural–urban disparities, as noted earlier. Exploitation in the majority urban rental sector
was also apparent. Rent control had been introduced in 1939, but was
circumvented by the demand for 'key money', and, in Havana in
particular, by the growth of condominiums, whereby new apartments
were sold on instalment plans with very high mortgage rates (Spitze
and Alfaro, 1959). By the mid-1950s, 70,000 private evictions were
annually reported, from a total urban rental stock of 460,000 units
(Fernandez-Nunez 1976). In 1953, tenants represented nearly 60 per cent
of urban households and 75 per cent of those in Havana. Despite rent
controls, they paid on average nearly a quarter of their incomes on rent.
In response to such situations, early housing policy saw both sweeping
legislation and innovative construction programmes.

In 1959 all evictions were halted and most rents were reduced by
between 30 and 50 per cent, with the greatest reductions for the lowest
rents. Ten-year tax exemptions were offered for owner-occupied houses
built in the following two years to discourage rental construction and
stimulate investment in home ownership (Hamberg, 1986). The 1960
Urban Reform Law established the concept of housing as a public
service, and aimed to make it free from 1970: an ideal which was later
indefinitely postponed. Private renting was prohibited, but landlords
were allowed to retain their homes and a vacation house. Sitting tenants
had the first priority to buy, the price being amortized by continued
regular rent payments of between five and 20 years. *Cuarterias*, inner-
city slum housing with families living in one or two small rooms and
having to share facilities, became government property, with tenants'
payments credited towards the purchase of replacement housing.

Little actual redistribution of housing took place to try to match
need with availability, apart from dwellings vacated by emigrants. It
was argued that eliminating the use of housing for profit had been the
main goal of reform, along with attempting to achieve greater equality
by improving conditions for those in the worst housing, and eliminating
social and racial segregation. Through such policies, the overwhelming
majority of tenants became owner-occupiers, joining the one-third of
urban families owning their homes before 1959. From May 1961, long-
term leaseholding saw families assigned new or existing government-
owned dwellings with lifetime occupancy, and paying no more than 10
per cent of family income for rent. No other tenure forms were
permitted. From 1963, with the continuing US blockade, priorities

moved significantly away from housing, such that between 1964 and 1970, only 44,000 government-built dwellings were completed, and between 1968 and 1971, just 5,000 units per year were built (Hamberg, 1986).

Further, Barkin (1980) suggests that out of a total of 560,000 new housing units constructed between 1959 and 1972, many were built by families and individuals with relatively crude materials, such that only some 295,000 could be considered adequate.

A Revolutionary Response to the Housing Problem: Micro-brigades

The problem of attempting to ameliorate the housing situation was initially confounded by shortages of building materials and bottlenecks in their supply. By 1971, however, lack of labour became the major constraint, as improved supplies of cement and the inauguration of new building material plants eased the earlier problems. Given this new situation, and the apparent willingness of the populace to participate in mass mobilization activities, a 'revolutionary' measure was adopted to tap a new source of labour for building construction, raise economic production efficiency and reduce employment turnover, just at a time when such policies were otherwise on the wane.

Resembling a system rather unsuccessfully attempted in the Soviet Union known as the Gorkii method, workers in employment centres were to be encouraged to raise productivity in order to be able to release colleagues for up to two years to undertake housing construction in 'micro-brigades'. This was seen to be an important factor in the early 1970s, before the new economic planning and management mechanisms were introduced. Micro-brigades therefore comprised 25 to 35 released workers – manual, professional, bureaucratic – usually with little experience of construction work, who would be supervised by skilled men provided by the Construction Ministry, who also made available the necessary materials, land and equipment. The construction work usually took place close to the employment centre, such that when completed, the dwellings would be distributed amongst the workforce back at the employment centre according to need and merit, as agreed at general meetings of the workers. Micro-brigade members were therefore not automatically entitled to a dwelling from their own efforts. But distribution based in part on employment performance did appear to help raise worker efficiency and reduce labour turnover.

The new residents of such apartments – usually in blocks of four- or five-storey walk-ups comprising 20 or 30 separate flats – would pay only 6 per cent rather than 10 per cent of family income for rent, the lower level acknowledging the 'surplus work' contributed either as a micro-brigade worker or as a worker maintaining production levels at the employment centre.

Originating in Havana, the system rapidly took on the responsibility of contributing a major part of new government-sponsored housing nationally. But micro-brigades were essentially urban, and were specifically aimed at redressing the capital's housing deficiencies. By September 1971, Havana had 218 micro-brigades working, and in 1973, the capital saw 8,500 new housing units completed largely as the result of micro-brigade activity. This reflected both an official recognition of the deteriorating nature of the capital's ageing housing stock, and a return to a general growth policy for Havana. Symbolic of this emphasis was the Alamar housing project (1971–74), involving 84 micro-brigades of 2,700 workers, producing an integrated complex of housing, schools, clinics, sports centres and some small industrial plants.

In its first flush of enthusiasm, the micro-brigade system constructed some 37,500 units between 1971 and 1975, although this was still far from adequate to meet the nation's housing requirements, and by the late 1970s, the process had slowed down dramatically. At its peak in 1975–6, the system saw 1,200 micro-brigades of some 25,000 workers, producing 27,000 dwellings per annum. But, with claims that they were incompatible with economic efficiency, micro-brigades began fading into the background, and it seemed that yet another of Castro's ideals had run its course. In 1978, the government proposed either transforming micro-brigades or phasing them out altogether. Basically, micro-brigade work was low quality and high cost: the workers themselves were being paid more than untrained building workers, materials and techniques incurred higher unit costs, since appropriate techniques had to be employed which required relatively low assembly skills, and entailed a minimum number of different designs. Productivity was also hit by bottlenecks in the availability of such materials. A further problem focused on the housing allocation process operating exclusively through the workplace, which often left out some of the most needy households, especially those in emergency shelters. In addition, the labour situation had changed, and it was now more difficult to remove workers from their workplace without disrupting production.

However, during the first half of the 1980s, Havana's housing situation had sufficiently deteriorated to a position whereby the state was forced to recognize that it alone could not solve the urban housing problem, and that by the middle of the decade nothing short of a crisis was apparent. In response to this, December 1984 saw new housing legislation which: (a) converted tenancy to home ownership: 460,000 remaining rent-paying households (representing about 20 per cent of all households) were to become owner occupiers by amortizing the price of their dwelling through monthly rent payments; (b) allowed for all new government-built housing to be sold to highest priority families, the distribution and allocation priority being undertaken by local public agencies, rather than by the workplace; and, (c) sanctioned the free market sale of land and housing and short-term private renting, permitting owner-occupiers to rent rooms out to no more than two households at any one time: with 140,000 dwellings having at least one spare room, it was estimated that such spare capacity could release up to 6 per cent of the total housing stock. But 'wild' property speculation soon abused the spirit of the law, and within a year, the state was obliged to intervene to retrieve a monopoly role as broker of property transactions, although private house-swapping arrangements continued.

An official report revealed that 56 per cent of the capital's housing was in a poor condition, nearly 72,000 houses were propped up to avoid collapse, and a further 10,000 were also in need of such physical support. Over 15,000 families were temporarily living in state shelters as a result of being moved out of uninhabitable dwellings; yet officially, the city had only 50 shelters with 3,751 beds, although a priority was set in 1987 to build sufficient for an extra 2,500 spaces (*Granma Weekly* 7 February 1988). This situation was given greater urgency and poignancy in July 1987 when four people, including two children, were killed when an apartment block collapsed in Havana (Geldof, 1987).

Under such circumstances, the micro-brigade concept was resuscitated as part of the 'Rectification of errors and negative tendencies' campaign, which, from the autumn of 1986, focused on Havana to help redress the years of neglect and explicit discrimination against the city, and also to soak up some of the re-emerged over-manning in offices and industry, with the objective of 'transforming' the capital by the end of the century. During 1987, 20,000 workers – 3,000 of them women – joined the micro-brigades in the capital, with 9,000 housing units projected for 1987, and 12,820 for 1988 in addition to a range of other constructions such as family doctor 'home-offices' (1,300 in two years) and day-care centres (100) over and above five-year plan provision (*Granma Weekly*, 11 October 1987, 17 January 1988).

The Consequent Pattern of Urbanization

Two major methodological problems exist when attempting statistically to examine patterns of urban growth before and after the revolution: (a) a 17 year gap exists between national censuses spanning the first 10 important post-revolutionary years; and (b) the census definition of an urban population has continued to change, a problem the Cuban census authorities readily acknowledge (CEE, 1983: 8). Currently 'urban' entails a settlement of 2,000 or more people, or one of at least 500 people and four of the following: paved streets, piped water system, sewer system, medical services, educational centres; or alternatively, one of at least 200 people and all of the above five infrastructural characteristics plus electric street lighting (CEE, 1982: 59).

As Table 4.1 showed, by 1953, 57 per cent of Cuba's population was officially recognized as being urban, a much higher level than for most of Latin America. By 1970, this had risen to 60.5 per cent, while the 1981 census recorded 69 per cent, higher than for South America (66.2 per cent), Central America (60.2 per cent) and the Caribbean (53.3 per cent), and only slightly lower than for the Americas as a whole (69.1 per cent) (CEE, 1983: 8). National estimates since the last census place the 1986 urban population at just over 7.3 million, or 71.3 per cent of the total population (Comité Estatal de Estadísticas (annual)).

The 1981 pattern of urbanization by province (Table 4.2),

Table 4.2. Degree of Cuban urbanization and population densities by province 1981.

Province	Urban population				Persons per urban dwelling	Province pop. density per sq km*
	'000s	%	% incr. over 1970	% of nat. total		
Cuba	6,712.0	69.0	8.5	100.0	4.2	91.6
Pinar del Rio	312.6	48.8	10.7	4.7	4.3	61.1
La Habana	428.3	73.1	5.0	6.4	4.1	107.2
Cuidad Habana†	1,929.4	100.0	0.0	28.7	3.9	2,769.9
Matanzas	422.7	75.6	13.4	6.3	4.1	48.8
Villa Clara	526.0	68.7	14.7	7.8	4.0	90.0
Cienfuegos	235.2	72.1	12.9	3.5	4.2	82.5
Sancti Spiritus	249.3	62.3	11.5	3.7	4.3	61.4
Ciego de Avila	214.1	66.7	12.0	3.2	4.0	49.6
Camagüey	483.4	72.4	7.5	7.2	4.0	44.2
Las Tunas	217.9	49.8	15.6	3.3	4.3	70.5
Holguin	457.0	50.1	11.1	6.8	4.5	102.5
Granma	375.6	50.8	10.9	5.6	4.6	91.3
Santiago de C.§	566.8	62.0	10.7	8.4	4.8	154.1
Guantanamo	246.3	52.9	12.1	3.7	4.9	77.0
Is. de la Juv.‡	47.4	81.6	–	0.7	4.7	28.2

* 1985 figures, as used in Figure 4.1.
† Hereafter referred to as Havana City.
‡ Isla de la Juventud, a 'special' municipality hereafter referred to as the Isle of Youth (formerly the Isle of Pines).
§ Santiago de Cuba, hereafter referred to as Santiago.

Sources: CEE (1981a: 12–14; 1982: iv–v; 1983: 15, 61–9); *Cuba en Cifras* (1986: 20–5); author's additional calculations.

emphasizes that apart from the City of Havana, which by definition is totally urbanized, the highest levels of urbanization are found in the western and central provinces of Matanzas (75.6 per cent urbanization), La Habana (73.1), Camagüey (72.4), Cienfuegos (72.1), and Isle of Youth (81.6), which rapidly developed as an educational centre in the 1970s. The lowest levels of urbanization are found in Pinar del Rio (48.8) in the far west, Las Tunas (49.8), Holguin (50.1), Granma (50.8), and Guantanamo (52.9) in the far east. With the exception of Camagüey, all provinces outside Havana show urban population increases for 1970–81 above the national average of 8.5 per cent. Further reflecting the positive discrimination against Havana City, adjacent La Habana province reveals a mere 5 per cent increase for the period, compared to 11 provinces experiencing more than double that rate. Las Tunas province reveals the greatest increase in urban population between 1970 and 1981 – 15.6 per cent, averaging 4.5 per cent per annum during the period, although together with Pinar del Rio, it remains the only province with an urban population below 50 per cent.

The policy of provincial redistribution and balance has emphasized the role of provincial capitals, especially since their administrative reorganization in the mid-1970s. In this respect, Table 4.3 reveals the minimal growth of Havana City throughout the 1975–85 period, but witnesses a ten-fold increase in growth rates from 1981, representing a

Table 4.3. Growth of provincial capitals in Cuba 1975–85

Capital	Population in thousands			% annual average increase		
	1975*	1981	1985*	1975–81	1981–5	1975–85
Pinar del Rio	87.3	96.7	100.9	1.8	0.9	1.4
Havana City	1928.1	1929.4	2014.8	0.01	0.1	0.04
Matanzas	95.3	100.8	105.4	1.0	0.9	1.0
Santa Clara**	149.7	172.1	178.3	2.5	0.7	1.7
Cienfuegos	93.9	102.8	109.3	1.6	1.3	1.5
Sancti Spiritus	63.7	71.9	75.6	2.1	1.0	1.7
Ciego de Avila	66.3	74.3	80.5	2.0	1.7	1.9
Camagüey	224.1	245.5	260.8	2.3	1.2	1.5
Las Tunas	64.8	85.9	91.4	5.2	1.5	3.7
Holguin	153.0	186.9	194.7	4.1	0.8	2.5
Bayamo**	79.8	100.6	105.3	4.3	0.9	2.9
Santiago	319.6	347.3	358.8	1.4	0.7	1.1
Gunatanamo	149.1	167.3	174.4	2.0	0.9	1.5
Nueva Gerona**	27.3	31.1	34.4	2.3	2.1	2.4

* Official estimates.
** All provinces take their names from their capitals except Granma (Bayamo), Villa Clara (Santa Clara) and the special municipality of Isla de la Juventud (Nueva Gerona).

Source: *Cuba en Cifras* (1986: 26); author's additional calculations.

partial reversal of policy. By contrast, those capitals revealing high 1975–81 growth rates – Holguin, Bayamo and Las Tunas – experienced a considerable slowing down between 1981 and 1985, partly due to the emphasis being placed on the development of smaller towns, and also to the greater resource expenditure on Havana. Over the whole 1975–85 period, however, they still show the greatest growth rates: 2.5, 2.9 and 3.7 per cent per annum respectively. All other capitals also reveal a slowing down in growth rates after 1981.

Havana City's primacy is still clear (with a population now above two million). No other urban centre has a population of more than 400,000, and of the eight between 100,000 and 400,000, each is located in a different province as provincial capitals. Nevertheless, as a result of regional redistribution and induced growth in provincial capitals, Havana's share of national population had been reduced from 20.8 per cent in 1953 to 19.8 per cent by 1981. On an index of two cities, for example, the capital's primacy over the same period had been pared down from 7.46 to 5.53 (Acosta and Hardoy, 1972: 169; author's calculations from 1981 census). But internal migration balances reveal the continued appeal of the capital. Between 1976 and 1981 Havana City recorded the largest numbers of in- and out-migrants for any province in both gross (90,100) and net (33,300) terms, although their proportions are relatively small in comparison with the city's total population. However, despite government policies, in the first five years of territorial-administrative reform, Havana City still managed to attract an annual internal migration balance of 33,000, averaging an increase of 1.7 per cent per annum. Slater (1982) argues for caution in interpretation here, since many of the internal migrations to and from the capital appear to be only of a temporary nature.

That the Havana region continues to exert a migratory pull is also reflected in La Habana province's 1976–81 net migratory gain with every other province apart from neighbouring Matanzas and the rapidly developing Isle of Youth. Havana City has net deficits only with the Isle of Youth (200) and surrounding La Habana province. By contrast, Guantanamo province had net deficits with every other province.

The predominant internal migratory movement for the 1976–81 period was between neighbouring provinces, the greatest flows being between La Habana and Havana City: 6,200 into the city, and 8,800 out, providing La Habana province with a net gain of 2,600 (CEE 1983: 14; 17–18).

Urban Structure

General Characteristics

Little systematic research appears to have been undertaken, either before or since the revolution, on the internal structure of Cuba's major urban areas. However, the essential elements of Cuban urban internal structure can be summarized as: (a) a colonial core: typified by large courtyard houses, and grand squares, the best examples being in Old Havana and Trinidad. Much replacement, infilling, subdivision and change of use have taken place in many colonial cores, with cultural and administrative functions found alongside residential and commercial activities, although the more important cores, such as the examples cited, are now under the protection of the state; (b) nineteenth- and early twentieth-century additions: comprising mixed land uses, with significant quality variations in buildings and environments; (c) single family detached and semi-detached dwellings characterizing suburban development but also representing the early form of socialist new town and continued early post-revolutionary growth of Havana, incorporating nodal service centres; (d) neighbourhoods of four- and five-storey walk-up apartments as the ubiquitous post-revolutionary urban housing form; (e) limited numbers of tower blocks in the centres of Havana and Santiago; (f) 'temporary' elements such as shelters and spontaneous settlements; and (g) peripheral industrial zones segregated from residential areas.

Housing and Land Use

Although urban housing reforms were undertaken in the early years of the revolution, and a substantial planning superstructure was established, urban land itself was not nationalized. The requirement to set maximum prices at a low uniform rate severely restricted speculation, but it was largely unable to eliminate the underlying differences related to variations in topography, location and infrastructure. This continued to pose problems, both practical and ideological. A number of other socialist societies had sought the wholesale public ownership of urban land and the implementation of comprehensive urban land use allocation processes through centralized planning mechanisms. Ironically, by the mid-1970s, planners and economists in such countries were seeking new mechanisms to overcome 'misallocation' of central land uses and indicators for attributing notional functional values to urban land. Notable in this respect was the work of Kabakova in the Soviet Union (Bater, 1980) whose land value surrogates – presence of infrastructure and access to services – revealed concentric patterns outward from city centres when mapped according to their notional value. From the 1980s, with the requirement for higher population densities on government-owned land, similar types of surrogates were evolved in Cuba in order to reflect such factors as distance from city centre, accessibility and infrastructure (Gonzalez, 1982). Such an approach was considered to be consistent with Cuba's stage of transition to socialism (Hamberg, 1986).

In terms of residential characteristics, race and locality had, arguably, always been stronger divisive forces in pre-revolutionary Cuba than social class (Amaro and Mesa-Lago, 1971). However, Afro-Cuban or 'black' ghettos appear not to have developed. Low-income residential neighbourhoods saw a general inter-mixing of groups (such as in El Cerro and Luyano in Havana). High-income areas, by contrast, such as the Miramar and Biltmore suburbs of the capital, were almost exclusively white. By 1953, the Afro-Cuban urbanization rate was about 60 per cent, just above the national average.

After the revolution, although the urban reform law did not substantially change racial distribution in housing, a number of policies, however indirectly, did aid the virtual elimination of exclusively white residential areas. Detailed empirical evidence, is, however, rather meagre.

Havana

Old Havana occupies the crowded tip of a peninsula jutting out between the bay and the harbour channel on the east, largely made up of two- and three-storey buildings fringing narrow, grid-iron streets. The line of the former wall, which began to be demolished in 1865, can be traced in the spaces immediately beyond, which have been subsequently occupied by a major boulevard and parks, and large buildings such as the presidential palace (now the National Revolutionary Museum), and the main railway terminus.

Before the revolution there had been a post-war trend to reverse what had been an increasing concentration of people and activities here. Between 1919 and 1943, Old Havana's population increased by more than 50 per cent, from 45,000 to 72,000, largely due to the renovation of unused dwellings and the replacement of old, smaller buildings by large apartment blocks. By contrast, between 1943 and 1953, the population declined by 18 per cent to 59,000, reflecting both the expansion of non-residential land uses – commercial, financial and industrial – and the migratory pull of new suburban residential developments.

The densely settled *repartos*, or subdivisions, which early spread beyond the wall, occupied large areas to the west along the coast and to the south along the highways penetrating the interior of the country. The built-up area along the coast, known as Vedado, developed as a high-status residential area, but in the 1950s its character changed decisively as a business district grew to become the new commercial centre of the capital: large, co-operatively owned apartment blocks were constructed alongside multi-storey offices and a major shopping and recreation centre.

With better transport and improved accessibility to the city from outlying areas, substantial suburban development took place, further extending the built-up area of the city and physically linking pre-existing settlements such as Guanabacoa and the large industrial centre of Marianao. Urban development to the east of Havana was stimulated by the completion of a tunnel under the entrance to Havana Bay and the wide Via Blanca. This trend was continued in the post-revolution period.

According to final 1981 census data (CEE, 1983: 31), Havana City contained 21.8 per cent of all the country's dwellings, but possessed no less than 62.6 per cent of all apartments, with no other province recording more than 4.4 per cent of the total. A similar pattern emerged for *cuarteria* dwellings, essentially characteristic of urban inner areas. Havana City held 59.9 per cent of the national total, again almost three times its share in proportion to size. *Bohios*, by contrast, were almost non-existent within Havana City, being represented there by just 0.05 per cent of the country's total. Only 44.5 per cent of the city's dwellings are houses (*casa*) – by far the lowest province figure. The city has the highest proportions of apartments – 42.7 per cent of its total stock, and *cuarteria* dwellings, 12.8 per cent: by contrast, suburban and rural La Habana's figures are 8.0 and 2.7 per cent respectively.

Contemporary Havana City contains 15 municipalities, each of which exhibit very different characteristics. Old Havana is now the only section of the city to reveal *cuarterias* as the largest class of dwelling – 51.4 per cent, as well as having the second largest number (16,900) within the city. Centro has the largest number – 19,600 – representing 36.8 per cent of its total, where the number of apartments are the second highest within the city and represent 41.1 per cent of the municipality's total stock. Together with 22.1 per cent of houses, Centro, in fact exhibits the most balanced representation of urban dwelling types in Havana City. By contrast, Plaza de la Revolución, an area of 1940s and 1950s developments, and La Havana del Este, a post-revolutionary development, are dominated by apartments – representing 66.2 and 71.1 per cent respectively of their total dwelling stock. The previously wealthy suburban areas of Arroya

Naranjo and Cotorro are predominantly of family houses (67.5 and 77.9 per cent) as is San Miguel del Padron (67.9), while a number of other municipalities, such as Cerro, Playa and Diez de Octubre contain a relatively equal balance of houses and apartments, but with few *cuarterias* (CEE, 1981b, with author's additional calculations).

From the mid-1960s, a National Monuments Commission began to study the problems of Old Havana, but it was not until a decade later, following the declaration of the area as a 'national landmark', that indiscriminate demolition was halted, and preparations for a comprehensive plan were inaugurated. It was found that over 90 per cent of highly valued buildings occupied just 8 per cent of Old Havana (Capablanca, 1985: 60). Plans were subsequently drawn up for the restoration of the area's important buildings and for the revitalization of the area as a whole. The Old Square has been a particular focus of attention, and UNESCO's declaration of the area to be of 'world cultural heritage' status has had a knock-on effect for the greater care of other historic areas in the country (Hamberg, 1986; M'Bow, 1985).

Conclusions

Several indicators suggest the existence of a considerable degree of social and spatial equality within Cuba at different scales. Although Havana's dominance in the national space-economy has been diminished, it certainly continues. Concentrating investment in provincial capitals and their linked urban systems has complemented attempts to cluster rural settlements, thereby offering improved access to services and better integration of the population. This has been made easier by the mid-1970s' administrative-territorial reforms producing a more homogeneous and rational structure.

But while most observers agree that contemporary Cuba exhibits a greater degree of social and economic equity than existed before 1959 (Brundenius, 1981; Seers, 1974, 1975), the extent of this equity and the cost incurred in reaching it have long been matters for intense debate. Let us take just two contentious areas: income and health.

Most indicators would suggest that regional and urban–rural disparities in Cuban incomes have been reduced. Programmes aimed at improving living conditions in rural and low-income urban areas have complemented the discrimination against Havana. Mesa-Lago (1981) examined surveys conducted in 1953 and 1957, and calculated that a ratio of about 17:1 existed between average urban and rural incomes. Dumont (1970) pointed to a 20 per cent rural wage increase during the first two years of the revolution: as a consequence of the Agrarian Reform Law of May 1959 and the guarantee of stable employment to

350,000 cane cutters, for example, their wages were almost doubled. In urban areas, the Rent Reduction Law of 1959 contributed to a substantial income redistribution of an estimated 80 million pesos. As a consequence of acts such as these, by 1982, based on a national value of 100, the median salary in each province ranged from 91.6 to 106.2 – a very low ratio of 1.16:1 (Susman, 1987b).

However, the 1980 wage reform, as the focus of new material incentives within the revised economic system, did result in individual wage differentials increasing to 5.3:1 in 1981, from a low of 4.3:1 in 1963 (Brundenius, 1984; Mesa-Lago, 1981); but contrasting with a ratio of 24:1 for Peru and Brazil (Susman, 1987b), to remain the most egalitarian pattern of income distribution in Latin America. Overall, wage rises of 15 per cent and productivity increases of 35 per cent also followed between 1977 and 1981 (Perez-Stable, 1985). Susman (1987b) argues that when looking at total salaries paid, a very strong correlation ($r = 0.95$) is revealed between the proportion of the national workforce in each province, and the proportion of total national salary paid in each province in 1982, reinforcing the claim of a high degree of income equality.

Yet ironically, Cuba is one of the most heavily rationed countries in the world, and while this has an equalizing effect on consumption, it does little for surplus disposable income apart from helping to generate black markets. Diverting such income into housing helps in two ways. By encouraging owner-occupation, disposable income is committed and is available to the state, while the responsibility of upkeep of a large housing stock is to some extent shifted from a public to a private burden.

Cuba's health service has been extolled as a model for any developing society (Diaz-Briquets, 1983), yet on paper it appears very urban biased. Because health services are organized on central place principles, the much lower population per physician ratio in urban areas, and especially large cities, is not necessarily an indicator of inequality in terms of access. Primary care facilities are almost ubiquitous, located in rural as well as in urban areas of all sizes, while secondary and tertiary health facilities, free and accessible to all, are found in towns and cities throughout Cuba. But as noted earlier, the census definition of an urban area may rest on the very presence of medical services. By definition, therefore, a rural settlement may lack medical services and rely upon nearby urban facilities. With a consistent spatial scale of analysis, the distribution of medical services reveals a high degree of equality: for example, all 1982 provincial figures of hospital beds per thousand inhabitants were around 4.8, except for Havana City (9.2), which had the most hospitals and higher order facilities to serve the rest of Havana Province, of which it was a part until 1976, as well as the national population as a whole (Susman, 1987b).

However, critics of Cuban socio-economic performance argue that much unemployment is disguised, that rural–urban disparities continue (Del Aguila, 1984), and that (as in most other 'socialist' societies) élite privileges have re-emerged, including privileged housing, department stores, vacation villas, access to hard currency and luxury goods (Packenham, 1986). They suggest that most social benefits entail high political costs, directly and necessarily associated with the state apparatus which provides food, housing, health care and educational opportunity, thereby wielding substantial manipulative power over individuals and groups. Such observers conclude that many of the revolutionary aims and achievements could have been gained by alternative means and without incurring Cuba's substantial economic problems.

Cuba's pre-revolutionary relations with the United States in particular, and with world markets in general, possessed all the essential ingredients of a classic dependency relationship: (a) the prosperity and growth of the Cuban economy was primarily a function of international economic and political events; (b) economic surpluses appeared to be channelled to developed countries, particularly the United States; and (c) the domestic benefits of the Cuban dependent economy fell largely on an economic and social élite.

The post-revolutionary position poses more of a problem: Cuba is clearly still highly dependent on external, controlling factors, but most dependency models have been based upon conditions of capitalist development: how is the development path of a socialist society to be accommodated within a model constructed to emphasize capitalist exploitative processes?

The first Soviet credits were received in 1960 (Bach, 1987) although it was not until 1972 that Cuba joined the Soviet bloc Council for Mutual Economic Achievement (CMEA). The two-way flow of Cuban sugar to the Soviet Union (and to other CMEA countries) and Soviet oil to Cuba has provided at least an assured market for around 60 per cent of Cuba's sugar harvest at relatively stable, guaranteed prices, through times when world prices have fluctuated, and an important and regular source of fuel for this generally energy-deficient island. Both commodities have been critical, and despite varied attempts at economic diversification (Hall, 1981a) and the discovery and exploitation of limited supplies of indigenous oil (producing around a million tonnes per annum – about a tenth of the country's needs), the economic relationship remains a dependent one for Cuba (Smith, 1985).

However, Cuba has been able to use this relationship to its financial advantage, selling a proportion of its subsidized Soviet oil at market prices for hard currency to prop up its own foreign exchange stocks. A perverse symmetry has been established in recent years when world market sugar prices have been lower than Cuban production costs: Cuba has bought cheaply on world markets to sell, as its own sugar, to the Soviet Union and other CMEA members for guaranteed higher prices (Duncan, 1986). Indeed, one particular transaction actually reported by the Cuban National Bank in 1985 saw the Cubans arriving at a 'surplus' of over $600 million, representing over half of the country's hard currency earnings for the year, by selling other countries' cheaper sugar to the Soviet Union for subsidized oil which was then resold at a higher price.

Overall, trade with the Soviet Union is running at a value of eight billion roubles per year, some 50 times the 1960 level, and Soviet investment in Cuba has been reckoned at four to five billion dollars per year, representing around 51 per cent of all Soviet aid to developing countries (Duncan, 1986: 46, 51). Certainly within Cuba, the Soviet relationship is explicit both in the USSR's involvement in over 400 joint industrial projects (*Granma Weekly*, 14 February 1988: 6), and in relation to exploiting Cuba's strategic location: the largest intelligence information gathering installation outside Soviet territory employs around 3,000 of an estimated 19,700 Soviet military and civilian technicians and advisers on Cuban soil (Erisman, 1985). Debate continues as to how far Cuban military and civilian participation in Angola, Mozambique and Ethiopia since the mid-1970s has been at the behest of the Soviet Union (Dominguez, 1982; Valenta, 1981).

By the mid-1980s, a succession of disappointing sugar harvests – partly due to adverse weather conditions – and low world prices for sugar, tobacco and nickel witnessed desperate shortages of hard currency and a significant slowing of the growth rate, that for 1988 being just 1.4 per cent rather than the projected 5 per cent. Repayments on debts to the West (estimated at three billion dollars) were suspended in July 1986.

The importance of CMEA assistance in general, and Soviet aid in particular, is heightened under such circumstances. Sugar represented 78 per cent of all Cuban exports in 1986, yet only 17 per cent of all exports are to non-socialist countries. By 1988, CMEA prices paid for Cuban sugar were four times world market levels, although for 1986–90, the Soviet price was reduced from 915 to 850 roubles a tonne (Hurtado, 1987). In 1986, Cuba was to have started repaying Soviet debts, estimated at $125 million, a repayment which would have continued until 2010; but the USSR deferred this requirement until 1990. For the period 1986–90, a 50 per cent increase in Soviet economic aid and trade was envisaged, providing credits worth three billion dollars.

Two papers have addressed the question of Cuba's 'socialist

dependency'. Leo-Grande (1979), employing time-series data up to 1976, compared pre- and post-revolutionary conditions, and concluded that Cuba remained vulnerable by virtue of its highly concentrated trade and aid relationship with the Soviet Union. But, he argued, if this unequal partnership could be referred to as 'dependency', then it was substantially different from accepted notions of dependency and thereby required a new conceptual basis for analysis.

The second study (Packenham, 1986), attempted to take up this challenge by examining in detail some nine major indicators of dependency. Packenham concluded that since 1959, six indicators had shown no change, two had revealed increased dependency, and only one, comparing trade partner concentration with the USA before 1959 and the USSR since the revolution, could be interpreted as expressing less dependency.

In the Gorbachev era, the future of Cuban–Soviet relations remains uncertain. The extent to which economic requirements can be divorced from ideological considerations, both within and outside the Soviet bloc, may be critical for future Cuban developmental paths. Domestically, policies continue to swing back and forth. At the time of writing, Havana is being promoted, no doubt at the expense of other settlements, as a 'world class' capital city. Mass mobilization concepts are back in favour. Will either of these thrusts be sustained? When reforms elsewhere in the socialist world might suggest otherwise, will the collectivized nature of agriculture, around which so much settlement policy has revolved, remain intact? Presently, the questions remain open. One thing is certain, however. Cuba's future development path will contain no shortage of interest.

ACKNOWLEDGEMENT

Grateful thanks are due to Pat Luck for the cartography.

REFERENCES

Acosta, M. and Hardoy, J.E. (1972) 'Urbanization policies in revolutionary Cuba', in: Geisse, G. and Hardoy, J.E. (eds) *Latin American Urban Research*, Vol. 2, Beverly Hills: Sage, 167–77.

Acosta, M. and Hardoy, J.E. (1973) *Urban Reform in Revolutionary Cuba*, New Haven: Yale University.

Agencia de Información Nacional (1983) *Cinco Años de Esfuerzos y Realizaciones: Nueva División Político-administrativa*, Havana: Editora Politica.

Amaro, N. and Mesa-Lago, C. (1971) 'Inequality and classes', in:

Mesa-Lago, C. (ed.) *Revolutionary Change in Cuba*, Pittsburgh: University of Pittsburgh Press, 341–55.

Anon (1981): *Socioeconomic Guidelines for the 1981–5 Period*, Havana: Political Publishers.

Bach, Q.V.S. (1987) *Soviet Economic Assistance to the Less Developed Countries*, Oxford: Oxford University Press.

Barkin, D. (1978) 'Confronting the separation of town and country in Cuba', in: Sawers, L. and Tabb, W. (eds) *Marxism and the Metropolis*, London: Oxford University Press, 317–33.

Barkin, D. (1980): 'Confronting the separation of town and country in Cuba', *Antipode*, **12** (3), 31–40.

Bater, J.H. (1980) *The Soviet City*, London: Edward Arnold.

Bellows, I. (1964) 'Economic aspects of the Cuban revolution', *Political Affairs*, **43** (1), 14–29.

Brundenius, C. (1981) *Economic Growth, Basic Needs and Income Distribution in Revolutionary Cuba*, Lund: Research Policy Institute, University of Lund.

Brundenius, C. (1984) *Revolutionary Cuba: the Challenge of Economic Growth with Equity*, Boulder, Colorado: Westview Press.

Butterworth, D.S. (1980): *The People of Buena Ventura: Relocation of Slum Dwellers in Post Revolutionary Cuba*, Urbana: University of Illinois Press.

Capablanca, E. (1985) 'La Habana Vieja: anteproyecto de restauración', *Cuidad y Territorio*, 57–64.

Carciofi, R. (1983) 'Cuba in the seventies', in: White, G. *et al.* (eds) *Revolutionary Socialist Development in the Third World*, Brighton: Wheatsheaf, 193–233.

CEE (Comité Estatal de Estadísticas) (1981a) *Acerca de los Resultados Preliminares del Censo Nacional de Población y Viviendas de 1981*, Havana: CEE.

CEE (Comité Estatal de Estadísticas) (1981b) *Censo de Población y Viviendas 1981 Cifras, Preliminares*, Havana: CEE.

CEE (Comité Estatal de Estadísticas) (1982) *Estudios y Datos sobre la Población Cubana*, Havana: CEE.

CEE (Comité Estatal de Estadísticas) (1983) *Acerca de los Resultados Definitivos del Censo de Poblacion y Viviendas de 1981*, Havana: CEE.

Comité Estatal de Estadísticas (Annual) *Cuba en Cifras*. Havana: CEE.

Del Aguila, J. (1984) *Cuba: Dilemmas of a Revolution*, Boulder: Westview Press.

Diaz-Briquets, S. (1983) *The Health Revolution in Cuba*, Austin: University of Texas Press.

Dominguez, J.I. (ed.) (1982) *Cuba: Internal and International Affairs*, Beverly Hills: Sage.

Dumont, R. (1970): *Cuba: Socialism and Development*, New York: Grove Press.

Duncan, W.R. (1986) 'Castro and Gorbachev: politics of accommodation', *Problems of Communism*, **35** (2), 45–57.

Dyer, D.R. (1957) 'Urbanism in Cuba', *Geographical Review*, **47**, 224–33.

Edwards, M. (1979) 'Urban and rural planning', in: Griffiths, J. and Griffiths,

P. (eds) *Cuba: the Second Decade*, London: Writers and Readers Publishing Group.

Erisman, H. (1985) *Cuba's International Relations: The Anatomy of a Nationalistic Foreign Policy*, Boulder: Westview Press.

Fernandez-Nunez, J.M. (1976) *La Vivienda en Cuba*, Havana: Editorial Arte y Literatura.

Fernandez-Nunez, J.M. (1985) 'Dos decados de planificación regional y urbana en Cuba', *Ciudad y Territorio*, 63–4, 95–8.

Garnier, J-P. (1973) *Une Ville, une Révolution: La Havane*, Paris: Editions Anthropos.

Geldof, L. (1987) 'Havana patches up its homes', *The Guardian*, 18 November.

Gonzalez, A. (1982) 'Las sombras de viento en el diseño de conjuntos urbanas', *Arquitectura y Urbanismo* 3, 14–32.

Gonzalez, E. (1974) *Cuba under Castro: Limits of Charisma*, Boston: Houghton Mifflin.

Gugler, J. (1980) 'A minimum of urbanism and a maximum of ruralism': the Cuban experience', *International Journal of Urban and Regional Research*, 4 (4), 516–35.

Hall, D.R. (1981a) 'External relations and current development patterns in Cuba', *Geography*, 66 (3), 237–40.

Hall, D.R. (1981b) 'Town and country planning in Cuba', *Town and Country Planning*, 50 (3), 81–3.

Hamberg, J. (1986) 'The dynamics of Cuban housing policy', in: Bratt, R. *et al.* (eds) *Critical Perspectives on Housing*, Philadelphia: Temple University Press, 586–624.

Hurtado, M.E. (1987) 'Invoking the powers of revolutionary will', *South*, 91, 33–4.

Leiner, M. (1985) 'Cuba's schools: 25 years later', in: Halebsky, S. and Kirk, J.M. (eds) *Cuba: Twenty-five Years of Revolution 1959–1984*, New York: Praeger, 27–44.

Leo–Grande, W.M. (1979) 'Cuban dependency: a comparison of pre-revolutionary and post-revolutionary international economic relations', *Cuban Studies*, 9 (2), 1–28.

M'Bow, A.M. (1985) 'Campana internacional para la salvaguarda de la Plaza Vieja de la Habana', *Ciudad y Territorio*, 63–4, 65–71.

Mesa-Lago, C. (1981) *The Economy of Socialist Cuba: A Two Decade Appraisal*, Albuquerque: University of New Mexico Press.

Morse, R.M. (1971): *The Urban Development of Latin America 1750–1920*, Stanford: Center for Latin American Studies.

Packenham, R.A. (1986): 'Capitalist dependency and socialist dependency: the case of Cuba', *Journal of InterAmerican Studies and World Affairs*, 28 (1), 59–92.

Perez-Stable, M. (1985) 'Class, organization and *conciencia*; the Cuban working class after 1970', in: Halebsky, S. and Kirk, J.M. (eds) *Cuba: Twenty-five Years of Revolution 1959–1984*, New York: Praeger, 251–69.

Pollitt, B.H. (1984): 'The Cuban sugar economy and the Great Depression', *Bulletin of Latin American Research*, 3 (2), 3–28.

Portillo, R.D. and Pereira, J.C. (eds) (1978) *Atlas de Cuba*, Havana: Instituto Cubano de Geodesia y Cartografía.

Roca, S. (1977) 'Cuban economic policy in the 1970s: the trodden paths', in: Horowitz, I.L. (ed.) *Cuban Communism*, New Brunswick: Transaction Books (third edition), 265–301.

Roca, S. (1986) 'State enterprises in Cuba under the New System of Planning and Management (SDPE)', *Cuban Studies* 16, 153–79.

Schroeder, S. (1982) *Cuba: A Handbook of Historical Statistics*, Boston, Massachusetts: G.K. Hall & Co.

Seers, D. (1974) 'Cuba', in: Chenery, H.B. *et al.* (eds) *Redistribution with Growth*, London: Oxford University Press, 262–68.

Seers, D. (ed.) (1975) *Cuba: The Economic and Social Revolution*, Westport, Connecticut: Greenwood Press.

Slater, D. (1982) 'State and territory in post revolutionary Cuba: some critical reflections on the development of spatial policy', *International Journal of Urban and Regional Research*, 6 (1), 1–34.

Smith, J.T. (1985) 'Sugar dependency in Cuba: capitalism versus socialism', in: Seligson, M.A. (ed.) *The Gap between Rich and Poor*, Boulder: Westview Press, 366–78.

Spitze, R.G.F. and Alfaro, A.G. (1959) 'Property rights, tenancy laws of Cuba and economic power of renters', *Land Economics*, 35, 277–83.

Susman, P. (1974) 'Cuban development: from dualism to integration', *Antipode*, 6 (3), 10–29.

Susman, P. (1987a) 'Spatial equality and socialist transformation in Cuba', in: Forbes, D. and Thrift, N. (eds) *The Socialist Third World*, Oxford: Basil Blackwell, 250–81.

Susman, P. (1987b) 'Spatial equality in Cuba', *International Journal of Urban and Regional Research*, 11 (2), 218–41.

United States Department of Commerce (1956) *Income in Cuba*, Washington DC: US Dept. of Commerce.

Valenta, J. (1981) 'The Soviet–Cuban alliance in Africa and the Caribbean', *The World Today*, 37 (2), 45–53.

White, G. (1987) 'Cuban planning in the mid-1980s: centralization, decentralization, and participation', *World Development*, 15 (1), 153–61.

[5]
Barbados

Robert B. Potter
and
Mark Wilson

Introduction

Viewed by the casual observer, Barbados might seem to share little in common with most Third World nations, including many of its Caribbean neighbours. The country is relatively prosperous, ranking thirty-fourth in the list of 142 countries reporting to the World Bank in 1985 in respect of its Gross National Product (GNP) per capita, putting it ahead of European nations such as Portugal and Greece (World Bank, 1985). In 1986, the level of GDP per capita was US4,580 per annum. In fact, real growth has been recorded in GDP annually since 1983, standing as high as 5.1 per cent per annum in 1983 and 2.2 per cent in 1987 (Central Bank of Barbados, 1988). There are almost 35,000 cars, or 52 per 1,000 households (Barbados Licensing Authority, 1988) – and for those who may doubt the figures, the visual evidence is daily apparent in the central business district of the capital, Bridgetown. There is an efficient and comprehensive system of public transport with strongly subsidized fares. The population growth rate is a manageable 0.35 per cent per annum. Official statistics point to a much-quoted 97 per cent level of literacy. Small wonder then, perhaps, that in a recent statement, Dr Courtney Blackman, a former Governor of the Central Bank of Barbados, commented that government policies have 'made Barbados one of the most egalitarian societies in the world' (Blackman, 1987: 16).

Indeed, it would be hard not to conclude that in overall terms, Barbados has made great advances during the latter half of the twentieth century, with respect both to its economic and social welfare systems. This is in part a product of recent economic developments, which have replaced sugar and its by-products with tourism, services and light manufacturing as the mainstays of the economy. But to present this argument devoid of its wider social and spatial contexts would be very misleading. The relative prosperity enjoyed by Barbados is, and always has been, somewhat of an optical illusion. Quite patently, the wealthier sections of the economy, of the society, and of the national space are, of course, those which are most visible and conspicuous. Physically and socially less accessible, there is a considerable amount of real poverty in Barbadian society. In 1985, officially recorded unemployment was running at 18.7 per cent, and although this had decreased marginally to 17.9 per cent by 1987, it is a considerable increase from the level of 10.9 per cent which pertained in 1981 (Central Bank of Barbados, 1988). The degree to which even a substantial number of middle-class Barbadians are unaware of this is perhaps suggested by the general tenor of Dr Courtney Blackman's remarks.

Historical Perspectives on Urbanism in Barbados: an Outpost of the Metropolitan Economy

The higher level of economic development experienced by Barbados today is not simply a result of recent economic growth. Barbados was settled by the English in 1627, and although starting life as a tobacco and cotton producing colony, by the 1640s, it had become a sugar economy run on the basis of plantations and with its massive labour needs being supplied by the cruel and harsh system of black slavery. During the colonial period, from the first settlement through to independence in 1966, the island performed a dual role: on the one hand, it was a dependent sugar colony, suffering from disadvantageous terms of trade and unequal exchange in the classic manner analysed by dependency theorists such as Frank (1969) and Beckford (1972). But all dependency is relative dependency, and Barbados was always a commercial, and to a lesser extent, an administrative centre for British colonialism in the Windward Islands as a whole, and even, at certain junctures, in Trinidad and Guiana. As the most easterly of the Caribbean islands (Figure 5.1 inset), Barbados derived great relative advantage as the firt port of call for transatlantic ships and also for those from North America.

However, its function was not limited to that of an entrepôt port. It was also the main banking centre in the Eastern Caribbean, and until the early 1970s, still acted as a processing centre for agricultural products like copra from islands such as Dominica and St Lucia. Because of this higher level of commercial activity, and also due to the history of free settlement, Barbados housed a substantially larger commercial and administrative white population than the other colonies, and in addition, a much higher proportion of the planter class was actually resident on the island. To a degree, therefore, in articulating the flow of capital from the peripheral satellite to the metropolitan core, Barbados

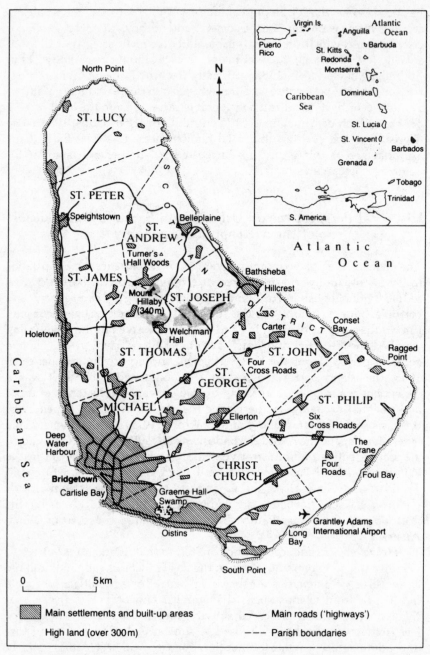

Figure 5.1. The principal settlements and built-up zones of Barbados.

became a quasi-autonomous centre for the accumulation of capital and social surplus product, legacies which persist through to the present day. The sobriquet 'Little England' which is so often applied to Barbados, while primarily intended as a cultural comment, has always had a certain economic ring to it as well, for it had a head start in terms of the accumulation of infrastructural and financial capital.

The first European settlement, Jamestown, was located half-way along the sheltered leeward or west coast at what is now known as Holetown (Figure 5.1). Shortly afterwards, rival settlements were formed at what are today Bridgetown, Speightstown and Oistins. Indeed, the major feature of the development of urban settlements in Barbados in the colonial period was their remarkable persistence and durability, for these four settlements remain as the contemporary urban foci, forming a continuous linear urban corridor (Figure 5.1). However, over time, despite the early ascendancy of Speightstown as a sugar port in the north, the locational advantages of Bridgetown became pre-eminent. These included the best natural harbour in the form of Carlisle Bay (Figure 5.1), as well as a coastal inlet known as the Constitution River, an area of low terrain inland and good access to the agricultural interior.

During the colonial period, Bridgetown thereby became the focus of the Barbadian economy within this static coastal-oriented settlement pattern. First and foremost, Bridgetown was the point of attachment of the economic outpost to the 'mother country'. Secondly, it acted as the centre of financial and political control for the dependent colonies elsewhere in the Eastern Caribbean, and thirdly, as a retailing and service centre for the planters and the rest of the rural population of the island.

Throughout the Caribbean region, as elsewhere in the developing world, linear-coastal settlement patterns are the norm, illustrating the regional outcome of dependent urbanization and development (Potter, 1985b). The pattern discernible in Barbados is highly reminiscent of the mercantile model of territorial evolution put forward by Vance (1970). The point is explored in Potter (1985a: 49–79 and Potter, 1986a) and only a brief summary is provided here. The first stage recognized in the Vance sequence involves the initial search phase of mercantilism, where the prospective colonizing power seeks to acquire information as the immediate precursor to the second phase wherein any natural resource storage that is offered by the territory is harvested. The establishment of permanent settlers is seen as a third distinct stage, and they proceed to produce agricultural staples and consume manufactured goods from the mother country. During this era, the settlement system of the colony becomes clearly established, focusing on a coastal point of attachment and exhibiting a far more coastal-linear form than might be expected on the basis of either economic or social expediency. In Barbados, by the end of the seventeenth century, Bridgetown had quite literally become what Campbell (1978) has described as 'the city of the merchants'.

Bridgetown's primate role was an established component of the Barbadian space economy from these early times onward. During the 1800s, the metropolitan parish of St Michael accounted for a roughly constant proportion of the total population, at just under 30 per cent (Potter, 1983a). In 1981, the population density of St Michael was 3.4 times the national average. Outside St Michael the density of population of the rural administrative zones was remarkably similar (with an average of 320 per sq km and a standard deviation of 40). There was a clear split between the urban administrative and trading sector and the rural zone consisting almost entirely of sugar plantations.

In the period 1891–1960, the proportion of the total population living in St Michael grew rapidly to around the 40 per cent mark (Potter, 1983a), and the density of population in the metropolitan parish was 4.5 times the national average recorded in 1946. At the same time, there were the beginnings of a growing demographic differentiation between the rural parishes (which recorded a mean population density of 342 sq km in 1960, and a standard deviation of 100). The more remote parishes of St Philip, St Joseph, St Andrew and St Lucy lost population and what were becoming essentially the suburban parishes of Christ Church and St James experienced corresponding population gains.

Urbanization in the Twentieth Century: Neo-dependent Polarization or Growth?

The essentials of these demographic changes are summarized for the period between 1871 and 1980 in Figure 5.2. Since 1960, although the proportion of the national population living in St Michael has fallen slightly (with a population density 3.9 times higher than the national average in 1980), the pattern of increasing differentiation among the suburban and rural areas has been accentuated (mean population density in 1980 of 361 per sq km, with a standard deviation of 141). The more remote parishes on the eastern coast actually support lower populations than they did back in 1881. On the other hand, there has been very rapid growth around St Michael, particularly in the suburban coastal parishes of Christ Church and St James, but more recently, in the inland suburbs of St George and St Thomas, and coastal St Philip.

While in one sense these changes can be regarded as a form of spreading out of wealth and development, in another sense they can be viewed as a more graded but nevertheless stark form of socio-spatial concentration. In fact, the pattern can be interpreted as the development

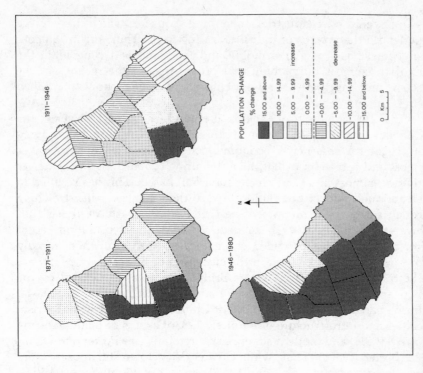

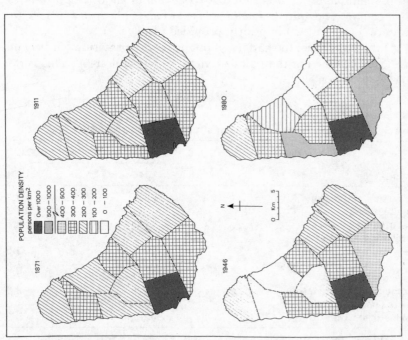

Figure 5.2. Demographic change 1871–1980 in Barbados.

of a nascent 'post-industrial' one in a country which has scarce experienced the process of industrialization itself. Thus, the urban core is showing signs of social, economic and demographic decline, while the 'suburban' zone is burgeoning and prospering. In the meantime, the eastern and northern rural-agricultural parishes show continued depression and decline.

What forces have brought this about? Over the past 40 years, the Barbadian economy has grown swiftly and there has been a shift away from sugar towards newer economic activities such as tourism, other services and to a lesser extent, manufacturing (Table 5.1). Of the newer activities, almost all are urban or suburban-based. This has resulted in the continued shift of population toward the urbanized belt, stretching through Bridgetown along the west and south coasts of the island. However, as might have been deduced from the account on recent demographic change provided earlier, by no means all these rapidly growing functions are based in the city areas of Bridgetown. Many are to be found in the wider Greater Bridgetown area, as defined by the Town and Country Development Planning Office, or in the coastal suburban areas of St James and Christ Church. This is as true of tourism facilities and infrastructure (see Potter, 1983b) as it is of manufacturing (Potter, 1981), and modern supermarket retailing (see Potter and Dann, 1986; Potter, 1989a). Thus, while Greater Bridgetown still houses 70 per cent of manufacturing jobs, and 67–70 per cent of all job opportunities, 77 per cent of retail outlets and 92 per cent of all public sector offices, the rural areas are noticeably poorly provided (Table 5.2).

At the same time, the pattern of public service provision has become more acceptable from the point of view of the rural areas. This is not

Table 5.1. Changes in the employment structure of Barbados, 1946–86.

	Total employment ('000s)	
Sector	1946	1986
Agriculture and fishing	28.9	8.1
Manufacturing	3.5	11.3
Construction	7.9	8.8
Distribution, commerce and tourism	12.4	23.6
Transport and communications	3.2	4.4
Public sector	3.0	37.4
Electricity, gas and water	0.4	2.5
Others (including craft industries)	32.5	3.3

Sources: Worrell, 1982; Central Bank of Barbados, 1986.

Table 5.2. Employment opportunities in the urban and rural areas of Barbados (*ca.* 1980)

Sector	Percentage of total establishments located in		
	Central Bridgetown	Greater Bridgetown	Rest of Barbados
Manufacturing jobs	←——————70——————→		30
Retail outlets	43	34	23
Private sector offices	61.5	26	12.5
Public sector offices	33	59	8
Tourism	←——————50——————→		50
Fishing	33		67
All employment	←——————67–70——————→		30–33
Total population	1	43	56
Area of country	←——————8——————→		92

Sources: Town and Country Development Planning Office, 1970, 1983, 1987.

true, however, of private sector services. If the national distribution of lawyers, banks and general practitioners are scrutinized in detail, then their paucity in non-metropolitan Barbados is clearly evident (Table 5.3). On the other hand, the same cannot be said of the wide range of services provided by the public sector (Table 5.3). The pattern of closely fought elections and the evenly balanced two-party system, involving the Barbados Labour Party (BLP), and the Democratic Labour Party (DLP), has generally ensured that politicians neglect the more basic and obvious forms of rural development at their peril. Polyclinics, branch libraries, community centres and schools are generally quite evenly spread across the island. The flat-fare public bus service can also be explained by the political need to integrate the rural areas more effectively into the national space economy, so that urban services are accessible to all, albeit at a cost of time and effort, if not money. Children from even the most remote villages may choose to attend Bridgetown secondary schools such as Queen's College and Harrisons rather than local institutions. Moreover, telephone ownership rates in Barbados are very high indeed, standing at almost 400 per 1,000 of the population (Barbados Telephone Company 1988), and calls within the country are free of charge.

The implications of urban primacy for the rural population in Barbados are, therefore, infinitely less serious than in the case of many larger and/or poorer Caribbean countries, which generally possess less well developed transport networks: and the cases of Haiti, the

Table 5.3. Private and public sector services in the urban and rural areas of Barbados

Sector/service	Numerical Provision in		
	Central Bridgetown	Greater Bridgetown	Rest of Barbados
Private Sector			
Retail floor space (m^2)	69,254	85,140	20,003
Lawyers	76	77	0
Banks	17	32	16
Medical doctors	95	52	19
Public Sector			
Polyclinics	0	4	4
Libraries	1	2	6
Secondary schools	4	11	10
Police stations	2	3	11
Fire stations	1	2	3
Post offices	1	5	11

Sources: Town and Country Development Planning Office, 1970, 1983, 1987; Barbados Telephone Directory, 1987.

Dominican Republic, Jamaica, Guyana and even St Vincent and Grenada readily spring to mind. Clearly, where the state has intervened over the market place, a more equitable planned pattern of service provision has emerged. This is well illustrated by the distribution of health as against manufacturing facilities in Barbados in the early 1980s.

At the same time, increased levels of car ownership and the improved public transport system have meant that the coastal belt has increasingly come within commuting distance of most rural areas. In this sense, there are no parts of the island which would not, in a larger country, be regarded as forming part of a widely defined 'Bridgetown Metropolitan zone'. It is such a reality that has given rise to the much quoted aphorism that: 'Barbados is a city where sugar cane grows in the suburbs'. Every settlement is within reach of an hourly bus service to Bridgetown, with a flat fare equivalent to 50 cents US. In no case is the bus journey to central Bridgetown longer than 80 minutes, or 20 minutes to the nearest part of the urbanized coastal belt. Access to the main labour market is therefore physically possible from all parts of the island. However, some commentators might suggest that this relatively easy access and the resultant close interaction between urban and rural zones (Potter, 1989a; Potter and Dann, 1986) has allowed strong socio-spatial polarization to continue to an extent not consistent with social welfare considerations, being premised on the possibility of frequent travel within such a small community. But access, like poverty, deprivation and, indeed, all welfare issues, is a relative concept and not an absolute one. For example, a local song refers to the northernmost parish of St Lucy as an island off the shore of 'mainland' Barbados, such is the perception of its relative inaccessibility and isolation.

Whether these changes are seen as progressive enough is very much a matter of personal political persuasion. Some may see them as the beginnings of incipient spread effects resulting directly from a period of strong capitalistic growth. As a basic justification for sharp spatial and social cleavages, such plaudits suggest that you can only share that which you have acquired in the first place. Those of a more radical persuasion are likely to counter that the cost of this has been the opening of the economy and a basically top-down, neo-dependency form of development which stresses economic and material growth, but which largely ignores social development, the quality of life and indigenous culture. Such commentators on the scene will argue that recent development has led to higher average levels of wealth, but greater disparities about this overall mean figure, so that relative as opposed to absolute disadvantage has increased.

The Internal Structure of Metropolitan Bridgetown and the Urban Crescent

As a service centre for a population in which those with money to spend were either British or deeply anglicized, it is hardly surprising that the capital city Bridgetown took on the appearance of an English market town from an early date. Almost all the early travellers who wrote about Barbados stress this point. As early as 1700, Père Labat commented that the town was 'Handsome and large . . . the houses are well built in the English taste, with many glazed windows and magnificently furnished' (Schomburgk, 1848). In 1862, Trollope commented, some might feel gratuitously, that 'Bridgetown, the metropolis of the island, is very much like a second or third rate English town. It has none of the peculiarities of the West Indies, except the heat' (Trollope, 1862: 194). In a similar vein, but closer to the present, Patrick Leigh Fermor (1950) described it as 'a completely English town, a town on the edge of London, and the wide clean streets (appear) to be almost as full of the white as of the coloured Barbadians. All the familiar landmarks were there – the one-price bazaars, the chemists with well-known names and the multiplicity of teashops.'

But the absence of a strong military presence in the urban landscape is a notable feature. Most of Britain's other possessions in the Caribbean were military conquests. But Barbados did not become an important military base until the late eighteenth century. Thus, the Garrison buildings constructed in the nineteenth century are situated some two kilométres from the city centre, and there is no central parade ground, and no fort dominating the Careenage.

Another 'British' element of Bridgetown is its irregular street plan. Trollope wrote that the streets are 'narrow, irregular, and crooked'. The regular grid plan and central square, features which are common to the morphology of most other Caribbean cities, are missing here. This characteristic of the cityscape is also related to the fact that Bridgetown was not developed through a single military, administrative or large-scale private initiative, but as the result of piecemeal operations on a small-scale basis by individual settlers. Some 30 years after the first colonization of the island, Ligon (1673: 25) described how: 'One house being set up, another was erected, and so to a third, and a fourth, until at last it came to take the name of a town'.

But once again, it is possible to suggest that the appearance of a prosperous English market town – or 'a tropical Tewkesbury-upon-Sea' (Potter and Dann, 1987) – so remarked upon in the eighteenth, nineteenth and early twentieth centuries was, to a considerable extent, another facet of the age-old optical illusion. The central business district, based on Broad Street, certainly looked and still looks English enough. So did, in their way, the all-white late nineteenth-century residential suburbs of Belleville and Strathclyde. But at about the same time that Leigh Fermor was comparing directly Bridgetown to London, living conditions in the lower-income residential districts of Barbados were very different from those found in the metropole. According to a Housing Board Survey produced in 1944:

> In a great many cases, particularly in the smallest houses, there is no covered cooking accommodation. In wet weather, the inhabitants are frequently unable to get a hot meal. Since there is no water laid on in the block, no washing facilities exist . . . in exceptionally wet weather (the ground) becomes waterlogged and partially flooded. Pit latrines cannot properly be used, since the water table is 2'6" to 3' below ground level . . . 80% of the houses use bucket latrines. Local people are employed to clear the buckets twice a week at a charge of 6 cents for each clearance. . . . Though difficult to prove, it was fairly evident that many people made as little use as possible of their latrines and used empty plots and the Emmerton ditch. Many houses have no proper separate bucket privy in the yards. Shallow surface wells are very common, and are used for watering the very rare cultivated vegetable beds and for clothes washing. A case of a surface well only 2'6" from a pit latrine was recorded.
> (DeSyllas, 1944)

Although in many respects conditions have improved greatly in Barbados since the 1940s, housing and general residential conditions still display wide variations within the city. The poorest housing is, of course, generally found in a broad elliptical zone which exists to the north, east and south of the city centre. Here the majority of houses are over 20 years old, are constructed entirely of wood and make use of pit latrine toilets. The patterning of residential quality in Bridgetown has been summarized by means of a statistical analysis of the 1980/81 census data at the enumeration district level which has recently been carried out by Potter (1987, 1988, 1989b).

This research ended with a factorial analysis of eight leading housing variables. These were reduced to their first principal component, this effectively representing a summary measure of poor housing conditions. The final result of the analysis is reproduced as Figure 5.3. The broad zone of housing disamenity encircling the city

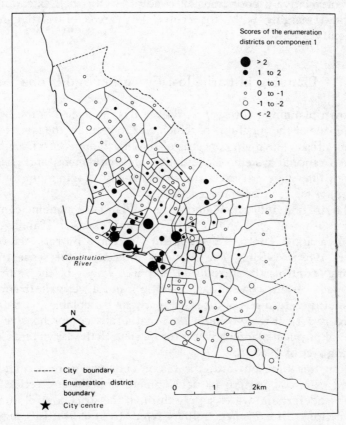

Figure 5.3. An index of housing disamenity for Bridgetown.

centre of Bridgetown is clearly discernible. Outside the city centre, the pattern of residential quality is best described as conforming with a broad Hoyt-type wedge or sectoral pattern. Particularly prominent in this respect is a southern sector of relatively high residential quality. This area runs along the south coast, through districts such as Hastings and Worthing toward the high socio-economic status zones which exist in the parish of Christ Church. This merges with an eastern area of generally sound residential conditions which is discernible on the south-eastern urban periphery (Figure 5.3). This latter area contains the large post-World War II government housing estates of Wildey and Pinelands. The northern sector of the metropolitan area of Bridgetown also stands out as being of generally medium to high residential status. It is within this area, close to the University of the West Indies campus, that a number of middle-class residential developments have proceeded at places like Cave Hill, Wanstead, Lodge Hill and Eden Lodge. Finally, the middle western periphery of the Bridgetown urban area stands as a sector of relatively poor housing conditions, this belt extending right into, and merging with, the central city areas of relative housing disamenity.

Planning in Barbados: Evolution and Scope

The town planning process in Barbados has its origins in the Board of Health, one of the functions of which was to regulate the layout of new housing areas. The main concerns of the Board appear to have been to ensure a rational system of circulation and movement, and residential densities that were not excessive. Accordingly, a minimum lot size of 223 square metres was enforced.

The rise of a fully articulated system of land use planning came with the establishment of the Office of Town and Country Planning under the Town and Country Development (Interim Control) Act of 1959 (Potter, 1983a, 1986b). The Act was interim in the sense that the planning controls it introduced applied only to the intensively developed western coastal agglomeration and a very short stretch of coast on the eastern side of the island between Belleplaine and Bathsheba (see Figure 5.1). It was not until 1965 that a fully comprehensive spatial system of physical planning was introduced with the Town and Country Planning Act of 1965.

From this time onward, the major concerns were regulating the detailed cadastral pattern of development and the protection of the island's underground water supply through the strict control of all new construction. Practitioners often refer to the British legislative framework under which the planning process operates and its direct emanation from the British Act of 1947. But the prevailing ethos of planning in Barbados leads to an approach which varies in emphasis from current British practice, in so far as very little attention is given to the landscape and urban design aspects of most applications, and a great deal to matters such as building lines, setbacks from plot boundaries, and the overall density of new developments.

Since the mid-1960s, the Planning Department has produced two strategic physical development plans for the nation as a whole (see Potter, 1986b for a summary). More recently, a draft structure plan for Bridgetown has been formulated (Town and Country Development Planning Office, 1987). However, as in other countries, there have been problems in the precise implementation of these overall strategic plans, and the constraints faced do not always relate to issues which fall within the remit of the planning professionals themselves. These include the place of town planning within the overall apparatus of government, the degree of functional integration between ministries, and the pattern of politics and land ownership in Barbadian society as a whole.

In a small nation, many questions, if they cannot be resolved by inter-departmental discussion, will be resolved at Cabinet level. If a clear political decision is taken once the alternative options have been considered, then there is a basis for the healthy evolution of an agreed strategy. If, however, no clear decision is taken and different departments take distinct approaches, then strategic town planning may degenerate into the production of abstract documents which have little meaning in the context of overall government policies or for the realities of development control.

Further, while planners see their discipline as playing a central role in formulating a strategy for the physical management of social and economic change in a mixed economy, this view is not generally shared by all other professionals, or indeed by those who set political goals. Planners are frequently perceived as people who sit at drawing boards and draft maps, who are concerned with detailed questions of site planning and layout; and who should be concerned with the physical aspect of the implementation of plans which are drawn up by other agencies.

Urban Planning Problems in Barbados

Rather than considering the issues faced by urban planning in the Barbadian context along with their institutional and theoretical foundations on a primarily chronological basis, we shall examine two of the most important sets of planning problems in a thematic manner in this section. These are: (a) the planning of the national settlement system, and (b) housing planning and upgrading.

Planning the National Settlement System

The preparation of major strategic studies commenced with the Physical Development Plan for Barbados (Town and Country Development Planning Office, 1970). The major aims of the plan have been summarized by Potter and Hunte (1979) and Potter (1986b). The plan's starting point was the argument that a major economic loss was resulting from the rapid intensification of commercial activity and congestion that had occurred in Bridgetown. Accordingly, the major policy of the plan was an unequivocal call for the decentralization of population, industry and social infrastructure away from the primate capital. It was advocated that by 1980, a spatial rationalization should have been set in motion, culminating in the establishment of a clearly defined and integrated hierarchy of settlements below the level of Bridgetown. The plan, which was produced with technical assistance and personnel from the United Nations Development Programme, was clearly inspired by the theoretical constructs of classical central place theory.

A summary of its proposals is provided by Figure 5.4. Speightstown and Oistins were designated as major urban foci for the northern and southern regions, both serving total populations in the order of 100,000. Below, seven district level centres were proposed. These were to be based on the existing settlements of Belleplaine, Holetown, Welchman Hall, Nessfield, St John (Carter-Small Hope), St George (Parish-Glebe Lands) and Six Cross Roads. It was envisaged that these would all reach populations of between 3,000 and 6,000 by 1980. Finally, some 58 village clusters were identified, which were to be enhanced to perform as local service centres. These were dotted across the entire face of the island.

Given the physical environmental and socio-demographic relations of the island, the 1970 plan seemed almost utopian in the planned settlement hierarchy it advocated. In particular, little or no credence of the existing distribution of high-grade agricultural land, water catchment areas and socio-economic infrastructure seemed to have been taken. Instead, the 1970 plan appeared as an over-technical and over-theoretical palliative, so that it fell into the category of 'eminently publishable, but hardly practicable plans' (Potter, 1983a: 10). It is not suggested that the aim of decentralization was anything less than highly desirable, but rather that the spatial configuration finally suggested to promote it was never really likely to be practical in the short- to

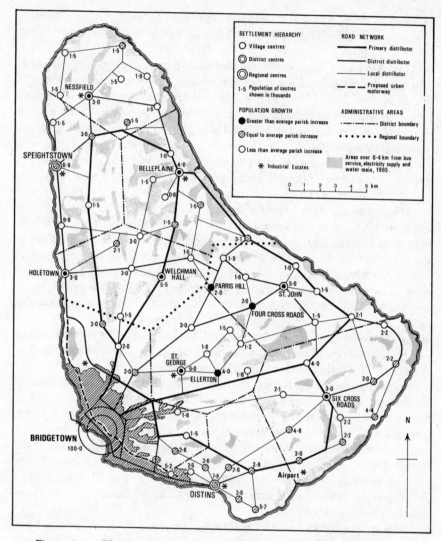

Figure 5.4. The main proposals of the Physical Development Plan 1970.

medium-run periods. In the 1979 paper, Potter and Hunte argued that a less ambitious initial programme of decentralization into an inner and outer ring of settlements might conceivably be followed.

In the event, the Revised Physical Development Plan was produced in 1983 (Town and Country Development Planning Office, 1983). The survey component of the plan notes the continued urban primacy of Bridgetown, for in 1980, of a total national population close on 250,000, the Bridgetown area remained home to 108,500 or 43 per cent. Of greater salience, 152,000 or 62 per cent lived in the continuous linear urban corridor running from Speightstown in the north to Oistins in the south.

The Revised Plan accepts the shortcomings of the earlier blueprint, albeit in an understated manner. Specifically, it is argued that changes in the economy post 1970 have continued the tendency toward urban-oriented employment growth, resulting in a strong process of suburbanization during the 1970–80 plan period. It is accepted that it is 'now no longer possible to reinstate fully the strategy of planned settlement development to the extent envisaged in the first plan' (Town and Country Development Planning Office, 1983, p. 80). The 1983 plan seeks instead to modify this ongoing trend and to 'rationalize the emerging linear urban corridor within which various urban areas are integrated into one metropolitan zone' (p. iv). A major feature of the plan is the definition of a boundary limiting the urban zone. This is shown clearly in a summary of the Revised Plan presented in Figure 5.5. The maximum urban core delimited runs from the central point of the west coast in the parish of St Lucy in the north, through the entire west, south and south-eastern coasts. Within this zone, three principal axes of urban growth have been designated. One is the area which runs north along the coast from Speightstown to Checker Hall. The other two are located at Warrens Cave Hill to the north of the Bridgetown area, and to the north of Oistins respectively (Figure 5.5).

It is also envisaged that a number of centres for more limited expansion will be established. One of these is Holetown, which it is intended will witness the growth of its commercial sector, this being primarily related to the tourist industry. Other settlements for expansion are Nessfield in the north, Belleplaine, Welchman Hall, Parish Lands (St George) and St Martins. These areas of growth are counter-balanced by strong restrictions being placed on further development in Central Bridgetown, Worthing, Wildey and Six Cross Roads (Figure 5.5).

The net outcome of the instigation of these changes would be a distinct five-level settlement and service centre hierarchy. Bridgetown would naturally be the national centre at the pinnacle. Below it, Speightstown and Oistins emerge as major centres of true urban status. Holetown, on its own, represents a third tier of the urban mesh. As a fourth level, Warrens, Worthing and Wildey emerge as important settlement nodes. Outside these areas, a number of potential urban growth points are recognized in the plan, being based on existing village clusters, most of which were designated as growth points in the 1970 Physical Development Plan.

In the article on which the above account is based (Potter, 1986b), it is argued that the Revised Physical Development Plan represents the

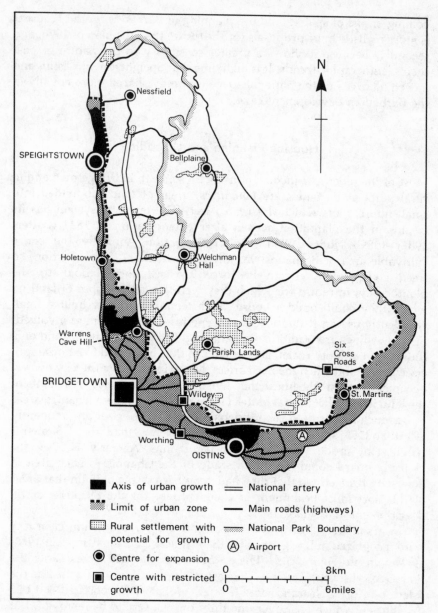

Figure 5.5. The main proposals of the Revised Physical Plan 1983.

coming of age of spatial land use planning in Barbados, both because it is more realistic in its proposals for the future than the plan of 1970, and secondly, because it shows a greater sensitivity to the nature of past socio-demographic trends. It is high time that Speightstown, Oistins and indeed all areas of the national space economy shared more equally in the Barbadian development cake.

Housing Planning and Upgrading

Most of the older low-income housing areas, both in Bridgetown and in rural parts of Barbados are *tenantries*, areas of land subdivided into small house spots which are rented out. The tenantry system has its origins in the plantation system after emancipation in 1834 (Potter, 1987; 1989b; Jones 1987). On emancipation, virtually the entire cultivable area of Barbados was already owned and in production, so freed slaves were effectively forced to sell their labour to the plantocracy, in return for which they were allocated a spot of land on which they could build a house. Such tenants normally built a small wooden house on it due to the extreme insecurity of tenure involved. Such dwellings are traditionally lightweight structures which stand on a foundation of loose rocks, and which can thus be moved to a house spot elsewhere if and when the need arises. Many families are thereby owner-occupiers as far as the house they live in is concerned, but are tenants of the land itself. The general pattern is for densities in these tenantry areas to be much higher than is considered desirable. Lot sizes are frequently less than 185 square metres and setbacks less than the 1.8 metres required by modern day planning regulations. As early as 1944, the Housing Board commented in a study of the Chapman's Lane area of inner-city Bridgetown that they had 'long been of the opinion that areas of this sort must be bought in their entirety for the purposes of re-development' (DeSyllas, 1944).

In a similar vein, four clear categories of priority slum clearance were recognized in Bridgetown by the Physical Development Plan 1970, as shown in Figure 5.6. These totalled some 250 acres, and the Emmerton district located to the east of the port was designated as the sole top-priority clearance area (Potter, 1985a). This consisted of 1,025 dwellings of which well over one-third or 392 were to be removed. But redevelopment of this sort has actually taken place in very few low-income areas, and the Revised Physical Development Plan still attaches the highest priority to redeveloping the New Orleans, Nelson Street and Church Village districts. However, site and service schemes and public housing projects were instituted from the 1950s on what was then the periphery of the built-up area some 2–4 kilometres from the city centre,

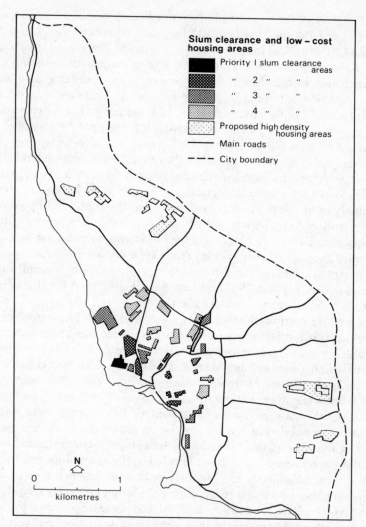

Figure 5.6.   Housing policy zones for Bridgetown in the 1970s.

as for example at the Bayland and Belfield-Pine Housing Areas and these
relieved, to some degree at least, pressure on older housing areas.
However, there was no large-scale relocation and replanning of existing
tenantries and other housing areas, except where housing land was
purchased for major road projects or infrastructural developments. One
reason for this was that to redevelop at an acceptable density would
have resulted in high infrastructural costs and would have necessitated
large-scale overspill developments, as indicated previously in the case of
the Emmerton area.

At the same time, somewhat contradictory policies were enacted with respect to these areas. While comprehensive redevelopment remained a theoretical long-term objective of the Planning Department, other agencies proceeded to improve and resurface the existing road network, and installed public services such as electricity and water mains. At the same juncture, planning policies effectively acted as a restraint on the replacement of low-grade housing. Landowners were refused permission to sell substandard plots to existing tenants; and naturally, tenants were reluctant to replace wooden structures with permanent concrete buildings unless they could purchase the land. Even where tenants or small landowners did wish to rebuild, lot sizes made it difficult to obtain planning permission. Solutions of an *ad hoc* nature were likely to be adopted, of course; not least, the tradition of piecemeal wall-by-wall reconstruction, which made it very difficult to enforce planning controls, particularly when a house was surrounded by a high temporary corrugated iron paling. From 1965, tenants of house spots in most tenantries generally did have security of tenure as a result of the Tenantries Control and Development Act. It became difficult for most landlords to evict tenants or to raise the rent. Partly as a result of this legislation and partly reflecting rising living standards too, some tenants built more substantial wooden structures on permanent foundations of concrete, or even built a permanent structure from concrete blocks. However, adherence to high standards of road width and density still acted as a significant barrier to land sales and redevelopment, even where landowners were willing to sell the freehold in house spots to their tenants. In the case of one large tenantry, landowners were refused permission to subdivide for sale to the tenants over a 20 year period while negotiations on the relocation of tenants and reorganization of the layout of the tenantry took place. This led to the anomalous situation in which it was difficult for the landowner to gain any real benefit from ownership either by raising rents, selling the land or evicting tenants and converting the land to another use. At the same time, tenants might make a substantial investment in a permanent structure, but would in theory at least be in breach of the terms of their lease if they did so; a situation which might lead to a complex predicament, particularly in cases where a tenant died intestate or wished to part with a property.

The Tenantries Freehold Purchase Act, which was passed in 1980, was an attempt to resolve this impasse (Potter, 1986c). Landlords were given the right – or more accurately, the duty – to sell lots in most cases to long-standing resident tenants who wished to buy them, irrespective of the overall layout of the area, unless lots were specifically certified as unsaleable. However, implementation of the Act in urban areas has not always been a simple and straightfoward process.

Owners of the large rural 'plantation' tenantries have in general been prepared to sell lots to residents at the statutory price of US$0.50 per square metre (effectively, about one-thirtieth of the open market price of development land in most areas). However, the owners of the urban or 'non-plantation' tenantries have generally been more reluctant to sell, in spite of the fact that sales were to be at the 'market price' for tenantry land and not at a fixed statutory price. These urban tenantries are often quite small, and the owner will, in many cases, have a long-term intention of using some or all of the land to build a house, for himself or to provide for a family member. There has been considerable political debate about this aspect of the Tenantries Freehold Purchase Act, and recent comment in the press has suggested that it is the intention of the government to amend the legislation. However, it is difficult to envisage an amendment which would give landlords the right to make use of existing tenantry land but which would also not lead to the eviction of tenants who have lived on their house spots for many years and made substantial investments in building permanent structures there. Simply removing the 'right to purchase' which was granted by the 1980 Act, without removing the security of tenure granted by the Act of 1965 would lead to a situation which is satisfactory neither for tenants nor for landlords.

The Tenantries Development Act, which was also passed in 1980, was an attempt to complement the Tenantries Freehold Purchase Act by introducing a workable method for replanning tenantry areas which did not meet minimum town planning standards of layout and infrastructural provision. In many ways an admirable piece of legislation, it allowed for a wide range of objectives and envisaged the preparation of improvement schemes for those tenantries which needed upgrading. Such schemes were not to be finalized until there had been a thorough process of public consultation involving both landowners and tenants in the areas affected. In practice, however, while large numbers of tenantries have been 'designated' as in need of improvement, formal improvement schemes have proved difficult to prepare and implement. As a result, the legislation has actually been by-passed in most cases, and agencies such as the Ministry of Transport and the Water Authority have carried out widespread improvements to tenantry areas on an *ad hoc* basis.

This pattern of piecemeal improvement, together with widespread land purchase by tenants on some tenantries under the Freehold Purchase Act, has had the result of perpetuating the existing pattern of layout, which is sometimes haphazard and does not generally conform with planning standards. At the same time, however, it has led to a considerable improvement in living conditions, which has been of great benefit to the residents of these areas. Inner-city areas like Chapman's Lane – the subject of the 1944 study – have never been comprehensively redeveloped, in spite of frequent declarations of intent on the part of various government agencies. However, they have been materially improved as a result of a combination of small-scale private initiatives by tenants and residents, and a series of improvements on many separate occasions by different government agencies. Areas like this now generally have paved roads, electricity, and water mains; some have piped natural gas supply and sewer connections. Many houses are well-built concrete block structures with indoor plumbing, and one of the most pressing problems is the provision of sufficient parking spaces.

Clearly, the effects of post-1980 housing planning have been to promote upgrading. But it must not be forgotten that such policies were necessitated in the first place as a result of the long-standing barriers which existed to the process of spontaneous improvement as a direct result of insecurity of residential tenure. It is generally agreed, therefore, that while the quantity of shelter available in Barbados is not a problem, its overall quality most certainly is (Potter, 1987: 1989b). As well as upgrading, the National Housing Plan (Ministry of Housing and Lands, 1986) and White Paper on Housing (Ministry of Housing and Lands 1984) both advocate the stimulation of the private sector to build expandable starter homes and wet core units; and a brief overview of these policies is provided in Potter (1988). In short, much remains to be done if housing conditions are to be brought into line with general socio-economic conditions in contemporary Barbados.

Concluding Comments

Many of the contemporary issues that Barbados faces can be fully understood only in relation to the country's colonial history of plantation slavery, its pattern of land ownership and the dependent nature of its development path. There is no doubting the fact that the rise of systems of physical, economic and social planning has contributed directly to the amelioration of long-standing inequalities and inequities. But although a great deal has been achieved in the overall domain of public services, there remains much spatial inequality with respect to the private sector. In contrast to public services, developments in light manufacturing, tourist, service and retailing activities in the post-independence period, while undoubtedly having transformed Barbados into a More Developed Country, have tended to continue bolstering the spatial hegemony of the coastal zone (Potter, 1981; 1983b). In this respect, the present planning machinery envisages the development of employment opportunities at the extreme northern and southern ends of the linear urban corridor as vital to the process of decentralizing employment opportunities. Whether this is seen as enough is a matter of personal persuasion and a subject for debate. But certainly, there seems much in the argument that recognition must be given to integrated policies of planning and development, which focus specifically upon the needs of all areas of the national space, both rural as well as urban. While the clarion call of development theory is for imperatives 'from below', rather than 'from above' (Stöhr and Taylor, 1981), it has to be recognized that small dependent nations – even those like Barbados that have prospered in relative terms over the past several decades – cannot seek to cut themselves off internationally in the way that China has from time to time in the past in an effort to promote a sustainable indigenous base for development (Potter, 1989a). Although the attraction of foreign capital, enclave industries and tourists is a fact of life in Barbados, future planning needs to stress rural locations above urban ones, and small-scale family enterprises above multinationals. At the very least, in Barbados as elsewhere in the Caribbean region, much will have been achieved if it comes to be fully accepted that social rather than economic factors need to be stressed in planning the future physical distribution of human activities in space.

ACKNOWLEDGEMENTS

The authors thank Graham Dann and David Weeks for reading and commenting on a draft of this chapter.

REFERENCES

Barbados Licensing Authority (1988) Personal communication.

Barbados Telephone Company (1988) Personal communication.

Beckford, G.L. (1972) *Persistent Poverty: Underdevelopment in Plantation Economies of the Third World*, New York: Oxford University Press

Blackman, C. (1987) 'The economy: a review', *The Nation*, Wednesday 2 December, 16–19.

Campbell, (1978) 'The town of the merchants', *Bajan and South Caribbean*, **296**, 6–8.

Central Bank of Barbados (1986) *Annual Report 1985*, Bridgetown: Barbados.

Central Bank of Barbados (1988) *Annual Report 1987*, Bridgetown: Barbados.

DeSyllas, L.M. (1944) *Report on Preliminary Housing Survey of Two Blocks of Chapman's Lane Tenantry, Bridgetown*, Bridgetown, Barbados.

Fermor, P.L. (1950) *The Traveller's Tree: A Journey through the Caribbean Islands*, London: John Murray.

Frank, A.G. (1969) *Capitalism and Underdevelopment in Latin America*, New York: Monthly Review Press.

Jones, A. (1987) 'The housing experience of Barbados', *Cities*, **4**, 52–7.

Ligon, R. (1673) *A True and Exact History of the Island of Barbados*, London.

Ministry of Housing and Lands (1984) *White Paper on Housing*, Barbados Government Printing Office.

Ministry of Housing and Lands (1986) *Barbados: The National Housing Plan*.

Potter, R.B. (1981) 'Industrial development and urban planning in Barbados', *Geography*, 66, 225–8.

Potter, R.B. (1983a) 'Urban development, planning and demographic change 1970–80 in Barbados', *Caribbean Geography*, 1, 3–12.

Potter, R.B. (1983b) 'Tourism and development: the case of Barbados, West Indies', *Geography*, 68, 44–50.

Potter, R.B. (1985a) *Urbanisation and Planning in the Third World: Spatial Perceptions and Public Participation*, London: Croom Helm and New York: St Martin's Press.

Potter, R.B. (1985b) 'Environmental planning and popular participation in Barbados and the Eastern Caribbean: some observations', *Bulletin of Eastern Caribbean Affairs*, 11, 24–30.

Potter, R.B. (1986a) 'Spatial inequalities in Barbados, West Indies', *Transactions of the Institute of British Geographers*, New Series, 11, 183–98.

Potter, R.B. (1986b) 'Physical development or spatial land use planning in Barbados: retrospect and prospect', *Bulletin of Eastern Caribbean Affairs*, 12, 24–32.

Potter, R.B. (1986c) 'Housing upgrading in Barbados, West Indies: the Tenantries Programme', *Geography*, 71, 255–7.

Potter, R.B. (1987) 'Housing in Barbados: good, bad or beautiful?', *The New Bajan*, 1, 26–34.

Potter, R.B. (1988) 'The structure and provision of housing in Barbados: a research agenda', *Bulletin of Eastern Caribbean Affairs*, 14, (in press).

Potter, R.B. (1989a) 'Rural–urban interaction in Barbados and the Southern Caribbean: patterns and processes of dependent development in small countries', ch. 9, in: Potter, R.B. and Unwin, T. (eds) *The Geography of Urban–Rural Interaction in Developing Countries*, London and New York: Routledge, 257–93.

Potter, R.B. (1989b) 'Urban housing in Barbados, West Indies: vernacular architecture, land tenure and self-help', *Geographical Journal*, 155, (in press).

Potter, R.B. and Dann, G. (1986) 'Core–periphery relations and retail change in a developing country: the case of Barbados', in: Cassassas, L. and Metton, A. (eds): *Commercial Change*, Barcelona: Catalan University.

Potter, R.B. and Dann, G. (1987) *Barbados: World Bibliographical Series*, Oxford and Santa Barbara, 'Introduction', xiii–xxxiii.

Potter, R.B. and Hunte, M.L. (1979) 'Recent developments in planning the settlement hierarchy of Barbados: implications concerning the debate on urban primacy', *Geoforum*, 10, 355–62.

Schomburgk, R. (1848) *The History of Barbados*, London: Longmans, Brown and Green.

Stöhr, W.B. and Taylor, D.R.F. (1981) (eds) *Development from Above or Below? The Dialectics of Regional Planning in Developing Countries*, Chichester: Wiley.

Town and Country Development Planning Office (1970) *Physical Development Plan for Barbados*, Barbados: Government Printing Office.

Town and Country Development Planning Office (1983) *Barbados Physical Development Plan, Amended 1983*, Barbados: Ministry of Finance and Planning.

Town and Country Development Planning Office (1987) *Greater Bridgetown Physical Development Plan (Draft)*, Bridgetown, Barbados.

Trollope, A. (1862) *The West Indies and the Spanish Main* (fifth edition), London.

Vance, J.E. (1970) *The Merchant's World: The Geography of Wholesaling*, Englewood Cliffs, New Jersey: Prentice-Hall.

World Bank (1985) *World Development Report 1985*, London: Oxford University Press.

Worrell, D. (1982) (ed.) *The Economy of Barbados 1946–1980*, Bridgetown: Central Bank of Barbados.

[6]

Guyana

Alan Strachan

The mainland South American country of Guyana owes its Caribbean links to the political, social and economic heritage forged during nearly a century and a half of British colonial rule. Unlike those of many of its neighbours, the problems facing Guyana are not due to overpopulation and rapid rates of urbanization, but are the result of economic decline and social inequalities. Its population of some 801,000 (1980) lives at a density of only 3.73 per sq km, and even using the broadest definition, only 49.1 per cent reside in urban communities. The absence of population pressure is largely accounted for by excessively high rates of emigration.

The highly skewed population distribution can be explained by reference to the geography of the area and the manner in which it was colonized. Extending over an area of 214,970 sq km, Guyana is similar in size to Britain, but 90 per cent of the population live on the coastal plain, a narrow belt of alluvial mud between 15 and 65 km wide. Three major rivers, the Essequibo, Demerara and Berbice, divide it into four distinct parts (Figure 6.1), and the only bridge is that across the Demerara (Strachan, 1980b). The area to the north-west of the Essequibo is characterized by a landscape of farms, scattered holdings and small villages and has no urban service centre of any consequence. The much broader west and east Demerara coastlands form the country's heartland, large agro-villages line the coast road and at its centre lies Georgetown with a population of 200,00 in 1980, the capital and only major urban area in Guyana. South of the Berbice River the coastal strip is serviced by the port and small town of New Amsterdam (20,000 in 1980).

Inland from the coastal fringe lies the rainforest zone where the terrain rises inland to the Pakaraima Mountains and the spectacular flat topped Kaieteurian plateau. This is home to the remnant Amerindian population, around 40,000 in number in 1980, whose small villages are

140

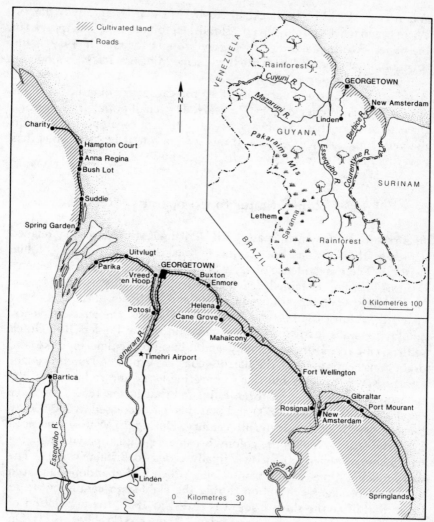

Figure 6.1. Guyana: location map.

to be found along the principal rivers. The discovery of gold and diamond deposits around 1900 resulted in an influx of prospectors who established Bartica (estimated population 4,000 in 1980), located at the junction of the Essequibo and its tributary the Mazaruni (Figure 6.1). Early optimism was unfulfilled and Bartica is now a much reduced service centre. The discovery of large deposits of bauxite some 100 km inland along both the Demerara and Berbice rivers soon after the turn of the century was to be more important in the long term for the economy of the country. Mining began in 1916 but its major growth came during and after the World War II. A new town, Mackenzie, and two villages, Wismar and Christianburg, were established to house those employed in the mines. All three communities were brought together in 1969 as the town of Linden, named after the then Prime Minister. In 1975, it had an estimated population of 27,000.

The savanna zone was opened up for cattle ranching but this has gone into decline over the past 20 years. The small population working the extensive ranches has always been insufficient to support more than the very small service centre and mission station at Letham which has never had more than a few hundred residents.

From Colonial Status to Co-operative Republic

In a continent in which Spanish and Portuguese colonization reigned supreme, the Guianas are unique in their north European colonial heritage. There is evidence of early Spanish exploration and settlement, but this was not sustained, leaving a vacuum which was filled by the Netherlands when it renounced its allegiance to Spain at the end of the sixteenth century (Barber and Jeffrey, 1986). Over the next 200 years, employing skills learned in the reclamation of the Polders, the Dutch settlers embarked on an equally ambitious programme of dyke and drain construction along the narrow coastal strip. The Dutch brought African slaves to carry out this engineering work and to labour on the tobacco plantations. It has been estimated that in the 1660s, the slave population was around 2,500 and that this had increased to 100,000 by the first decade of the nineteenth century. During the War of American Independence (1775–82) the colony became a political pawn, changing hands several times until it was finally ceded to Britain in 1814. The working conditions on the plantations, which had abandoned tobacco in favour of sugar cultivation during the eighteenth century were so harsh that after the slave trade was ended in 1807, the population of British Guiana fell steadily to around 98,130 in 1838 (Webber, 1931). On gaining their freedom in 1834, the former slaves began to leave the plantations and established villages on abandoned estates and in so doing, laid the foundations of the agro-village communities which continue to be a feature of the settlement pattern along the coastal strip (Figure 6.1). Manpower shortages led to the introduction of the indentured labour system thus initiating the ethnic plurality which is now such an important feature of Guyanese society. Portuguese workers were the first to come, followed by Africans, Indians and Chinese. Between 1834 and 1917, when the indentured system ended, it is estimated (Webber, 1931) that 340,541 individuals entered the colony: 70.1 per cent from India, 12.4 from the West Indies, 9.2 from Portugal,

4.1 from China and 3.9 from Africa. In the absence of alternative employment in the colony, the majority of workers continued to live close to the sugar plantations once their contract period had expired. The Portuguese were an exception, for they established themselves as traders and retailers in the villages, and increasingly in Georgetown as well.

The administration of the colony was overseen by a Governor appointed by the British government and a small élite group of estate and property owners, the great majority of whom were white. However, in the 1930s, the labour unions were instrumental in extending adult suffrage and in so doing, brought about a radical change in British Guiana's political life. The period up until the 1980s was dominated by two major personalities, Cheddi Jagan, an Indo-Guyanese, and Forbes Burnham, an Afro-Guyanese, whose political philosophies and rivalry helped shape not only the country's political ideology but also its present economic and social status. Jagan formed the radical socialist People's Progressive Party (PPP) in 1950, and he became its Leader and Burnham its Chairman. This party fought and won a resounding victory in the 1953 election but, claiming that the country was under threat of communist subversion, the Governor almost immediately suspended the constitution. The British government's fear of 'Jagan socialism' and the latter's unwillingness to temper his political views dominated life in British Guiana in the 1950s and were instrumental in delaying its progress towards independence. Internal disagreements led to Burnham establishing a rival party, the People's National Congress (PNC), after the PPP's electoral victory in 1957. Although not apparent in the beginning, the two parties have become racially oriented, with the PNC having the support of the Afro-Guyanese, and the PPP the Indo-Guyanese. Notwithstanding the PPP's electoral support, confirmed in the 1961 election, the British government could still not bring itself to give independence to a colony whose legislature was so avowedly socialist. Indeed it went so far as to introduce a system of proportional representation which gave the PNC victory in the 1964 election and independence was granted two years later. The British government's expectations that the new nation would follow a moderate political course were not fulfilled. As early as 1961 there had been clear evidence that Burnham and the PNC favoured a co-operative form of social and economic development. This was confirmed in 1970 when the country's official title was changed to that of the Co-operative Republic of Guyana. Although it remained within the Commonwealth, the new Republic established close links with many countries in the Eastern Bloc and embarked on a programme of nationalization which was to see some 80 per cent of the country's economy become government controlled by 1980. In successive

elections during the 1970s and 1980s, the PNC used its urban power base
and blatant ballot rigging to stay in power (Spinner, 1984). Burnham,
who became President in 1980, remained the dominant political figure
until his death in 1985. The former Prime Minister Desmond Hoyte
became President and the PNC retained its political supremacy.

Over the past 40 years, Guyana's racial plurality has become an
increasingly important dimension of its daily life. Differential fertility
and emigration rates have combined to alter the country's demographic
structure. Persistently high levels of emigration since the late 1940s by
Afro-Guyanese and out-migration of Indo-Guyanese only over the last
20 years has resulted in the latter group accounting for just over 50 per
cent of the total population (Tables 6.1 and 6.2). Until quite recently,
rural to urban movement linked to the administrative, service and
industrial development of Georgetown was mainly by the Afro group,
as was migration to the new mining villages. The resultant dominance of
the Afro population in urban areas has provided the PNC with an easily
mobilized and assertive power base which it has used to counter the
increasing trend towards racially determined voting behaviour. The
traditional agro-villages, established first by freed African slaves, have
been taken over by the Indo-Guyanese. This sets them apart from all
other groups who, in response to real and perceived opportunities, have
moved into the emerging urban areas, particularly Georgetown. This is

Table 6.1. Population of Guyana 1831–1984 and level of urbanization, 1931–80.

Year	Total	Per cent change	Per cent change	Per cent urban
			(Per annum)	
1831	98,000	–		
1841	98,154	0.1	0.01	–
1851	135,154	37.6	3.76	–
1861	155,907	15.3	1.53	–
1871	193,491	24.1	2.41	–
1881	252.186	30.3	3.03	–
1891	278,328	10.3	1.03	–
1911	296,041	6.3	0.31	–
1921	297,691	0.5	0.05	–
1931	310,933	4.4	0.44	25.0
1946	369,678	18.8	1.88	28.0
1960	560,330	51.5	3.67	29.0
1970	699,848	24.8	2.48	31.7
1980*	793,000	13.3	1.33	48.1
1984*	801,000	1.0	0.33	49.1

* Estimate

Source: Government of Guyana, 1970; World Bank, 1984; Hope, 1986.

Table 6.2. Racial composition of Guyana and
Georgetown (*ca.* 1980).

Race	Guyana	Georgetown
	(per cent)	(per cent)
East Indian	50.2	27.4
African	30.0	53.7
Mixed	10.3	13.2
Amerindian	4.6	0.6
Portuguese	1.0	4.2
Chinese	0.6	1.3
Others	3.3	0.5

Source: Hope, 1986; Dodd and Parris, 1977.

clearly seen in the proportional distribution of races between the nation
as a whole and the capital Georgetown, a point highlighted by Table
6.2. However, the East Indian urban population is growing very rapidly
at the present time as a result of accelerated rural to urban migration and
high fertility rates among those already living in towns.

The Present Rate and Pattern of Urbanization

It is necessary to preface any discussion of Guyana's economy and
society by emphasizing the almost total absence of up-to-date statistics.
As a consequence of the government's decision not to publish the results
of the 1980 census, analysts are forced to rely on estimates, of variable
accuracy, based on 1970 census date (Government of Guyana, 1970).
An official Statistical Bulletin which contained a limited range of
standard information was produced quarterly until 1979. Data included
in statistical digests such as those published by the World Bank (various
dates) and Lloyds Bank (1986) lack the precision usually associated with
such sources. It is not possible therefore to write with any certainty
about something as fundamental as even population size (Table 6.1) and
even less so about such important matters as rates of urbanization,
levels and nature of emigration, racial composition (Table 6.2), social
class, employment characteristics and housing conditions.

Guyana's economic difficulties have their origins in the colonial
period, but matters have not been helped by the policies followed since
independence. The dominance of the sugar plantation/estate continued
unchallenged until the twentieth century when the discovery of bauxite
and the introduction of commercial rice cultivation broadened the
economic base (Scherm, 1987). However, these developments did
nothing to reduce the country's total dependence on external markets for
its products and on overseas producers for much of its food

requirements and almost every form of manufactured good. There has been very little industrial diversification and there is no significant income from tourism so that as world demand for its staple products has declined, Guyana's economy has collapsed. In 1983, sugar accounted for 37.4 per cent of exports, followed by bauxite (35.5), rice (11.2) and timber (2.3). The World Bank (1984) estimated that its 1982 per capita income of US$490 was lower than in 1970, and that it had fallen by over a third between 1975 and 1982. Real wages have fallen by over 60 per cent between 1975 and 1983, unemployment is now in the region of 50 per cent, and the government deficit in 1984 amounted to 74.5 per cent of GDP (Lloyds Bank, 1986). The impact of this crisis has been felt by all sections of the community, but without question, most acutely by those living in Georgetown, Linden and New Amsterdam where the people are not able to fall back on garden cultivation to meet essential food requirements.

The World Bank (1983) and others (Cross, 1979; Hope, 1983, 1984b, 1986) suggest that nearly 50 per cent of Guyanese now reside in urban areas. This statistic is somewhat misleading for it is based on the number of people living in settlements with in excess of 5,000 inhabitants and does not take account of the history of settlement in Guyana. The large agro-villages which were established along the coast-road (Figure 6.1) have no urban pretentions. They do not exhibit the type of employment specialization and residential and functional structure that is usually associated with urban areas. There are only three truly urban areas in Guyana: the capital and dominant city Georgetown (200,000 in 1980), the mining community of Linden (27,000 in 1975) and the small port town of New Amsterdam (20,000 in 1980). To these might be added the small river crossing communities of Bartica, Parika and Rosignol (Figure 6.1) which because of their nodal positions have emerged as very small, but significant service centres. Using this more restricted definition the proportion of the population resident in urban areas falls to around a third.

A quarter of Guyana's total population lives in Georgetown. The rate of urban growth has been significant over the past 50 years (Table 6.3). Georgetown increased by 187 per cent and New Amsterdam by 150 per cent. In the case of Georgetown, this was most rapid between 1946 and 1960 (57.8 per cent) followed by a lull during the 1960s and more rapid growth, over 20 per cent, during the following decade. The figures for Linden are incomplete owing to its fragmented village structure prior to 1969. However, the combined populations of the three villages expanded rapidly during the 1960s (+27.1 per cent). However, with the decline in mining its subsequent growth has been much more modest. Starting from a very modest base in 1931, New Amsterdam had doubled in size by 1970, but cut-backs in both sugar and bauxite exports made

Table 6.3. Rate of urban growth in Guyana 1911–80.

Year	Georgetown		New Amsterdam		Linden	
	Number	Per cent	Number	Per cent	Number	Per cent
1911	57,677				(not founded)	
1921	59,594	+3.3			(not founded)	
1931	69,663	+16.9	8,002		(not founded)	
1946	94,035	+34.9	9,567	+19.5	*	
1960	148,391	+57.8	14,053	+46.8	18,845	
1970	163,939	+10.4	17,782	+20.9	23,956	+27.2
1980†	200,000	+21.9	20,000	+12.4	27,000	+12.7

* Two separate mining villages
† Estimate

Sources: Government of Guyana, 1970; World Bank, 1983; Lloyds, 1986.

this small town less attractive to migrants during the 1970s. Although significant, these rates of increase would have been far higher had it not been for the high levels of emigration experienced by Guyana since the late 1940s (Standing and Sukdeo, 1977). Strachan (1980a, 1983) calculated that the net migration loss between 1950 and 1965 was nearly 30,000 and that over the following 10 years the figure was around 50,000. This population haemorrhage has become even more acute over the past decade with estimates of 20,000 Guyanese leaving the country each year (Catholic Institute for International Relations, 1984). The World Bank (1984) noted that Guyana's population had risen by no more than 7,000, from 793,000 to 801,000, between 1980 and 1984. The sharply falling annual rate of population increase over the past 30 years (Table 6.1) is clear evidence of the scale of emigration. There are two main reasons why this has occurred. Firstly, the shortage of all forms of employment as a result of the collapse of the economy since independence has been responsible, and second, the growing conviction on the part of Indo-Guyanese that there is no acceptable role for them in Guyanese society or economy. Emigration has been selective involving mainly the young, and within this group, a high proportion of the more highly educated and skilled. It is a reflection of Guyana's commercial and industrial stagnation that despite these massive losses, there is no shortage of suitably qualified people to fill all available positions. Although there is a steady flow of return migrants (Strachan, 1980b; 1983), the situation is serious since emigration has robbed the country of those who would be best able to help overcome its present problems. However, it could be argued that given the disastrous policies followed by the government, emigration has acted as a relief valve against even greater poverty, unemployment and housing deficiency. Rural to urban migration is taking place for all the well-documented reasons, it is male dominated and the majority of Guyanese made at least three intermediate moves before finally arriving in Georgetown (Hope, 1982; Hope and Ruefli, 1981). Migrants accounted for 51 per cent of urban growth during the 1970s (Hope, 1986) and there is little evidence that high urban unemployment has in anyway reduced the magnitude of rural to urban movement. Since migrants are now mainly Indo-Guyanese there will be further changes in the racial composition of Georgetown's population (Table 6.2).

The links between urbanization and the patterns of economic development are most obvious in Guyana's two smaller urban areas. Linden – the first – owes its existence entirely to the discovery and development of bauxite deposits. The Demerara River, which is navigable for small ocean-going ore carriers upstream as far as the mine, is used to export the ore, but a paved road had to be built over quite difficult terrain from Georgetown. The mines were operated by the

Canadian ALCAN company (nationalized in 1971) and a subsidiary of the US owned Reynolds Metals (nationalized in 1975). Three communities were established to house the workers; a town – Mackenzie, and two villages – Wismar and Christianburg (Guyana Information Service, 1979). The amalgamation of these communities has created a town with some 27,000 inhabitants and a layout which exhibits a hybrid combination of imported and indigenous community structures. In the absence of any resident population on which they could draw, the mining companies were forced to provide accommodation not only for foreign-born engineers and administrators, but also for the Guyanese labour force: the latter was drawn overwhelmingly from the Afro-Guyanese community. This took the form of a new town, Mackenzie, which incorporated many of the design features to be found in comparable communities being developed in Britain in the 1950s. The town centre, with its modest public buildings, offices and shopping mall, is surrounded by a series of residential neighbourhoods. These were developed for different social groups. The managers and engineers were provided with detached bungalows and ranch-style houses, many having good views over the river. Semi-detached or four-in-a-block were the norm for skilled and semi-skilled workers. Where it was provided, the housing for the unskilled labour force took the form of much more modest terraces and cottages. The arcuate street pattern with small recreation areas and strategically placed schools and churches is typically 'new town'. This imported settlement form stands out in sharp contrast to the much more informal layout of the essentially indigenous villages of Wismar and Christians-burg. Away from the core, with its limited range of shops and services and orderly street pattern, these villages merge almost imperceptibly into the forest where scattered shanty-type holdings are to be found. Several self-help housing projects were developed adjacent to these villages in the 1970s. The decline in bauxite production consequent upon indifferent management since nationalization and falling world demand has hit Linden very hard. The potential of the minerals in the area for the production of ceramics and paint has been investigated, but neither has proved commercially viable. The effects of the recession have been severe and as a result, growth has declined sharply and unemployment is very high among all age groups. Hardship is widespread, particularly among the poorer townspeople, and migration to Georgetown or abroad is increasingly seen as the only option, especially by the young.

The second town – New Amsterdam – owes its foundation to the need for a port and service centre to meet the requirements of those plantations located on the east bank of the Berbice River. Its limited hinterland and shallow harbour restricted its growth throughout the nineteenth century and its population in 1931 was only 8,002 (Table

6.3). The period of most rapid growth came during the 1950s and early 1960s, when New Amsterdam and the adjacent riverside community of Everton became the trans-shipment point for the bauxite ore mined upriver. However, cutbacks in world demand have seen production concentrated more and more on the Demerara deposits, with a consequent decline in port activity at New Amsterdam and a marked reduction in its rate of growth. Structurally, the town shows clear evidence of each new phase in its economic development. The old town focuses on the port area, and here there is the assemblage of buildings, both official and industrial, associated with the movement of goods and people. Adjacent to the port, a small business area developed, with a town hall, market, a range of shops and a small number of professional offices. The homes of the more affluent families were located to the north where they could benefit from sea breezes. As population densities in the established working class areas became excessive, new houses spread southwards along the river and to a more limited extent inland. Streets lined with very small cottages, each with its own yard, are typical of these areas, along with a few general stores, drinking/rum shops, the occasional primary school and a scattering of churches. On the edge of the town this more formal urban structure gives way to a fringe of smallholdings, intermixed with a growing number of fairly rudimentary shacks. With the decline in bauxite exports, the living standards and housing standards of established residents have fallen and there is little prospect of work for newcomers. Faced with this bleak prospect, many young people have moved on to Georgetown (Hope and Ruefli, 1981) or, like many before them, have opted to emigrate.

The Urban Geography of Georgetown

Georgetown, the capital, is located at the mouth of the Demerara River, at the centre of the highly productive coastal plain. It has a tolerably good harbour and its only drawback is that it lies some 3.5 m below sea level. Undeterred, the Dutch chose this as the site for their capital Stabroek and set about draining and protecting the area. This work was continued by the British so that Georgetown, by virtue of its spacious layout and gracious architecture, came to be regarded as the most attractive garden city in the whole of the Caribbean. A regular grid of grass and tree-lined drainage canals and ditches was constructed and the area was protected by a high embankment which served on the seaward side as a modest promenade, and along the river as the harbour and its associated quays. A system of sluice gates, more recently replaced by pumps, was developed to allow surplus water to be released into the river at low water. The presence of ornamental gardens and walkways

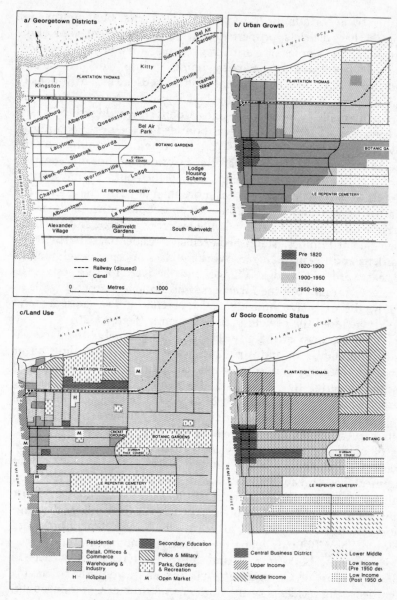

Figure 6.2. Urban geography of Georgetown.

added greatly to the environmental quality and residential desirability of the city's northern districts of Cummingsburg, Alberttown, Queenstown and Kingstown, as did the wide streets created by the subsequent culverting of the north-south ditches (Figure 6.2). The plantation owners, administrators and merchants built impressive mansions in these districts, properties which today represent some of the finest remaining examples of Caribbean colonial architecture. Southern Georgetown has traditionally been home to the working classes. Centred on Stabroek, the original Dutch settlement, high-density residential districts came into being in Lacytown, Bourda, Werk-en-Rust, Wortmanville, Charlestown and Albouystown (Figure 6.2a and 6.2b). The compact built-up area was bounded to the north and north-east by sugar estates, to the east by the extensive grounds of the Botanical Gardens and the D'Urban Race Course, to the south-east by the very large Le Repentir Cemetery and to the south by more sugar plantations. Post-1945 expansion has more than doubled the area of the city. Earlier movement by middle-income households towards the north east at Newton, Kitty and Campbellville was consolidated and extended as upper-income families established exclusive residential suburbs at Bel Air Gardens and Prashad Nagar. Working-class housing developments spread eastwards in Lodge Village and Lodge Housing estate to effectively surround both the racecourse and Botanic Gardens, while to the south, the extensive housing developments at La Penitence and Ruimveldt enclosed the cemetery at Le Repentir (Figure 6.2b).

The land use map of the city (Figure 6.2c) highlights the expected riverside dominance of industry and warehousing, including sugar refineries, a distilling and soft drinks company, several other food processing concerns, timber yards and a number of small engineering businesses which provide the bulk of Georgetown's meagre industrial employment. The continuity of the city's central business district (CBD) from its earliest foundation through to the present can be seen in the cluster of public buildings, shops and offices adjacent to the river in Stabroek. Government, and to a much lesser extent private, office development has spread eastwards from the CBD to form an almost continuous business thoroughfare as far as the racecourse. More recently, retailing, offices and hotels have taken over some of the large mansions along Main Street to form an intermittent northward extension of the CBD paralleling the industrial waterfront.

Open spaces, both formal and informal, have always been a prominent feature of Georgetown's cityscape. In addition to having large gardens, the residents of the northern suburbs of Cummingsburg, Alberttown and Queenstown also have access to two recreation grounds and the delightful Promenade Gardens, a miniature botanic garden (Figure 6.2c). By contrast, the poorer central and southern districts are almost completely devoid of formal open space, with the exception of Bourda Green, which is no longer grass covered, and the banks of the drainage canals. This contrast has been heightened over the past 30 years with the conversion of much of the very extensive Plantation

Thomas on the seafront to public, sports club or educational open space, whereas in the southern La Penitence and Ruimveldt housing areas, open space is limited to a few small plots, many of which have not been properly landscaped or tended. The Bourda Cricket Ground, Botanical Gardens and racecourse are now in the heart of the urban area and continue to provide recreation facilities for the whole community.

Georgetown established an early, and excellent, reputation for the quality of its educational provision. Primary schools abound and a cluster of long-established senior schools is to be found in the heart of the city. In response to growing demand, a schools campus was developed at Plantation Thomas. The University of Guyana and the College of Education are located on adjacent green field sites some five kilometres east of the city at Turkein. Since independence, however, financial stringencies and the persistent 'brain drain' of teachers has placed considerable strain on the educational system, and recent reports (Catholic Institute for International Relations, 1984) suggest that the previously high standard of educational provision is not being maintained.

Churches and temples are an important feature of Georgetown's urban scene. Most prominent are the cathedrals on the edge of the CBD, with St George's, the largest wholly wooden building in the Caribbean, being the most striking. A plethora of churches belonging to a multiplicity of groups and sects is to be found throughout the middle- and lower-income areas.

The present residential structure of the city reflects the history of the settlement (Figure 6.2b). The northern districts of Cummingsburg, Kingston, Alberttown and Queenstown have preserved their high socio-economic status – but not without change. As Georgetown's population has grown over the past 30 years, the large garden plots in these districts have come under increasing pressure for development. Original plots have been subdivided to accommodate an average of between three and six houses (Strachan, 1981). This has greatly increased residential and population densities and reduced the social standing of these districts. As the number of white collar workers increased, mainly after 1946, Newtown and Kitty were developed as middle-income suburbs with higher housing densities. This pattern was later replicated in both Campbellville and Subryanville. The high-status tradition of this northern coastal belt was reinforced by the outward thrust of upper-income detached houses, each with their own fair-sized garden, through Bel Air Park to Prashad Nagar and Bel Air Gardens on the urban periphery. The riverside and the southern districts of the city have always housed the lower income groups. The old working class areas of Lacytown, Bourda, Werk-En-Rust, Wortmanville, Charlestown and Albouystown (Dodd and Parris, 1977; Heins, 1978), characterized by a mixture of terraced properties and modest detached houses, have experienced a steady decline in social status through multiple occupancy and the subdivision of what were already quite small plots (Strachan, 1981). The more recently developed Lodge, Lodge Housing Scheme and Tucville extend this zone of low socio-economic status eastwards to the urban fringe. To the south, the suburbs of La Penitence, Riumveldt Gardens and South Riumveldt contain a mixture of social groups. Initially the cottages in these areas were developed to house skilled manual and junior office workers, but as the economy has faltered and the pressure for urban housing has increased, these areas have slipped down the social scale. Housing has become an increasingly more critical problem in Georgetown as the construction of new homes has failed to keep pace with demand.

This situation can in part be accounted for by the central role that the state has always played in the provision of houses for all sections of the community. It built direct contract houses either for sale or rent at Lodge, Lodge Housing Scheme and parts of La Penitence and Riumveldt, access to which has become increasingly politically controlled, with preference given to the Afro group, particularly with regard to rented property (Peake, 1986). The rapidly expanding East Indian urban population has had to solve its own housing problem by intensifying the already high levels of occupancy and multiple occupancy within the existing housing stock. For middle-income groups, the government often initiated residential developments by undertaking the task of acquiring the land, levelling it, constructing sewers and providing road access. This prepared land was then sold or rented to groups who built their own houses with loans from the Credit Corporation, a body which made loans to 'credit worthy' groups (Peake, 1986). This form of development was common in the suburbs of Subryanville and Campbellville and to a lesser extent in Riumveldt to the south of the city. Private development was a feature of the upper-income suburbs to the east of the city at Prashad Nagar and Bel Air Gardens. A number of self-help projects, often in the form of co-operative organizations, were undertaken in the southern suburbs, but these were beyond the financial reach of the poor (Heins, 1978). Slum clearance and redevelopment for housing has seldom been undertaken, and very little house building has occurred during the 1980s. Overcrowding and poor maintenance are features of all but the most affluent housing areas. Both building and maintenance are hampered by the financial situation and by the lack of even the most mundane 'raw materials' such as nails and paint.

Housing is only one of a number of serious problems facing the inhabitants of Georgetown and the other urban areas. All of the evidence points to a marked decline in the quality of life and standard of living over the past 25 years, and to the fact that this trend is accelerating. The primary cause has been the progressive collapse of the country's economy. The adoption by the government of a policy of state ownership has not been accompanied by essential restructuring as demand for sugar and bauxite has declined. The manufacturing sector, which is to be found mainly in Georgetown, has not been developed and consequently makes a minor contribution to the country's GDP (12 per cent) and provides only a small number of jobs (15 per cent of the labour force). By contrast, the service sector accounts for a disproportionately high 51 per cent of employment, mainly in government offices and retail outlets in Georgetown. However, this sector has not escaped unscathed. During the 1980s, wage levels have not kept pace with inflation and the number of jobs has been cut by nearly a third. Unemployment levels are currently estimated to be around 30 per cent (Lloyds Bank, 1986), but much higher, up to 50 per cent, among the young (Hope, 1982; 1984a) and the trend for all groups is up. In order to survive, households have increasingly turned to the black market. This varies in scale from the illegal export of gold, diamonds and agricultural produce and the use of the money so gained to import goods and food items no longer readily available in Guyana, to participation in small-scale commerce such as market stalls, home made alcohol and the sale of cooked and uncooked food. The city has four flourishing outdoor markets (Figure 6.2c) which provide outlets for those wishing to sell surplus produce or goods and in which essential purchases can be made at a minimal and often negotiable price. Shortages are commonplace, affecting everyday items such as milk, flour, cooking oil, soap, drugs, domestic fuels, gas and kerosene and have been known to include local staples such as rice and sugar (Catholic Institute for International Relations, 1984). A measure of the severity of the situation has been an increase in the incidence of malnutrition in Georgetown and the other urban areas where households do not have sufficiently large gardens to enable them to grow much of their own food (Hope, 1984b). The situation in Georgetown is aggravated by the near collapse of public utilities – water purity cannot be guaranteed, breaks in the electricity supply are frequent and the health service has deteriorated sharply to the extent that the Public Hospital in Georgetown, the country's major medical institution, has been said to constitute a health hazard (Catholic Institute for International Relations, 1984). Reference has already been made to the deterioration of the education service. In such circumstances it is not surprising that the incidence of crime has increased very dramatically over the past two decades with rates of 164 per 10,000 population over the age of 10 recorded in Georgetown, 204 in New Amsterdam and 146 in Linden, compared with 97 in rural areas (Jones, 1981). Within the city, the lower socio-economic districts were found to have the highest crime rates (Dodd and Parris, 1977). As the quality of life within Georgetown, and indeed in the country as a whole has progressively declined, it is not surprising that so many of its citizens have opted to emigrate.

Planning and Politics

Having brought the country to independence, the ruling PNC immediately set about consolidating its position. By promoting cooperative ownership, the government seemed to be advocating a twin policy of top-down and bottom-up planning; a partnership in development. This strategy received popular acclaim with numerous cooperatives in such areas as housing, education, transport, agriculture, savings and retailing coming into being with an estimated membership of over 120,000 in 1974 (Peake, 1987). However, having launched the idea, the government then sat back and let it run its course. No effort was made to co-ordinate projects either by sector or administrative district and little encouragement was provided, other than in the area of housing. Not surprisingly, therefore, many failed, while those that survived made little progress and the number of new co-operatives fell dramatically. There are many reasons for this failure to respond to the needs of co-operatives, these include a lack of understanding of the development process, administrative incompetence and the downturn in the national economy. It might also have been a deliberate part of the PNC's strategy to secure its power base. Ever mindful of the electoral threat posed by Jagan's PPP, the policies and actions of the PNC have had the express aim of concentrating power into as small a group of party officials as possible. This was to be achieved by bringing as much of the Guyanese economy as possible under direct or indirect government control. Capitalizing on the enthusiastic acclaim for cooperatives, the majority of which were headed by PNC party members in 1970, the country's name was changed to The Co-operative Republic of Guyana. This was followed by an aggressive programme of nationalization which not only included all of the main industries but also banking (Hope, 1975), communications, the media, the civil service, the police, the judiciary and the education system. The PNC further consolidated its position through the establishment of the Guyana Defence Force, overwhelmingly manned by Afro-Guyanese, and the promotion of the Guyana National Service for young people. In 1977, it was estimated that one in 35 of the population was in one or other of these organizations (Peake, 1987). The power of the ruling élite was secured in the new constitution of 1980, under which a parliamentary system is notionally retained, but all power flows from and through the President. At the national level, obsessed with its primary goal of securing power, the PNC government failed to recognize and address the fundamental economic problems facing the newly independent country. Of the three National Development Plans produced, the first, 1966–72, was abandoned half way through leaving a weak industrial sector, high unemployment and substantial debt (Greene, 1974; Hope, 1977). The second plan, 1972–76, which aimed to improve housing conditions, bring about industrial diversification and regenerate agriculture fell short on all counts as world markets for Guyana's staple products declined. The effects of this collapse were compounded by widespread managerial and administrative incompetence in the now state-owned industries, factors which were also to undermine the third development plan, 1977–81 (Chandisingh, 1983). Throughout the 1980s, no real attempt has been made to plan for economic development. With the failure of co-operative socialism, the government was forced to look elsewhere to help prop up its collapsing economy and it is a reflection of its pragmatism that it did not hesitate in turning to the International Monetary Fund (IMF) in 1976. Since then, dependency on loans from this agency has increased, with the result that the IMF's requirements now influence all sectors of the Guyanese economy.

Although a system of local government is still in place, the conditions under which it operates have been radically altered. At independence the government inherited a long established four-fold system of local government based on urban sanitary districts, village districts, county districts and rural sanitary districts. The need to update the system had long been recognized and this was done in a package of Acts passed in 1969. However, the promise of increased local autonomy was not fulfilled. The introduction in 1973 of a new development policy based on 10 regions added another tier of bureaucracy. Each of the regions has its own Minister appointed directly by the Prime Minister (the President after 1980). This strengthened the control that the government has over every aspect of life in Guyana. In the absence of elections – the last local election was held in 1970 – positions on city and town councils are reserved for loyal party members and patronage is important in the appointment of officers and staff. The Local Democratic Organs Act 1980 reaffirmed the administrative, management and revenue raising role of local authorities and went on to say that they should also take the lead in promoting economic development. This was a totally unrealistic expectation as the maladministered local authorities are fighting a losing battle to maintain, never mind improve, social and economic conditions (Spinner, 1982).

Despite the slogan of the 1972–76 Second Development Plan to 'feed, house and clothe the nation' (Government of Guyana, 1972) the absence of an identifiable housing policy has been a feature of the post-independence period. Urban planners have been further handicapped in their work by the unavailability of data to predict housing need, a lack of skilled construction workers, material shortages and a fragmented pattern of land ownership. In the absence of enforceable controls, the private developer has had a relatively free hand to build houses where and when they please providing they are prepared to pay the high land and building costs involved. These costs are transferred to the purchaser, which means that only the very affluent can afford to live in new subdivisions (Peake, 1986). The housing options available to the great majority of the population are very restricted. Up until the mid-1970s, the colonial and PNC governments built rented housing, ostensibly as part of slum clearance programmes but in reality, simply to rehouse families from overcrowded inner city areas. In 1985, it was estimated that the government owned somewhere between 2,000 and 7,000 rented dwellings, the majority of which are in Georgetown. Mainly as a consequence of preferential allocations procedures, some 99 per cent of tenants are Afro-Guyanese. Although no rented properties have been built during the past 10 years and the existing stock is at a premium, rents charged are minimal. Maintenance is non-existent and the houses are deteriorating rapidly, so much so that the government now intends to divest itself of this burden and gain some much needed income by selling them.

Self-help housing has been an important dimension of Guyanese housing policy for the past 30 years with an estimated 4,000 dwellings built by 1982 in numerous small schemes (Peake, 1986). Although the concept was introduced as early as 1952, it was only after independence, as part of the co-operative movement, that self-help was actively promoted. The movement reached a peak in the 1970s, but has now virtually come to an end. Self-help schemes took two main forms: the Aided Self-Help Housing Society (ASHS) and the Co-operative Self-Help Housing Group (CSHG). In the former, members had to pay for the land and its development and repay the Ministry of Housing for the materials provided. This usually required that a loan be secured from the Guyana Co-operative Mortgage Finance Bank to be repaid at an agreed rate over a specified number of years. On the other hand, CSHG members undertook to pay a fixed percentage of their income towards the cost of their house spread over a number of years, based on each family's particular circumstances. This has proved the more popular of the two schemes and as ASHS members have run into repayment problems, they have been encouraged to convert to a CSHG form of mortgage repayment. Self-help housing developments are to be found in all three urban areas and in many of the larger villages.

In the country as a whole, the number of private, rented and self-help houses built has failed to keep pace with demand, but the shortfall has been most serious in Georgetown where population growth has been greatest. Here multiple occupancy has resulted in excessive overcrowding in houses and districts with inadequate and disintegrating facilities, a bleak prospect about which little can or will be done in the absence of effective planning policies and the finances necessary to implement them.

Epilogue

Is there any prospect of improvement in Guyana's critical situation? Perhaps there is a glimmer of hope in the change of leadership that came about with the death of Forbes Burnham in 1985. The new President, Desmond Hoyt, has softened the party line and has increasingly acknowledged the need to adjust and respond to changing circumstances. This has brought about a partial rapprochement with the United States which has resulted in the relaxing of loan constraints. A short breathing space has been secured, but if this is not to be squandered the PNC has to introduce realistic policies for economic regeneration, promote effective racial integration and respond more positively than in the past to the now united opposition parties. There is little in the government's record to give grounds for optimism, but without change, the vicious circle of economic decline, social inequality and emigration will not be broken.

REFERENCES

Barber, C. and Jeffrey, H.B. (1986) *Guyana: Politics, Economics and Society*, London: Frances Pinter.

Catholic Institute for International Relations (1984) *Guyana Comment*, London: Catholic Institute for International Relations.

Chandisingh, R. (1983) 'The state, the economy, and the type of rule in Guyana: An assessment of Guyana's 'socialist revolution'', *Latin American Perspectives*, **10** (4), 59–74.

Cross, M. (1979) *Urbanization and Urban Growth in the Caribbean*, Cambridge: Cambridge University Press.

Dodd, D.J. and Parris, M. (1977) 'An urban plantation: socio-cultural aspects of crime and delinquency in Georgetown, Guyana', *International Journal of Criminology and Penology*, **5** (1), 32–61.

Government of Guyana (1970) *Population Census, 1970*. Georgetown: Guyana Statistical Bureau.

Government of Guyana (1972) *Guyana Development Plan 1972–76*. Georgetown: Government Printer.

Greene, J.E. (1974) 'The politics of economic planning in Guyana', *Social and Economic Studies*, **23** (2), 186–203.

Guyana Information Service (1979) *'Guyana in Brief'*, Georgetown: Government Printer.

Heins, J.J.F. (1978) 'Spatial inequality in Guyana. A case study of Georgetown', *Tijdschrift voor Economische en Social Geografie*, **69** (1/2), 36–45.

Hope, K.R. (1975) 'National cooperative commercial banking and development strategy in Guyana', *American Journal of Economics and Sociology*, **34** (3), 309–22.

Hope, K.R. (1977) 'Development administration in post-independence Guyana', *International Review of Administrative Sciences*, **43** (1), 67–72.

Hope, K.R. (1982) 'The employment problem, rural–urban migration and urbanization in the Caribbean', *Population Review*, **26**, 42–53.

Hope, K.R. (1983) 'Urban population growth in the Caribbean', *Cities*, **1**, 167–74.

Hope, K.R. (1984a) 'Unemployment, labour force participation, and urbanization in the Caribbean', *Review of Regional Studies*, **14**, 9–16.

Hope, K.R. (1984b) 'Urban population growth and urbanization in the Caribbean', *Inter American Economic Affairs*, **39** (1), 31–49.

Hope, K.R. (1986) *Urbanization in the Commonwealth Caribbean*, Boulder/London: Westview Press.

Hope, K.R. and Ruefli, T. (1981) 'Rural–urban migration and the development process: a Caribbean case study', *Labour and Society*, **6** (2), 141–48.

Jameson, K.P. (1981) 'Socialist Cuba and the intermediate regimes of Jamaica and Guyana', *World Development*, **9** (9/10), 871–88.

Jones, H. (1981) *Crime, Race and Culture: A Study in a Developing Country*, Chichester: John Wiley & Sons.

Lloyds Bank (1986) *Guyana. Economic Report 1986*, London: Lloyds Bank.

Peake, L. (1986) 'Low income women's participation in the housing process: a case study from Guyana', *Gender and Planning Working Paper 10, Development and Planning Unit, Bartlet School of Architecture and Planning, University College* London.

Peake, L. (1987) 'Guyana: a country in crisis', *Geography*, **72** (4), 356–60.

Scherm, G. (1987) 'The Guyanan countries', *Applied Geography and Development*, **29**, 27–43.

Spinner, T.J. (1982) 'Guyana update. Political, economic, moral bankruptcy', *Caribbean Review*, **11**, 8–11, 30–2.

Spinner, T.J. (1984) *A Political and Social History of Guyana*, Boulder/London: Westview Press.

Standing, G. and Sukdeo, F. (1977) 'Labour migration and development in Guyana', *International Labour Review*, **116**, 303–13.

Strachan, A.J. (1980a) 'Government sponsored return migration to Guyana', *Area*, **12** (2), 165–69.

Strachan, A.J. (1980b) 'Water control in Guyana', *Geography*, **65** (4), 297–304.

Strachan, A.J. (1981) 'Housing patterns and values in a medium sized Third World city: Georgetown, Guyana', *Tijdschrift voor Economische en Social Geografie*, **72** (1), 40–6.

Strachan, A.J. (1983) 'Return migration to Guyana', *Social and Economic Studies*, **32** (3), 121–42.

The World Bank (1983, 1984) (published annually) *World Development Report*, New York: Oxford University Press.

Webber, A.R.F. (1931) *Centenary History of British Guiana*, Georgetown: The Argosy Company.

[7]
The Netherlands Antilles

Mike L. Samson

Historical Aspects of Urban Development

With the establishment of the Dutch West India Company in the Netherlands Antilles in 1631, mercantilism gained a stronghold. Like the English and Spanish, the Dutch were interested in expanding their commercial interests and influence in the New World. They were looking primarily for relief ports in the archipelago. In doing so, they occupied the island of St Maarten in 1631, followed by Curaçao in 1634, Aruba, Bonaire and St Eustatius in 1636 and Saba in 1640. From a mercantile point of view, however, the Netherlands Antilles brought the company little economic benefit, as they did not find the expected quantities of salt and gold. Nevertheless, the company decided to keep the islands, issuing charters to Dutch settlers with the intention of converting these islands into agrarian colonies, with emphasis on the slave and sugar trades. As such, these islands prospered, especially Curaçao and St Eustatius. Today, the Netherlands Antilles consist of the three larger leeward islands of Aruba, Bonaire and Curaçao located off the north coast of Venezuela (Figure 7.1), together with the smaller territories of Saba, St Eustatius and St Maarten located to the Windward. The latter island is shared between the Netherlands and France.

Primary Production

During the mercantile period, the plantation culture served a dual purpose. First of all it was associated with cultivation of the soil and food for the settlers. Secondly, it became the provider of food for the slaves. When around 1648 the company made a contract with the Spanish and Portuguese holders of the slave *asiento*, the slave trade in

161

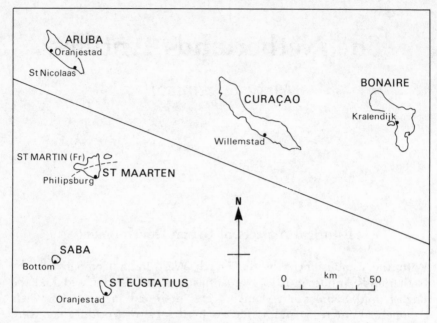

Figure 7.1. The Netherlands Antilles: location map.

the Netherlands Antilles, in particular Curaçao, increased in importance. With the increase of the slave trade, the number of plantations also increased. Around 1700, the company owned nine plantations in Curaçao, situated at Oostpunt (East Point), Duivels Klip (Devil's reef), Koraal Tabak, Noordkant (North side), Rio Canario, Hato, Piscadera, St Maria and Lelienberg (*Encyclopedie van de Nederlandse Antillen*, 1985).

The products of the plantations in Curaçao were for local use only. Besides corn, beans, peanuts and fruits, some cattle breeding took place for milk, butter and cheese, while cattle were sold on the local market. Later, the selling of firewood and charcoal took place. Some plantations also produced the pods of the dividivi tree as a material for the local tanneries. In Aruba, aloe culture was introduced around the 1840s. It became very popular with small farmers. It was mainly used as a raw material in the pharmaceutical industry, particularly in Europe. As such, it became a very important export product. With respect to salt, the plantations near the coast of Curaçao and Aruba engaged in salt export, mainly to the United States and Europe. However, the profits were modest because of price fluctuations on the world market, and fierce competition from other countries. In Bonaire, the production of salt and a chalk distillery were important. In order to provide food for the slaves, the few plantations cultivated corn, while some cattle were kept.

On the Windward Islands, emphasis was placed on commercial crops like cotton, sugar and indigo. This was possible as the Windward Islands, in particular St Maarten, received more rainfall. Cultivation of cereal crops, fruits and cattle breeding took place on a small scale. The economic boom of St Eustatius in the late eighteenth century had the effect of stimulating the sale of agricultural products on St Maarten.

In 1789, there were 92 plantations on St Maarten, of which 25 cultivated sugar as the main export product; the remainder produced for the local market. In St Eustatius, the emphasis was on tobacco and sugar for export. Other important agricultural products were yams, sweet potatoes, vegetables and some cattle breeding for local consumption. Saba was not a typical plantation island. It became a self-sufficient community of small planters and a few slaves. The small lots were used for the cultivation of food crops for local consumption.

Commerce and Trade

The economy of the Dutch colonies during the sixteenth and seventeenth centuries was led by the slave and schooner trades. Agriculture, particularly in the early colonial days had a supportive role. The plantations provided food for the numerous slaves, while the flourishing slave and schooner trades provided the planters with high prices for their products. As a consequence of this system, many planters also invested in the schooner trade, while some were even to be found at sea, leaving the plantation in the care of supervisors.

The change in emphasis from the production of tobacco to sugar increased the demand for slaves. Curaçao and St Eustatius became the foremost transit ports for the slave trade in the Caribbean. Beside trading in slaves and sugar, Curaçao and St Eustatius traded in European merchandise with the surrounding British and French settlements. In particular, St Eustatius experienced an economic boom between 1752-75. Not only did it become the foremost slave depot and trading post of the company, but it also developed into a rock of contraband in gold, while trading arms with the rebelling colonies in North America. This prosperity gave St Eustatius the name of the 'Golden Rock', but it also initiated its downfall. When England waged war against the Republic of the Netherlands, its intention was to attack St Eustatius. On 3 February 1781, Admiral George Brydges Rodney attacked the island, and took possession of all its goods at a value of £3,000,000. The archive and the city were destroyed completely, houses were looted and the slaves ill-treated (Bor, 1981).

During the second half of the nineteenth century, Curaçao lost two of the most important pillars of its trade, namely, the slave trade through the abolition of slavery in 1863, and the sugar trade, due to the much cheaper price of French sugar beet. Since agriculture and trade were closely linked, these economic drawbacks were strongly felt in the plantation culture. The income of the planters decreased, and many could not pay their debts. Consequently, they were forced to sell their plantations and move to the city of Willemstad (Figure 7.1), where most of them owned a house. Others lost interest and also moved to the city, leaving the plantations in the care of mostly inexperienced factors.

This development marked the decay of the primary economic sector of the Netherlands Antilles. The freed slaves who stayed on in the rural districts faced many problems. First of all the 'pagatera' (pay-soil) agreement, whereby the liberated slaves were offered a lot by the former owner in return for a certain number of days of free labour created a financial burden. Secondly, frequent droughts causing crop failure and an absence of know-how in cultivating the land added to the financial burdens of farmers and agricultural labourers. Owing to the deplorable situation in the agricultural sector, many were forced to look elsewhere for their living. During the first two decades of the twentieth century, the Cuba trek was popular. Many agricultural labourers from Curaçao, Aruba and Bonaire took part in these seasonal migrations to the sugar cane plantations of Cuba, where the labour demand rose owing to the increasing demand on the international sugar market. The workers could earn up to f6.25 (Antillian guilders) and supervisors f7.50, compared to f0.45–f0.65 per day at home (Dekker, 1982: 58). The stream of seasonal migrants ebbed away when the oil refineries in Curaçao (Shell, 1915) and Aruba (Exxon, 1927) were established. Many of the agricultural labourers and small farmers from the rural districts were recruited as navvies and moved to the outskirts of the city.

In St Maarten, St Eustatius and Saba, agriculture was in a deplorable state by 1900. Efforts by government to revive cotton production in St Maarten and St Eustatius failed, mainly because of low prices on the world market and because many left for the oil refineries in Curaçao and Aruba. There they settled in the suburban areas of Curaçao and in the residential quarters such as Esso Heights and the village in Aruba (Gill, 1983).

The spiral trend of decline in agriculture, which started after the abolition of slavery, and the decrease in commerce and trade, continued into the twentieth century. The industrial revolution brought about by the establishment of the oil refineries further contributed to the bleeding of the agricultural sector, as many labourers left the rural areas for better wages in the oil refineries. Last but not least, poor soil structure, frequent droughts, irregular rainfall, hurricanes (particularly in the

Windward Islands) and a lack of agricultural know-how also contributed to the decay of the agricultural sector.

Social Structure

One of the researchers who has conducted much work on social structure in the Netherlands Antilles, in particular Curaçao, is Hoetink (1974). In his studies he considers the society of the Netherlands Antilles during the nineteenth century as consisting of different socio-cultural groups. Across these groups, the colour barrier cuts through as a sharp social dividing line. Thus, whether you approach the problem of social stratification from the point of view of socio-cultural or socio-economic groups, colour will serve as a feature dividing people into groups and classes.

In order to visualize the social structure of the nineteenth century society in the Netherlands Antilles, a slightly modified social structure scheme, as used in Dekker (1982) will be discussed in this section. This is shown in Figure 7.2. The model indicates that above the colour barrier, there are two groups, the old Jewish and Protestant families, who emigrated from Holland and Brazil during the mercantile days, and who formed the upper class. The class with the highest living standard was that of the Jews, in particular the merchants. The higher Protestant classes, owners of plantations, state officials and some merchants, did not seem to possess the same capitalistic mentality towards profit

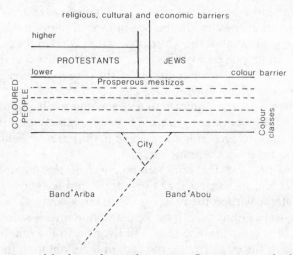

Figure 7.2. A model of social stratification in Curaçao towards the end of the nineteenth century. (Source: Dekker, 1982: 93).

making as the Jews. As a result of this difference, many of the Protestants became debtors to the Jews (Dekker, 1982: 95). Beside these old Protestant families, there were Protestant families of lower status, who occupied less important jobs. During the nineteenth century, however, the lower Protestant group advanced somewhat, because of a boom in the schooner trade. Some of them became captains, some ship owners, while others established themselves as craftsmen. Nothwithstanding these developments, the division between the classes was maintained in order to mark the difference in social standing between these two Protestant groups.

Together with the lower Protestant groups, the prosperous coloured groups formed, economically speaking, the middle class of the nineteenth century. Although the well-to-do coloured population had the same economic opportunities as the lower Protestant group, they were not able to surpass the colour line, and socially speaking they could not reach higher on the social ladder. Within the coloured group itself there were differences, since social mobility was based on the shade of the skin and prosperity. The lighter the skin, the better the possibilities for social mobility. Some of the coloured people were nearly white and if they were also well-to-do, they belonged to the middle classes.

The lower part of the model is occupied by the largest and socially speaking the lowest ranking group, the blacks. At the top of this group, were the blacks living in the city, as they were more liberated from the behaviour common to slaves. At the bottom were the blacks living in the rural districts Band'Ariba and Band'Abou, where they still practised the style of living common to the slaves.

During the rapid urbanization processes in the city of Willemstad, due to modern industrialisation after 1920, a significant part of the black population lived in the city. In the pre-industrial period (as depicted in the model), 6–8 per cent of the white population lived in the city. By that time more than 45 per cent of the total population lived in the city. In other words, the non-white population of the City must have been more than 40 per cent of its inhabitants (Dekker, 1982: 97). According to Dekker, different sources indicate that of the non-white population, the blacks formed the dominant group. They were mostly occupied in the service sector as kitchen maids and porters in the harbour, while some of them were occupied in the trade sector.

The literature and the occupational lists of the commercial and governmental sectors suggest that Protestants and Jews lived mainly in the city. As stated earlier, many of the Protestants, and to a lesser degree Jews, possessed plantations. But as the plantation business declined, due to the abolition of slavery and severe drawbacks in the schooner trade, many moved to the city, leaving the care of the plantation in the hands of factors.

The coming of modern industrialization by means of the establishment of the oil refineries brought changes in the social structure of the nineteenth century. Not only did it change the socio-cultural structure through the coming of immigrants from different parts of the world, but also through socio-economic changes affecting the lowest social group, like higher wages and changes of occupation. However, Dekker points out that the increased social mobility after 1920, meant an infringement on the old class structure. Notwithstanding these changes, the most elementary division line between the classes, the colour differences, did not decline in significance; in fact, it was further accentuated by the coming of the new Dutch and American white population. They occupied new top positions at the Shell and Exxon oil refineries and in government. Government functions were in particular the dominion of the Protestant white population (Dekker, 1982: 102).

The social structure of the Netherlands Antilles is the consequence of its history of settlement: this has deeply affected, and still does, socio-economic, socio-cultural and urbanization patterns. Modern industrialization brought more social and geographical mobility to the lower social classes, but it also accentuated ethnic and cultural differences. The black population who moved from the rural districts to the city and its outskirts, occupied the lowest paid jobs in the service sector or in the oil refineries, while the top jobs in government or the oil refineries were reserved for the white population. Today the majority of top functions in government, and in some private sectors, are held by locals, but even then, colour differences cut through the classes and sub-classes as a clear demarcation line in a society with a rich mosaic of cultures. Against this background, and the fact that the islands differ in size, ecology, strategic location and natural resources, national identity becomes a very subjective mix of feelings, within each island and between the individual islands.

Population Change 1930–80

It is impossible to make estimations of future population trends without an understanding of past and present population developments. For this reason, this section deals briefly with population change from 1930 onwards. As in other countries, industrial development in the Netherlands Antilles triggered changes which had a dramatic impact on demographic and economic circumstances. The impact on the population was particularly felt during the 1930s and 1940s, when the Netherlands Antilles experienced a growth of 31,559 or 41.3 per cent and 54,793 or 50.8 per cent respectively. The bulk of these increments took place in Curaçao and Aruba (Table 7.1). These significant

Table 7.1. Population change in the Netherlands Antilles 1930–80.

	Neth. Antilles		Aruba		Bonaire	
Year	N	%	N	%	N	*
1930	76,332	–	15,687	–	5,733	–
1940	107,891	(41.3)	30,614	(95.2)	5,616	(2.0)
1950	162,684	(50.8)	51,000	(66.6)	5,079	(−9.6)
1960	192,538	(18.4)	56,910	(11.6)	5,812	(14.4)
1970	223,827	(16.2)	60,734	(6.7)	8,191	(40.9)
1973	234,374	(4.7)	61,717	(1.6)	8,213	(0.3)
1974	237,788	(1.5)	61,788	(0.1)	8,400	(2.2)
1975	239,788	(0.8)	61,982	(0.3)	8,785	(4.6)
1976	242,869	(1.3)	62,288	(0.5)	8,838	(0.6)
1977	245,049	(0.9)	62,755	(0.7)	8,861	(0.3)
1978	246,424	(0.8)	63,049	(0.5)	8,918	(0.6)
1979	249,878	(1.4)	63,931	(1.4)	8,879	(0.4)
1980	253,334	(1.4)	64,797	(1.4)	9,061	(2.0)

Sources: Island registry offices, Aruba, Bonaire, Curaçao, Saba, St Eustatius and St Maarten 1930–80.

increments were due to labour migrations, principally to the oil refineries. The migrants came from the Windward Islands and other islands in the region, Holland, the United States, Surinam, Venezuela, Colombia, Madeira and Asia. The recruitment of foreign labour was necessary due to the rapid expansion of production at the oil refineries.

During the 1950s and 1960s, the absolute numbers of the population in the Netherlands Antilles increased at a much slower pace. This becomes evident by the decline of the percentage growth from 50.8 in 1950 to 16.2 per cent in 1970. The main contributors to this small amount of growth were Curaçao and Aruba. Both islands experienced a drop in their percentage growth, from 51.8 in 1950 to 16.5 per cent in 1970 for Curaçao, and 66.6 and 6.7 per cent for Aruba. After 1970, a definite turning point can be noticed in the population development of the Netherlands Antilles. Between 1970 and 1980, the population of the Netherlands Antilles increased by only 13.2 per cent compared to 16.2 per cent in the period 1960–70. The small growth of the population must be considered against the background of demographic and socio-economic conditions on the islands.

Besides the decrease in fertility, the relatively small population growth of the Netherlands Antilles after the 1960s was also due to net migration losses, in particular from Curaçao. During the 1960s and 1970s many labourers were discharged from the oil refinery because of rationalisation and automation. Many of them migrated back to their place of origin. Within this context, the rapid population growth experienced by the island St Maarten is quite remarkable. Between 1970

Curaçao		Saba		St Eustatius		St Maarten	
N	%	N	%	N	%	N	%
50,165	–	1,457	–	955	–	2,235	–
67,317	(34.2)	1,210	(16.9)	1,130	(18.3)	2,004	(14.2)
102,206	(51.8)	1,129	(−6.7)	970	(14.2)	2,300	(14.2)
125,094	(22.4)	980	(−13.2)	1,014	(4.5)	2,728	(18.6)
145,707	(16.5)	956	(−2.4)	1,358	(33.9)	6,881	(152.2)
152,229	(4.5)	965	(0.9)	1,421	(4.6)	9,829	(42.8)
154,928	(1.8)	951	(−1.5)	1,411	(−0.7)	10,310	(4.9)
156,209	(0.8)	991	(4.2)	1,363	(−3.4)	10,458	(1.4)
158,022	(1.2)	979	(−1.2)	1,363	(−)	11,379	(8.8)
158,882	(0.5)	999	(2.0)	1,345	(−1.3)	12,207	(7.3)
159,067	(0.1)	1,017	(1.8)	1,342	(−0.2)	13,031	(6.7)
161,075	(1.3)	105	(−0.2)	1,256	(−6.4)	13,722	(5.3)
162,362	(0.8)	1,008	(−0.8)	1,008	(7.0)	14,762	(7.6)

and 1980, the population of St Maarten increased by 7,881 persons or 114.5 per cent. The rapid population growth of St Maarten was due to the fast growth of its industrial sector, in particular that of tourism. This caused a wave of labour migration to the island from neighbouring islands and also from the Leewards.

The Economy and Employment

In considering urbanization and planning, an appreciation of the recent economic history and employment structure of the Netherlands Antilles is required. By the early 1980s, the pillars of the Antillian economy were: (1) oil refining; (2) tourism; (3) offshore banking; (4) ship repairing (the CDM company in Curaçao); (5) aviation (National Aviation Company ALM); and (6) shipping.

Modern industrialization in the Netherlands Antilles started with the establishment of the oil refinery in Curaçao (Shell, 1915) and Aruba (Exxon, 1927). They were established to serve the American market, and brought wealth to the islands. Until 1980, their activities sustained a prosperous, if vulnerable, economy with a standard of living only one-third lower than that of Holland and much higher than the neighbouring countries of the Caribbean and South America. In the wake of the oil refinery industry, other industries such as oil storage, trans-shipment, cargo handling and ship repair followed.

The steep rise in oil prices during the 1970s brought a wave of tourists from neighbouring Venezuela who spent their new wealth in the shops and casinos of Willemstad and elsewhere in the Leeward Islands. In St Maarten, tourism started to develop rapidly during the 1960s. The demand for labour exerted a strong pull on many in the neighbouring islands and also from the Leeward Islands. From the mid-1960s, Curaçao became an important centre for offshore banking, due to the favourable tax treatment accorded to interest payments to United States companies resident in the Antilles.

However, in the 1980s, these favourable economic conditions were curbed considerably. In the wake of the fall in world oil prices, the Venezuelan bolivar was devalued. This reduced the flow of tourists to less than a third, and hit Curaçao in particular. Secondly, the world recession of 1982–83 adversely affected port operations. Decreasing profitability caused both Shell and Exxon in Curaçao and Aruba respectively to cease operations in 1985. In Aruba this led to mass emigration to the Netherlands and elsewhere in the Caribbean. Fortunately, Curaçao was able to lease its refinery to the Venezuelan State Oil Company in October 1985 for a period of five years.

Owing to these drawbacks, unemployment increased in the Netherlands Antilles in the 1980s. In 1981, the level of unemployment stood at 16.1 per cent, compared to 14.6 per cent in 1972. Curaçao was particularly badly hit, its unemployment rate having increased from 13.8 to 20.3 per cent between these two dates. Against these changes, however, it is to be remembered that the standard of living in the Netherlands Antilles is relatively high, with an income per capita in 1984 of about US$6,600, almost equal to that recorded in some industrial countries.

Urbanization in the Twentieth Century

Urbanization in the Netherlands Antilles is basically an outcome of the last 70 years, and two main periods can be distinguished: the period 1920–55, marked by the introduction of modern industrialization and economic growth; and 1955 to the present, which has been characterized by the growth of the tourist and commercial sectors, followed by an economic recession after 1983.

Modern industrialization in the Netherlands Antilles started with the establishment of the oil refineries in Curaçao and Aruba. Economically, the oil refineries affected all the islands but mainly the Leeward Islands, in particular Curaçao and Aruba. The rapid population growth of Curaçao and Aruba (Table 7.1) was the result of mass recruitment by the oil refineries of labour from the Windward Islands and overseas. Moreover, the oil refineries promoted the increase of related activities like oil storage, trans-shipment, cargo handling and ship repair. The growth in these sectors, in turn called for improved transport facilities and infrastructure in Curaçao and Aruba. Water distillery plants and power stations were built and roads were paved mostly in the city and its outskirts, while communication and transport increased by the building of the national airport in the district of Hato in Curaçao.

As Koot (1979) notes, the oil refineries not only provided direct employment, but also promoted indirect employment, due to their significant contribution to overall economic growth of the Netherlands Antilles. There was enough employment and the wages were relatively high, which resulted in an increase of purchasing power. Concomitant with these developments, the central business districts of the cities, in particular Curaçao and Aruba, increased during this period. The increase in real income also promoted the increase of assortments of provisions and articles of luxury. Consequently, the import of these goods increased as local production could not anticipate this demand. Merchants from Syria, Lebanon and China were particularly active in this sector of trade.

While former plantation owners and merchants settled in the inner city and its immediate environs, the Shell oil refinery started to build residential quarters on the outskirts where during the 1920s and 1930s, suburbanization processes took place. Shell residential quarters such as Emmastad, Julianadorp, Bullenbaai, Biesheuvel, and Rust and Burgh, Rio Canario, Groot Kwartier and Suffisant were built at this time. From the rural areas, in particular Band'Abou, many agricultural labourers, who were attracted as workers to the oil refinery or as porters in the harbour, also settled in the outskirts. The difference in level of income and ethnic origin, however, was clearly reflected in spatial and social aspects of the urbanization processes during this period.

One of the main characteristics in the planning of the residential quarters of the oil refineries was the lack of social integration. This was particularly evident in Curaçao. The high Shell employees, who were mostly of Dutch origin, occupied dwellings in Emmastad, Julianadorp, Rust and Burgh, Bullenbaai and Biesheuvel. These residential quarters consist of villas with a distinct Dutch style. The lower employees of local origin and from other parts of the Antilles (St Maarten, St Eustatius) and South America, lived in much smaller and simple dwellings. They were located in the areas of Rio Canario, Suffisant and Groot Kwartier. The lowest group of employees at the oil refinery were the rural workers who settled spontaneously on plots in the outskirts of the city, in areas like Wishi, Coronet, St Jago and Monte Verde. Today, these form squatter areas on the outskirts of Willemstad. Contrary to this, areas like Poel, Vianen, Stuyvesant, Saartje and Marchena started out as planned but ended up as slums. Today, only Marchena exists, which is a border of the squatter area of Wishi. Both these areas suffer heavy pollution from the oil refinery. In Aruba, similar slum areas developed at Esso Heights and the Village near the capital Oranjestad (Gill, 1983).

Unlike the rapid occurrence of agricultural growth in England, urban industrial growth in the Netherlands Antilles exerted a negative influence on agriculture. The aggressive recruitment of agricultural labourers in the Netherlands Antilles led to the severe bleeding of the agricultural sector. This development had a downward spiral effect on agriculture. Urbanization and prosperity increased the demand for agricultural products in the city and the suburban areas. Consequently, foreign agricultural products had to be imported since the local market could not provide these products. As a result of this trend, the contribution of agriculture to GDP (excluding Aruba) amounted to only 15.6 per cent in 1985 (staff estimate, Central Bureau of Statistics, 1985).

The urbanization and economic changes of the present time are closely linked with those of the past. Between 1957 and 1984, the relative contribution of the industrial sector to gross national product, declined from 49 to 24 per cent. Leading to the decline were, on the one hand, the rationalization and automation processes of the refineries in the mid-1950s, and on the other, the reduction in world demand for oil and the fall in oil prices during the seventies. These developments obliged the refineries, in particular Shell, to make sharp reductions in personnel and in refining output. Between 1952 and 1982, the number of workers at the Shell refinery decreased from 11,138 to 2,583. Between 1978 and 1982, its output decreased from 13 million tonnes to 10 million (*Encyclopedie van de Nederlandse Antillen*, 1985).

Variations in population densities for the constituent islands of the Netherlands Antilles between 1960 and 1986 are shown in Table 7.2.

Table 7.2. Population densities in the Netherlands Antilles 1960–86.

Territory	Area in sq km	Density of pop. per sq km			
		1960	1972	1981	1986
Netherlands Antilles	993	193	288	237	233
Curaçao	444	281	329	334	346
Aruba	193	294	317	340	–
Bonaire	288	21	28	31	36
St Maarten	34	80	263	430	627
St Eustatius	21	48	66	68	87
Saba	13	75	74	74	75

Sources: Population Census 1960, 1981 and estimated figures for 1986. Central Bureau for Statistics, Willemstad, Curaçao.

The high density of occupancy of Aruba and Curaçao is clearly apparent. The most significant change signposted in the data is the emergence of St Maarten as the most densely populated area of the Netherlands Antilles after 1981. The other islands show much lower densities. These figures suggest that post-1960, urbanization was most pronounced in St Maarten, followed by Curaçao. Accordingly, the discussion which follows will concentrate on these two territories as examples. Unfortunately, lack of data makes it impossible to consider the other densely settled island of Aruba in detail.

Curaçao

When discussing social structure, mention was made of planters and a great portion of the non-white population moving to the city of Willemstad in the second half of the nineteenth century. The city then 'was quite small and the buildings were soundly built of brick, stone, timber and tiles and serviced with water supply, drainage and sewerage' (Department of Urban and Regional Development Planning and Housing, 1986:3). With the coming of modern industrialization after the establishment of the oil refinery in 1915, the city expanded rapidly from 15,775 inhabitants in 1924 to 50,102 in 1956. The expansion of the city also meant increased pollution, congestion and decay, which pushed many of the affluent families out of the city to suburban locations. Those remaining behind in the central areas were people with low-income jobs, who could hardly pay the rent.

According to census data, the population of Willemstad (Figure 7.1), the leading city, declined from 43,547 in 1960 to 31,883 in 1981. At the same time, the suburban districts of Curaçao grew from a population of 50,586 to 82,847. These statistics denote a shift of population from the city to the suburban areas and certain rural districts. The reasons for this movement out of the city are manifold and form part of the classic self-reinforcing downward spiral, whereby an initial decay sows the seeds for yet further decline.

Before 1920, one could speak of a circle of residential quarters, mainly around the Schottegat. With the establishment of the oil refinery and the building of residential quarters for workers, the original residential circle round Schottegat expanded towards the outskirts of the city. During 1920–55, the Shell company built residential quarters at Emmastad, Julianadorp, Asiento, and Suffisant. Later on in the 1950s, the government started social housing programmes for the lower income groups. Projects at Marie Pampoen, Steenrijk, Cher Asile, and Brievengat were built in the 1950s. In the 1960s and 1970s Koraal Specht, old Brievengat, Seru Fortuna, and Jan Doret were built.

Moreover, there were the affluent families who wanted their own villa according to their taste and thus from the 1930s onwards, villa quarters like Mahaai, Vredenberg, Korporaal, Jongbloed, Jan Thiel, Toni Cunchi, Francia, and Rooi Catochi came into existence. However, most of the residential quarters which were built during the period 1920–55, lacked systematic physical planning with respect to their land use. They were primarily built to function as commuting areas. With the exception of the houses built by Shell, they lacked good infrastructure such as paved roads (Raeven, 1983).

During the last 10 to 20 years, social housing programmes have contributed to a much better physical planning scheme. The new residential quarters show certain similarities in their construction, with an eye for the development of rural zones into city regions, and with strong links to the inner city. Jan Thiel, Tera Cora, respectively situated in the rural districts Band'Ariba and Band'Abou, and the rural–urban zone Ceru Mahuma are examples of such projects.

Although developments within the housing sector suggest decentralization towards the rural areas, with functional ties to the inner city, it would be premature to suggest that the rural areas are facing a rapid suburbanization process. The housing pattern as seen at the moment has not yet reached the state at which one can speak of a significant relief of the inner city. Industrial and commercial growth in the near future, however, will speed up suburbanization processes in these areas.

The provision of infrastructure is another significant area of concern. With the increase of prosperity, the number of vehicles on the island increased greatly. In 1966, there were about 15,747 privately owned cars and in 1983, 41,000, an increase of 38 per cent. Today in 1989, there are about 60,000 cars for a population of around 160,000 or one car for every three persons. Unfortunately, physical planning concerning roads has lagged behind the rapid growth of the motor car in Curaçao. The road pattern has mostly remained the same as in the days before the industrial revolution. This means that the majority of roads are still unpaved (Raeven, 1983). As most employment is concentrated in the inner city areas of Punda and Otrabanda and the sites north and east of Schottegat, at peak hours a great deal of traffic congestion occurs. Moreover, the widening residential circle away from the city and suburban area adds to the problems of traffic. It is against this background that plans for four-lane roads at a distance from the city are being considered. This will then lead to a second circular road by the 1990s.

A concomitant of industrialization and urbanization is the development of the water and electricity supply systems. Curaçao possesses a sophisticated water supply system, organised by the state-owned KAE (Kompania di Awa i Elektricidat). It desalinates sea water into potable water and it also produces power and sells it to KODELA (Kompania di Produkshon i Distribushon di Awa i Elektricidat). This company also handles the billing and collection of bills. In 1985, about 97 per cent of Curaçao's population had a house connection; a steady increase from 70 per cent in 1960. In 1984, there were about 41,000 domestic and 2,640 industrial/commercial connections. The average per capita consumption was 114 litres per day, high considering the expense of the service (*Encyclopedie van de Nederlandse Antillen*, 1985).

St Maarten

As indicated in Table 7.2 St Maarten was by 1981 the most densely populated island of the Netherlands Antilles. The dynamic behind this change was the rapid growth of tourism in the 1960s and 1970s. To a considerable extent, St Maarten took over from Cuba after 1959 as the Caribbean tourist paradise. As a direct consequence, in-migrants were attracted from the United States, Curaçao, Aruba and elsewhere in the Caribbean.

American investors in particular began constructing hotels along the seafront in the capital Philipsburg and elsewhere on the island (Koot, 1979). Although it is difficult to get accurate statistics concerning employment because of the importance of the informal sector, the available data do give certain indications as to the expansion which has occurred within the tourist and commercial sectors. Figures obtained from the Central Bureau of Statistics show that the number of persons employed within the wholesale/retail trade, hotel and restaurant sectors, increased from 58 in 1960 to 2,622 in 1981. A concomitant increase took place in the number of hotel rooms, from 1,015 in 1972 to 2,113 in 1980, an overall increase of 51.9 per cent. The rapid growth of tourism has promoted a degree of suburbanization, particularly in the Cul-de-Sac/Little Bay and Upper Princess Quarter areas, and this is reflected in housing and other developments.

Planning and Politics

The introduction of a national planning system in the Netherlands Antilles dates back to the second phase of development aid by the Netherlands during 1967–71. With a view to preserving national resources and sites, and the acquisition of land for physical development, empirical research became of primary importance to the government of the Netherlands Antilles. Such research was carried out by institutes from the Netherlands (Universities of Wageningen and Groningen) and France (Sogreah). Extensive surveys were carried out in Aruba, Bonaire and Curaçao.

Today, physical planning has become an integrated part of government policy in the Netherlands Antilles. In the 1970s, the Department of Urban and Regional Planning (DROV) was established in Curaçao. It has subsequently developed into a government institution with considerable capacity and a good deal of professionalism. Of all the islands, Curaçao is the best equipped to formulate and execute programmes of physical development planning. In the 1980s, some studies were made in Aruba concerning physical planning for the island, while in the other islands, a variety of studies have been carried out since 1975. However, none of these islands have been provided with the legal framework necessary, nor do they possess the full apparatus required to execute comprehensive programmes of physical planning. Only Curaçao has such a framework, the Eilandsverordening Ruimtelijke Ontwikkelingsplanning Curaçao (EROC), passed in 1983.

Having briefly considered the history of the planning system, we now turn attention to planning for housing. In absolute terms, it is the Leeward Islands of Curaçao and Aruba which show the highest number of people living under bad housing conditions. According to the 1981 census, these islands had 1,403 and 507 persons respectively living in 'bad housing'. Further, Gill (1983) estimates that Curaçao currently faces a housing shortage of 9,300 units, and Aruba one of 2,700. In a speech made during a symposium on Housing in the Netherlands Antilles held in 1982, the Head of the Department of Urban and Regional Development Planning in Curaçao, L.E.J. Butot, made the following comments: 'Claims on the land have become more numerous and urgent with the growth of population. The unplanned and unstructured fashion in which the urbanized areas have grown at a rather low density have created a series of serious problem areas. In the existing urban areas as well as in future extensions, housing, in comparison to other uses, takes up most of the land. Quantitative housing demand studies have shown that in an ideal building programme, 1,800 housing units per year would have to be built during the coming twenty years. This forms a sharp contrast with the actual production of houses on the island of Curaçao, which has been about 600 units per year the last series of years' (Butot, 1982).

In an effort to remedy the housing situation, a Public Housing Foundation (FKP) was created in Curaçao in 1978. This is a non-profit making private enterprise which runs on capital contributed by the island government of Curaçao and Dutch development aid. The former also contributes land for new public housing projects and provides some rent subsidies. Its principal goals are the construction of low-cost public housing and direct lending to low and low-medium income groups. It also functions as a mortgage bank to those practising self-help. Finally, it provides technical advice to smaller housing organisations on the other islands. In principle, all who are in need of housing can register with the FKP. As at 1 October 1983, some 4,914 persons were registered with the Foundation to rent a dwelling. Currently, there are approximately 8,000 such registrations. In order that applicants should get an equal chance to rent a house, a points allocation system was introduced. The criteria for the allocation of points are social situation, the physical condition of the house and the medical situation of its occupants. From one to three months after registration, applicants are informed as to how many points they have been awarded. From then on, applicants receive one extra point each month, regardless of their situation. Those with the highest number of total points are the first in line when units become available. Rents and profits from mortgages enter into a revolving fund geared for housing maintenance and upgrading. Both mortgages and rents are set in accordance with the income of the recipient; mortgage rates vary between 7 and 10 per cent a year. The average monthly rent for public housing is about f350, and collection is good. New tenants pay only 70 per cent of their rent and gradually contribute the full amount. The bulk of the applicants for public dwellings are from the unemployed and low-income. Given the increase in deprivation, the number of applicants is likely to increase in the near future. The number of persons on social benefit increased from 3,638 in 1976, to 11,118 in 1986.

According to the Department of Urban and Regional Planning, since 1978 some 3,100 plots have been used for public housing construction and a further 820 have been given over to self-help projects. These have undoubtedly contributed to the increase in population densities experienced in the suburban areas of the city, and this trend looks likely to continue. The government's plans for the provision of public housing have to be seen in the light of its attempt to relieve the enormous pressures which affect some parts of Willemstad and its outskirts.

Since the 1950s, progressive housing decay has affected the inner city areas, and added to this, the post-1983 economic recession has seen the decline of the central business district. The rehabilitation of low-income houses poses severe financial and social problems to the government's plans to revitalize the inner city. Due to the relative poverty of the majority of the families living in the inner city (the majority earn between f500 and f750 per month), the provision of publicly financed housing to acceptable standards will require subsidies beyond those implicit in the terms of granting of Dutch aid. On the other hand, the alternative of rehousing such low-income groups in peripheral suburban areas would impose unnecessary social and economic strains on them. They would become distant from their places of employment, their social and cultural ties would be uprooted; they would find it difficult to afford the cost of transport and would add to the already congested roads. Consequently, the government favours a policy which entails less dislocation, and ways are being explored to accumulate funds to maintain low-income housing in the inner city. These include a more aggressive lobbying for financial support in the private sector, the reassessment of property tax systems in the inner city and improving the system of collecting taxes, thereby increasing revenues which in turn can be used for repairs; and finally, using some of the revenues gained from tourism and upgrading the CBD, for low-income housing projects. The execution of rehabilitation programmes for the inner city should preferably be carried out by a joint group of existing agencies, under the co-ordinating supervision of the Public Housing Federation.

Finally, we turn to the case of Aruba, for after Curaçao it is the island with the largest housing need. As in Curaçao, the introduction of modern industry also witnessed a new phase of development with respect to urbanization. New residential areas were built, and the old city boundaries expanded. The urban area of San Nicolas expanded with the construction of the Village and Esso Heights areas. Although in one sense planned communities, the initial lack of infrastructure within these rental areas has meant that they have developed into slums. Currently, both of these areas are the focus of much needed urban renewal schemes. Like Curaçao, Aruba is wrestling with the problem of the financing of its housing programmes. Calculations made in 1983, for instance, indicate that for the next 10 years, 35 million Antillian guilders will have to be spent on housing. For the implementation of its housing programme, Aruba depends on aid from the Netherlands, as well as funds from local government and private institutions such as pension funds and banks. However, together these sources cover only one-third of the total costs. Thus, other measures have to be taken in order to cover the deficit, including avoiding expensive forms of construction and critically analysing building costs. In 1983, housing needs not only represented a problem for lower income groups, but also for those with better incomes. Because of this, new types of housing were introduced, such as apartments and trailers. Generally, however, the rental levels for these were too high, especially as most of the occupants were newly established families who had to pay half their monthly salary as rent.

In 1986, as a direct consequence of the closing of the oil refinery, thousands emigrated to the Netherlands, United States, or other places in the Caribbean. Unfortunately, at this stage, no data are to hand concerning the impact of mass emigration on housing need in Aruba. On the other hand, an aggressive recruitment drive for labour outside Aruba has been started in the last two years. The Prime Minister for example, went to the Netherlands in person in order to urge Arubans to return home. It would be interesting to see what the impact of an eventual mass return migration would be on the housing needs of Aruba. It goes without saying that these and other questions need to be addressed in order for the government to be provided with the necessary framework for improving housing in Aruba.

Conclusion

The establishment of the Shell and Exxon refineries at the beginning of the twentieth century saw the start of urbanization proper in the Netherlands Antilles. Between 1930 and 1950, the population of Curaçao doubled from 50,165 to 102,206, and in Aruba the increase was from 15,687 to 51,000 (Table 7.1). During this period, the principal urban places grew rapidly and marked social and spatial inequalities became apparent. The European and American employees of the oil refineries not only held the better-paid jobs, they also lived in exclusive and physically well-protected residential quarters. The non-white employees of the companies had to be content with less luxurious living spaces. The more recent rapid urban development that has occurred in St Maarten has been connected with the growth of the tourist industry. In all these places, urban development has been associated with the expansion of utilities, roads and commercial facilities, and has meant the need for new housing, and for urban renewal and upgrading. In the larger islands of Curaçao and Aruba, processes of suburbanization, both planned and spontaneous, now seem to be under way. Finally, it can be stressed how cultural, ethnic and economic differences on the one hand, and facts of size, location, natural resources and ecology on the other have manifested themselves in slight variations in urbanization and planning experiences during the past 70 or so years. These factors have led to interesting differences in urbanization patterns between the individual islands as summarized in this chapter. Moreover, they had led to a hybrid national identity in the Netherlands Antilles which is apparent to the extent that each island regards itself as having an independent and separate identity within the Netherlands Antilles as a whole, a factor which must be taken into account by both politicians and planners alike.

ACKNOWLEDGEMENTS

I would like to thank Systems and Office Support and Xerox Antilliana NV (Curaçao) for help in preparing this work for publication, Rob Potter for his encouragement, and my wife and daughters for all their patience and support.

REFERENCES

Bor, W.E. vanden (1981) *De Sociale Organisatie van een Kleine Caribische Samenleving*, St Eustatius, The Hague.

Butot, L.E.J. (1982) Unpublished paper delivered at a Symposium on Housing, University of the Netherlands Antilles.

Dekker, J. (1982) *Curaçao zonder/met Shell: een bijdrage tot bestudering van demografische, economische en sociale processen in de periode 1900–1929*, De Walburg Pers, Zutphen.

Department of Urban and Regional Development Planning and Housing (1986), *Revitalising Downtown Willemstad: executive summary*, Curaçao, Netherlands Antilles.

Encyclopedie van de Nederlandse Antillen (1985) De Walburg Pers, Zutphen.

Gill, R. (ed.) (1983) *Housing in the Netherlands Antilles*, University of the Netherlands Antilles.

Hoetink, K. (1974) *Het patroon van de oude Curaçaose samenleving* (Fourth edition) Aruba, Netherlands Antilles.

Koot, W. (1979) *Emigratie op de Nederlandse Antillen*, Leiden.

Raeven, L. (1983) Unpublished report on urbanization and physical planning in Curaçao, University of the Netherlands Antilles.

[8]

The Commonwealth Eastern Caribbean

Brian Hudson

Unity and Diversity

The English-speaking Eastern Caribbean islands have much in common physically, historically and culturally, and yet there is great diversity. Even in terms of language the common English heritage is diversified by strong infusions of French in some islands. In St Lucia and, particularly, Dominica, a French patois is widely spoken.

All are small island countries, ranging from minuscule Anguilla (90 km²) and Montserrat (102 km²) to the relative giant of Dominica (750 km²). Like Anguilla, Dominica and Montserrat, St Lucia is one single island, but St Kitts-Nevis and Antigua and Barbuda are 'twin island' states, while St Vincent and the Grenadines, and Grenada each comprise a main island and a number of much smaller ones. The British Virgin Islands comprise 16 inhabited islands and about 20 uninhabited islets and cays, with a total area of 150 km².

Typically the islands are ruggedly mountainous, rising to over 1,400 metres in Dominica, and with very little flat or gently sloping land. Most show evidence of geologically recent volcanic activity, and St Vincent's Soufriere, which has erupted with deadly violence this century, remains a threat to property and life. Earthquakes are experienced throughout the region. Of the larger islands, Antigua is the least mountainous, a central clay plain separating the 300–400 metre old volcanic mountain remnants from an area of rolling limestone upland, which rises to little more than 100 metres. Anguilla and Barbuda are both largely flat and low-lying with coral terraces rising to about 60 metres above sea-level.

With a latitudinal extent of less than seven degrees, the islands display climatic variations that are related mainly to relief which is responsible for the great differences in rainfall. The low, dry and often scrubby islands contrast with the high wet ones with their luxuriant

181

vegetation. All of them lie in the hurricane belt, Dominica, St Lucia and St Vincent having suffered severely from hurricanes in recent years.

Politically and economically, too, there is diversity, Anguilla, the British Virgin Islands and Montserrat still being British colonies, the rest having gained independence from Britain. All but the Commonwealth of Dominica, which like Trinidad and Tobago is a republic headed by a president, recognize the Queen as Head of State.

While, on the whole, it is true to say that these countries are economically dependent on the export of agricultural products such as bananas, cocoa, spices, citrus, sugar and rum, together with earnings from tourism, the main exports vary from island to island. The role of tourism varies considerably. It is the main contributor to GNP in Anguilla, the British Virgin Islands and Antigua, but it is little developed in Dominica with its black volcanic sand beaches and poor accessibility. Industrial development, too, is very uneven, nowhere being on more than a modest scale.

Generally poor by world standards, these islands nevertheless display a considerable range of wealth. In 1985, per capita GNP figures were as low as US$850 and US$900 for St Vincent and the Grenadines and Grenada, respectively, but more than the total of these two combined in Antigua and Barbuda at US$2,020 (World Bank 1987: 269). Unemployment is widespread, commonly 20 per cent of the workforce, possibly having been as high as 50 per cent in Grenada before the 1979 revolution.

Historical Perspectives on Urbanism and Planning

Unlike the pre-Columbian civilizations of nearby mainland Central America, the Arawak and Carib peoples of the Antilles developed no urban settlements. In the West Indian islands towns came into existence with the arrival of the Europeans (Hudson, 1980: 1). Many of the early European settlements were established with little or no thought as to layout, although their siting often reflected considerations of water supply, defence and the safe accommodation of shipping, hence the location of most of the important towns on the leeward coasts of the islands (Figure 8.1). A remarkably large number of West Indian towns do show evidence of planning in their layout, however, and in the Lesser Antilles, as well as elsewhere in the Caribbean, the grid pattern of streets, sometimes with a central square, is a common form.

While in the Greater Antilles it was the Spaniards, followed by the English and French, who established the first towns, in the Lesser Antilles it was mainly the English, French and Dutch who did so. In the islands under discussion the mark of the English and French colonizers

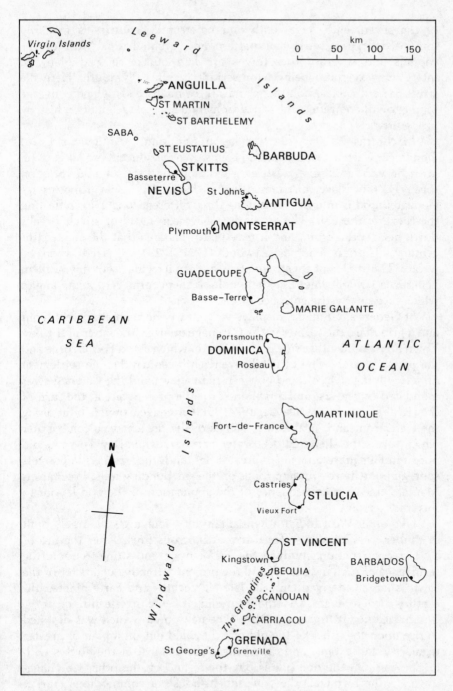

Figure 8.1. The Commonwealth Eastern Caribbean: location map.

of the seventeenth, eighteenth and nineteenth centuries is indelibly imprinted on the settlement pattern and urban form. Most of the capitals and several other towns are laid out on a grid plan, an interesting exception being Montserrat's capital, Plymouth. Here the street pattern is based on the island's three main roads which converge on the town, and reflect the topography and coastal reclamation history of the area.

In contrast to this adaptive layout, St John's, Antigua; Roseau, Dominica; Castries, St Lucia; and Kingstown, St Vincent are laid out on grids of various kinds. Castries is notable for its Columbus Square, formerly the Place d'Armes (Breen, 1844: 16), while Kingstown's elongated grid is unusual for having three different long axes, reflecting the curve of the bay. The regularity of Roseau's grid of streets breaks down near Fort Young, and it may be to this area that the eighteenth-century historian Thomas Atwood (1791: 172–3) referred when he wrote, 'The streets of this town are also very irregular, not one of them being in a straight line; but the whole of them form very acute angles which face nearly the entrance of each other.'

St George's, Grenada, displays very clearly both an adaptive layout and a grid plan, the former in the Carenage quarter, the latter in the Bay Town area on the other side of the ridge on which stand Fort George and the parish church. The original seventeenth-century French settlement on a low-lying strip of land between the Lagoon and the Carenage was inundated by the sea and abandoned for the present site at the turn of the eighteenth century (Devas, 1974: 66). Carenage Town is built along the waterfront and on the steep slopes of the breached volcanic crater which forms the sheltered deepwater harbour, while Bay Town is laid out round a square on a small area of flat land, the strict grid of streets soon giving way to winding roads on the surrounding hills. Precipitous Market Street is a consequence of the application of the grid layout to this hilly terrain.

Like other West Indian towns, many of which are still largely built of timber, St George's suffered from disastrous fires. After the fire of 1771, reconstruction involved the use of brick and stone to avoid the recurrence of such a disaster, and the present attractive character of the town is largely derived from its late eighteenth- and early nineteenth-century development. At the beginning of the nineteenth century, Thomas Coke (1810: 58–9) wrote, 'The new town, which was destined to rise upon the ashes of the old one they laid out on a plan of greater regularity and extent, and raised the walls of most of the houses with brick . . . . On the one side is Bay-town, and on the other Carenage-town. In the former is the government-house, a commodious market place, and an elegant square; and in the latter, the merchants and others, who are engaged in commercial transactions, take up their abode.'

Half a century later John Davy (1854: 510–1) was much less complimentary about West Indian towns in general: 'Relative to the towns in the West Indies, I shall offer but a few remarks; and, I regret to think that these can seldom be laudatory – no just principle having been acted on either in the selection of their sites, or in their construction, – expediency, or immediate profit in the way of business, having been in all respects more considered than the sanitary circumstances, every where so important, and more especially so in a tropical climate.

'Most of the towns, with the objects just mentioned in view, are situated on the leeward coast, close to the sea, and mostly in low situations equally unfavorable for ventilation and drainage, for coolness consequently, and the absence of malaria or noxious effluvia. Not one of them that I am acquainted with, is provided with sewers, or is sufficiently drained, or is well supplied with water, – great and fatal omissions in regard to the health, comfort, and welfare of their inhabitants'.

Improvements to these towns were implemented during the following hundred years or so of colonial government, including drainage, sewerage and water supply works, but problems such as poor housing conditions persisted, and others such as urban sprawl, traffic congestion and refuse disposal grew with increasing population and developing technology. Rural areas, too, suffering from the decline of the sugar plantations and other ills, presented problems which exacerbated an already difficult situation by encouraging migration from country to town.

In response to these growing problems, legislation, based largely on that of Britain, was introduced to combat slums, tackle housing problems, and to promote better town planning. After World War II, particularly with the approach and achievement of political independence, planning legislation was introduced throughout the West Indian islands, although, in the absence of proper planning machinery and trained personnel, it was often largely ineffectual. Nevertheless, planning, including economic development planning, began to receive more serious attention. 'Official interest in planning in the early sixties and seventies stemmed from a policy of the British Government which sought to tie approval of grants and loans to the preparation and approval of development plans' (St Vincent Central Planning Division, 1986: 1).

From 1966 to 1976, the United Nations, through the United Nations Development Programme, UNDP, co-operated in a series of three projects to provide technical assistance in physical planning to the governments of the Eastern Caribbean Common Market countries, plus the Cayman Islands' and Turks and Caicos Islands' governments (UNDP, 1977). The 10 participating governments were helped in establishing planning units, formulating physical development plans and strategies, drafting of effective legislation to control land development and training of national staff in these fields.

Physical Planning Units were established in all 10 participating countries, although the organizational form and ministry responsible differed among governments. In some countries, including St Lucia, Dominica and St Vincent, the planning function was concentrated in the office of the Premier, and on the recommendation of the UNDP project, a number of governments combined socio-economic and physical planning functions where economic planning activities were established.

Not all the physical planning units survived the departure of the UNDP staff, however. In Grenada, where the locally trained technicians were dispersed, most leaving the island, and technical documents were lost, planning came virtually to a halt until the 1979 revolution. The People's Revolutionary Government of 1979–83 created a comprehensive Macro Planning Unit incorporating a newly established Physical Planning Unit set up with the assistance of the European Economic Community. The collapse of the revolution, and subsequent US invasion in 1983, led to the dissolution of Grenada's Macro Planning Unit, but the Physical Planning Unit survived.

One of the reasons for the ability of the re-established Grenadian unit to continue, albeit now mainly in the limited role of development control, is the presence of local fully trained professional planners. This reflects the Caribbean-wide growth of local planning expertise, most, if not all of the Commonwealth Caribbean countries having West Indian planners with recognized professional qualifications. Many of these men and women are geography graduates of the University of the West Indies, Jamaica, and elsewhere who have completed masters degrees in planning overseas, while others have diplomas in planning technology from Jamaica's College of Arts, Science and Technology. The growing strength and influence of the profession in the West Indies is indicated by the establishment of national planning associations in Jamaica, Barbados, Trinidad and Tobago and St Lucia, and recent attempts to forge regional professional links.

Today, the problems which confront planners on the islands of the Commonwealth Eastern Caribbean are generally similar to those of the larger West Indian countries, but extreme smallness in terms of limited land area, most of which is mountainous, and population whose numbers and incomes cannot provide a good market for local products, together with the particular vulnerability of small island ecosystems, exercerbate many of the difficulties.

To avoid unnecessary repetition, this chapter, which discusses nine different and widely scattered countries, makes no attempt to treat each one comprehensively. Instead, it discusses some of the major topics common to the Eastern Caribbean as a whole, using examples from the various islands under consideration.

Diversification of the Economy: Industry and Tourism

Industry

Throughout the Caribbean, the post-war years and, particularly, the period after political independence, saw attempts by the different governments to decrease the islands' economic dependence on their limited traditional primary products and on their traditional markets, mainly Britain in the case of the countries discussed here. The declining or fluctuating prices for major crops, particularly sugar, made it necessary to find alternatives, notably banana production in the Windward Islands. Bananas, too, are liable to market price fluctuation and are particularly vulnerable to disease and natural disasters such as the hurricanes of 1979 and 1980 which devastated crops in Dominica, St Lucia and St Vincent, and the eruption of Soufriere which destroyed plantations in St Vincent in 1979.

While it was generally recognized that agriculture would remain an important sector, the need to diversify the economy was universally accepted, and, like most other developing countries, the Eastern Caribbean islands looked to manufacturing and tourism. At the same time, considerable effort has been made to reinvigorate and diversify agriculture (Rojas and Meganck, 1987). A recent example is a World Bank project in Grenada to promote the cultivation of non-traditional crops, including fruits and vegetables, ornamental plants and cut flowers (World Bank, 1986: 6). Innovative developments of this kind generally require improved international as well as internal transport links, and it was largely for this reason that Grenada's People's Revolutionary Government made the construction of an international airport a cornerstone of its economic development policy (Bishop, n.d.: 180–8).

The lack of adequate air-cargo facilities is considered a major obstacle to the development of manufacturing, particularly in small countries with a heavy dependence on the export market (Dominica/UNDP, 1985: 30–1). Nevertheless, in practically all of the countries under discussion, manufacturing industries are being strongly promoted to increase export earnings, reduce imports, create jobs and broaden the economic base.

Most of the islands have long supported agro-industries, notably rum-distilling which continues to make a useful contribution to the economy, although among the countries discussed here only Antigua exports a significant quantity. Among the few industries which have developed to serve local needs and utilize local raw materials, furniture manufacture is one of the more important, but until recently, the range and output of goods remained small. Since the 1960s, however, the number of manufactured goods produced in the islands has increased markedly, and the emphasis has moved to exportation as well as import substitution. The range of light manufacturing tends to be very similar in each island, typically including the processing of local agricultural produce and the production of textiles, soft drinks, cigarettes, building blocks, electrical goods and the retreading of tyres. This does not encourage intra-regional trade, and in only a few cases does the factory of one island produce goods largely for consumption in the neigbouring countries. St Vincent's flour mill, which serves the Windward Islands, is one example. Local craft industries have been stimulated by the growth of tourism, and Dominica has managed to export its high-quality craftwork to other Caribbean islands (*Latin America and Caribbean*, 1984: 206).

The nature and pattern of industrial development in the West Indies today is largely the result of government policies vigorously pursued since independence from Britain. Like Puerto Rico, the Eastern Caribbean islands tried to attract foreign – mainly US – investors with the prospect of cheap labour and the offer of incentives including tax holidays, exemption from duties on imported capital equipment, and freedom to repatriate all profits. Governments established bodies to promote economic development, including industry, and it is on this sector that St Vincent's Development Corporation and St Lucia's National Development Corporation, set up in 1970 and 1971 respectively, have concentrated their efforts (Browne, 1985: 82; St Lucia/UNDP, 1977: 27).

Governments also provide factory space because foreign investors are often unwilling to construct their own. Dominica, for example, recognizes that the lack of factory buildings is an obstacle to industrial development there, and the island's Industrial Development Corporation has built factory shells at Canefield near the second airport which serves the capital, Roseau (Dominica/UNDP, 1985: 30). Other island governments have also constructed factory shells to attract overseas entrepreneurs, usually near to the capital or a major airport. In Grenada the new international airport at Point Salines was built near the capital, St George's, in an area where much of the island's industry was already concentrated. This great improvement in air-cargo facilities has further boosted the potential for industrial expansion and recently factory shells have been built at nearby Frequente.

In St Lucia, Vieux Fort, with the country's main international airport and second seaport, and not Castries the capital, has been identified as the main industrial development area. However, the capital, which has the main port and second airport, will remain an important manufacturing centre (St Lucia/UNDP, 1977: 27–8). St Lucia has established two free zones, to further stimulate industry, an approach adopted elsewhere in the Caribbean where inevitably it is the subject of considerable controversy.

Criticism of Eastern Caribbean industrialization policies is well expressed by the Vincentian planner, Bentley Browne (1985: 86–8) whose comments on his own country are equally valid elsewhere in the region. He acknowledges that manufacture has helped to increase the gross domestic product and employment levels (the manufacturing sector's contribution to St Vincent's GDP rose from 4 per cent in 1974 to 12 per cent in 1984 and provided over 3,000 new jobs) but cautions that, while manufacturing activities contributed to economic growth, they have done little to stimulate development. The emphasis is on largely foreign-owned and enclave-type export manufacturing industries producing goods with a high import content and which involve a very low level of value added. Moreover, the government's expenditure on the provision of infrastructure and the fiscal exemptions enjoyed by foreign companies greatly offset any contribution made by the manufacturing sector to the island's economy.

Technological advances, and the resultant fall in demand for large quantities of cheap labour, are reducing the advantages of locating industries outside North America, a trend which is reinforced by protectionist policies, making it increasingly difficult to re-export manufactured goods to the USA. With low investment in fixed capital, it is relatively easy for foreign companies to leave once the tax holiday period is over or when local wages rise. Hence 'The development and continued expansion of export oriented "screw driver industries" . . . is dependent on a series of external conditions which the state cannot influence and on internal factors which will be difficult to control, or if they are controlled, would lead to great social, economic and political repercussions on the society' (Browne, 1985: 86). No less dependent on external conditions is the oil refining industry which, in the islands under discussion, is represented only in Antigua and St Lucia. The small refinery near St John's has had a chequered history, during much of which it has been out of production and used only for storage (Mulchansingh, 1988).

In the 1970s, the government of St Lucia turned to the petroleum industry to provide a catalyst for development which, it was hoped, would emancipate the island from its dependence on bananas and tourism, and alleviate its economic problems, including unemployment conservatively estimated at 25 per cent of the workforce (Koester, 1985; 1986). The government entered into an agreement with the US-based multinational Amerada Hess Corporation, and in 1977, plans were announced for the establishment of a petroleum storage facility and super-port on the leeward coast south of Castries, and the eventual construction of a refinery there. 'The petroleum project was perceived at all levels of St Lucia's society as a way of securing a stable source of revenue, as a magnet for continuing to attract mutli-national investments, and as a means of employing large numbers of people' (Koester, 1985: 270).

The original agreement between the Amerada Hess Corporation and St Lucia included a 20 year tax holiday, complete exemption from import duties or exchange controls, and a mere two cents a gallon royalty to government. In mid-1982, a 201 million gallon capacity trans-shipment terminal storing up to US$4,176 million-worth of crude oil was opened at Cul de Sac, providing the government with a new source of revenue amounting to about US$43 million a year (*Latin America and Caribbean*, 1984: 233). It is, however, unlikely that the proposed oil refinery as outlined in the agreement will be built because the Caribbean oil refinery industry has been badly hit by world over-supply and shifts in patterns of production and distribution (ICFTU/CCL, 1986: 11; *Latin America and Caribbean*, 1984: 233).

On completion of the massive project with its initially heavy demand for labour and relatively high wages, few jobs remained, almost none of them for women. The local agricultural economy had been severely disrupted, and, as Koester (1985: 277) observed, 'A paradox common to large-scale development efforts is that this local level self-sufficiency is often sacrificed to a national goal aimed at lessening economic dependence.' Another large-scale project on the leeward coast of St Lucia, at Gros Islet, similarly disrupted the local economy in a scheme intended to help achieve national economic goals. Here it was not industry but tourism which promised a path to development.

Tourism

Caribbean tourism is relatively long-established, and Aspinall's comprehensive tourist guide to the region was first published as early as 1907. By the time of the 1935 edition, in addition to the frequent steamship services from Britain, Europe, the USA and Canada, there were daily air services between Miami and Cuba with less frequent flights to other parts of the Caribbean, including a weekly service to Antigua on the Miami–Paramaribo route (Aspinall, 1935: 488). At that time St Lucia, though not on a major international route, had an airport with links to other Caribbean islands (Aspinall, 1935: 175; Gaile and Hanink, 1984: 274; 276).

The era of mass tourism did not arrive until after World War II when the airliner, particularly the jet passenger aircraft, replaced the banana boat as the chief international tourist carrier. The closure of US military bases established in the Caribbean during the war benefited tourism in several islands, including Antigua and St Lucia, by providing those countries with international airports. Countries without adequate airport facilities were at a serious disadvantage in the highly competitive tourist business, and despite the accusations of the USA, this was the main reason for the construction of Grenada's new international airport (Bishop, 1982: 164–5; Hudson, 1983: 51–6).

While it is true that all of the islands of the Caribbean possess attractions which appeal to tourists, notably sun, sand, sea and scenery, and are close to rich markets, especially those of North America, not all are equally endowed. Antigua, for example, has a deeply embayed coast with many superb white sand beaches, a particularly dry, sunny climate, a number of picturesque historical sites, and an international airport which developed from a US military base established under the war-time lend-lease arrangement. All this, together with publicity generated by the American millionaires' resort of Mill Reef, gave Antigua an early start in tourism development which accelerated greatly in the 1950s (Macpherson, 1980: 116–17; Richards, 1983: 29).

In contrast, Dominica, despite its magnificent scenery with beautiful forest-clad mountains and cascading rivers, suffers from its lack of attractive beaches, most of them being of black volcanic sand, high rainfall, and relatively difficult access in the absence of an airport capable of handling large jet aircraft. Consequently, tourism is only slightly developed in Dominica whereas in Antigua it dominates the economy, generating about 40 per cent of the country's GNP and providing three-quarters of the jobs (*Latin America and Caribbean*, 1984: 177).

The large inter-island disparities in tourism development are paralleled within the individual countries themselves, and hotels and resorts are generally concentrated in a few coastal areas. The spatial distribution of tourist facilities naturally reflects, to a large degree, the location of attractions and infrastructure (Hudson, 1987: 49–51). Development tends to concentrate mainly around the best and most accessible beaches, at, for example, Grenada's Grand Anse, but also at other major attractions such as yacht harbours, including St Vincent's Calliaqua, and at famous scenic spots, notably the luxury resort high above the sea near St Lucia's celebrated Pitons. In Antigua, the scenically beautiful and historic Nelson's Dockyard is also one of the Caribbean's major yacht harbours, a combination which has greatly stimulated tourism in that area, while the close juxtaposition of one of the region's finest beaches and arguably the most picturesque town in the West Indies contribute to the heavy concentration of tourism near to and south of St George's, Grenada.

Among the Eastern Caribbean islands there is a tendency for the main concentrations of tourism to occur near the capitals of their respective countries, these being, with the exception of Basseterre in Guadeloupe, the largest towns in each case. This is largely because the area round the major town is invariably the most developed part of the country and is the best equipped in terms of infrastructure such as roads, electricity and water supplies and telephone service. Moreover, there is a readily available large pool of labour on which the tourist industry can draw.

Although this concentration tends to exacerbate the problem of regional disparities within individual countries, it can make more economic the provision and utilization of costly infrastructure. This was recognized in Grenada's *Proposed Physical Area Development Strategy 1977–1990* which states, 'conceptually, the area development strategy for Grenada presupposes concentration of resources in one geographic area and the creation of an economic and social growth axis . . . from St George's to Grand Anse in the south-west corner . . .' (Grenada/UNDP, 1977: 68). The economic generator for this growth was to be tourism.

In contrast, Dominica's planners rejected the recommendations of foreign consultants to develop relatively large-scale beach-related tourist resorts with concentrations in the vicinity of the two largest towns, Roseau and Portsmouth. Instead, they proposed a more dispersed pattern reflecting the distribution of the island's scenic resources and natural attractions, and related to other sectoral development programmes such as agriculture and forestry (Dominica/UNDP, 1976: 41; 83; Dominica/UNDP, 1985: 90; 126–8). This strategy recognizes that Dominica's tourist development is constrained by its generally inferior beaches and that its greatest potential probably lies in the island's superb inland scenery, including mountains, forests, rivers and lakes.

Dominica's modest efforts to harness tourism to its overall economic development strategy and Grenada's much more vigorous promotion of the tourist industry as a key element in its economic policy both reflect the attitude, widespread in the developing world, that tourism not only provides a valuable new source of income and employment, but can strengthen and stimulate other sectors of the economy. As is well known, however, the economic impact of tourism is often disappointing and there are commonly undesirable social and environmental consequences which are particularly strongly felt in small island countries such as those of the Pacific and Caribbean (Britton and Clarke, 1987). These problems, as experienced in the Caribbean, have received considerable attention, and it is not appropriate to attempt a comprehensive discussion of them here (Beekhuis, 1981; Browne, 1985; Hawkins, 1976: 129–40; Richards, 1983: 15–35). Instead, it will suffice to consider briefly three examples: Antigua, which has the most developed tourist industry in the countries under consideration, St Vincent and the Grenadines where tourism is less developed partly because of relatively poor air links, and Grenada where between 1979 and 1983 an attempt was begun at developing a 'New Tourism'.

Antigua's early start in tourism has already been noted, and its rapid development is reflected in the proliferation of its hotels, with room numbers increasing from 560 in 1961 to 2,496 in 1975 (Richards, 1983: 29). This period saw a structural change in the economy of Antigua and Barbuda, with 'the decline and ultimate collapse of the sugar plantocracy . . . coupled with the emergence of an industry of modern vintage which displaced agriculture from its primary position' (ibid.: 30). While agriculture's contribution to the gross domestic product fell from 35.2 per cent in 1953 to 4.8 per cent in 1968, tourism's share rose from 7.7 per cent to 14.1 per cent over the same period. In 10 years, from 1960 to 1970, employment in agriculture declined from 33 per cent of the workforce to 14 per cent, while tourism's share rose from 2 per cent to 5 percent, trebling its number of workers and agricultural employment fell in absolute terms (ibid.: 30).

With the growth of tourism as the dominant sector, the economy of Antigua and Barbuda remains 'extremely vulnerable to external economic developments', particularly so in this island where the very fickle high-income tourist plays a major role. Furthermore, the majority of the hotels are foreign owned, 90 per cent of tourist beds being owned by expatriates in 1968 when most of those locally owned were in guest houses. 'Since then the ownership pattern has moved somewhat in favour of national ownership, due to the real or fabricated insolvency of several large foreign-owned hotels and the subsequent government take-over. It is important to note, however, that these state-owned hotels are still under expatriate control' (ibid.: 31).

An important benefit of tourism has been the creation of new jobs, but as Richards (ibid.: 31–2) observed, employment in the tourist sector displays features similar to those of plantation agriculture. These include a high proportion of semi-skilled and unskilled workers, largely women; a high proportion of non-nationals in the managerial and skilled jobs; and high seasonality of employment.

In terms of foreign exchange earnings, tourism's substantial gross income is much reduced by leakages. In 1963, 41 per cent was spent on imports alone, and to this amount should be added the repatriated earnings of non-nationals. Tourist spending has had very small impact on income-generation in Antigua and Barbuda where substantial links between tourism and other sectors of the economy have not developed.

In Antigua, as elsewhere in the Caribbean, 'tourism does not now serve to strengthen linkages between the sectors of the economy, to place greater control of the economy into national hands and to reduce dependence on and vulnerability to changes in external situations' (Carrington and Blake, 1976: 8, quoted in Richards *op. cit.*).

Browne (1985) and Nanton (1983) find similar problems in St Vincent and the Grenadines where 'enclave tourism has exacerbated a dependence on imports and disrupted small communities to little local advantage' (Nanton, 1983: 234). Among the adverse effects of tourism there have been soaring land prices and the loss of agricultural land to tourist-related uses as at the Peniston Estate which has been developed for a golf course and hotel facilities (Browne, 1985: 72). Problems of tourism-related speculation in land have arisen even in this relatively undeveloped country. In the small Grenadine island of Bequia, for example, two North American companies subdivided a quarter of the land for tourist-residential development, but a decade later most of the plots remained vacant while local people were unable to buy housing land at the inflated prices (ibid.: 72).

Noting the occurrence in St Vincent of many of the common problems of tourism in developing countries, including the encouragement of migration from rural areas, the development of urban sprawl along major coast roads, and adverse social and cultural side-effects, Browne (ibid.: 77), proposed 'An indigenous form of tourism based on the state's physical and human resources and their carrying capacities'.

The creation of such an 'indigenous form of tourism' was a major component of revolutionary Grenada's economic development policy, and 'The New Tourism', as it was called, was the theme of a speech by Prime Minister Maurice Bishop as early as 1979, the year in which he came to power (Bishop n.d.: 67–74). After summarizing the problems associated with the 'Old Tourism', Bishop outlined the nature of Grenada's 'New Tourism' which he saw not merely as a business but as an instrument of world peace and understanding. The economic aspects were emphasized, however, and tourism was intended to be used as a stimulus for national development by forging links between it and other sectors, including agriculture and agro-industry. Local cuisine and Grenadian culture were to be encouraged rather than allowing the island's culture to be 'determined by some pre-conceived notion of what the tourist might expect' (ibid.: 72).

Understandably, in the face of US hostility to the Grenadian government, great emphasis was placed on the diversification of the tourist market, there being considerable potential in Latin America and Europe. Linked with this was the encouragement of non-white visitors, particularly West Indians, by which it was aimed 'to break the relationship between tourism, class and colour' and to provide 'a useful complement to other visitors in the so-called "off season" ' (ibid.: 72).

Acutely aware of the difficulties arising from intra-Caribbean rivalry and competition, Bishop pledged Grenada's support for a regional approach to problems of tourism. Not the least important aspect of this is air transportation, which largely determines the possible level of tourist development. St Vincent, for instance, is seriously disadvantaged because its airport cannot provide for air services linking it with places beyond the basin itself (St Vincent/UNDP, 1976: 87). Until recently, Grenada was in a similar situation and most of its visitors came via Barbados, where normally an overnight stay was necessary (Hudson, 1983). The construction of Grenada's new airport changed this, and, indeed, may also have helped St Vincent by providing an additional international gateway to the region (Republic of France, 1985: 46).

While ease of access is clearly an important aspect of mass tourism, there may also be advantages in maintaining a certain exclusivity and limiting development. The international jet airports of Antigua, St Lucia and Grenada increase the danger of an overwhelming tide of tourism which could threaten the particular attractive qualities of those islands. In order to encourage large airlines to use Grenada's new airport it is necessary to increase the number of hotel rooms on the island to at least 1,000–1,200, and recent plans for four new hotels, each providing 250–350 rooms, suggest that the Grenadian government is now yielding to pressure from investors to allow a somewhat larger scale of building than was previously regarded as acceptable (World Bank, 1986: 6).

Problems of Human Settlements

Migration and Urban Development

The impact of industry and tourism on the scale and pattern of development has already been briefly noted, but contemporary problems of human settlements need explicit consideration here.

Even in the mid-nineteenth century there was a considerable concentration of population in the largest town of each West Indian island. The 1844 census records that the proportion of population living in the largest town ranged from just over 15 per cent in Grenada and Montserrat to nearly 25 per cent in Antigua (Davy, 1854: 512–13). Partly in consequence of migration from rural areas, the concentration of population in the larger towns, especially the capitals, has increased, some countries having up to a third or more of their people living in and around the capital.

The impact of rural–urban migration has been greatly reduced by migration to North America, the UK, and other Caribbean territories experiencing hotel and other construction booms. In St Vincent, out-migration reduced population growth to one-third of the natural increase in the 1960s and 1970s, while in Dominica it halved the population growth (St Vincent/UNDP, 1976: 2; Dominica/UNDP, 1976: 76–90). Since then, opportunities for migration overseas have greatly diminished, tending to increase pressures within the islands.

While out-migration relieved pressures of unemployment and boosted income from remittances sent home by migrants, this population movement has been selective and has led to a serious brain drain, as well as to an age distribution shift in favour of the very young (St Vincent/UNDP, 1976: 2). This latter also reflects sustained high fertility, and with greater restrictions on overseas migration together with continuing internal migration, increased pressures on urban areas can be expected. By the year 2,000, more than 64 per cent of the population of the entire Caribbean region may be living in urban areas, compared with 38 per cent in 1960 (Hope, 1983: 167), a general trend which can be observed in the individual small countries under discussion.

Nevertheless, the very smallness of these islands makes it possible for many people to work in town and yet to reside in the country, some holding office or other urban jobs while operating small farms. The extent to which this can occur depends on topography as well as on distance. In the case of Antigua, size and topographical character-istics allow for high accessibility with short travelling times between various places on the island. 'A kind of residential dispersed develop-ment is emerging in such a way that although the biggest concen-tration of services, commerce and industries is produced along the St John's–Airport corridor, residential areas are dispersed' (Soler, 1987c: 41).

Dominica's relatively large size, and particularly its very rugged terrain, make travel much more difficult. Over 50 cent of the island's settlements are more than an hour's drive from Roseau, over 25 per cent being more than a two-hour road journey away. 'Larger distances make Roseau a less accessible place on a day-to-day basis to approximately half of all human settlements in the country. Consequently, dual urban–rural emplacement or small town–large city emplacement is less possible in Dominica' (Soler, 1987a: 29).

Roseau's workforce, however, includes many who commute daily from outside the town, mainly from nearby settlements such Massacre, Mahaut, St Joseph and Pointe Michel. During working hours these people swell the town's population, and demands on Roseau's services such as water supply, sewerage, refuse collection and sanitary facilities, are greater than its recorded resident population would indicate. They also contribute greatly to traffic congestion (Dominica/UNDP, 1985: 51).

Despite topographic limitations, Roseau has begun to sprawl along the coast, in pockets of flat land and on the gentler slopes, in a linear form of development found in the vicinity of major towns throughout the Caribbean. Tourism has greatly added to these sprawling ribbons of development along the coast. In St Vincent, this 'has led to uncontrolled urban/suburban extension in a linear fashion along the major Windward highway' (Browne, 1985: 72), while in Antigua, too, coastal development and urban sprawl are occurring 'without clear reference to any rational management of land as a resource' (Soler, 1987c: 41).

Thus, while there is a common tendency for development to concentrate in one particular part of the country, normally along the coast near to the capital, it often takes an unco-ordinated, scattered form which in part reflects the topography, but is also a consequence of haphazard growth. Government housing schemes no less than private residential developments contribute to the urban sprawl (Soler, 1987c: 41). Apart from being a wasteful use of limited land resources, scattered development of this kind is relatively difficult and expensive to provide with utilities and services.

Regional Disparity and Urban Hierarchy

It is for reasons such as those mentioned above that planners propose the concentration of development in the south-west of Grenada, though here, too, development has been largely scattered and unco-ordinated. Even in an island as small as this, where it is not unusual for people to commute daily between settlements in the extreme north and east and the St George's area in the southwest, there is some concern about regional disparities. This problem was recently exacerbated by the opening of the Point Salines Airport which replaced the one north of Grenville. The proposed establishment of an industrial estate at the old Pearls Airport site is an attempt to retain jobs in the north-east (Blaize, 1985: 11; Smith, 1988).

Notwithstanding Grenada's policy of development in accordance with the overall trend towards concentration in the south-west, here, as elsewhere in the Eastern Caribbean, planners have proposed an urban hierarchy, with a secondary growth centre at Grenville, the second largest town, and tertiary centres at Gouyave, Victoria and Hills-borough continuing to serve their respective parishes (Grenada/UNDP, 1977: 68–70).

The relatively large and most rugged of the islands discussed here, Dominica, well illustrates the problems of the both highly dispersed settlement and urban primacy. The spatial distribution of Dominica's population is determined largely by the terrain and the pattern of road development, itself a function of terrain. Most of the settlements are on low-lying land near the coast, in river valleys or on hillsides near river valleys. Of the approximately 80 settlements, 53 settlements (66 per cent) are on the coast, and another seven (9 per cent), lie within a mile of the sea (Dominica/UNDP, 1985: 44). On the leeward or western side of the island, where slopes are generally less steep and road construction began earlier, most settlements are of the nucleated or linear type, with densities much higher than those found in the dispersed settlements characteristic of the windward and interior settlements. About half Dominica's settlements have fewer than five hundred people, and 85 per cent of all settlements have fewer than 1,200 each. In 1981, some 35,000 people, about 48 per cent of the island's population, lived in these small, scattered settlements, while almost 38,000 people, over 51 per cent of the national total, lived in the eight largest settlements, including greater Roseau, the largest with over 19,000 inhabitants, or some 26 per cent of Dominica's people (ibid.: 46).

This highly dispersed settlement pattern in a country with very limited financial resources severely constrains the provision of basic services. Excessive concentration of investment and resources in one relatively large urban area, however, despite certain economic advantages, 'does not permit the optimum utilization of the nation's resources and can hardly be justified on grounds of social equity and the necessity to achieve and maintain national cohesion' (ibid.: 106). Moreover, the physical constraints of Roseau's site make the diversion of growth to other centres highly desirable.

In response to these problems, planners have recommended a strategy based on the 'integration of all settlements of the island into a comprehensive hierarchical system of inter-related and functionally linked settlements' (ibid.: 107). To prevent congestion in Roseau, Portsmouth, planned as the capital of the island in 1765 (Honychurch, 1984: 46), has been proposed as a major growth centre with industrial development and the provision of services and facilities similar to those of the capital. It is envisaged that Portsmouth will absorb many of the migrants from rural areas who would otherwise have settled in the Roseau area (ibid.: 112).

With the expansion of Portsmouth, very careful planning and control will be required to minimize the loss of good agricultural land; but here, as in most of the settlements selected as main service centres, future development will inevitably be at the expense of cultivated areas (ibid.: 48–9). This is particularly so because of the expense of developing the steeper slopes and the economic advantages of building on flatter areas which often contain the best agricultural land. Dominica's planners recommend that residential development, particularly low-income schemes, should be mainly confined to slopes of less than 25 per cent in order to minimize construction costs, while industrial development should ideally be on land with less than a 15 per cent gradient (ibid.: 95).

Housing

Commonly, as in St Kitts-Nevis, all the most easily accessible non-agricultural land suitable for housing has already been settled (Soler, 1987b: 22), and almost any new development scheme involves either the loss of land in cultivation or that which has agricultural potential. While government officials may try to minimize the transfer of high quality agricultural land to urban uses, their task is often made all the more difficult by the absence of well-defined criteria for land selection (Soler, 1987c: 41).

In places, the problem of urban sprawl and loss of agricultural land is exacerbated by premature subdivision, a widespread phenomenon in the West Indies which, as we have seen in the case of Bequia, is often associated with land speculation related to tourism. Tiny Montserrat, where tourism consists mainly of retiree homes, may serve as an example. By 1976 only about six hundred of the 3,700 lots subdivided on the island's west coast had been built on, there being an over-supply of land for urban development and a wasteful provision of costly, under-used infrastructure. The vacant subdivided area, mostly suitable for vegetable and fruit cultivation, had a holding capacity of about 20,000 in a country whose population was then estimated at 13,500 and was expected to grow by no more than 2,200 by 1990 (Montserrat/UNDP, 1976: 7–8). This projected growth did not occur and the 1980 census recorded Montserrat's total population as 11,519, with recent estimates putting the figure at about 12,000.

Subdivisions of this kind are normally designed for the relatively wealthy, including expatriate owners, and by wastefully consuming land and inflating land prices can hinder the solution of the most important housing problem – the provision of adequate homes for people with lower incomes. The usual bad conditions of poor housing in developing countries are found in the islands discussed here, though not on the scale or to the degree which make the slums of, say Lagos, Calcutta, or even Kingston, Jamaica seem so intractable. Inner urban slums of decaying, overcrowded houses, formerly the homes of middle-class families, and peripheral settlements of shacks clinging to hillsides, the banks of gullies and in other odd corners of land are common in and around the larger towns, while the rural areas, too, are characterized by overcrowded dwellings of poor construction, often without adequate basic services.

The flimsy construction, poor repair and often dangerous sites of these dwellings in town and country make them particularly vulnerable to natural hazards, especially hurricanes. In 1979, for example, Hurricane David destroyed 2,000 and severely damaged 6,700 of Dominica's houses, rendering 60,000 people homeless and adding considerably to the squatter problem (Dominica/UNDP, 1985: 10; 84). Fire, too, remains a serious threat, and that which destroyed much of Castries in 1948 led to the redevelopment of the central area, including the building of public housing schemes in the form of apartment blocks.

Perhaps the most serious housing problem is overcrowding. The 1980 census records that in St Vincent the occupancy rate was 1.59 persons per room, but that in the Bridgetown area, the mean exceeded two persons per room. Dominica has a similar occupancy rate, averaging 1.5 persons per room. This is expected to continue to the end of the century while the government focuses its efforts on the provision of infrastructure and the improvement of existing accommodation (ibid.: 102).

As in slums and squatter settlements in many parts of the world, the spirit of self-help is evident in the Eastern Caribbean. Castries, for example, has spontaneous settlements in which the erection of wooden dwellings and associated workshops indicate that 'the inhabitants . . . are doing their utmost to thrive in a situation of severe social and economic deprivation . . . and despite much poverty, there is a genuine air of improvement and progress about the settlement' (Potter, 1985: 110).

Attempts have been made to harness this initiative and energy for self-help in government housing policies, partly through sites and services schemes such as those initiated by St Lucia's Urban Development Corporation (St Lucia/UNDP, 1977: 38–9), and in variety of financial assistance schemes including loans for house construction and repairs. A Grenadian proposal for assisted house construction involving government technical advice and the use of local materials as well as local financing is intended to provide new houses at a cost of EC$20,000 each (World Bank, 1986: 8), while in Dominica there is a housing scheme for low-income earners involving the AID Bank, the Caribbean Development Bank and the Dominican Social Security Administration which sets the maximum loan limit at $30,000. Nevertheless, even this relatively small sum 'puts the scheme out of the range of the capacity to pay of low income earners, unless several household members can combine to obtain loans as joint borrowers' (Dominica/UNDP, 1985: 85).

The construction of houses by government bodies, often with

overseas financial and technical assistance, while sometimes meeting specific needs, such as supporting industrial or tourist development projects, may be generally considered as little more than symbolic schemes. The number of units added to the housing stock this way is relatively small and their cost usually puts them out of reach of those in most need (Dwyer, 1975: 97). Indeed, in the islands of the Eastern Caribbean, as in most of the Third World, efforts to improve housing conditions generally have little effect on the lot of the very poor. Improved housing usually requires improved incomes to pay for it.

Housing, including squatter settlements and middle-class subdivisions, has contributed greatly to the urban expansion which consumes large areas of the island's limited land resources. In order to make more efficient use of building land and to achieve economies in construction, it may be necessary to adopt new approaches to house design and residential development in the islands. The recent National Development plan for St Kitts-Nevis recommends the introduction of non-traditional housing types such as semi-detached units, row houses and low rise apartments to reduce unit cost and minimize land requirement (Soler, 1987b: 22), and Grenada's People's Revolutionary Government adopted a row house design for one of its public housing schemes near Grand Anse.

Town Centres, Renewal and Conservation

While the fringes of urban areas are undergoing rapid development, town centres are experiencing renewal at different rates, some, such as Roseau, showing little sign of redevelopment, others, notably Castries, having something of a building boom with new office blocks rising near the waterfront and Columbus Square.

Problems of the town centres include the decayed state of many old buildings, commonly between one and two centuries old, and the often equally decayed and overloaded infrastructure. Drainage and sewerage problems are widespread and sometimes acute, and the road systems are often unable to cope adequately with traffic flows. Traffic congestion, parking problems and pedestrian–vehicular conflict are particularly severe in St George's where the town's streets are narrow, winding and often very steep.

To help ease congestion and facilitate expansion and redevelopment of downtown areas, several land reclamation schemes have been undertaken and others are planned. This is not a new practice in the Eastern Caribbean where the sites of many towns have been formed partly by infilling coastal swamps and shallows, notably at Castries and St John's (Breen, 1844: 14; Coke, 1810: 416). One of the most recent reclamations is that on the Kingstown waterfront where a cultural centre, a bus terminal and a major car park are among the uses proposed for the area. The new complex on reclaimed land at Pointe Seraphine, Castries, however, is mainly devoted to tourism, with two cruise ship berths, a shopping mall, restaurant/bar and other related facilities. Indeed, many of the proposed downtown and waterfront schemes are being planned at least partly to improve tourist-related facilities (OAS, 1985).

The antiquity of many of the streets and individual buildings, and the commonly hilly sites of the towns or their suburbs, while posing problems, may also be regarded as an opportunity for the enhancement and diversification of the 'tourist product'. Some of these towns are already recognized as major tourist attractions in themselves, picturesque St George's being widely regarded as one of the most beautiful places in the Caribbean and Grenada's main tourist sight (Hudson, 1987: 56–7). Nevertheless, relatively little has been done to exploit this resource, and the loss of the unique architectural heritage of the region continues, through neglect, ignorance and inevitable redevelopment pressure. Architectural heritage conservation is costly and is unlikely to achieve high priority in poor countries, but there are signs that the value of this resource is now beginning to be recognized in the Eastern Caribbean. In several islands, proposals have been put forward to conserve and develop it (Jackson, 1985). Elsewhere in the Caribbean, notably in the old towns of San Juan and Havana, successful heritage conservation schemes show what can be achieved under different political and economic systems.

Environment, Planning and Conservation

Conservation of the built and natural environment has become an important planning issue in the Eastern Caribbean as public and political awareness of environmental problems has increased. While the Caribbean does not yet have environmental problems on the scale of the Mediterranean, in some areas the situation is already critical. Rapid population growth and urbanization contribute to pollution from cities and to increased pressure on agricultural resources which, in turn, leads to deforestation and soil erosion with consequent damage to mangroves and coral reefs, adversely affecting fisheries (Anon, 1981).

These problems are most severe in the more developed and industrialized countries such as Puerto Rico and Jamaica, and in very poor, environmentally degraded Haiti, but the islands under discussion here are experiencing similar problems which, if on a smaller scale, are all the more serious because of their tiny areas and the fragility of their ecosystems.

One of the greatest environmental threats to these countries is, of course, the tourist industry (Hudson, 1986; 1987), and the case of St Lucia's Rodney Bay provides an excellent example of the way in which poorly conceived tourist development schemes can have disastrous environmental, social and economic consequences. Rodney Bay, the unofficial name by which Gros Islet Bay has become better known, attracted tourism development in the early 1960s when Canadian investors built a hotel on Reduit Beach, just south of the offshore Pigeon Island with its historic buildings associated with Admiral Rodney. Further development was inhibited by the local sandfly nuisance thought to be caused by a nearby swamp. A Jamaican entrepreneur, owner of a large marine dredging and construction company, offered to solve the problem and, at the same time, increase the development potential of the area by a dredge-and-fill operation which would create a new lagoon, provide additional building land, and connect Pigeon Island to the mainland by a causeway. This proposal was accepted by the St Lucia government which participated in the development in partnership with the Jamaican entrepreneur and the Commonwealth Development Corporation.

The serious environmental and social problems which this ambitious large-scale development created are discussed in detail by Towle (1985). Unanticipated consequences of the scheme include beach erosion, which has necessitated costly remedial action including a gabion blanket near one hotel and an offshore breakwater. Ecological and physical changes brought about by the development scheme have also largely destroyed fishing in the area, to the detriment of the inhabitants of Gros Islet, whose involvement in the tourist industry has been adversely affected rather than enhanced (ibid.: 234-8). Ironically, the new causeway itself suffers erosion, and remains an undeveloped, unused expanse of sand, while sandflies still abound in the area.

In his analysis of the Rodney Bay scheme, Towle (ibid.: 240) succinctly expresses the underlying problems which all the islands experience: 'The political decision-making process is inexorably inclined to optimize short-term, sectoral development aimed at generating employment, investment and income in a problem-solving mode within the shortest time-frame. This is a fact of life, but it is especially risky when the developmental "quick fix" involves the allocation of small island coastal resources, usually involving complex, closely coupled dynamic natural ecosystems with an overlay of an equally closely coupled human ecosystem, constrained by both the insular vulnerability and limited option factors characteristic of smaller islands'.

More gradual, smaller-scale development seems most appropriate in these circumstances, but even this has its dangers as imperceptibly, slow incremental change can alter an environment as completely as a rapid large-scale development. Large numbers of small developments, many of them tourist-related, are having this effect in the Caribbean, and are contributing to the widespread transformation of the very environment which attracts and supports tourism, including beautiful beaches and landscapes (Hudson, 1986; 1987).

The despoliation of many West Indian environments is so advanced that now some islands are attempting to woo the tourist by claiming to have avoided this fate. St Lucia, despite unfortunate developments such as Rodney Bay and the Hess oil terminal, boasts, on its tourist information kit folder, of being 'One of the last truly unspoiled Caribbean islands', while a publicity brochure for a hotel on the tiny Grenadine island of Canouan invites the prospective visitor to 'Relax on perhaps the last unspoiled island in the Caribbean'. It will require much stricter planning control than hitherto to preserve the tropical island paradise image which makes the West Indies so attractive to tourists.

Among the many problems raised by this issue, however, is the difference in attitude and taste between residents and tourists. The environment which attracts and enchants visitors may not be valued by those who experience it daily, and who might, in fact, wish to see it changed. Tropical forests and historic buildings which appeal to many tourists could be regarded as signs of undevelopment and backwardness by local residents who may rather see the forest cleared for farming and modern buildings in place of the old (Hudson 1986: 120–1; 1987: 55–6; Ringel and Wylie, n.d.).

Nevertheless, there have been notable successes in the fields of architectural heritage and natural area conservation, including the restoration of Antigua's celebrated Nelson's Dockyard, and the establishment of Dominica's Morne Trois Pitons National Park. The designation of conservation areas such as national parks often arouses opposition and causes resentment, as in the case of that on the US Virgin Island of St John (Olwig, 1980; Olwig and Olwig, 1979), and the Levera National Park in Grenada (ECNAMP, 1983; Frederick, 1987: 63–7).

The Levera project was one of the initiatives of Grenada's People's Revolutionary Government, and this regime's strong commitment to development on sound ecological principles was most clearly demonstrated by the establishment in 1983 of an Environmental Conservation Council with the Head of the Physical Planning Unit as its executive secretary. At the first meeting of the Council it was announced that the PRG 'intended to strengthen the nation's environmental management system by the establishment of a post of Secretary for the Environment to be held by a person of Cabinet rank', and that the

Attorney General was reviewing existing legislation relating to the environment with a view to making necessary changes. 'By the end of 1983, most of the institutional and legal instruments were in place to allow for the preservation and management of Grenada's natural resources' (Jules, 1986: 283), but by that time the Grenada Revolution had collapsed. Although the Environmental Conservation Council was short-lived (Frederick, 1987: 47–8), the post-1983 Grenadian government continued the previous administration's collaboration with the Eastern Caribbean Natural Area Management Programme, ECNAMP, on the Levera Project (Renard, 1988). Happily, Levera is one of several national parks recently established in Grenada.

Based in St Croix, ECNAMP, itself, is a collaborative effort involving the Caribbean Conservation Association, CCA, with its head office in Barbados, and the University of Michigan School of Natural Resources. Many of its activities contribute to the implementation of elements of the world-wide International Union for the Conservation of Nature/World Wildlife Fund Conservation Programme for Sustainable Development, and a major ECNAMP project was a survey to provide the CCA with 'the information to devise a logical, systematic and effective strategy for conservation action in the Lesser Antilles' (Putney, 1982: vii). Among the results of this survey are Preliminary Data Atlases for the 25 islands or island groups in the region, including all those discussed in this chapter.

The CCA, for which the survey was undertaken, came into existence as a result of a meeting held in the US Virgin Islands in 1965, and, while concerned with the entire Caribbean, it is most active in the English-speaking countries, most of whose governments are members of the organization. The Association is concerned with all aspects of the environment, not only natural ecosystems, and is involved in the Caribbean Plan for Monuments and Sites, CARIMOS, a programme dealing with the conservation of the region's architectural heritage. Perhaps the most important roles of the CCA are environmental education in the region, and acting as 'a "broker" between governments and non-government organizations, on both a regional and a national basis' (Sheppard, 1986: 354).

Conclusion

With the creation of a vigorous regional environmental organization, the proliferation of national development plans and legislation, the establishment of physical planning units, and the emergence of a growing body of highly qualified West Indian planners, the Eastern Caribbean islands may appear to be well prepared for wise management of their natural and human resources and the planning of their settlements. Despite these considerable achievements, however, many serious problems remain.

Of the many plans prepared, largely with UNDP assistance, few were ever formally accepted by government and given official status. Their recommendations, therefore, are difficult to implement. Moreover, there is commonly lack of official local plans which is a serious impediment to development control, the major function of physical planning units in the region.

Development control, while quite effective in the main urban centres, tends to be less so in peripheral areas and beyond, especially in relation to the quickly built little wooden houses of the poor. In these areas planning authorities are often unable or unwilling to impose unrealistic standards, and accept the construction of substandard dwellings erected without permission as long as they are not built of 'permanent' materials such as concrete blocks. Inevitably, however, 'temporary' buildings are improved by their occupants as funds and fortune permit, and wooden planks and corrugated metal sheets are gradually replaced by more permanent materials. On suitable sites and with appropriate layout, this may be a process to be encouraged and assisted, but often the original 'temporary' dwellings have been built on land which is unsuitable for permanent residential development in areas which are difficult to service and which may even be dangerous. Commonly, the layout is haphazard and inappropriate for modern urban conditions, and the emerging unofficial permanent settlements may impede official development plans.

The work of processing development applications, including site inspection and monitoring unofficial developments, occupies most of the time and energy of government planners in the Eastern Caribbean. Lack of sufficient qualified staff means that plan preparation usually has to be neglected until assistance comes in the form of overseas technical aid such as the UNDP projects.

The pursuit of balanced, long-term development policies is made even more difficult in micro-states, such as those under discussion, when their governments deal with large foreign and multinational corporations. The contract between St Lucia and Amerada Hess, America's forty-third largest industrial corporation, well illustrates the dependent position of small island nations, such as those of the Eastern Caribbean, and 'it also suggests why planning tools like preconstruction social, economic, and environmental assessments are an exception for developing countries' (Koester, 1985: 277). The oil company put pressure on the St Lucia government to come to a quick decision on the proposed development at Cul de Sac by making obvious overtures to Bonaire about building it there. As we have seen in the case of Rodney Bay, even when dealing with a company from a small country such as Jamaica, a micro-state is often at a disadvantage. This extreme weakness and vulnerability is further illustrated by the adverse effect on Dominica's main industrial enterprise, manufacturing coconut products and soap, when Jamaica and some other importers in the region reduced their demand (Dominica/UNDP, 1985: 30).

Development problems associated with smallness and fragmentation, in terms of land area, population, wealth and power, have been mentioned frequently in this chapter, and are discussed at length elsewhere (Benedict, 1967; Connell, 1988; Farrell, 1982), with Connell focusing on Third World island micro-states. West Indian economist Trevor Farrell (1982: 7–13), identifies three groups of disadvantages which small states must face: the relatively limited range of activities in which they can engage; loss of 'agglomeration economies'; and 'the phenomenon where a small state finds itself needing to carry out the same range of functions as a large state, but not on the same scale' (ibid.: 9). All three sets of problems have serious implications for planning and development in the Caribbean, not least in the organization and deployment of local planning expertise in the region.

A small island state has as much need of highly qualified planning staff as a large country. Indeed, the enormous pressures on limited resources and the fragility of the ecosystems require the very highest level of expertise, and yet lack of funds makes this very difficult to pay for. Furthermore, while a small country may not need as many experts as a large state requires, certain activities, such as research and planning, often require a minimum scale of operation for the meeting of enough bright minds to achieve the best results. While it may not be practical to establish such a planning team in each island country, it might be possible to make better use of the highly qualified planners who are now scattered across the Commonwealth Eastern Caribbean. Perhaps there is merit in the suggestion that countries of the region combine 'to create a team of peripatetic planners – a planning equivalent of the West Indies cricket team' (Hudson, 1984).

Many scholars believe that ultimately successful solutions to problems of development in the Eastern Caribbean depend on greater economic and political integration. Bentley Browne (1985: 141) is not exceptional in believing that his country 'cannot survive alone and must seek greater levels of interdependence with Caribbean and other third world states'. Farrell (1982: 22–3) argues that 'production/resource integration in the Caribbean will ultimately and inescapably demand political integration at some level', warning that, without achieving this in the foreseeable future, 'the developmental effort of the LDC's is *ceteris paribus* going to be that much more difficult, and some pessimism about its eventual success is hard to avoid'. Recognition of this by economists, political scientists and planners in the region may, perhaps, give cause for optimism.

ACKNOWLEDGEMENTS

The author gratefully acknowledges the assistance of West Indian planners, librarians and others who kindly provided information and gave other invaluable help in gathering material for this chapter. Special thanks are due to the staff of the Geography Department and Library of the University of the West Indies, Mona, and to Carlton Frederick, Bentley Browne and Mervin Williams for their kind co-operation and hospitality. The generous assistance of the Queensland University of Technology, which granted the author leave and travel expenses for research in the West Indies, is also very gratefully acknowledged.

REFERENCES

Anon (1981) 'About this issue . . .', *Ambio*, **10**, 6: 272.

Aspinall, A. (1935) *The Pocket Guide to the West Indies*, London: Sifton, Praed and Co. Ltd.

Atwood, T. (1791) *The History of the Island of Dominica*, 1971 facsim. edn., London: Frank Cass and Co. Ltd.

Beekhuis, J. (1981) 'Tourism in the Caribbean: impacts on the economic, social and natural environments', *Ambio*, **10**: 325–31.

Benedict, B. (1967) *Problems of Smaller Territories*, London: Athlone Press.

Bishop, M. (n.d.) *Selected Speeches 1979–1981*, Havana: Casa de las Américas.

Bishop, M. (1982) *Forward Ever! Three Years of the Grenadian Revolution*, Sydney: Pathfinder Press.

Blaize, H.A. (1985) 'Budget speech to the House of Representatives, Grenada, 26 April 1985', St George's: Government of Grenada.

Breen, H.H. (1844) *St Lucia. Historical, Statistical and Descriptive*, 1970 facsim. edn., London: Frank Cass and Co. Ltd.

Britton, S. and Clarke, W.C. (eds) (1987) *Ambiguous alternative: Tourism in Small Developing Countries*, Suva: University of the South Pacific.

Browne, B.A. (1985) 'The environment, planning and development in small island states. The case of St Vincent and the Grenadines WI', unpubl. MA dissertation, Institute of Planning Studies, University of Nottingham.

Carrington, E. and Blake, B. (1976) 'Tourism as a vehicle for Caribbean economic development', in: Caribbean Tourism Research Centre, *Economic Impact of Tourism*, Barbados.

Coke, T. (1810) *A History of the West Indies*, Vol. 2, 1971 facsim. edn., London: Frank Cass and Co. Ltd.

Connell, J. (1988) *Sovereignty and Survival. Island Microstates in the Third World*, Research Monograph No. 3, Department of Geography, University of Sydney.

Davy, J. (1854) *The West Indies Before and Since Slave Emancipation*, 1971 facsim. edn., London: Frank Cass and Co. Ltd.

Devas, R.P. (1974) *A History of the Island of Grenada, 1498–1786*, St George's, Grenada: Carenage Press.

Dominica/UNDP (1976) *Dominica National Structure Plan 1976–1990*, Roseau: Dominica.

Dominica/UNDP (1985) *Commonwealth of Dominica National Structure Plan 1985*, prepared by the Economic Development Unit with the assistance of UNDP/UNCHS. Project DMI/81/003.

Dwyer, D.J. (1975) *People and Housing in Third World Cities*, London and New York: Longman.

Davy, J. (1854) *The West Indies Before and Since Slave Emancipation*, 1971 facsim. edn., London: Frank Cass and Co. Ltd.

Devas, R.P. (1974) *A History of the Island of Grenada, 1498–1786*, St George's, Grenada: Carenage Press.

Dominica/UNDP (1976) *Dominica National Structure Plan 1976–1990*, Roseau: Dominica.

Dominica/UNDP (1985) *Commonwealth of Dominica National Structure Plan 1985*, prepared by the Economic Development Unit with the assistance of UNDP/UNCHS. Project DMI/81/003.

Dwyer, D.J. (1975) *People and Housing in Third World Cities*, London and New York: Longman.

ECNAMP (1983) 'Outline of the management alternatives for the Levera area', prepared by the Eastern Caribbean Natural Area Management Program and presented at the Environmental Conservation Workshop, St George's, Grenada, March 1983.

Farrell, T.M.A. (1982) *Small Size, Technology and Development Strategy*, Research Paper No. 4, Department of Economics, University of the West Indies, St Augustine, Trinidad and Tobago.

France, Republic of (1985) *St Vincent and the Grenadines: Economic, Financial and Social Situation*, Ministry of Foreign Relations, Co-operation and Development.

Frederick, C. (1987) 'An evaluation of physical/environmental planning and development control in Grenada: 1955–1985', unpublished MA dissertation, Institute of Planning Studies, University of Nottingham.

Gaile, G.L. and Hanink, D.M. (1984) 'Caribbean airline connectivity and development', *Caribbean Geography*, 1: 272–83.

Grenada/UNDP (1977) *Grenada. Proposed Physical Area Development Strategy 1977–1990*, prepared for the Government of Grenada by the United Nations Physical Planning Unit in association with the Ministry of Communications and Works, St George's, Grenada.

Hawkins, I. (1976) *The Changing Face of the Caribbean*, Bridgetown, Barbados: Cedar Press.

Honychurch, L. (1984) *The Dominica Story: a History of the Island*, Roseau: The Dominica Institute.

Hope, K.R. (1983) 'Urban population growth in the Caribbean', *Cities*, 1: 167–74.

Hudson, B.J. (1980) 'Urbanization and planning in the West Indies', *Caribbean Quarterly*, **26**: 1–17.

Hudson, B.J. (1983) 'Grenada's new international airport', *Caribbean Geography*, **1**: 51–7.

Hudson, B.J. (1984) 'Human resources for physical planning in Caribbean territories. The experience of Grenada'. Paper presented to the Regional Conference of Physical Planners, University of the West Indies, Mona, Jamaica, 19–22 September, 1984.

Hudson, B.J. (1986) 'Landscape as resource for national development: a Caribbean view', *Geography*, **71**: 116–21.

Hudson, B.J. (1987) 'Tourism and landscape in Jamaica and Grenada', in: Britton, S. and Clarke, W.C. *op. cit.* 46–60.

ICFTU/CCL (1986) *An Economic Policy for the Caribbean*, International Confederation of Free Trade Unions/Caribbean Congress of Labour Conference and Special Session of the General Council, Barbados Workers' Union Labour College, Barbados, April 1986.

Jackson, I. (1985) 'Upgrading tourism-related facilities in downtown and harbourfront areas in Antigua and Barbuda, Dominica, Grenada, St Christopher and Nevis, Saint Lucia, and Saint Vincent and the Grenadines', in: OAS, *Improving Tourism-related Facilities in Downtown and Harbourfront Areas*, 71 et seq.

Jules, D. (1986) 'A note on environmental and conservation policy in revolutionary Grenada', *African Environment* 'Hors-serie', Caribbean Environment No. 2,279–90.

Koester, S.K. (1985) 'Industrial development from a marginal point of view: the effects of a petroleum project on a rural economy', in: Geoghegan, T. (ed.), *Proceedings of the Caribbean Seminar on Environmental Impact Assessment*, Institute for Resource and Environmental Studies, Dalhousie University, Halifax, NS and Caribbean Conservation Association, St Michael, Barbados, 270–8.

Koester, S.K. (1986) 'From plantation agriculture to oil storage: economic development and social and economic marginalization', *African Environment* 'Hors-serie', Caribbean Environment No. 2: 229–50.

Latin America and Caribbean 1984, World of Information, Saffron Walden.

Macpherson, J. (1980) *Caribbean Lands* (fourth edition), Trinidad and Jamaica: Longman Caribbean.

Montserrat/UNDP (1976) *Montserrat National Physical Plan Vol. 1, Written Statement*, St Lucia: UNDP Physical Planning Project.

Mulchansingh, V. (1988) Personal communication.

Nanton, P. (1983) 'The changing pattern of state control in St Vincent and the Grenadines', in: Ambursley, F. and Cohen, R. (eds) *Crisis in the Caribbean*, Kingston, Port of Spain, London: Heinemann.

OAS (1985) *Improving Tourism-related Facilities in Downtown and Harbourfront Areas*. Final Report of OAS Regional Workshop, St John's, Antigua and Barbuda, 16–20 September 1985. Organization of American States, Executive Secretariat for Economic and Social Affairs, Department of Regional Development, Washington DC.

Olwig, K.F. (1980) 'National parks, tourism and local development. A West Indian case', *Human Organization*, **39**: 22–31.

Olwig, K.F. and Olwig, K. (1979) 'Underdevelopment and the development of "Natural Park" ideology', *Antipode*, 11: 16–25.

Potter, R.B. (1985) *Urbanisation and Planning in the Third World*, London and Sydney: Croom Helm.

Putney, A.D. (1982) *Survey of Conservation Priorities in the Lesser Antilles. Final Report*, Caribbean Conservation Association, Caribbean Environment Technical Report No. 1. St Croix: ECNAMP.

Renard, Y. (ed.) (n.d.) *Perceptions of the Environment*, Barbados: Caribbean Conservation Association.

Renard, Y. (1988) Personal communication, ECNAMP.

Richards, V.A. (1983) 'Decolonization in Antigua: its impact on agriculture and tourism', in: Henry, P. and Stone, C. (eds) *The Newer Caribbean. Decolonization, Democracy and Development*, Philadelphia: Institute for the Study of Human Issues.

Ringel, G. and Wylie, J.(n.d.) 'God's work: perception of the environment in Dominica', in: Renard, Y. (ed.) *op. cit.*, 39–50.

Rojas, E. and Meganck, R.A. (1987) 'Land distribution and land development in the Eastern Caribbean', *Land Use Policy*, 4: 157–67.

St Lucia/UNDP (1977) *St Lucia National Plan*, Castries Government of St Lucia.

St Vincent Central Planning Division (1986) *St Vincent and the Grenadines Development Plan 1986–1988*, Kingstown: Ministry of Finance and Planning.

St Vincent/UNDP (1976) *St Vincent National development Plan 1976–1990 Vol. 1, Survey and Analysis*. Prepared for the Government of St Vincent by the UNDP Physical Planning Project, St Lucia.

Sheppard, J. (1986) 'The Caribbean Conservation Association', *African Environment*, 'Hors-serie', Caribbean Environment No. 2, 351–4.

Smith, A. (1988) Personal communication from the Director, Budget and Planning Division, Ministry of Finance, St George's, Grenada.

Soler, F. (1987a) *Development Control and Physical Planning: The Case of the Commonwealth of Dominica*, Organization of American States Department of Regional Development. Organization of Eastern Caribbean States Natural Resources Management Project. Economic Base Resource Management Plurinational Project.

Soler, F. (1987b) *Development Control and Physical Planning: The Case of St Kitts and Nevis*, OAS.

Soler, F. (1987c) *Development Control and Physical Planning: The case of Antigua and Barbuda*, OAS.

Towle, E.L. (1985) 'St Lucia–Rodney Bay/Gros Islet', in: Geoghegan, T. (ed.) *op. cit.*, 228–43.

UNDP (1977) *United Nations Development Programme Assistance in Physical Planning (Phase III) Caribbean: Multi-island Country Project*, New York United Nations.

World Bank (1986) *Grenada Updating Economic Memorandum*, Report N. 6292, GRD.

World Bank (1987) *World Development Report 1987*, New York: Oxford University Press.

[9]
Belize

G.M. Robinson
and
P.A. Furley

The 1981 Census of Belize recorded the country's population as being 160,000 or just seven people per sq km. Even allowing for a degree of under-enumeration, these figures immediately set Belize apart from most of its Caribbean neighbours. For example, although it is twice the area of Jamaica, it has only 7 per cent of Jamaica's population. With a total surface area of 8,867 sq miles (22,700 sq km), it is larger than all of the ex-British Caribbean islands put together. Furthermore, there are large uninhabited areas of the country, although, like neighbouring Petén in Guatemala and the Yucatán Peninsula in Mexico, they represent the *despoplados* or regions depopulated since late-Mayan times. Consequently, there is relatively little pressure of population upon available resources at present. Nevertheless, with nearly one-third of the inhabitants living in the major settlement, Belize City, and around 55 per cent of the population classed as urban, the country has some of the urban problems, albeit on a smaller scale, that are found in the more populous Caribbean states.

A pronounced feature is the concentration of people in the larger settlements on the coast, the chief exceptions being the closely settled rural population in the Belize River valley and the flatter northern plains. The current distribution of population reflects a recent history of movement from the littoral towards the interior, the reverse pattern to that of the ancient Mayan New Empire which was centred in the heartlands of the Petén and Yucatán. In addition, Belize has the distinction of having established a new planned capital, Belmopan, which is currently one of the world's smallest with only 4,000 people, and also has a significant proportion of its citizens living outside the country, mostly in the United States.

The nature of the problems associated with the growth of Belize City and the planning of Belmopan form two of the main elements of this chapter. However, emphasis is also placed upon the economic development of the country, which is related to the pattern of urban settlements. The basis of the economy has been the export of primary produce: timber under early colonial rule and, more recently, sugar cane and citrus fruit. As a consequence, all developments have started on the coast and subsequently penetrated inland. The growth of the main port, Belize City, has been tied to the primary sector, and the country's prosperity has depended upon overseas markets.

The nature of urbanization in Belize can be approached, therefore, by means of an analysis of the settlement pattern and an examination of the nature of its overseas dependence. Attempts to diversify the economy in recent years are considered as a means of highlighting the impact of government policies on resource use and the settlement system.

The Evolution of the Settlement Pattern

Estimates place the population of Belize at half a million in the tenth century (Coe, 1971; Turner and Harrison, 1983), but this had fallen to under 50,000 at the time of the Spanish Conquest of Middle America in the sixteenth century. The Spanish never occupied and settled the area of present-day Belize, though Spanish armies may have passed close by in Guatemala. Depopulation, which was partly a result of the population migrations resulting from the decline of the established Mayan centres over hundreds of years, was accelerated by disease contracted and subsequently spread by the colonists. Today the Maya Indians, who once had complex settlements such as Altun Ha and Xunantunich, based on intensive 'raised bed' and milpa farming, represent only a small element in the Belizean population. The Mestizos, a cross between the Indians and the Spanish, form the predominant group (Table 9.1). When British traders first began to show an interest in the timber and logwood to be found along the Yucatán coast in the seventeenth century, there was a very small indigenous population in the area. The Spanish opposed any permanent British presence, but by the 1650s, there were small British settlements extracting logwood along the eastern coast of the Yucatán, including some in the vicinity of the Belize River (Waddell, 1961).

These settlements therefore evolved on the coast, from which there was penetration inland by river, particularly along the Belize River Valley. In the first half of the eighteenth century, exports of logwood from the Belize River Valley to Britain gradually increased and were then succeeded by exports of mahogany which became popular for both furniture and shipbuilding. Under various Anglo-Spanish treaties, permanent British settlement was prohibited, though boundaries of 'the

Table 1. Population by ethnic group and district in Belize, 1980.

Ethnic groups	Districts and percentage of total population						
	Belize	Corozal	Orange Walk	Stann Creek	Toledo	Cayo	Total
Creole	75.1	16.1	11.3	32.9	11.9	31.0	40.0
Mestizo	13.1	58.4	64.5	10.5	5.9	49.0	33.4
Garifuna (Carib)	3.2	2.3	2.3	45.6	12.7	1.9	7.6
Maya	0.7	13.8	6.8	5.2	25.4	4.6	6.8
White	1.1	1.7	13.5	0.5	1.0	8.0	4.2
Kekchi	0.1	0.3	0.2	0.2	31.5	0.4	2.7
East Indian	1.5	2.9	0.2	2.0	8.6	1.1	2.1
Others	5.2	4.5	1.2	3.1	3.0	4.0	3.2
Total	100.0	100.0	100.0	100.0	100.0	100.0	100.0

Sources: Ministry of Education, Belize (1984); Regional Census Co-ordinating Committee (RCCC) (1984).

British settlement of Honduras' were described in Treaties in 1783 and 1786. When Mexico and Guatemala achieved independence from Spain in the 1820s, British settlers were cutting timber over an area from the Rio Hondo in the north to the Sarstoon River in the south (Figure 9.1). These boundaries, plus a north–south line between the two rivers, have been the ones claimed consistently from 1835 onwards by Britain, but disputed by Guatemala despite the 1849 Anglo-Guatemalan Commercial Treaty and the 1859 Anglo-Guatemalan Treaty (Bianchi, 1959; Bolland and Shoman, 1977).

Despite disputes with Spain in the eighteenth century and bans on permanent settlement, a rough census of the semi-permanent coastal population in 1823 recorded 5,178 people, including 216 'whites' and 2,468 'slaves'. The latter had originated in Africa, while other settlers included black Carib Indians and Yucatecan Indians. Just 25 years later a similar census, in what was now known as British Honduras, enumerated approximately 25,000 people, reflecting the growth of the mahogany trade (at its peak in 1845) and an influx of migrants, including Yucatecan, Kekchi and Mopan-mayan Indians, who were fleeing the unrest in other Central American countries (Dobson, 1973: 243–5). The majority of the population were Creoles, a term used in Belize to refer to those of African descent, and mostly the descendants of slaves brought into the country to work the timber reserves.

Although the greater number of new settlers worked in the mahogany and logwood industry, smallholders spread into areas not cultivated since the days of the Mayan civilization. From 1838, land

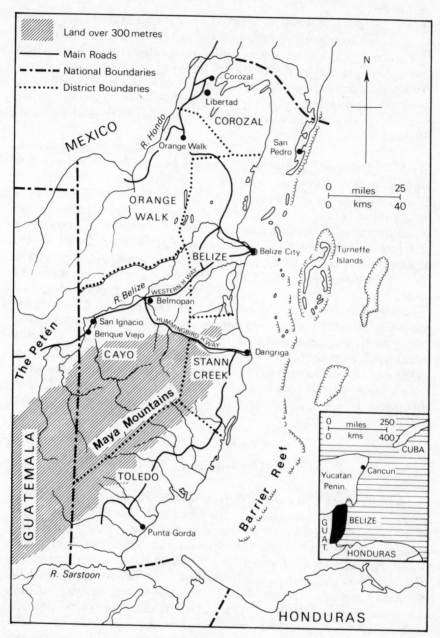

Figure 9.1. Belize: location map.

grants and sales of land for cultivation were authorized. In 1859, a Lands Title Registry was established and in 1872, regulation was placed on Crown Lands. Unfortunately, as land was 'alienated' in large blocks and at high prices, small farmers and prospective immigrants found it extremely difficult to acquire land. In addition, much land went into the hands of owners interested in exploiting timber reserves, and this tended to retard permanent settlement over substantial parts of the interior (Bolland, 1977).

As exports of mahogany and logwood declined, more attention was focused upon agricultural production for which no traditional base had been developed. Numerous settlement schemes based on exploiting the country's agricultural potential were begun, only to fail through poor organization and a lack of understanding of the particular constraints posed by the environment. However, both the number of settlements and farm exports increased steadily during the second half of the nineteenth century. For example, by 1867, there were four sugar estates along the Sittee River, one in the south of the country and six in the north. But with most of the labour engaged in the timber trade, East Indians had to be imported to assist with the cane harvest. This added to the polyglot nature of the population as did an influx of 1,200 black immigrants from Jamaica and Barbados in the 1880s to work on newly established banana plantations. Other schemes involving Chinese, Italians and Germans proved less successful, but descendants of many of these groups, together with families of Middle East traders and a few permanent British immigrants, can be found throughout the country today.

Population Growth and Distribution

In 1900, the population was just over 37,000. It doubled in the next 50 years and then doubled again in the next 25 (Figure 9.2). During this time, Belize City remained the largest single centre of population, but gradually more land in the interior was brought under cultivation. Major agricultural developments were limited though, as much of the best land was alienated. Despite the fact that Crown Land could be purchased cheaply, few small farmers were willing or able to buy unimproved land. However, from 1945 a 'Location Ticket' system enabled farmers to purchase land through annual cash instalments and the demonstration of satisfactory husbandry of the land over a five-year period. Four main areas of agricultural settlement developed (Figures 9.1 and 9.3):

(1) *Northern Belize*: Growth occurred initially through colonization in the nineteenth century by Yucatecan Indians, and from the 1930s by sugar cane growers. In 1937, the colony was awarded an export quota of

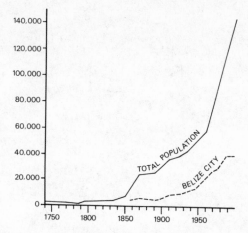

Figure 9.2. Population growth in Belize, 1740–1990.

1,000 tons of sugar per annum in the International Sugar Agreement. Subsequently, sugar production assumed a much more important role in the country's economy, replacing timber as the most valuable export commodity in the 1950s. For some years, only one major refinery was in operation (at Libertad), but a second was opened in the 1960s near Orange Walk Town by the British firm, Tate and Lyle, thereby helping to treble output within 12 years. The number of growers increased from 196 in 1954 to 2,153 in 1969, and the small towns of Corozal (1980 population: 6,862) and Orange Walk (1980 population: 8,441) grew as market and administrative centres (Black, 1972).

(2) *The Stann Creek Valley*, inland from Dangriga along what is now the Hummingbird Highway. The principal settlement, Dangriga (1980 population: 6,627), on the coast 50 km (30 miles) south of Belize City, was one of several locations selected along the Caribbean coast of Central America by Carib Indians or Garifuna. 'The Caribs are descended from the original Red Carib Amerindians who occupied many of the West Indian islands when they were discovered by Columbus' (Dobson, 1973: 255). Inter-marriage between the Caribs or Garifuna and the Creoles has produced the present-day Black Carib community of Belize, which has been established in the country since 1797 when they were expelled from their homes in Dominica and St Vincent.

In the hinterland of Dangriga, many experimental schemes growing tropical crops under the plantation system were tried unsuccessfully before citrus production flourished, partly through exports of orange juice concentrate to Britain during World War II. International companies have dominated production, although much of the production has been achieved by small growers (Bull, 1972).

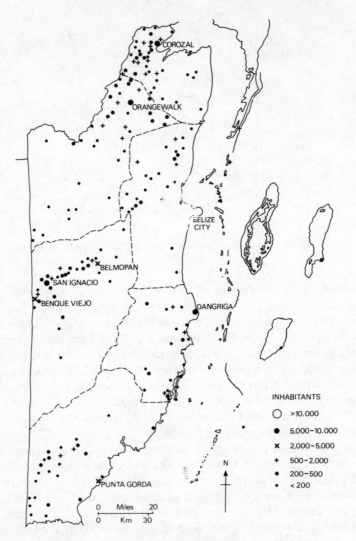

Figure 9.3. The distribution of settlements in Belize.

(3) *The Belize River Valley*: Settlement has been largely restricted to the upper part of the Valley, within 50 km (30 miles) of the Guatemalan border. This area is sufficiently far inland to avoid the worst effects of the frequent hurricanes which affect the Belizean coast, and it also lies beyond the low-lying, swampy coastal plain which would require extensive drainage for productive commercial agriculture. Agriculture has developed in the western half of the Valley on a mixture of alluvial deposits and soils derived partly from the Mayan Mountains and partly

from the extensive limestones which underly the northern half of the country (Jenkin *et al.*, 1976; Robinson, 1983a). These support a range of tropical crops, though the typical staples have been maize and beans. The crops are grown on smallholdings, 50 per cent of which were recorded as being under 4 ha (10 acres) in the 1973/4 Agricultural Census. However, the extension of the Location Ticket system, promoting holdings of at least 20 ha (50 acres), has increased both the area cultivated and the size of holding (Robinson, 1983b, 1985a). The opening of the Western Highway from Belize City to the Guatemalan border in 1954 also stimulated agricultural development as well as the movement of settlement from along the river to the road. Hence, the road is now the main focus for a series of small villages with populations under 300, such as Teakettle, Ontario Village and Georgetown, and river traffic has been replaced by road haulage. The 1949 bridge over the river at San Ignacio, the capital of Cayo District, marked the start of this transformation and contributed to the growth of this small town (1980 population: 5,606) as a market centre for the western part of the Valley. Ten kilometres (6 miles) closer to Guatemala, Benque Viejo del Carmen (1980 population: 2,466) has assumed a similar function.

The Belize Valley has two further distinctive features which developed post-1945: a large area occupied by Mennonite groups, and the country's new capital, Belmopan. The Mennonites arrived from North America and Mexico in the 1950s, and with a 46,540 ha (115,000 acres) allocation of land at Spanish Lookout, farm with modern agricultural techniques using motorized equipment (Everitt, 1983; Sawatzky, 1971). Today, the Mennonites in the Belize Valley and in two other large colonies in the north of the country, dominate commercial production of poultry-meat and eggs, supplying Belize City and much of the Belize River Valley. The Mennonites are also the only commercial dairy producers, those at Spanish Lookout supplying pasteurised milk to Belize City and Belmopan (Robinson, 1983a: 56–7).

Belmopan, the capital of Belize, is an artificial creation, following the destruction caused by Hurricane Hattie in 1961. Belize City suffered from severe flooding and damage to property, and it was felt that government offices should be relocated some distance inland, away from the main destructive force of violent storms. The decision to create a new capital, 80 km (50 miles) inland, was also an attempt to encourage a new pole of economic growth around an important road junction and perhaps provide an inland counterbalance to the dominance of Belize City. In 1970, when the new residences in Belmopan were first occupied, the population of the new capital was just under 3,000 (Furley, 1971; Kearns, 1973). This has hardly changed subsequently (1980 population: 2,932), though there are believed to be at least 1,000 illegal refugees who have settled around its forested outskirts. However, the presence of the new capital has succeeded in stimulating agricultural production in this part of the Belize Valley and has developed a small market for farm produce.

(4) *Toledo*: The southernmost part of Belize is also the most inaccessible, the most constantly humid, and the area containing the greatest concentration of Indians. The Indians, living in designated reserves, represent a number of Mayan groups (principally Mopan and Kekchi), many of whom have moved into Belize during the past 150 years seeking a safe haven away from various disputes in neighbouring countries. Much of the agriculture in Toledo District is for subsistence purposes only, and is reliant upon hand-tool methods. The largest settlement is Punta Gorda (1980 population: 2,219), the district capital, from which a ferry service runs to Livingston in Guatemala.

Although Belize's population has increased rapidly in the last three decades, much of the country remains sparsely populated. Since the 1920s, half of the population has lived in the seven largest towns, and the rural population has also been concentrated within the four settlement zones described above. The Maya Mountains, occupying over one-quarter of the country, provide a major area of undeveloped land while coastal and some inland swamps and large parts of the western and north-western borders are also little settled. This comparative lack of pressure of population upon resources distinguishes Belize from many of its Caribbean neighbours. However, with them, it shares a rapid increase in population, reaching 21 per cent in the 1970s, though this official figure is probably an under-estimate. There are also growing numbers of young dependants – 58 per cent were under 20 years of age in 1980 compared with 49 per cent in 1946 (Ministry of Education, 1984: 31).

The character of the settlements in the country is clearly related to the predominance of one or other of the ethnic groups. Thus, the Mestizo areas have largely Hispanic-looking towns, often around a central plaza (a notable example was San Ignacio before its recent destructive fire). The Creole areas have a close mesh of either indigenous organic growth or colonial grid-iron streets reminiscent of much of the Caribbean, while the Indian settlements stretch back from a central, and usually clear, communal area. The current distribution of the main ethnic groups as indicated by primary spoken languages, illustrates this diversity (Figure 9.4). Of the six administrative districts of the country, only Belize, containing Belize City, has an English-speaking majority, although many of the coastal inhabitants are also predominantly English-speaking. In the two northern districts, Spanish-speaking Mestizos predominate while in Stann Creek there is a significant Carib or Garifuna element, and, in Toledo, Mayan and other Indian groups are important (Table 9.1). This multi-ethnic and multi-cultural character

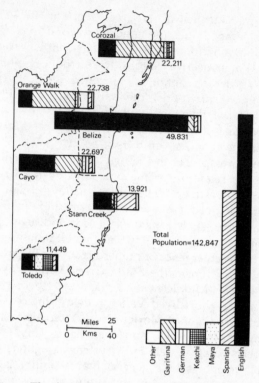

Figure 9.4. The distribution of ethnic groups in Belize by district.

has been further accentuated by the recent influx of refugees from El Salvador and Guatemala. These have been largely Mestizo and Indian groups, and they have tipped the balance of the population in favour of Spanish-speaking Catholics. Increasingly, the Creoles of Belize City are becoming an island of the English-speaking Caribbean as Spanish Central America absorbs rural Belize (Bolland, 1986).

The Economy

As suggested earlier, the settlement pattern and the nature of urban centres closely reflect the development of the economy. Throughout the nineteenth and early twentieth centuries the export of timber and timber products to Britain dominated the economy. Outside Crown Lands, timber companies dominated, and agricultural and other forms of development were limited. Belize City was the one urban growth point as it represented the main entry point and port. However, the timber industry was part of a 'robber economy' in which extraction dominated over the proper management of resources (Dobson, 1973: 126–34). The timber industry slumped once the larger hardwoods has been removed and it was not until a national Forestry Department was formed in 1922 that there was a concerted effort to introduce intensive forest management in order to obtain a sustained yield. Even then, the emphasis was upon softwoods, the hardwoods having never been systematically replaced. The fact that in the 1920s timber still accounted for around 90 per cent of the colony's exports, indicates the low level of diversification in the economy up to that point.

Agricultural development in the first half of the twentieth century was limited by the retention of the best land by the Crown and by insufficient capital investment. The larger, mainly foreign, landowners controlled plantation production which generated irregular exports of a range of tropical crops, such as bananas, cocoa and sugar. None of this production stimulated large-scale settlement, although growing sugar production led to the emergence of numerous small villages in the north, and the citrus production in the Stann Creek Valley gave rise to the plantation village of Middlesex and increased the size of smaller settlements along the short-lived Valley railway. Internal communications were limited, roads into Mexico and Guatemala were little more than muddy and rutted tracks, and even Belize City could only be served from ocean-going vessels by a system of lighters. The limited nature of development and its general inaccessibility is summarized aptly in the often quoted comment by Aldous Huxley in the 1930s, 'If the world had any ends, British Honduras would be one of them.' It is only with the great increase in transport (particularly by air) and telecommunications (especially satellite television) over the past decade that this isolation has been overcome.

The barrier of inaccessibility has been broken down only gradually, but major economic changes post-1945 have transformed the Belizean economy at least in terms of increasing agricultural exports and developing a small manufacturing sector. The International Sugar Agreement of 1937 awarded British Honduras a quota of 1,000 tons of sugar per annum and helped to encourage regular production. In the 1950s, further quota arrangements with the United States and the Commonwealth Sugar Agreement encouraged modest expansion. But sugar did not become the chief earner of export revenue until the British firm, Tate and Lyle, invested in Belize in the 1960s. Increased sugar prices and the need for the United States to seek new supplies, following the loss of its Cuban canefields, promoted expansion. Tate and Lyle's subsidiary, Belize Sugar Industries Ltd. (BSI), established a new refinery and extended cane-growing to a large part of northern Belize (Figure 9.5).

The result was dramatic in that, by 1970, sugar represented 40 per

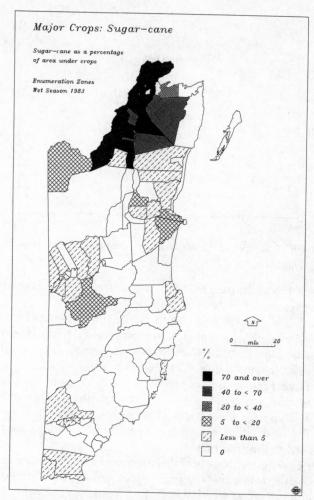

Figure 9.5.   The distribution of sugarcane in Belize, 1983.

cent of total exports by value and the numerous small settlements of the northern plains expanded rapidly. Output continued to rise in the 1970s (Figure 9.6). However, this represents the classic situation of heavy reliance upon a fluctuating world market, and in the 1980s, prices fell, reducing revenue to both refiners and cane-growers. BSI has sold off virtually all its own caneland so that production is now dominated by private growers, mostly smallholders, the majority producing less than 300 tons per annum. A more substantial cost-cutting measure by BSI was the recent sale of the older of its two refineries (at Libertad) to

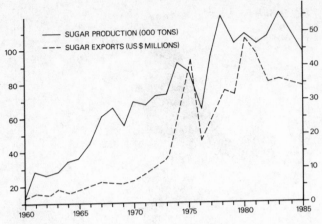

Figure 9.6.   Belize's production and export of sugar, 1960–85.

Petrojam, a Jamaican firm that will use sugar cane to make ethanol for export to the United States.

The other export crop to rise to greater prominence from the 1960s has been citrus. Again, subsidiaries of foreign firms dominated the expansion of citrus production, the firms having large estates in the Stann Creek Valley (Figure 9.7). As with sugar production, Belizean interests have now assumed greater control of both the growing of grapefruits and oranges as well as processing. Improved harbour facilities at Dangriga have assisted an increased export of both frozen orange juice and citrus concentrates, but the volatility of the world market is still a limiting factor.

Other changes within the Belizean economy have come about from the early 1960s, following the granting of full internal self-government in 1964, and the change of name from British Honduras to Belize. The newly elected government produced a Development Plan for the remainder of the 1960s, expressing the intention of supporting domestic agriculture. Subsequently, and with later Development Plans, production of food for the domestic market has been increased, though with significant imports continuing even of tropical foods. The 1964 Plan and its successors encouraged small, semi-commercial producers through measures aimed at regulating marketing, reducing the amount of alienated land and guaranteeing security of tenure. For example, the 1966 Rural Land Utilization Tax exempted all smallholdings under 40 ha (100 acres) as well as land which had been permanently improved. It also increased taxes on unimproved lands in order to discourage absentee landowners. Further stimulus was given to the Location Ticket system enabling farmers to purchase land by annual cash instalments

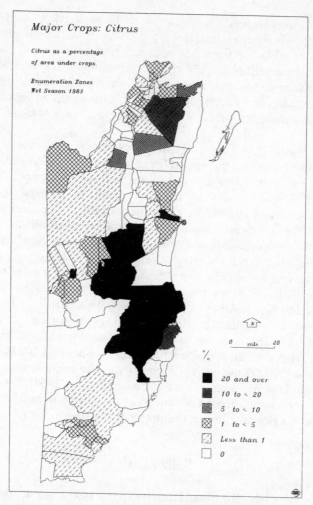

Major Crops: Citrus

Citrus as a percentage of area under crops

Enumeration Zones Wet Season 1983

0   mls   20

°/₀

■ 20 and over

▨ 10 to < 20

▦ 5 to < 10

▨ 1 to < 5

▨ Less than 1

□ 0

Figure 9.7. The distribution of citrus crops in Belize, 1983.

(Bennett and Furley, 1986). Having cultivated the land successfully for five years while making the necessary payments, the land was then surveyed, plans registered and a Crown Grant awarded. This scheme had its greatest effects in the Belize Valley, though many of the farmers here farm only on a part-time basis. More recently, further encouragement to smallholders has been given by allowing squatters to establish certain rights to Crown Land after a period of continuous occupation of land.

The encouragement to domestic food production has had only a gradual influence upon economic development. In such a small market as Belize, a few traders have dominated the market, with limited numbers of wholesalers/retailers purchasing from large numbers of producers. In addition, there has been much trading of fruit, vegetables and poultry by smallholders direct to the consumers. A greater degree of commercialization has characterized the smallholder sector during the past two decades, but a high proportion of farmers are either only semi-commercial producers or farm on only a part-time basis (Robinson, 1985a; 1985b).

There has been relatively limited development of manufacturing industry. For example, the hoped-for growth of an industrial estate in Belmopan has not materialized beyond a few workshops. Thus the revenue from the export of primary products is used to import manufactured goods, especially consumer durables. The chief manufacturing activity is located in Belize City in the forms of out-worker production of clothing, and the manufacture of beer and cigarettes. Increasingly, the tourist industry is being regarded as a major potential growth area and in recent government plans receives a priority second only to agricultural development. The country's attractions are being championed in North America by the national Tourist Board: 'We have the Caribbean Sea, Barrier Reef, crystal clear waters, snorkelling, diving, Maya ruins, mountains, caves, thousand foot waterfalls . . .' Gradually, the number of visitors has risen – to around 100,000 in 1984 and perhaps 150,000 currently – especially to the offshore coral islands, the Cays, and the main resort of San Pedro (Pearce, 1984). Some of this tourist development has also produced an expansion in hotel accommodation and tourist facilities in the major town, Belize City.

Belize City

Belize City is nearly five times larger than the next biggest urban centre in the country and houses between half and one-third of the country's population. This dominance was established from the foundation of the settlement as the only major port for the small colony, though until the mid-nineteenth century it was merely 'a trading post attached to a massive timber reserve' (Bolland, 1977: 6). Its site was not a promising one: on swampy ground, barely above sea level, among the distributaries of the Belize River. Some sources refer to the town being established on land only elevated above sea level by a base of mahogany chips and gin bottles! However, it was from this point that access could be gained to the Belize River and the interior. The initial alluvial and estuarine site of the town was around the distributary, Haulover Creek, but subsequent growth involved laborious infilling of mangrove swamp, encouraged by some periodic government funding, and draining,

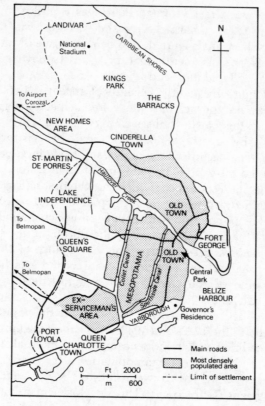

Figure 9.8. Belize City.

notably the construction of the Burdon Canal in the 1930s. The town is surrounded on three sides by the sea (Figure 9.8) and at no point is it more than a few feet above sea level. The susceptibility to hurricane damage and the difficulty of providing proper drainage have given a particularly storm-battered character to the settlement. Hurricane Hattie in 1961 inundated the settlement to a depth of some 5 metres (15 feet), demolishing about one-third of the buildings and severely damaging a further third.

Despite the disadvantageous site, some substantial buildings were erected in the nineteenth century. These included large merchants' houses, a Government House on the sea-front, still an imposing white-painted residence, several churches and St John's Cathedral, 'the first Protestant Episcopal Church founded in Spanish America' (Lewis, 1976: 2). Indeed, in the Victorian 'heydays', travellers such as Stephens (1841) looked upon Belize as the bastion of controlled government and civilized living in the region. The main area of settlement was to the south of Haulover Creek, though there was a bridge built across the Creek and, in 1815, a barracks for the garrison was established on the northern side. Canals were dug to help improve drainage, but little development in the nineteenth century seems to have prevented such descriptions as 'dilapidated' and 'dirty' (Burdon, 1934). New building was required quite frequently because of repeated fires amongst the wooden houses, but the lack of suitable land helped limit spatial growth. The dense packing of the houses and poor sanitation helped foster disease, and the portrayal of the town by visitors was often unfavourable. The decline of the mahogany trade increased unemployment and limited the capital available in the country to invest in improvements to the main settlement which, for the first half of the twentieth century, remained a down-at-heel, dilapidated and remote outpost of British rule. The population had remained overwhelmingly Creole, the descendants of the original slave population brought into the country to work the timber resources. This ethnic dominance of the Creoles has continued throughout the twentieth century and has helped to give Belize City some of the character of a mini-Kingston, Jamaica, or Georgetown, Guyana.

Change to Belize City was brought about by population growth and, eventually in the 1970s and 1980s, some increased prosperity. Both of these factors have had an influence upon the internal structure of the city. For example, the increase in population after World War I and the return of war veterans led to expansion to the west and south of the original settlement (Old Town). This development involved construction of a new canal to assist drainage and some further infilling. The area settled reflected its site in its name, and with canals on three sides, was known as Mesopotamia. This was a high-density housing area with 1,000 dwellings accommodating 6,000 people on 28 ha (70 acres) (Everitt, 1985: 100). At the same time, land to the north of the Creek was reclaimed to form the Fort George area which extended the harbour frontage east of the Old Town (Figure 9.8).

In 1931, a major hurricane caused widespread destruction, especially in Mesopotamia (Anderson, 1952: 32), but this prompted a loan from the Imperial Treasury and some major rebuilding which included drainage improvements. The quality of some of the housing was upgraded, but the character of Belize City remained largely unchanged. It stayed a small urban centre, its population concentrated in a limited area, with narrow streets, poor sanitation, with most older buildings storm-battered alongside their distinctive steel water tanks and vats, and it was a town lacking industry. At that time Belize City was 'a commercial town which lived on the merchant business connected with the forest industries, by arranging and financing exports and providing for imports of food supply' (Grant, 1976: 68).

However, World War II brought about several changes to Belize City and to the country as a whole. A number of Belizeans served overseas, not necessarily in the military; for instance a group from the Forest Service went to Scotland where they released local foresters for war service. The returning Belizeans, and changes in attitude resulting from greater communication with the outside world, accompanied a minor economic surge resulting from war-time demand.

Post-1945, major change has accompanied the increased rate of population growth and, recently, greater wealth and some economic diversity. The first of a series of extensions of the built-up area came in the early-1950s when Cinderella Town, King's Park and Caribbean Shores (Figure 9.8) were built on landfill sites to help overcome the acute housing shortage. Cinderella Town was a government-financed scheme offering homes on hire-purchase. In contrast, Caribbean Shores comprised stone-built houses designed by private architects for government ministers, merchants and businessmen. This development has remained physically separate from the rest of Belize City (Everitt, 1985: 104). The post-1945 equivalent of Mesopotamia, though on a smaller scale, was built to the south-west of the city, but proved highly susceptible to flooding.

In 1955, a Housing and Planning Department was formed as part of the national administration. Its early survey work reported on the many problems faced by Belize City, but it took few steps to stimulate remedial action. Instead, it was Hurricane Hattie in 1961 that prompted not only the foundation of a new inland capital, but also rebuilding in Belize City (Everitt, 1984). Some of the rebuilding reduced the congestion south of Haulover Creek by adding new housing north of Cinderella Town and along the road towards the airport. The former development, King's Park, added to the initial 1940s growth in this area and is a combination of government-funded houses and large private residences. Part of this expansion was a leasehold scheme, with the option to buy at some future date upon fulfilment of the conditions of the lease. However, in 1980, such tenure accounted for only 2.5 per cent of the total number of households in Belize City, compared with 36 per cent for private freehold and 48 per cent rented from private owners (Farazli and Leathem, 1987: 112).

More recently, expansion has occurred towards the International Airport, northwards along the coast and southwards to the new deep-water docking area. However, Belize City still suffers from a growing housing deficit. This totals at least 5,000 houses according to a recent ministerial estimate, which complained about the lack of overseas donors willing to provide the type of long-term loan required to make a large-scale housing policy viable (*The Courier*, 101 (1987), p. 18). Even so, major investment from the Canadian government has facilitated substantial improvements to roads and drainage within the town in the 1980s.

Belize City in the 1980s is still largely an overcrowded, compact and isolated town – not much different from the childhood memories of Zee Edgell in her novel *Beka Lamb* (1982) set in the 1950s. It has developed some more affluent suburbs, such as King's Park and Caribbean Shores, but much of the town is still poor and densely populated, with people living in a variety of West Indian two-storey 'cottage-design' housing common throughout the British Caribbean. Although influenced increasingly by American tastes and capital, Belize City has been little altered by twentieth century technology, despite the widespread acquisition of television.

> Still, the majority of Belizeans live in the cramped quarters of the old town, linked to the city's core and to each other by their feet. Regularly blown down by tropical storms, the city stubbornly rights itself while maintaining its familiar form. (Price, 1987: 14)

Formal development planning for Belize City has been lacking, though this has been recognized by government since Belize attained its independence in 1981 (Robinson and Furley, 1983). A physical development plan is intended for the city for the early 1990s and a preliminary study has been commissioned as an initial step (Farazli and Leathem, 1987). This study highlights the general lack of use of basic urban land management (see Dunkerley, 1983), and also illustrates the growing role, post-1945, of particular agencies in shaping the urban form. The most important government agency has been the Central Housing and Planning Authority (CHPA), under the jurisdiction of the Ministry of Housing. The CHPA has implemented city ordinances relating to building standards, drainage, water supply and sewerage, thereby introducing minimum design standards for new development. Similarly, the City Council has increased its own powers to regulate development. Other agencies, such as the six credit unions in Belize City and government finance organizations, have encouraged the building of better privately owned residences. However, until a detailed development plan for the city is implemented, both the acute housing shortage and the necessary infrastructure for economic growth will not begin to be addressed in a systematic fashion.

Belmopan and the District Capitals

As indicated earlier, Belmopan was constructed as a direct response to the devastation of Hurricane Hattie in 1961, but also because of an existing awareness of a need to encourage growth outside the coastal zone and to relieve the problems faced by Belize City (Ministry of Overseas Development, 1974). There was also a political drive to build a new capital by the newly elected People's United Party under George Price, the Premier at that time. A Reconstruction and Development Corporation was established to oversee both the repair to hurricane damaged properties and the installation of the new capital. The building of Belmopan, aided by a loan from the British government, cost less than £6 million. However, although there were comprehensive site surveys and the location was strategically sound (Furley, 1971), there were few if any long-term resource or planning evaluations on the impact or likely development of the new capital. Furthermore, some of the initial plans, for example for a university, were unrealistic in all but the long-term period, and finances were insufficient to establish much in the way of social or economic infrastructure.

There are several respects in which the building of Belmopan has achieved its original objectives and a number of ways in which it has failed. There is little doubt that it is a safer, better constructed capital than Belize City. It acted as a focus for the drive towards independence, and a base from which the newly established nation of Belize could evolve. It has ample space for future development and infilling, and is well located with regard to the main highways (existing and planned) and the country's main river valley. The establishment of the capital has given new impetus to the upgrading and metalling of the road system, particularly the Western Highway from Belize City to the Guatemalan border near Benque Viejo, the Northern Highway to the Mexican border at Santa Elena, the Hummingbird Highway, which is a top priority for upgrading at present, from Belmopan to Dangriga and thence via the Southern Highway to the Toledo District.

However, Belmopan has not grown to the extent originally envisaged. A series of growth stages had been planned, from a starting point of 5,000 inhabitants in 1972 to an equilibrium of 25,000 to 30,000, mainly by siphoning off people from crowded Belize City (Everitt, 1984: 140). Recent estimates suggest that the population is still less than that intended in the initial stages of development. Belmopan was built as the seat of government, and while it now houses the National Assembly and government offices, there has been little development of other sources of employment. The new housing is not traditional to Belize and it has tended to be too expensive for low-wage earners, although, more recently, lower cost housing units have been built. It has not proved a counter-attraction to Belize City, partly because the latter has itself improved in terms of better and more varied housing, better drainage and sanitation, better communications and port facilities, but also because there have not been the devastating storms of earlier decades to exert a critical 'push' to would-be migrants. This situation could change rapidly, but, without some 'pull' of industrial and commercial employment opportunities, the growth of Belmopan will depend upon 'push' factors (storms, unacceptable crowding and poor conditions). These are not the best providers of migrants for Belmopan when compared with the advantages of North America which is attracting significant numbers of Belizean migrants – official estimates record over 25,000 since 1970.

The lack of planning to provide employment, for example, the processing of agricultural produce for which the local region is well suited, was noted in an evaluation in the mid-1970s (Ministry of Overseas Development, 1974), and has scarcely changed since. Belmopan has not proved a counter-attraction to the primacy of Belize City, which is unlikely to lose its predominance as a trading and commercial centre. One of the main problems is the small population, both of the region around Belmopan and of the country as a whole. There is therefore a very limited internal market. It is difficult to see medium- or large-scale investment in agro-business concerns being attracted to the area at present, and, in any case, their presence would be totally out of proportion to the modest level of development. In this respect it is perhaps as well that Belmopan reflects the scale of the country and is in a position to adjust flexibly to change.

The remaining urban settlements in Belize are essentially the capitals of the six administrative districts. Belize City is itself a capital of one of the districts, but the remaining five are important in marketing and social terms and have minor central business district functions.

Corozal (Corozal District) lies on an attractive coastal bay site, 13 km (8 miles) south of the Mexican border. Its proximity to the fast-developing Mexican town of Chetumal and to agricultural and tourist developments in the Mexican state of Quintana Roo, have given it a recent filip and added an entrepreneurial role to its old administrative status. It has always had a considerable Mestizo population and strong links with Mexico. The sugar refinery at Libertad symbolizes the region's relationship with the fate of the sugar industry, which may now be resurrected by the refinery's recent take over by a Jamaican firm intending to produce ethanol.

Orange Walk Town (Orange Walk District) is the current centre of the sugar industry, with the remaining sugar refinery and increasingly diversified agricultural activities, including, it is widely believed, the lucrative trade in marijuana. The greatly improved Northern Highway now permits rapid transport and communication with Belize City. The projected link road between Belmopan and the Northern Highway is also likely to influence the development of Orange Walk.

San Ignacio (Cayo District) is another inland town, at a crossing point of the Belize River. Until 1949, the town was reached by boat from

Belize City, a journey which could take many days upstream at low water. The Western Highway now permits rapid travel along the length of the main river valley and its potentially rich agricultural hinterland. The town and its smaller neighbour, Benque Viejo, may achieve greater importance if the political dispute with Guatemala can be resolved, permitting the trade of goods into the Petén, which is most easily approached from the Belize River Valley.

Dangriga (Stann Creek District) lies at the mouth of the Stann Creek river and was the natural shipping point for the production of citrus. It was one of several Carib settlements located on this coast. Once reliant upon a small railway along the valley, it is now connected by the Hummingbird Highway to Belmopan, although its natural direction of trade is by sea. The lack of a deep-water channel and port facilities make future development unlikely and the town would seem to have to depend upon lighters for some years to come.

Punta Gorda (Toledo District) is the most southerly and isolated of the District capitals. Although it has a good coastal site, its remoteness from the rest of the country and the relative lack of development, until recently, of its hinterland, much of it being an Indian Reserve, has meant that it has shown the least growth of the major settlements in Belize. However, there have been a number of recent changes which are affecting the area. These include the continued upgrading of the Southern Highway along which a number of tourist and agricultural development projects have taken place, for example, the Toledo Rural Development Project and work by Britain's Overseas Development Authority, which is looking at ways of improving agricultural production, particularly that of rice (King et al., 1986). Although the area may grow in economic importance and is strategically significant, the distance from the Belmopan–Belize City axis may inhibit growth in the short term.

Conclusion

Belize has developed more by accident than design. Although the evolution of the pattern of settlement from the coast inland does follow, in general terms, Taaffe, Morrill and Gould's (1963) model of port and transport development, much of the growth has been adventitious and the notion of longer-term development planning has really only taken hold since the 1960s.

Two factors determine the urban pattern – the historical colonization from the coastal littoral, and the changing focus of the economy over time. Within this pattern, there are different ethnic and social patterns. The Mestizo, Indian, Creole and Carib groups have engendered subtly different features in the broad structure of settlement.

Different waves of economic development have left their mark – the early timber and logwood industry is perhaps least evident today, but survives in the mills of the Haulover Creek area and in the small softwood centre of San Luis in the Maya Mountains. The sugar industry has left an inheritance of numerous dispersed villages, a settlement pattern quite unlike any other part of Belize. The citrus industry has had little impact outside the long narrow strip of the Stann Creek Valley, but its associated settlements are distinctive – seasonal plantation villages such as Middlesex, the scattered settlements along the main road, the canning factories at Melinda, and the port outlet for Dangriga. The growth of indigenous agriculture has produced a number of village communities, generally with less than 500 people. However, outside investment has also had an impact on the settlement pattern, for example, rice production in Toledo District, the scattered banana plantations in Stann Creek and Toledo Districts, the Hershey cocoa plantations along the Hummingbird Highway, the land colonization scheme of the United Nations High Commission for Refugees (Valley of Peace, near Roaring Creek). In contrast, the Mennonite settlements at Spanish Lookout near San Ignacio and at Blue Creek in the north-west have added a European/North American style of landscape to the countryside.

It is also possible to identify the probably short-lived British military presence in the major installations close to the International Airport and in smaller scattered camps throughout the country. Most recently, there has been a strengthening of some coastal settlement through the growth and success of fishing and the establishment of fishing co-operatives. Finally, perhaps the most powerful impact on urban settlement will be the growth of tourism. Tourism has resulted in the growth of hotel accommodation in the small resort of San Pedro on Ambergris Cay, and has affected the success and growth of the International Airport and internal air system, the development of hotels in Belize City, Belmopan and the district capitals, and in the growth of service industries. The scale may be slight but the impact on such a small population has been striking over the past 20 to 30 years (Pearce, 1984).

In contrast to one of its near neighbours of similar size, El Salvador, Belize is a nearly empty country. It has grown extremely slowly but has the diversity of natural regions and the framework of a modern transportation network to form a sound base for successful development. Its lack of natural resources, the principal reason for slow growth, may have saved it from some of the excesses exhibited in other parts of Middle America. The promise of more detailed future planning of economic and urban growth may mark a significant change in Belize's development. However, after less than a decade of independence, it is perhaps too soon to expect Belize to break away from its dependence on the export of primary produce and overseas investment to bring about even limited economic growth.

REFERENCES

Anderson, A.H. (1952) *Brief Sketch of Belize*, Government Printing Office, British Honduras.

Bennett, A. and Furley, P.A. (1986) 'Land tenure, land colonization and re-settlement in Belize', 7–71, in: Furley, P.A. and Robinson, G.M. (eds) 'The Agricultural Census of Belize, Part Two: Land colonization and the adoption of new crops', *Occasional Publications, Dept. of Geography, University of Edinburgh*, No. 3.

Bianchi, W.J. (1959) *Belize: the Controversy between Guatamala and Great Britain over the Territory of British Honduras in Central America*, Las Americas Publishing Co., New York.

Black, I.H. (1972) 'The state of the sugar cane industry in Belize', 132–51, in: Furley, P.A. (ed.) *University of Edinburgh Expedition to Central America, 1970: General Report*, Dept. of Geography, Univ. of Edinburgh.

Bolland, O.N. (1977) *The Formation of a Colonial Society: Belize from Conquest to Crown Colony*, Johns Hopkins University Press, Baltimore.

Bolland, O.N. (1986) *Belize: A New Nation in Central America*, Westview Press, Boulder, Colorado.

Bolland, O.N. and Shoman, A. (1977) *Land in Belize, 1766–1871*, Kingston Institute of Social and Economic Research, University of the West Indies, Mona.

Bull, C.J. (1972) 'The small scale citrus grower in British Honduras', 110–31, in: Furley, P.A. (ed.) *University of Edinburgh Expedition to Central America, 1970: General Report*, Dept. of Geography, Univ. of Edinburgh.

Burdon, J.A. (1934) *The Archives of British Honduras*, Sifton Praed, London.

Coe, M.D. (1971) *The Maya*, Pelican Books, Harmondsworth.

Dobson, N. (1973) *A History of Belize*, Longman Caribbean, Trinidad and Jamaica.

Dunkerley, H.B. (ed.) (1983) *Urban Land Policy: Issues and Opportunities*, World Bank/Oxford University Press, Oxford.

Edgell, Z. (1982) *Beka Lamb*, Heinemann, London.

Everitt, J.C. (1983) 'Mennonites in Belize', *Journal of Cultural Geography*, 3: 82–93.

Everitt, J.C. (1984) 'Belmopan, dream and reality: a study of the other planned capital in Latin America', *Revista Geográfica*, 99: 135–44.

Everitt, J.C. (1985) 'The growth and development of Belize City', *Journal of Latin American Studies*, 18: 75–111.

Farazli, C. and Leathem, T. (1987) *Belize City: Background Planning Study*, School of Urban Planning, McGill University, Montreal.

Furley, P.A. (1971) 'A capital waits for its country', *Geographical Magazine*, 43: 713–20.

Grant, C.H. (1976) *The Making of Modern Belize: Politics, Society and British Colonialism in Central America*, Cambridge University Press, Cambridge.

Jenkin, R.N., Innes, R.R., Dunsmore, J.R., Walker, S.H., Birchall, C.J. and Briggs, J.S. (1976) 'The agricultural development potential of the Belize Valley, Belize', *Land Resource Study, Minist. Overseas Dev.*, No. 24.

Kearns, K.C. (1973) 'Belmopan: perspective on a new capital', *Geographical Review*, 63: 147–69.

King, R.B., Baillie, I.C., Bissett, P.G., Grimble, R.J., Johnson, M.S. and Silva, G.L. (1986) *Land Resource Survey of Toledo District, Belize*, Land Resources Development Centre, Overseas Development Administration, Surbiton.

Lewis, D.G. (1976) *The History of St John's Cathedral, Belize*, Cubola Publications, Belize.

Ministry of Education, Belize (1984) *Belize Today – a Society in Transformation*, Sunshine Books Ltd, Belize City.

Ministry of Overseas Development, UK (MOD), (1974) *Belmopan: An Ex-post Evaluation*, MOD, London.

Pearce, D.G. (1984) 'Planning for tourism in Belize', *Geographical Review*, 74: 291–303.

Price, M.D. (1987) 'The persistent neglect of Belize City', *Focus*, 37 (4): 10–14.

Regional Census Co-ordinating Committee (RCCC) (1984) *1980–1981 Population Census of the Commonwealth Caribbean*, Caribbean Community Secretariat, Port of Spain.

Robinson, G.M. (1983a) 'The agricultural geography of Belize', 21–74, in: Robinson, G.M. and Furley, P.A. (eds) *Resources and Development in Belize*, Dept. of Geography, Univ. of Edinburgh.

Robinson, G.M. (1983b) 'Smallholder agriculture in the Belize Valley', 75–98, in: Robinson, G.M. and Furley, P.A. (eds) *Resources and Development in Belize*, Dept. of Geography, University of Edinburgh.

Robinson, G.M. (1985a) 'Agricultural change in the Belize River Valley', *Caribbean Geography*, 2: 33–44.

Robinson, G.M. (1985b) 'Agricultural innovation: the example of peanut-growing in the Belize Valley, Central America', *Singapore Journal of Tropical Geography*, 6: 116–26.

Robinson, G.M. and Furley, P.A. (1983) 'An independent Belize', *Geography*, 68: 43–6.

Sawatzky, H.L. (1971) *They sought a country: Mennonite Colonization in Mexico*, University of California Press; Berkeley.

Stephens, J.L. (1841) *Incidents of Travel in Central America, Chiapas and Yucatan*, Harper and Bros., New York, 2 vols.

Taaffe, E.J., Morrill, R. and Gould, P.R. (1963) 'Transport expansion in underdeveloped countries: a comparative analysis', *Geographical Review*, 53: 503–29.

Turner, B.L. and Harrison, P.D. (eds) (1983) *Pulltrouser Swamp: Ancient Maya Habitat, Agriculture and Settlement in Northern Belize*, University of Texas Press, Austin.

Waddell, D.A.G. (1961) *British Honduras: A Historical and Contemporary Survey*, Oxford University Press, London.

[10]

The French West Indies

Albert L. Gastmann
and
Scott MacDonald

Introduction

The increase in urban areas in the Developing World since World War II has been spectacular. This itself has been a result of the rapid rise in population and of the consequences of modern technology which have had a tremendous impact on the manner in which economic development has taken place in the nations and territories of Asia, Africa, Latin America and the Caribbean. The French tropical Antillean islands of Martinique and Guadeloupe, situated in the latter area, are no exception to this pattern, although their linkages to France have had a profound impact on the particular urbanization processes they have experienced. In March 1946, these islands, together with Réunion in the Indian Ocean and French Guiana in South America, voted to become Overseas Departments (*départements d'Outre-mer* or DOMs), which constitutionally, administratively, economically, and in part culturally, made them integral parts of the French nation-state. The relationship is theoretically equal to that between Hawaii and the United States. While this kept Martinique and Guadeloupe within the French fold during a period of liberation and independence elsewhere in the developing World, it also meant that France was to infuse substantial amounts of capital into the two Caribbean DOMs with the intention of making them as French as possible. The 'joining' of these Caribbean islands to European France has had a tremendous and ongoing influence on the nature of their socio-political and economic evolution, of which urbanization has been a significant offshoot.

The archipelago of Guadeloupe covers 1,780 square kilometres or approximately 583 square miles. Guadeloupe proper is formed by two islands, Basse Terre and Grande Terre separated by a narrow sea channel, the Rivière Salée (Figure 10.1). Nine-tenths of this department's population, which was 328,400 according to the census of 1982, live on

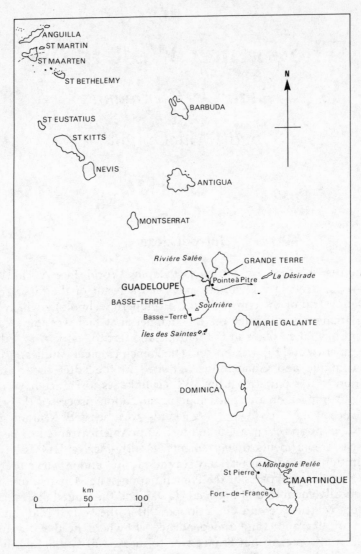

Figure 10.1. The French West Indies: location map.

these two islands. The rest live on the smaller islands of the archipelago which are known as Marie-Galante, La Désirade, and the tiny rocky islands of Les Saintes. Two hundred kilometres further north there are two more islands belonging to this conglomeration: St Bartholemew and St Martin. Half of the latter is a Netherlands dependency. Although the population density of Guadeloupe is great, being 184 inhabitants per square kilometre, it is exceeded greatly by that of Martinique which has

298 per square kilometre. The size of this latter island is 1,100 square kilometres or about 420 square miles, and its population in 1982 stood at 328,566. As both Guadeloupe and Martinique consist of high volcanic mountains, and in many areas along the coast large mangrove swamps, the areas that can be inhabited and cultivated are much smaller than the above statistics tend to indicate.

The historical evolution of urbanization on these islands was primarily influenced in the early years by their plantation economy. This economic structure has been dramatically changed in the post-World War II period, bringing about a new relationship between urban and rural areas. In the French Antilles, as in much of Latin America and the Caribbean, this was the most dynamic period of urban growth, including the development of shanty towns, urban spread, and efforts at urban renewal. While it is important to be aware of commonalities shared with the rest of the Caribbean, it is also important to understand that the nature of the relationship with France has added a different element due to that country's considerably greater wealth of resources to shape (or seek to shape) the region's development.

Historical Background

Martinique and Guadeloupe were originally inhabited by the Caribs who were driven out by the Europeans in the early 1600s. Settled by the French, the islands developed as major sugar producers, especially after Portuguese Jews and Dutch refugees arrived from Brazil with new production technology in the 1640s and 1650s. Society was thereafter dominated by the plantation system which, for its operation, needed vast numbers of African slaves. This created a social pyramid, with the small white planter class (often referred to as the *Grands Blancs*) at the top, under which was a small white-urban middle class (also known as the *Petits Blancs*). In time, the petits blancs were joined as a proto-middle class by mulattos, the offspring of European and African blood. The vast black rural majority of the population was at the bottom of the pyramid, providing most of the plantations' labour.

The first urban centres in Martinique and Guadeloupe were small port cities through which trade with France and Africa was conducted and which also functioned as administrative centres of both the civil and religious authorities. The mercantilist system, by which France sought to reap the benefits of the colonies, made these small ports the major link in the chain between the sugar plantations and the lucrative European markets. The oldest port cities in the French Caribbean are St Pierre on Martinique and Basse Terre on the Guadeloupean island of the same name (see Figure 10.1). The former was founded by Pierre Belain d'Esnambuc who took the island for France in 1635 and named the town he founded after his patron saint. Basse Terre was founded in 1643 by Charles Houel, the proprietor of the island. It stood in the shadows of Fort Saint Charles whose guns protected the small town in its early years and whose scenic views today are one of the major tourist attractions of the island. Although St Pierre and Basse Terre were the first urban centres of significance, they were both overshadowed in time by two other cities, Fort Royal on Martinique and Pointe-à-Pitre on Guadeloupe. After the French Revolution, the former became known as Fort de France.

In 1669, Governor General Jean Charles de Baas moved the capital of the French Antilles from St Kitts, where the earliest French settlement had been, to Fort Royal, Martinique. He did not choose St Pierre, the island's major port and commercial centre, because he felt that it was not well enough protected, and could easily be captured by enemy forces. Fort Royal grew in a half circle around the harbour which was easily defensible by Fort Saint Louis standing on the peninsula at its entrance. Pointe-à-Pitre was founded in 1759 by the English who captured and occupied the island of Guadeloupe during the Seven Years War. The name, which means Pieter's Point, derives from a Dutch Jewish refugee, who had settled there in 1654 after receiving permission from the aforementioned owner and governor of the island, Houël. Some merchants built their homes and warehouses here because the ships lying on its roadstead were well protected by the guns of nearby Fort Louis, but it was the English who actually developed it into a truly urban centre. From 1763, when the French again took possession of Guadeloupe, until the present, the city expanded in new forms to become with its twin city, Les Abymes, the major urban complex of the island. Pointe-à-Pitre, as well as Fort de France, St Pierre and Basse Terre, grew in the eighteenth century, not only because all the trade with France passed through these four port cities, but also because some French artisans established small handicraft industries here. In time, these cities attracted the growing mulatto class who worked for the artisans or started their own shops.

St Pierre was, throughout the eighteenth and nineteenth century, the centre of finance of the Antillean islands. This resulted in its having the largest white population and being the most prosperous and well developed city in the French Caribbean possessions. It was in those years the centre of the Béké élite, the name by which indigenous whites are known on Martinique. Here French commissioners and traders handled the credit facilities for the plantocracy of the islands of the Lesser Antilles, and acted as factors in the exporting of sugar and the importing of plantation supplies, and in the earlier days also slaves (Sleeman, 1986).

As the planters of Martinique were the closest to the sources of finance in St Pierre, they had the opportunity in many cases of becoming economically independent in their own right. This, as the writer on Martinique plantation economy Jean Crusol (1973) indicates, had the effect, unlike that which happened on the other islands, of preventing the transfer of estates in Martinique into the hands of the Metropolitan mercantile interests.

From early colonial days onward there also came into existence on these islands, besides the four major cities, smaller towns known as bourgs. The bourg, according to a very wide definition, was a small township directly linked to the plantation system. They developed along the major thoroughfares of the islands at a distance of about 10 kilometres or six miles from one another. Here in the days of the monarchy were the church and sometimes institutions of the religious orders to serve the spiritual and worldly needs of parishioners, including education and at least a rudimentary form of health care. Furthermore, the royal authorities entrusted with maintaining law and order were stationed here as well as the functionaries in charge of the documents on fiscal and other matters concerning the plantations (Bertile, 1985: 25).

During the period between the 1790s and the 1840s, the pattern of urbanization in the French islands changed considerably. Influenced by the ideas and consequences of the American and French revolutions, this period witnessed fundamental changes in the colonial administration and in attitudes towards slavery (Knight, 1978: 17). The creation of the First French Republic had an enormous impact on church organizations. Many of them were disbanded and the services they rendered were taken over by civil authorities. The successful Haitian revolution had its repercussions on Martinique and Guadeloupe. One of the key figures here was Victor Hugues, a Jacobin and an ardent revolutionary who in 1794 was sent by the committee of Public Safety of the Assembly of the First Republic to the West Indies with a fleet transporting 1,150 revolutionary soldiers. His orders were to free the slaves and institute a republican form of government. When he arrived in the West Indies he discovered that the island of Guadeloupe was in British hands. With the help of the slaves whom he encouraged to rebel against the planters, Hugues managed to re-establish French rule. He then proceeded to destroy the planter élite. Most white members of this class in Guadeloupe were massacred, ending forever the power of the plantocracy (Chaleau, 1973: 210). The same did not happen on Martinique. There the békés and their British allies managed to keep Hugues and his forces at bay. As a consequence, the béké planters remained at the apex of colonial society in Martinique, and are to this day an influential élite.

Although Napoleon when he came to power reinstituted slavery, he and his successors could not crush the spirit of freedom that now existed on the islands. Louis Delgres, the mulatto officer who fought Napoleon's general Richepanse on Guadeloupe in 1802, preferred to die rather than to surrender. To this day, he is remembered on the island as the people's hero. The demand for the abolition of slavery remained strong on the islands and found its echo in France in the abolitionist societies. In 1836, the French politician and statesman Victor Schoelcher visited the West Indies and promised to abolish slavery and in 1848, when he was in the forefront of the establishment of the Second Republic, he succeeded in doing so. In his honour, a town in Martinique was named after him, and this is now a major suburb of Fort de France.

The fact that as a consequence of the Napoleonic years Martinique retained an élite class of whites, the *Grands Blancs*, meant that more luxurious quarters were built for the wealthy in St Pierre and Fort-de-France than in Basse Terre and Pointe-à-Pitre. Didier, an elegant suburb of Fort-de-France, is a good example of this (Bertile, 1985: 36). The abolition of slavery in 1848 made it possible for the plantation workers to leave the land and as time went by, more and more blacks moved to the cities and the so-called bourgs of the islands changed their character and size, and became small urban centres.

Partly through this, the Caribbean sugar industry underwent a profound depression as the owners of the plantations struggled to find cheap labour. They were also increasingly pressed in international markets by beet sugar competition in Europe. To offset these difficulties the French state intervened in the 1860s. This intervention especially benefited the béké élite of Martinique. A crucial piece of legislation was the establishment of the Crédit Colonial in 1861. The purpose of this organization was to provide loans to sugar syndicates or, as was mostly the case in Martinique, to individual proprietors so that sugar factories, in conformity with new technology in that industry, could be constructed in the French colonies and also assist in the modernization of the old sugar plants where possible (Minister of Colonial Affairs, 1860).

Michael Sleeman (1986), in his article 'Sugar in Barbados and Martinique', notes two important points about the legislation as related to the sugar industry in Martinique. Long-term credit for major capital projects was now available, which resulted in the construction of a central factory ('*usine centrale*') system. This was an important step since this intervention was especially beneficial for the *Grands Blancs*. It allowed the béké planters to modernize the local sugar sector and make it more cost efficient, thus giving them the opportunity to compete with beet sugar on the world market. The second important point for the Martiniquan plantocracy was that the creation of the Crédit Colonial made it possible for them not to lose their land to

Metropolitan creditors as they now had new capital resources at their disposal. Béké land owners could now join French commercial and industrial interests as equal partners in this venture of modernization (Minister of Colonial Affairs, 1860).

The changes in the sugar industry, in the 1860s, increased the pace of development for the bourgs. New central *usines*, of which there were 17 by 1884, were constructed in or around the bourgs of Martinique and made these towns important as local distribution and administrative points in the chain of production. The *usines* added an industrial element to the bourgs, complete with what can be called in very broad terms an agro-proletariat. The same happened on Guadeloupe. After the 1880s, however, new economic conditions affecting the production of sugar and other changes caused most of the bourgs to decline in importance. A few that in this century grew to important urban centres in Martinique were, among others, Rivière-Pilote and Morne-Vert (Bertile, 1985: 46). Others, like Schoelcher, became part of Greater Fort-de-France in Guadeloupe. Baie-Mahault and Le Gosier became part of the urban agglomeration of Pointe-à-Pitre-Abymes and Baillif and others of Basse Terre (Bertile, 1985: 47).

Competition in sugar production grew more fierce in the 1880s as cane sugar became an ever increasing export crop for Cuba, Peru, Indonesia, and other tropical and semi-tropical countries. Furthermore, in Europe beet sugar production was also increased. In those years it became evident that there was no easy answer to the lack of cheap labour. An attempt was made to recruit plantation workers from India, but the numbers that came to the French colonies were insignificant in comparison to those that went to the British Caribbean colonies of Guyana and Trinidad. Nevertheless, for the next half century, sugar remained the principal export for Martinique and Guadeloupe. Especially in the latter island, the large metropolitan companies managed to keep the operations going, even though some companies and individuals tried to replace sugar by growing with some success bananas and pineapples. In Martinique, several béké planters also became active in trying to cultivate these products.

As the abolition of slavery and the building of central *usines* caused the black plantation workers to drift to the bourgs, so the bleak years in the sugar economy of the last two decades of the nineteenth century caused the *usines centrales* to need fewer workers and the unemployed began to drift to the larger cities, specifically Fort-de-France and Pointe-à-Pitre in search of work. The bourgs lost their economic significance as the centres of production, and their commercial value also diminished and the exodus of workers accelerated. In the early decades of the twentieth century the transportation revolution caused people to leave at yet a quicker pace.

The rapid ascendency of the 'big city', the most amazing phenomenon of the present age, had been given its start.

As automobiles, buses and trucks were introduced, the communication infrastructure of the islands improved. Better transportation created new freedom for people, allowing them easier access to the attractions of the larger cities. This process became especially marked in the post-World War II period as more French public and private funds became available for modernizing the two cities, Fort-de-France and Pointe-à-Pitre. However, already prior to the war, new public building and commercial edifices had started to change the character of the administrative and business centres.

Historically, the development of Fort-de-France and Point-à-Pitre had been accompanied by tragic disasters. In 1890, a large fire destroyed Fort-de-France. Only in the Carenage section were the wooden houses of the previous era spared; the rest of the city had to be rebuilt from scratch. Most public buildings, and the cathedral, were constructed in or after 1895. Today some of the older houses are also to be found in the residential quarter of Didier on the hills above the city. Pointe-à-Pitre was almost completely destroyed in 1843 by an earthquake. It was quickly reconstructed and overtook completely Basse-Terre in importance. On Martinique, St Pierre remained the hub of commerce and the centre of the béké society until 1902. As much as 50 per cent of the white population lived here. In that year, the eruption of Mount Pelée, on whose foothills the city was built, buried it under waves of molten lava, mud and ash (Wright, 1976: 192). The impact of this catastrophe was to shift the business emphasis of the French islands away from St Pierre to Fort-de-France and Pointe-à-Pitre. New commercial houses were rapidly established in Fort-de-France by the *Grands Blancs*, who without the competition from the merchant interests in St Pierre gained a virtual monopoly 'in the tertiary sector' as agents of French enterprises, wholesalers and exporters (Sleeman, 1986: 70). Suddenly, the sleepy small town became a vibrant business centre. By the early 1920s, these *Grands Blancs* had established an 85 per cent share of the export trade and held a similar percentage in the town's business houses. In Guadeloupe, they also became the owners of between one-fifth and one-quarter of the island's land resources, as well as setting up commission houses, sugar factories, and distilleries.

The funds of the Crédit Colonial in the 1860s and later on those of other French financial institutions for assistance have made it possible for the béké élite of Martinique to remain in the economic driver's seat and to maintain and enjoy strategic alliances with the political, commercial and industrial élites in France (Sleeman, 1986). Because of the centralized structure of the French state, this gave the békés the capacity to influence significantly local politics, and behind the scenes to control much of the decision-making process of their island. The white inhabitants of Guadeloupe were far less influential as, since the days of the French Revolution, there was no important group of them that controlled the property and owned land in the manner the *Grands Blancs* did in Martinique. Since the middle of the nineteenth century, therefore, the expanding mulatto middle-class has gained political power in Guadeloupe. In Martinique, their participation in the political arena developed more slowly, and at a later date. After the establishment of the Third Republic in 1870, however, the possibilities for receiving a good education increased dramatically for those of Afro-European descent; this gave them momentum for upward social mobility and by the turn of the century, the mulattos began to play a more important political role owing to their ability to assimilate French culture (Wright, 1976: 174–7; Haliar, 1965: 31–2). They obtained not only positions in the administration, but also in the legal and medical professions. They started to look upon themselves as being the political leaders of the less advantaged blacks, who in large numbers remained rural and beyond the 'civilizing' influences of the cities, and where they were inhabitants of the urban environment were a poor and politically voiceless proletariat. The political influence of these blacks was not to become important until after World War II. The urban expansion and renewal which took place in the latter part of the nineteenth century and in the early decades of the twentieth was primarily for the benefit of the upper- and middle-status groups of the population. The *'gens de couleur'*, the mulattos, in government service or employed in the professions, built modest but decent middle-class homes adjacent to the old centres of the cities, and the wealthier among them had their homes constructed in sectors where the *Grands Blancs* were living.

The Urban Explosion, Development and Planning

When in 1946 Martinique and Guadeloupe became overseas departments (DOMs), the primary goal of the French government was to make social and economic conditions on the islands equal to those existing in France. How to achieve this has been the chief concern of the metropolitan authorities in the past 40 years. Major improvements, it was felt, were needed first in all forms of social services; second, in multiple aspects of infrastructure; and third, in ameliorating the poor housing conditions, both in the cities and in the rural areas. Urban planning for Fort-de-France and Pointe-à-Pitre was considered the primary step for attaining this goal. The populations of these cities were growing at a phenomenal rate in the post-World War II era due to the rural exodus and the large increase in the overall rate of population growth.

Fort-de-France and its suburbs grew between the years 1954 and 1982 from 58,763 to 97,814 inhabitants, and the twin city of Pointe-à-Pitre–Abymes and its suburbs from 57,300 to 107,149 (Bertile, 1985: 45–7). In the years after 1982, both have increased considerably in size and account for well over 40 per cent of the population of the respective islands.

The construction of new dwellings by the early 1950s was far too slow to house the new arrivals in the cities. At first they settled wherever possible into the dilapidated buildings found in the oldest sections of the urban centres. They were soon overcrowded and the newcomers started to squat on the marginal lands around the cities which were often public property. There they could build their shacks without building permits. However, those who found no plot, or who had some money, constructed or rented slum dwellings on privately owned lands. The 'bidonvilles', or shanty towns, that arose through these activities quickly became a major problem for local governments. During this time city planners on the islands received little money from France to tackle the urban crisis, because, as John Ardagh noted, the main emphasis on urban renewal was for the cities of France proper where there also was a terrible housing shortage owing to the neglect of the war years (Ardagh, 1982: 258). Nevertheless, when the situation became highly critical in the DOMs, the French parliament felt obliged to vote for funds for urban renewal of these territories in the mid-1950s. This was especially so as the new leaders in parliament such as Aime Cesaire who represented the black majority of the islands, did not fail to point out the discrepancy between living conditions in metropolitan France and in the Antilles. Earlier in 1952, the national government had provided for tax breaks for housing contributions.

The real push to do something in the Antilles, however, came after the visits of President Charles de Gaulle and of his Minister of State, André Malraux, in 1958 and 1960 respectively. He wanted the mushrooming shanty towns to be eliminated. Urban renewal plans were drawn up by his government. The most ambitious ones were for Pointe-à-Pitre where huge slum areas were demolished in the 1960s to make space for high-rise and other housing projects, as well as new administrative and other government institutions, and educational and health care centres. Private businesses were encouraged to construct new office buildings and to establish plants for small industries.

A comprehensive urbanization programme was not fully initiated, however, until 1964 when the inter-ministerial conference on urban renewal in Paris (FRU) approved the funds needed (Boquet, 1985: 80). The sections Henri IV, Malraux and Bergevin of Pointe-à-Pitre came into existence at this juncture. The realization of the projects here, and also the projects in other cities of the Antilles took many years. The people who had lived in the demolished areas were temporarily relocated in transitory housing arrangements. In Pointe-à-Pitre this involved about two-thirds of the population. Many of these people were worse off than they had been before in the years they had waited for new living quarters. Once they could move to the newly completed projects, new problems arose as many often found the new environment alien. In the shanty towns, although families had lived in a cramped environment, they often had a small plot at which they could even keep some chickens or rabbits. However, in the new buildings – often copies of those constructed for industrial cities in the northern climates – keeping animals in this manner was out of the question. Moving to these new buildings, mostly large blocks of flats with modern conveniences meant adopting a new kind of life-style which was contrary to the life-styles of these people. Where they had known their neighbours before (usually out of necessity or by lack of privacy), the new surroundings did not encourage the forging of such communal relations. In combination, all these factors meant that the physical maintenance of the buildings suffered, and the surroundings created alienation and not a genuine spirit of community collaboration. In the following decades and in subsequent projects, cultural aspects relating both to the people and the tropical environment were taken more into consideration.

Through the 1970s and 1980s, French building programmes continued, but the continuing influx of migrants to the cities made it impossible to successfully solve the housing problem. The French feeling and desire that the state should improve the standard of living in the French Caribbean to that characterizing Europe, and the projects implemented to achieve this, were harder to achieve than first thought. Many of the shanty towns constructed on hills or in swamps where conditions were detrimental to health remained. Nevertheless, many people moved to new dwellings which were a great improvement as far as hygiene was concerned. Between 1967 and 1982, housing units with running water increased in Guadeloupe from 47 per cent to a total of 69.4 per cent; in Martinique from 34 per cent to 78.5 per cent. Dwellings with modern toilet facilities increased in the former between 1967 to 1982 from 22 per cent to 55.7 per cent, and in the latter from 25 per cent to 63.3 per cent. Also in Guadeloupe there was a remarkable increase in homes having electricity. In 1967, 40 per cent of homes had electricity; in 1982 it was 77.2 per cent. In Martinique the level soared in those years from 32 per cent to 72.3 per cent (Bertile, 1985: 140–1). Nevertheless, even today, for one in two families of the low-income group, living conditions are still poor.

As the rural exodus in the 1950s was accelerated by continuing decline in sugar production, it meant that the principal reason for the poor coming to the cities was in search of work. However, the cities were the home of commercial and public administrative establishments and not of industrial enterprises or money earning service activities. Thus, newcomers were more often than not unable to find jobs. Long-term structural unemployment was the consequence and this created an unhealthy economic climate, which the French government finds difficult to resolve. The politically fragmented Caribbean does not form an economic market in which goods produced in the relatively high-wage areas of the French Antilles can compete. But France does not provide a market either for, as a member of the European Common Market, goods produced in Martinique and Guadeloupe are too expensive owing to transport costs and matters connected with these. For the highly urbanized labour, jobs consequently remain scarce in Fort-de-France and Pointe-à-Pitre and many families cannot afford the new dwellings for workmen. To have them pay rent, unemployment compensation would have to be raised. This remains a central problem, especially in the late 1980s. The Antillean situation is best reflected in the importance that the Social Security building has come to play in the life of most inhabitants of the islands. As Mort Rosenblum (1986: 379) noted of the Social Security building in Pointe-à-Pitre:

> And more than the church, that building symbolizes why
> independentistes face a long uphill struggle. When unemployment
> in the metropole hovers at nearly 10% in France, it is above 30%
> in Guadeloupe. Separatists blame that on Paris. But Guadeloupe
> produces almost nothing, and what jobs there are come largely
> from the government. Souvenir T-shirts are made in China; shells
> are packaged in the Philippines.

Although there was less money available for housing in the late 1980s, fortunately some building construction continued. This was largely due to the expansion in tourist activities. Beginning in the 1960s, the French islands became an increasingly popular tourist destination for visitors from the United States, Canada and Western Europe. The development of hotels and other tourist-related facilities has kept the construction industry occupied despite the decline in housing projects. Tourist-related construction has been particularly active in St Anne and Les Trois Illets in Martinique and in Le Gosier, St Francois, and other resort locations in Guadeloupe.

The smaller islands of St Martin and St Bartholemew have also profited from the development of tourism. With respect to the latter, an island of only 25 square kilometres where most of the 3,500 inhabitants are descendants of settlers from Normandy, the impact has been substantial. In the late 1960s, the tourist industry in the United States discovered the island, with long-standing implications. By 1980, the island had 19 hotels and was visited by more than 8,000 tourists a year. Moreover, many of the wealthier North American visitors built and maintain secondary residences on the island. The hotels and bungalows, together with the buildings housing the shops and other tourist facilities, have completely altered the physical aspect of Gustavia, the only town on the island.

Changes have also come to the economy of St Bartholemew. The tourist-oriented developmental mode has extended beyond the urbanization of the island. Traditional sectoral economic activity in fishing, salt mining and agriculture has been almost completely eliminated. In the late 1980s, 45 per cent of those working are in construction and most of the others are accounted for by the service industries connected with tourism. In addition, property values have risen from 5 francs per square metre in 1965 to 100 francs per square metre in 1970, 250 francs in 1980, and a few years later in some cases to over 400 francs (Bertile, 1985: 56).

The rapid upward spiral in real-estate prices was a trend shared throughout the French Antilles, including St Martin which had also become a popular tourist destination. On Guadeloupe and Martinique, the same trend was evident around certain beach front areas, but in a less spectacular fashion (Bertile, 1985: 56). These changes have had some positive aspects for the overall well-being of the French islands, but both economically and socially many of the consequences (for instance, the widening gap between the desire for property ownership and the capacity to reach such a goal) are negative for the majority of the people.

By the second half of the 1980s, urban expansion and urban renewal have slowed considerably in the French Antilles. The major reasons for this are: (a) that there is no longer strong population growth (the growth rate is under 1 per cent) and many of the younger people leave the islands to seek unemployment in France, hence the population remains relatively stable; (b) the rise in interest rates in France has diminished available credit for real estate and enterprise both in the private and public sectors; and (c) the costs of construction have risen steeply since the mid-1980s. Another important factor is that, in the present policies of the French government, centralized urbanization projects are no longer high priorities. The French government has instead opted to follow a policy that will bring about decongestion in the two major cities of the islands as well as the smaller urban areas. The focus is on the improvement of housing conditions in the rural areas. However, to remove the remaining bidonvilles around the major cities in the French Antilles, considerable urban renewal is still required and this remains one of the major political issues between Antillean and European Frenchmen.

The Antilles have made a gradual transformation from being predominantly rural societies to societies dominated by the urban sector. In this transformation, there has been a blurring of the lines that separated the 'village' and the 'city'. From the decline of sugar and the greater interlinking of the French Antilles with the wider international system, came the rise of consumerism, which had a distinctively urban orientation. All of this was symptomatic of the changing interrelationship between the countryside, as supplier of the means of subsistence, and the city, as a place of industry and commerce. The major shifts in the French Antilles, especially in the post-World War II era, were characterized by the decline of the countryside's role as supplier of the means of subsistence. What has replaced it has been an urbanized society, largely dependent upon imports from the metropole. This trend is likely to continue with the European Economic Community's move toward total market integration by 1992. There is some Antillean apprehension that competition for scarce jobs and business opportunities, mainly in the cities, will become even more competitive, especially within the tourist sector. In the latter, Antilleans have to compete with European French, some of whom are now settling in these overseas departments. Concern has been vocalized that if there is a 'flood' of white newcomers from the metropole and other EEC states, Antilleans could become alienated from the French political system and, perhaps more importantly, from the means of production. Development projects for the expansion of the tourist sector could become confrontational with overt racial overtones.

Conclusion

The French Antilles face the 1990s with many questions to be addressed, most of which are related to the ongoing nature of urbanization. Questions will be raised about ownership, continuation of housing programmes and the need for employment generation, especially in urban areas. The central element of planning in the French Antilles remains the problem of urban growth without employment-generation, related to industrial, agro-industrial, or service sector expansion. Directly related to this is concern about a possible wave of European newcomers, capable of purchasing and willing to purchase substantial tracts of the islands' property. The many grants provided by the French for housing and financial assistance to poorer families creates a dependency that causes an ambiguous perception of relations with the metropole. From a political viewpoint this creates a desire for greater autonomy and independence, especially among the younger generation.

At the same time, for economic reasons, the majority of Antilleans remain reluctant to loosen ties with the metropole.

REFERENCES

Ardagh, J. (1982) *France in the 1980s: The Definitive Book*, Harmondsworth, UK: Penguin Books.

Bertile, W. (1985) *Le Logement dans les Départements d'Outre Mer*, Paris: La Documentation française.

Boquet, M. (1985) 'La renovation de Pointe-à-Pitre', *Habitat – Les Dossiers de l'Outre-Mer*, Talence: Bulletin d'Information du CENADDOM, No. 78–9.

Chaleau, L. (1973) *Histoire Antillaise*, Point-à-Pitre: Emile Gros Desomeaux.

Crusol, J. (1973), 'La Martinique, economie de plantation et survol historique', *Les Cahiers du Cerag*, No. 28.

Haliar, A. (1965) *Dans les Départements d'Outre-Mer*, Paris: Editions Louis Soulanges.

Knight, F.W. (1978) *The Caribbean*, New York: Oxford University Press.

Minister of Colonial Affairs (1860): letter dated 8 September 1860, sent by the Minister of Colonial Affairs to the Minister of Agriculture, Commerce, and Public Works, Paris: Archives d'Outre-mer, General C32 D265.

Rosenblum, M. (1986) *Mission to Civilize: The French Way*, New York: Harcourt Brace Jovanovich.

Sleeman, M. (1986) 'Sugar in Barbados and Martinique: a socio-economic comparison', in: Paul Sutton (ed.), *Dual Legacies in the Contemporary Caribbean: Continuing Aspects of British and French Dominion*, London: Frank Cass and Co. Ltd.

Wright, E. (1976) *French Politics in the West Indies: A Study of the Assimilation Policy in the History of Martinique and Guadeloupe, 1789–1900*, Ann Arbor, Michigan: University Microfilms International.

[11]

The Bahamas

Thomas D. Boswell
and
James E. Biggs

Introduction

Urbanization in the Bahamas, especially the internal and international migration that has spawned the growth of Nassau and Freeport, is rooted in the overall character of this archipelagic republic. Encompassing 29 islands (22 of which are permanently settled), 661 cays, and about 2,387 rocks, it stretches some 760 miles in a south-easterly direction from approximately 50 miles off the south-eastern coast of Florida to about 90 miles from the south-eastern tip of Cuba (Figure 11.1). Its total land area is 13,864 square kilometres (5,353 square miles), about the same size as the state of Connecticut in the United States (Department of Statistics, 1988: 1).

Topographically, the Bahamas consist of low-lying islands and cays that are the products of limestone and sand accumulation. The highest elevation occurs on Cat Island and is only 206 feet above sea level. Karst landforms, complete with caves, sink holes (locally called 'blue holes'), and sub-surface drainage patterns typify the landscape.

Located astride the Tropic of Cancer, about one-third of the Bahamian islands lie within the tropics, whereas the remaining two-thirds are just north of this latitudinal belt. The prevailing climate is of the tropical savanna variety, with approximately 75 per cent of rainfall occurring during the summer months of May through to October. The annual precipitation varies from about 25 inches in the south at Inagua to almost 60 inches in the north on Grand Bahama. Because of the low topography, seasonality of rainfall, and annual variations in precipitation, water is a problem on many of the islands. Wells supply most of the water for local use, but on New Providence, the island containing Nassau, additional water has to be barged in from nearby Andros. Agriculture is limited everywhere in the Bahamas by both the lack of year-round rainfall and the thin limestone soils. As a result, the

252

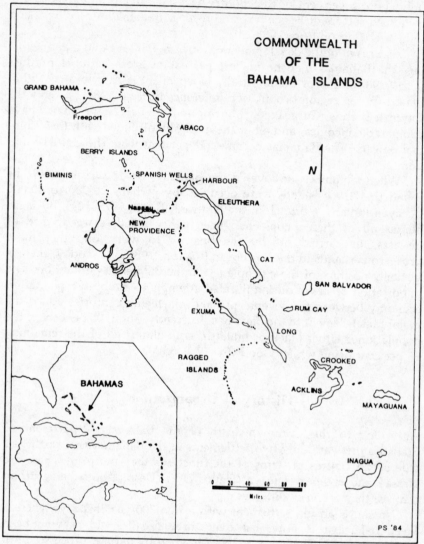

Figure 11.1. Commonwealth of the Bahamas: location map.

history of the Bahamas has not been dominated by the plantation system that played such a prominent role in the history of most of the islands in the Caribbean. Instead, the republic's history has been more dependent upon activities such as fishing, piracy, privateering, and smuggling. Since the 1950s, these activities have given way to tourism, banking and offshore manufacturing and it is these latter industries that have become the current economic mainstays of the Bahamas. Today, only about 5 per cent of the country's labour force is employed in the combined sectors of agriculture and fishing (Bahamas Agricultural and Industrial Corporation, 1988: 8).

As a result of the development of tourism, banking and manufacturing, the Bahamas has the highest per capita gross national product (US$7,190) of any of the politically independent islands located within the Caribbean region (Population Reference Bureau, 1988: 1). Only the Cayman Islands, Curaçao, St Martin, and the US Virgin Islands have comparable incomes, and all of these are still affiliated with their colonial powers. The Bahamas became independent from the United Kingdom in 1973.

When Columbus discovered the Bahamas on 12 October 1492 he found that these islands were occupied by perhaps 20,000 to 40,000 Lucayan Indians, a branch of the Arawaks (Segal, 1975: 104). By 1520, almost all of these people had been either killed, starved, died of diseases, or carried off by the Spanish to work on other more prosperous islands in the Caribbean (Craton, 1986: 39). Today, there is virtually no trace of these people left in the Bahamian population. The importation of slaves during ill-fated attempts to establish a plantation economy between the seventeenth and nineteenth centuries added the major racial element to the Bahamas. Currently, about 85 per cent of the population is either black or mulatto, with almost all of the remaining 15 per cent being white (Goodwin, 1988: 88).

History of Urbanization

According to the Commonwealth of the Bahamas Department of Statistics there are only two settlements in the Bahamas that qualify as true urban centres in terms of the functions they perform. These are Nassau and Freeport–Lucaya (Figure 11.1). Despite both being urban centres, they are very different.

Nassau is an old settlement with a rich 300-year history, whereas Freeport-Lucaya is only just over three decades old, having been founded in 1955. Furthermore, Nassau grew by natural processes until the late 1960s, while Freeport–Lucaya has been a planned community from its inception. Nassau has a much larger population, with over 150,000 residents, and produces a wider array of goods and services. Nassau is also the political capital of the Bahamas and is, in almost every other respect (except manufacturing), the country's primary city. Freeport–Lucaya has a population of only about 37,000 and its economy is highly dependent upon tourism and manufacturing. Given its size and lack of economic diversity, Freeport–Lucaya is more of a town than a city.

Nassau

Although Nassau was not the first settlement in the Bahamas it is one of the oldest. The Spanish were the first Europeans to claim the Bahamas as a result of the arrival of Columbus in 1492, but they paid little attention to this area because it compared unfavourably with the other Spanish possessions in the Caribbean and on the Latin American mainland. There was no gold or silver to be mined and, as previously mentioned, the Indian population quickly died out or was transplanted to other more prosperous colonies. In 1629, the British laid claim to the Bahamas and in 1648, the first permanent English settlement was established on the island of Eleuthera. Eighteen years later, in 1666, Nassau was founded on the north-eastern side of New Providence Island (Craton, 1986: 46–61). Originally known as Charlestown, it was renamed Nassau in honour of the Prince of Orange, Nassau, who became William III of England (Whittier, 1987: 98).

Nassau quickly became the chief settlement in the Bahamas. It was favoured by having a superb shallow-draught harbour that would accommodate any ship during these early times. Later it would need to be dredged to a greater depth, but it is well protected from storms by Paradise Island located several hundred yards north of New Providence. In addition, although most of the Bahamian islands are surrounded by shallow waters, New Providence is fortunate in being located astride the north-east Providence Channel, one of the few tongues of deep water that crosses through the Bahamas. Thus, it was favourably situated to serve as an entrepôt port for trading with Europe, the United States, and the rest of the Bahamian islands. Another advantage that Nassau had over other possible sites on New Providence was that the northern coast is cooled by prevailing north-east trade winds, whereas the southern coast tends to be swampy, hot, infested with sandflies, mosquitoes, and other insects, and has only shallow water.

A formal plan for Nassau was drawn up in 1729 based on a rectangular street pattern that would have Fort Nassau, built in 1697, as its focus. Soon, however, it was deviated from so that today, the city has several narrow crooked streets superimposed over the general rectangular grid pattern. In addition to Fort Nassau, which was located on the site of what is today the Sheraton British Colonial Hotel near the centre of Nassau Harbour, three other forts were built to protect the city. Fort Montagu was built to protect the eastern entrance to the harbour in 1742, and both Fort Charlotte and Fort Fincastle were built during the late 1780s, the former to protect the western approach to the harbour and the latter on Nassau Ridge, over-looking the centre of the harbour from high ground. These forts were necessary because of the lawlessness and piracy that prevailed in the Bahamas until the 1730s (Albury, 1975: 58–76). With the exception of Fort Nassau, they can still be seen in the landscape of the city.

Nassau grew slowly during the 1700s. Unsuccessful attempts were made to plant sugar, but these operations were never competitive with those developed elsewhere in the Caribbean because of inadequate rainfall and the poor and shallow soils of the island. The decline in privateering and piracy, several attacks by Spanish and French forces, and incompetent governance caused the economy to wane.

However, the American Revolution was to change this state of affairs. Between 1783 and 1788 approximately 8,000 Tory Loyalists and their slaves emigrated from the newly independent United States causing the population to triple, with most settling in Nassau. This influx also changed the racial composition of the population. In less than five years the proportion of the population that was black increased from about half to three-fourths (Craton, 1986: 148–57). By 1801, there were 11,300 people living in the Bahamas, with 55 per cent residing in Nassau (Table 11.1). The city of Nassau stretched from Culmer Street (now Elizabeth Avenue) westward to Augusta Street (today's Nassau Street) and from Nassau Harbour inland several hundred yards to the crest of Nassau Ridge (Craton, 1986: 161). By 1815 the administrative heart of the city was pretty well defined, much as it appears today. The gaol, now the main library, was raised between 1796 and 1800 and the buildings that surround Parliament Square, including the structures that house the Assembly, the Council, and the Supreme Court, were built between 1803 and 1812.

Table 11.1. Population of New Providence and the rest of the Bahamas, 1788–1980.

	New Providence		Rest of the Bahamas		All of the Bahamas
	Number	% of total	Number	% of total	Year (Number)
1788 (1)	3,472	39.5	5,312	60.5	8,784
1801 (1)	6,211	55.0	5,089	45.0	11,300
1861 (1)	11,503	32.6	23,784	67,4	35,287
1901 (2)	12,534	23.3	41,201	76.7	53,735
1911 (2)	13,554	24.2	42,390	75.8	55,944
1921 (2)	12,975	24.5	40,056	75.5	53,031
1931 (2)	19,756	33.0	40,072	67.0	59,828
1943 (2)	29,391	42.7	39,455	57.3	68,846
1953 (2)	46,125	54.4	38,716	45.6	84,841
1963 (2)	80,907	62.1	49,313	37.9	130,220
1970 (2)	102,005	60.2	67,529	39.8	169,534
1980 (2)	135,437	64.6	74,068	35.4	209,505

Source: (1) Doran and Landis (1980:189); (2) Department of Statistics (1986a):

The American Civil War, fought between 1861 and 1865, provided a boon for the economy of the Bahamas. Because the South needed war supplies, the Bahamas became involved in the lucrative but dangerous trade of running the blockade being enforced by the Northern forces. Manufactured items and war materials were imported from Europe and smuggled across the Florida Straits to the United States mainland. The return voyages brought cotton goods from the South and carried them to Europe. Suddenly, Nassau became prosperous for the first time in its history. Buildings sprang up and warehouses were built on the northern side of a widened Bay Street. But the flow of money dried up as suddenly as it started when the war ended and once again Nassau returned to being a quiet, poor town with a population of about 12,000.

Following the Civil War, the Bahamian government tried to promote tourism by attracting wealthy visitors from Great Britain and the United States. But the frictional effects of distance made these attempts unsuccessful. The large cities of the north-eastern United States were three to five days away by boat, and almost anything that could be had in the Bahamas could be found in Florida, which was cheaper and faster to get to over land. In 1873, Nassau received only 500 visitors, and this was the best tourist year before 1900 (Evans and Young, 1976: 21). There seemed to be a ray of hope in 1898 when Henry Flagler, who had been largely responsible for the development of tourism in southern Florida, signed an agreement with the Bahamian government to develop a hotel on the site of the old Fort Nassau. He also agreed to establish a steamship link with Florida, but these attempts were likewise doomed to failure. Between 1911 and 1921, the population of Nassau slightly declined, as did that of the rest of the Bahamas (Table 11.1). This was caused primarily by a large outflow of Bahamians to work as labourers in the agricultural and construction industries of South Florida (Mohl, 1987: 271–97).

The next boost to Nassau's economy occurred in 1919 when the United States passed the Volstead Act, which prohibited the sale and use of alcoholic beverages. Bootlegging became big business in Nassau, West End on Grand Bahama, and in the westernmost Bimini Islands. Enormous fortunes were made by some of the bootleggers and the Bahamian government also fared well through the taxes obtained on the liquor imported to the Bahamas before it was transported clandestinely to the American market. Land values soared in Nassau. The Sheraton British Colonial and Montague Beach hotels were built, as were a number of smaller hotels and guest houses. The city became modernized as its roads, sewers, electricity, and water supply were improved. Wealthy Americans, Europeans, and Bahamians built large and expensive houses along the northern coast both east and west of the downtown area. In 1929, daily flights of two and a half hours were started between Miami and Nassau. Nassau Harbour was dredged to a depth of 25 feet and Prince George Wharf was built. But, after a little more than 13 years of enforcement, the Volstead Act was repealed in 1933 thus ending Nassau's second economic boom (Albury, 1975: 171-81).

By the middle 1930s Nassau had slipped into the Depression that characterized most of the rest of the world at that time. As World War II began in 1941 the economy of Nassau began to revive. Money was spent in building two airports, one of which is used as the main airport today. The other, Oakes Field Airfield, was closed during the 1960s and its grounds have been used to erect the College of the Bahamas, a high school, a police training academy, and the city's main stadium.

Since the 1850s, Nassau had tried to promote itself as a tourist attraction, but it took almost a hundred years of waiting before these dreams would grow to fruition. Success did not begin to occur until the 1950s. A number of factors conspired to change the situation. Americans were making higher salaries that allowed more of them to afford a foreign vacation. Travel to Nassau became easier and cheaper, especially with the new international airport and development of jet airplanes. Many Americans visiting Florida found they could easily travel to Nassau and thereby expand their vacation experiences. Some visitors were yearning for a relatively inexpensive foreign vacation with an historical ambience combined with a tropical beach experience and Nassau seemed to fill the bill. But the most important impetus was the demise of Cuba's tourist industry with the success of the Castro revolution in 1959 (Evans and Young, 1976: 22-3). Suddenly, tourism in the Caribbean was a new ball game and the Bahamas was in an enviable position. Many new hotels have been constructed, especially along Cable Beach, west of downtown Nassau, and on adjacent Paradise Island.

The development of Paradise Island as an important tourist destination began during the 1960s. The five-mile long, half-mile wide island is connected to Nassau by a modern concrete bridge that arches over the harbour. It is home to 14 hotels (five of them high-rise structures), numerous restaurants, a large casino, an 18-hole golf course, apartments and condominiums. Its crowning glory came in 1981 when it overtook New Providence as the main island tourist destination in the Bahamas (Dupuch, 1988: 189-93; 327). Together, New Providence and Paradise Island received 1,658,580 tourists in 1987, accounting for almost 54 per cent of all tourists visiting the Bahamas that year (Ministry of Tourism, 1988a, Table 5: no pagination) and generating an expenditure of $607 million.

In addition to tourism, the Bahamian government worked hard during the 1960s to promote Nassau as a haven for the banking industry. As a result of these efforts, the Bahamas now has the largest offshore banking business in the Caribbean. The advantages that it has are no taxes, low registration and licensing fees, secrecy of accounts, a stable political atmosphere, a good communications system, and an English-speaking and well-trained workforce. Virtually all the international banking activities take place in Nassau, with a strong concentration in its central business district. Although some banks are visible, many are not because they tend to be small-scale operations often located on the second or third floors of buildings, the lower floors of which are used for other purposes.

The year 1953 marked a turning point in the history of urbanization of the Bahamas because it was the first, since 1801, in which more than half of all Bahamians were living in Nassau (Table 11.1). The fact that there was a majority living in Nassau in 1801 was a momentary aberration of history caused by the previously mentioned inflow of Tory Loyalists from the United States during the 1780s. From 1801 until 1901, Nassau's share of the Bahamian population fell, even though its absolute population rose. This was due to a higher rate of natural increase in the other islands. But since 1901, Nassau's share has been increasing, primarily as a result of internal and international migration. The city's most explosive increase has taken place since 1943, reflecting the economic growth that has taken place since then. Today, approximately 65 per cent of all Bahamians live in Nassau and in 1986, its population had reached over 150,000.

As previously mentioned, during Nassau's first 120 years, until 1788, its built-up area was confined to what is today the central business district and all of the city's buildings were located within several hundred yards of the harbour (Figure 11.2). During the next 100 years, growth was predominantly inland to today's Over-the-Hill area (see Figure 11.3). By 1988 the city had sprawled westward to Delaport Point and eastward to Culberts point. It had also grown inland across the island, almost to the south coast. Now Nassau occupies almost one-third of the area of New Providence Island. In fact, there are no legal limits to the city and its metropolitan area is usually considered to include all of the island, which is only 21 miles long and seven miles wide. The 1980 Bahamian population census results for New Providence, for instance, do not include separate social and economic statistics for Nassau, since the Department of Statistics regards all of New Providence as being synonymous with Nassau.

Creation of Over-the-Hill. The inner-city slum area located immediately to the south of Nassau's downtown is known as Over-the-Hill (Figure 11.3). It was given this name because it is south of Nassau Ridge and cannot be seen from the city itself. It is 'just beyond the hill'. It is not a slum in the typical sense of the term as used in the United States,

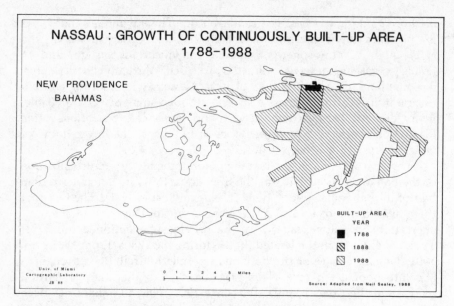

Figure 11.2. Growth of the continuously built-up area of Nassau, 1783–1988.
(Source: Adapted from Sealey, 1988).

because it was not created by the so-called housing filtering mechanism, whereby housing that was once occupied by higher-income families is passed down to those with lower incomes as the quality of the housing deteriorates through time.

Instead, Over-the-Hill started out as an area that was set aside to serve as a residence for the slaves of whites who lived in Nassau. Codified residential separation of the races in Nassau began during the 1790s. By this time, blacks had greatly outnumbered whites as a result of the immigration influx of American Loyalists and their slaves during the 1780s. The Bahamian government became alarmed by the successful slave insurrection that had occurred in Haiti in 1791. A resolution was passed that required blacks to be domiciled outside the limits of Nassau for better security. Upon completion of their daily chores in Nassau they were required to return to their own neighbourhoods at sundown, unless given special permission by their owners to do otherwise (Doran and Landis, 1980: 185–6).

The first two slave settlements were called Headquarters and Delancey Town, both being located behind Government House and the military barracks to facilitate their supervision in case of a potential uprising. They were separated by several hundred yards of underbrush. Headquarters was reorganized in 1821 to accommodate additional slaves who arrived on ships captured by the British Royal Navy after the

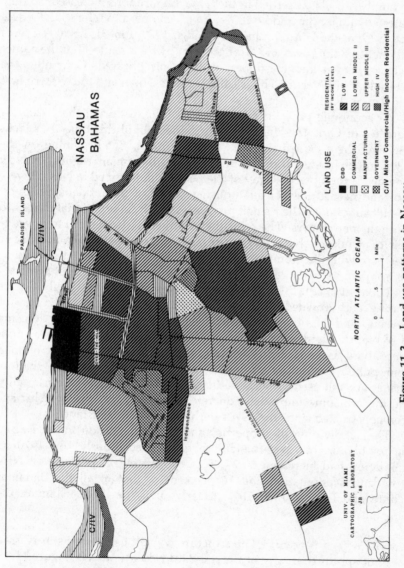

Figure 11.3. Land use patterns in Nassau.

slave trade had been outlawed, although slavery itself was not outlawed until the 1834–8 period. Thereafter, Headquarters was renamed Grants Town. Another similar settlement was started about the same time, just to the south of Delancey Town and became known as Bain Town. As the number of blacks settled in these neighbourhoods increased, so they coalesced and by the middle 1800s, it was common to refer to the whole area as Over-the-Hill (Doran and Landis, 1980: 186–9). Local residents still refer to Bain Town and Grants Town by their names, but the names Delancey Town and Headquarters have disappeared. Generally, the eastern half of Over-the-Hill is called Grants Town and the western half Bain Town (Figure 11.4).

As economic prosperity returned to Nassau during the 1920s the character of Over-the-Hill began to change. Until this time the blacks who lived here owned the land they occupied. But beginning on the 1920s, much in-migration from the other Bahamian islands to New Providence took place. Many of the people who arrived in Nassau were poor and needed inexpensive housing. Some of the residents in Over-the-Hill subdivided their small properties and built additional shacks to house the newcomers. The rents they charged allowed them to upgrade their own houses, but others were able to escape the area and move elsewhere with the money they received when they rented their land to the in-migrants. As a result, Over-the-Hill became an area of renters.

Today it is still the poorest area in Nassau, with the quality of its housing and crowded character testifying to this status (Ministry of Housing and National Insurance, 1984: 95). Most of the housing is of substandard quality, comprising small two- or three-room houses built of wood, many without plumbing. Water is often obtained from public standpipes provided by the government, and shallow latrines are still used by some residents. Mixed among the poor-quality housing are some improved concrete structures, most of which have been constructed since the 1970s with government assistance.

The subdividing of properties and the in-migration influx caused the population of Over-the-Hill to grow precipitously. By 1970 its population had increased to 27,257, representing 27 per cent of New Providence's population and 16 per cent of that of all the Bahamas (Doran and Landis, 1980: 187). Clearly, it is the largest slum in the Bahamas.

Morphology of Nassau.   The structure of land use patterns in Nassau does not appear to fit any of the standard western models (Figure 11.3). There is a well-defined Central Business District (CBD) that roughly corresponds with the limits of the entire city as it existed in 1788. In the CBD a mixture of functions are performed such as banking, shopping for both tourists and the local population, restaurants and fast food

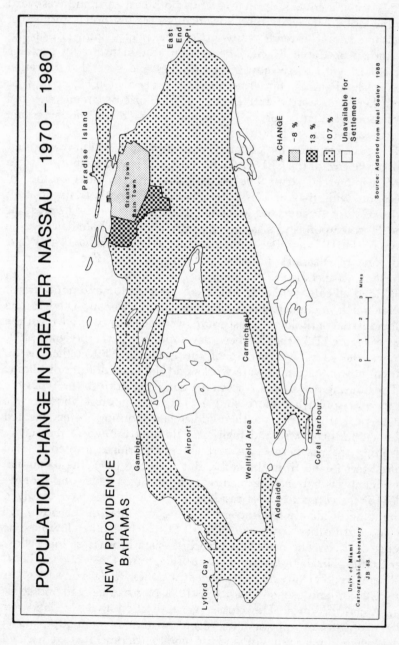

Figure 11.4. Population change in Greater Nassau, 1970–80. (Source: Adapted from Sealey, 1988).

enterprises, hotels and guest houses, apartments, government offices, and retail outlets. South of the CBD is the poor area of Over-the-Hill. There is a commercial strip that extends both eastward and westward from the CBD. The western section includes mainly hotels and eating establishments and extends westward off the map (Figure 11.3) to an area known as Cable Beach. The eastern section primarily contains retail stores, with a few government offices and several restaurants. Paradise Island and the far western section (as shown in Figure 11.3) of the northern coast are characterized by a mixture of commercial and high-income residential uses. The businesses in these two areas are primarily aimed towards tourists.

There is a combination of commercial strips that exhibit the form of an 'H' to the east of the CBD and which extends inland from the eastern coastal commercial strip. The western and eastern sides of the 'H' correspond with two of Nassau's major north–south transportation arteries, Collins Avenue and Mackey Street, respectively. The crossbar of the 'H' corresponds to a shopping centre known as Palmdale. At the bottom of the 'H' is another commercial strip that corresponds to Wulff Road, one of Nassau's primary east–west streets. The commercial establishments included in the strips that form the 'H' and the one on Wulff Road all cater primarily to the local population and not tourists.

Not much manufacturing activity occurs in Nassau. There is one small industrial park, located just south of Independence Drive (near the centre of Figure 11.3), that has been developed to attract foreign capital. Also, on the south–western tip of the island at Clifton there is an electrical power station, a waterworks and the Bacardi Rum distillery.

The housing patterns of Nassau are complex. Prior to the 1960s the pattern was somewhat more simple. Then the poorest housing was located near the CBD, with middle-class housing being located somewhat farther away and high-class housing located farther away still, along the northern coast and on several ridges located several hundred feet inland from the coast. But since the 1960s the Bahamian government has entered the picture as a housing builder and money-lender for the construction of residences. These projects have involved the building of mainly low-income housing and most of the sites have been located farther away from the CBD than the other low-income housing districts. The newer areas include such projects as the Yellow Elder Estates, Elizabeth Estates, Nassau Village and Pinewood Gardens.

Therefore, there are no neat concentric zones, wedges or sectors, or élite spines of land use, so characteristic of North American and some Latin American cities. The closest generalization that the land use patterns of Nassau approximate would be that of a multiple-nuclei model, where similar types of land use tend to agglomerate together and segregate themselves from other types. But even this pattern is not absolute because usually there are several agglomerations of the similar uses, rather than one dominant concentration.

As is typical of the majority of North American cities, most of the recent growth of Nassau has taken place in its suburbs (Figure 11.4). The area in the city centre experienced a decline in its population of about 8 per cent between 1970 and 1980, while the outermost zone increased by 107 per cent.

Freeport–Lucaya

Prior to 1955 the major economic activities on Grand Bahama Island were fishing, lumbering of native stands of pine, and a little agriculture. There had been a thriving sponge industry, but in 1938 a fungoid disease caused its demise. The 1953 Census indicated that the island's population was only 4,095 (Department of Statistics 1986a: 5). The largest settlement was located on the western end of the island (West End) and had considerably fewer than 1,000 inhabitants.

In 1955 an American entrepreneur, Wallace Groves, formed a company, the Grand Bahama Port Authority Limited and devised a plan to develop a settlement on the southernmost bend of the island (Figure 11.5), that would specialize in industrial activities. Land was cheap, the island was located only 85 miles from the United States, labour costs were less than in the USA, and there was an abundant supply of fresh, good-quality, underground water available. In that same year the Port Authority signed an agreement with the Bahamian government, called the Hawksbill Creek Agreement because the proposed settlement would be adjacent to a small creek of that name. Through this agreement the Port Authority committed itself to dredging a deep-water harbour to be named Freeport, encouraging private foreign capital to develop industrial and commercial businesses, and providing all the social services that the new population would need. In return, the government granted to the Port Authority 50,000 acres of land on very favourable terms, exemption of the port area from customs duties on non-consumable items, freedom from virtually all taxes, and authority to bring in whatever key personnel were needed without recourse to normal immigration requirements (Albury, 1975: 257). Essentially, the Port Authority had been given semi-autonomous authority to run the Freeport area like a company town without government control.

The first step was to dredge a deep-water harbour near Hawksbill Creek, and this was completed in 1959. A new international airport was opened in 1961. A ship bunkering depot was built, which allowed large oil tankers to anchor off the coast of Freeport alongside a man-made island. Because the United States limits the size of tankers that can enter its ports, larger super-tankers travel to Freeport and unload their petroleum products onto smaller vessels, which then proceed to nearby American ports. In addition, a large tank farm was established for storing oil that was not immediately transferred to the United States. Later, a cement plant, a petroleum refinery, and a pharmaceutical plant were opened. Today, Grand Bahama has the largest amount of manufacturing activity of any of the Bahamian islands. But the type of manufacturing that has been developed here is capital intensive, so it employs only about 12 per cent of the Freeport's labour force. Still, this is much higher than the proportion for the Bahamas as a whole, which stands at only 5 per cent (Sealey, 1988: 7).

Petroleum products and chemicals dominate the manufacturing of Freeport. Because the Bahamas does not produce any oil itself, all the crude oil it uses and processes must be imported from the Persian Gulf and Africa. In 1986, almost 74 per cent of all imports by value to the Bahamas were comprised of mineral fuels and related products. Conversely, 90 per cent of her exports were mineral fuels and another 8 per cent were chemicals (Department of Statistics, 1988: 71; 72). Virtually all of the imports and exports of these fuels and chemicals passed through Freeport.

By 1960, it became apparent that something else was needed to make the Freeport area a viable enterprise. As a result, a Supplemental Agreement was signed in 1960 between the Port Authority and the government that would allow the development of a tourism sector. The main resort facilities were to be built in an area east of the industrial zone that was named Lucaya. A beach was cleared and a system of canals built toward the interior of the island to allow for more property to have a waterside location. In 1963 the first hotel was completed in Lucaya, called the Lucaya Beach Hotel. Since then many additional hotels have been constructed, so that now tourism is second in the Bahamas only to that of the combined facilities of Nassau and Paradise Island. The first gambling casino was opened in 1963, providing a shot in the arm for tourism by creating an advantage over the tourist facilities in South Florida, which did not have casinos. Soon others were opened in Freeport City and in Nassau and Paradise Island. By 1980, 38 per cent of Grand Bahama's labour force was employed in tourism, about three times the percentage employed in manufacturing (Sealey, 1988: 7).

The year 1987 was a milestone in the island's short history of tourism because it was the first in which over one million (1,072,715) people visited the Freeport–Lucaya region, generating an income of $314 million (Ministry of Tourism, 1988b:6). Thirty-five per cent of all tourists travelling to the Bahamas visited Grand Bahama that year (Ministry of Tourism, 1988a: Table 5: no pagination).

In 1967 the black-dominated Progressive Liberal Party won the

Bahamanian national elections. Immediately it viewed the jurisdictional situation in Freeport with alarm. Its leader, Lyndon Pindling, argued that the Grand Bahama Port Authority had been given more control of Freeport than was warranted. Especially controversial was the control of immigration. Foreign whites dominated not only ownership of the businesses but also the population of Freeport–Lucaya. The 1970 Bahamian Census indicated that only 53 per cent of Grand Bahama's population was Bahamian and 63 per cent of the residents of Freeport were non-Bahamians (Department of Statistics, no date: 113; 114). In addition, immigrants held the highest-paying positions and occupied the best housing. Native Bahamians generally lived in much poorer housing, such as the poor communities of Eight Mile Rock and Pinder Point (Figure 11.5).

In 1969 the Grand Bahama Port Authority was sold to Benguet International. As a condition for approving this transfer, the Bahamian government required that it become a minority shareholder in the Port Authority, with representation on its Board of Directors. Henceforth, the government became responsible for granting all new licences and took over the quasi-government functions until then being performed by the Port Authority. Immigration and customs procedures in Freeport became standardized so they were the same as those elsewhere in the Bahamas (Craton, 1986: 282–3).

The favouritism that had been shown immigrants had come to an end. A new immigration bill was passed in 1970 that established rigid restrictions and conditions for the granting of entry and work permits. It formally stripped the Port Authority of the special powers and privileges it had exercised before with respect to immigration and in 1973 the government passed a new Citizenship Act that made it much more difficult for non-natives to obtain Bahamian citizenship (Segal, 1975: 108–12). Then the government embarked on a Bahamianization programme, designed to put pressure on local businesses to hire Bahamians for jobs, especially management positions from which they had been largely excluded.

The Bahamianization policy, the uncertainties caused by independence in 1973, and a recession in the United States brought about a downturn in the economy of Freeport–Lucaya until about 1978. As the economy recovered and businesses adjusted to using more Bahamian workers, the growth of Freeport took off again. By 1980, 79 per cent of the population living on Grand Bahama had been born in the Bahamas, thus signalling the success of the Bahamianization programme (Department of Statistics, 1986a: 115; 42).

The number of people living on Grand Bahama had increased to 33,102 by 1980, and in 1986 reached over 37,000, representing approximately 16 per cent of the Bahamas' total population. Today, the

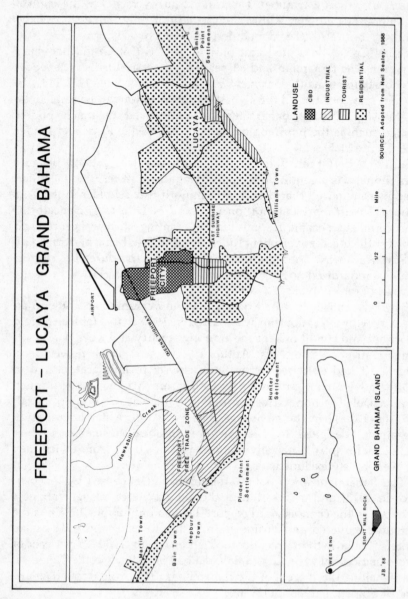

Figure 11.5. Freeport-Lucaya, Grand Bahama. (Source: Adapted from Sealey, 1988).

settled area of Freeport–Lucaya occupies three zones (Figure 11.5). The area to the west, surrounding the port and Hawksbill Creek, is the industrial zone and contains the petroleum refinery, oil bunkering facilities, cement plant, and pharmaceutical factory. It also includes the area that is within the free trade zone. To the east is the resort and residential area of Lucaya. Between Lucaya and the industrial zone is Freeport City. The city contains a small central business district comprising government offices, the building of the Port Authority, a post office, several banks, and a few commercial establishments. At the intersection of the main north–south and east–west arteries is a zone developed for tourism, containing a casino, the International Bazaar and several hotels. On the eastern, western and southern sides of the city are located middle-class residential areas. Some of the area east and north of Lucaya has had the infrastructure created for further residential expansion. Canals have been cut into the island in this area and roads and sewers laid out in anticipation of future growth, but most of this area is still vacant.

The metropolitan area of Freeport–Lucaya extends westward well beyond the three zones described above, to include the settlements of Eight Mile Rock and West End. Most of the people living in these two settlements travel to both work and shop in Freeport–Lucaya, even though the latter is about 25 miles away. The number of residents of Freeport–Lucaya and adjacent Eight Mile Rock was 22,301 in 1980, while that of the area surrounding West End was 9,173. If these two populations are added together they provide an estimate of 31,474 for the metropolitan area of Freeport–Lucaya, equal to 95 per cent of the population of Grand Bahama (Department of Statistics, 1986a: 114–15). It is for this reason that the Bahamas Department of Statistics did not report separate social and economic statistics for Freeport–Lucaya in the 1980 census.

The Demographics of Urbanization

Together metropolitan Nassau and Freeport contain approximately 80 per cent of the Bahamian population, giving the Bahamas the highest level of urbanization in the Caribbean (Population Reference Bureau, 1988; no pagination). With almost 65 per cent of all Bahamians living in Nassau it also has the highest level of urban primacy. Nassau is experiencing the same type of suburban flow that has characterized North American cities and some Caribbean primate cities, such as Kingston, Jamaica and San Juan, Puerto Rico.

Typically, rural to urban migration provides between one-third and one-half of the growth of cities in Third World countries (Potter,

1985: 80–3). For the entire Caribbean, it has been estimated that internal migration accounted for about 28 per cent of urban growth between 1970 and 1980, although there is considerable variation among the islands (Hope, 1986: 11–12; 46–7). However, it is also generally recognized that there is an inverse relationship between the percentage of a population that is urban and the percent of urban growth that is due to net migration (Drakakis–Smith, 1987: 29–30).

Given the high percentage of the Bahamian population that lives in Nassau and Freeport–Lucaya, it may be expected that migration has not played as important a role in the recent growth of these two urban places when compared to other Caribbean cities. This, however, is not the case. Migration has been very important in these cities, but in a different way than in most other Caribbean cities. What is distinctive about the urbanization of the Bahamas is that its primate city, Nassau, experienced negative net internal migration between 1970 and 1980; while its second city was the only significant gainer from internal movements (Table 11.2). Furthermore, internal migration played much

Table 11.2. Components of population change in new Providence, Grand Bahama and the Family Islands, 1970–80.

Components of change	New Providence (Nassau)	Grand Bahama (Freeport)	Family Islands
Population 1980(1)	135,437	33,102	40,966
Population 1970(1)	102,005	25,943	41,586
Change	33,432	7,159	−620
% Change (1970 base)	32.8%	27.6%	−1.5%
Internal in-migration (2)	5,027	7,376	4,411
Internal out-migration (2)	8,723	2,156	5,935
Net internal migration	−3,696	5,220	−1,524
As % of change	−11.1%	72.9%	−245.8%
Foreign born in 1980(2)	14,600	6,697	2,732
Foreign born in 1970(3)*	14,582	13,003	3,483
Estimates of net international migration	18	−6,306	−751
As % of change	0.0%	−88.1%	−121.1%
Estimates of natural increase†	37,110	8,636	1,655
As % of change	111.0%	120.6%	266.9%

Notes: * The numbers of foreign born persons by island were not published in the 1970 census results. To estimate these the number of individuals of Bahamian nationality who were born in the Bahamas was used for each island. The 1970 census indicated that the number of foreign born for all the Bahamas was 31,102. The total of the estimates for the individual islands is 31,068, indicating that the estimation procedure is 99.9 per cent accurate.

† Estimated using the residual method, whereby net internal migration and net international migration are subtracted from the change occurring between 1970 and 1980.

Sources: Numbers in parentheses refer to the sources listed below. (1) Department of Statistics (1986a); (2) Department of Statistics (1986c); (3) Department of Statistics (no date).

the same role for these two cities during the decade of the 1960s (Department of Statistics, Statistical Abstract, 1988: 39).

In fact, internal and international migration have played different roles in the growth of Nassau and Grand Bahama. This is a product of the development of Freeport–Lucaya as a new town and the government's Bahamianization programme. The continued growth of Freeport during the latter half of the 1970s siphoned off much of the internal migration that otherwise probably would have gone to Nassau (Boswell, 1986: 139–44). In addition, the government's successful Bahamianization of Freeport's businesses caused a net loss of more than 6,000 former immigrants. The loss of these people was almost balanced by its positive net internal migration. Thus, when the foreign element left Grand Bahama, most of their places were taken by in-migrants from other parts of the country. But even on Grand Bahama there was a negative total net migration of 1,086 persons.

While this was happening on Grand Bahama, the situation in Nassau was different. On New Providence there was a negative net internal migration of almost 9,000 people (Table 11.2). In fact, almost two-thirds of Nassau's loss went to Grand Bahama. At the same time net international migration was insignificant, as emigrants and immigrants tended to compensate numerically for each other. Clearly, the Bahamanization programme was more effective in Freeport–Lucaya than it was in Nassau. Still, it is important to keep in mind that the Bahamas' only two urban settlements both experienced negative total net migrations, an event that is highly unusual for Third World countries.

During the 1970s the Family Islands – that is, all the islands in the Bahamas minus New Providence and Grand Bahama – collectively lost population, a product of both negative internal and international migration. Only four of these other islands experienced positive net internal migration, Abaco, the Berry Islands, Harbour Island, and Spanish Wells, and in each case the net inflow was under 100 persons (Department of Statistics, 1986c: xxxv).

Internal Migration Patterns

The figures for the individual migration flows between New Providence and Grand Bahama and the rest of the islands in the Bahamas demonstrate several salient characteristics (Tables 11.3 and 11.4). First, there are very high correlations between in- and out-migration. This finding is in keeping with the well-known dictate that for each major migration stream there is a counterstream in the opposite direction.

A second finding is that the magnitudes of the in- and out-migration

Table 11.3. Internal migration to and from New Providence by island of origin and destination, 1970–80.

Island	In-migrants from:	Out-migrants to:	Net migration
Grand Bahama	1,439	5,758	−4,319
Abaco	256	546	−290
Acklins	158	58	100
Andros	973	664	309
Berry Islands	32	101	−69
Biminis	105	87	18
Cat Island	308	263	45
Crooked Island	90	73	17
Eleuthera	639	407	232
Exuma and Cays	334	242	92
Harbour Island and Spanish Wells	59	103	−44
Inagua	77	76	1
Long Island	338	188	150
Mayaguana	77	31	46
Ragged Island	25	10	15
San Salvador and Rum Cay	117	116	1
Totals	5,027	8,723	−3,696

1. Correlation coefficient between population size and in-migration ($r = 0.910$)
2. Correlation coefficient between population size and out-migration ($r = 0.973$)
3. Correlation coefficient between distance from New Providence and in-migration ($r = -0.368$)
4. Correlation coefficient between distance from New Providecne and out-migration ($r = -0.187$)
5. Correlation coefficient between in-migration and out-migration ($r = 0.833$)

Source: Department of Statistics, 1986c.

flows are not correlated with the distances that the individual islands are away from New Providence and Grand Bahama. A similar situation was found to be true for in- and out-migrations for New Providence during the 1960s (Boswell, 1986: 120). This violates the principle that most migration takes place over short distances and the notion that increasing distance creates frictional effects on all types of human interaction. The reason for this exception is that in the Bahamas the population is economically well off enough to be able comfortably to afford to travel back and forth between Nassau and Freeport–Lucaya and the other islands. It is probably true that most of those who migrate to either of these two cities from the Family Islands have visited them before. Furthermore, almost every Family Islander has relatives living in either Nassau or Freeport whom will help them adjust should they decide to move to either of these two cities. Finally, because communications are

Table 11.4. Internal migration to and from Grand Bahama by island of origin and destination, 1970–80.

Island	In-migrants from:	Out-migrants to:	Net migration
New Providence	5,758	1,439	4,319
Abaco	482	187	295
Acklins	22	2	20
Andros	457	232	225
Berry Islands	21	7	14
Biminis	55	49	6
Cat Island	55	17	38
Crooked Island	1	0	1
Eleuthera	162	103	59
Exuma and Cays	80	21	59
Harbour Island and Spanish Wells	19	8	11
Inagua	81	27	54
Long Island	130	33	97
Mayaguana	25	9	16
Ragged Island	8	7	1
San Salvador and Rum Cay	20	15	5
Totals	7,376	2,156	5,220

1. Correlation coefficient between population size and in-migration ($r = 0.998$)
2. Correlation coefficient between population size and out-migration ($r = 0.992$)
3. Correlation coefficient between distance from Grand Bahama and in-migration ($r = -0.285$)
4. Correlation coefficient between distance from Grand Bahama and out-migration ($r = -0.332$)
5. Correlation coefficient between in-migration and out-migration ($r = 0.996$)

Source: Department of Statistics, 1986c.

relatively good in the Bahamas, most people living in the other islands are well-informed of the opportunities that exist on Grand Bahama and New Providence.

A third notable finding is that the most important factor affecting the magnitudes of the migration flows between Nassau and Freeport–Lucaya and the rest of the Bahamian islands is the population size of the individual Family Islands. Almost without exception, islands with larger populations both send and receive larger numbers of migrants to and from New Providence and Grand Bahama. Surprisingly, other socio-economic variables appear to be of little importance. Population size was also found to be important in influencing internal migration to and from Nassau during the 1960 to 1970 period, but it was not as much of an overwhelming factor as it had been during the decade of the 1970s (Boswell, 1986: 120; see also Boswell and Chibwa, 1979: 140–51).

Immigration

Non-Bahamians comprise about 11 per cent of the total population residing in the Bahamas, but there are important variations among the islands. On Grand Bahama and New Providence they account for 21 and 10 per cent of the populations respectively; whereas in the Family Islands, non-Bahamians make up less than 7 per cent. In 1980, 88 per cent of all non-Bahamians lived in Nassau and Freeport–Lucaya (Department of Statistics, 1988: 40). As is the case in most countries, the two urban centres of the Bahamas clearly have more cosmopolitan populations than do the more rural Family Islands. During the decade of the 1970s, 83 per cent of the immigrants to the Bahamas came from four countries: Haiti (4,323), the United States (2,576), the United Kingdom (1,583) and Jamaica (1,148) (Department of Statistics, 1986c: xxxv).

The Haitians are clearly the poorest because they arrive in the Bahamas with little education and almost no knowledge of English (Marshall, 1979: 141–94). Because most arrive illegally and try to escape detection, the census figure of 4,323 is certainly too small. Estimates of their true number range from 15,000 to as high as 40,000 (Craton, 1986: 294). Many move through the Bahamas in a stage process with the ultimate goal of reaching South Florida (Boswell, 1983: 57–7). While in the Bahamas, the Haitians work mainly as low-paid labourers and service workers, often doing the types of jobs most Bahamians do not want to do themselves. Still, they are perceived as being a drain on the economy through their use of government-paid services. Occasionally, the government will round some of them up for deportation to Haiti, but officials have never succeeded in returning enough of them to make much of a difference and, as a result, the Haitians continue to arrive. In Nassau and Grand Bahama they tend to live in the poorest areas, such as those surrounding Carmichael Road and Over-the-Hill in the former, and Pinder Point and Eight Mile Rock in the latter. Haitians have been immigrating to the Bahamas since the late 1950s when the infamous dictator François Duvalier assumed power in their homeland.

Immigrants from the United States and the United Kingdom tend to occupy upper-level white collar occupations and make above average wages. The Americans have been migrating to the Bahamas in sizeable numbers for almost 200 years, whereas the British provided the original European settlers on Eleuthera and New Providence during the 1600s. Jamaicans tend to be most represented in the middle-classes, especially in such occupations as teaching and government service. They have been migrating in significant numbers to the Bahamas only since the 1950s.

Social and Economic Aspects of Urbanization

The impact of the process of urbanization is great in a country like the Bahamas where the population living in urban areas has climbed from 23 per cent in 1901 to almost 80 per cent today. In this section, attention will focus on the topics of housing, workforce characteristics, and crime. Comparisons will be made for these characteristics as they exist on New Providence, Grand Bahama and the Family Islands as a way of illustrating how the urban and rural areas of the Bahamas differ.

Housing Characteristics

Compared to the rest of the Caribbean and other Third World countries, the Bahamas is well off in terms of its housing situation. Approximately 60 per cent of its residences are classified as being in good condition and not requiring repairs. Only 15 per cent are so bad that they should be replaced. The average number of persons per room is only 1.2; whereas, in Jamaica, the comparable figure is 1.6 (Ministry of Housing and National Insurance, 1984: 34–6). Almost two-thirds of the housing in the Bahamas has adequate plumbing and sewage facilities. Although there is a problem with land titles in some parts of the Bahamas because of inadequate surveying, there are almost no squatter settlements in either Nassau or Freeport–Lucaya, unlike cities in most Third World countries and several in the Caribbean (Clarke, 1974: 228–9).

These, however, are generalizations that do not apply equally throughout the Bahamas (Table 11.5). For instance, on average, the quality of housing is highest in Grand Bahama and lowest in the Family Islands, with New Providence occupying an intermediate position. The fact that housing on Grand Bahama is better than on New Providence is clearly a product of the recency of construction of Freeport–Lucaya. Thus, Grand Bahama has the newest housing, the highest percentage of units with a piped water supply, the largest proportion of housing with flush toilets, and the highest percentage of units with electrical lighting. Conversely, the rural Family Islands have the oldest housing, less than half their units with piped water, more than half without a flushing toilet, and over 40 per cent relying on oil for their lighting. Clearly, except for the age of its units, housing conditions in New Providence are more similar to those in Grand Bahama than to those in the Family Islands.

The Bahamian government has become involved in the construction of new housing and the renovation of older housing in four ways. First, since 1962 it has had a mortgage insurance programme, whereby it insures money lent by private banks for the purpose of housing

Table 11.5. Housing indicators for New Providence, Grand Bahama, and the Family Islands.

Indicator	New Providence	Grand Bahama	Family Islands
Occupied dwelling units by age of construction: 1980			
(percentages)			
1960 or earlier	45	16	55
1961–69	28	60	24
1970–80	28	25	21
Occupied dwelling units by water supply: 1980			
(percentages)			
Piped into dwelling	66	74	42
Standpipe	22	6	16
Other*	10	20	42
Occupied dwelling units by toilet facilities: 1980			
(percentages)			
With piped system	10	10	2
With septic tank	62	65	42
Pit latrine	27	21	47
Other, including none	2	4	9
Occupied dwelling units by type of lighting: 1980			
(percentages)			
Electricity	87	91	58
Oil	12	9	42
Housing units completed under government mortgage insurance programme: 1962–83			
Number	2,478	200	7
Percentage of all Bahamas	92.3	7.4	0.3

* Includes piped into yard, public well or tank, and private not piped.

Source: Ministry of Housing and National Insurance (1984: 39–40; 112).

construction. Because their risks are lower, the lending institutions are able to charge lower interest rates on their loans, making them more affordable to Bahamians. Second, beginning in 1967, the government has become directly involved in the construction of several low-income housing projects, especially in Nassau. Third, in 1983 the Bahamas Mortgage Corporation (BMC) was created for the purpose of providing mortgage financing for housing for low-income families. Although the interest rates offered by BMC are similar to those offered by private lending institutions operating under the government mortgage insurance programme, the BMC loans have closing costs that are about one-third those of the private lenders. Fourth, the government had offered incentive grants of $1,800 to families building single-detached houses with construction costs of under $35,000 (Ministry of Housing and National Insurance, 1984: 10; 114–24).

The truth is, however, that most of the government's efforts to create better and more housing have taken place in Nassau. For instance, between 1962 and 1983, 92 per cent of all housing built under the government's mortgage insurance programme was constructed on New Providence (Table 11.5). There are two reasons for this concentration. First, population has become either stationary or is declining on most of the Family Islands, so there is less of a need for additional housing there. Second, most of the housing construction that has taken place on Grand Bahama had been built under the supervision of the Grand Bahama Port Authority and has used private capital.

Workforce Characteristics

It is generally true that Less Developed Countries have greater differences in the employment structures of their urban and rural labour forces than do More Developed Countries. As economic development proceeds, these differences diminish. At least this has been the experience of most countries in Europe and North America, and it also appears to be true of the Bahamas.

Today, the types of jobs that Bahamians have on the rural islands are not as different as they used to be from those held by urban residents. For example, in 1963 only 2 per cent of the labour force of New Providence was employed in agriculture, hunting, fishing, and mining; whereas for the combined labour force of the three islands of Abaco, Andros, and Eleuthera the figure was 50 per cent (Registrar General's Department, 1965, Table 35: no pagination). In 1986, the comparable figures were 3 per cent and 16 per cent respectively (Table 11.6), indicating a significant narrowing of the gap during the 23 year period. This has occurred primarily because of the development of tourism in the Family Islands, which has siphoned off some of the labour force that used to be employed in agriculture and fishing.

The indexes of difference for the Bahamian islands by industry of employment (Table 11.6) show that between one-fourth and one-fifth of the labour forces of New Providence, Grand Bahama, and the Family Islands would need to change their type of work to produce identical employment structures, far less than would be the case for many islands in the Caribbean. The differences that exist reflect three major contrasting tendencies. The first is the greater percentage of Nassau's workers employed in community, social, and personal services as a

Table 11.6. Labour force indicators for New Providence, Grand Bahama and the Family Islands.

Indicators	New Providence	Grand Bahama	Family Islands*
	Employed persons by industry group: 1986(1)		
	(percentages)		
Agriculture, hunting and fishing	3.3	4.1	15.4
Mining and quarrying	0.0	0.0	0.2
Manufacturing	5.0	7.5	1.5
Electricity, gas, and water	1.6	2.9	1.1
Construction	7.3	7.7	17.9
Wholesale and retail trade	12.9	11.7	12.1
Hotels and restaurants	17.7	30.8	19.6
Transport, storage, and communication	7.4	9.6	10.3
Financing, insurance, real estate, and business services	9.9	4.9	2.6
Community, social, and personal services	34.6	20.6	19.1
Not stated	0.3	0.2	0.2
Totals	100.0	100.0	100.0

Index of difference comparing New Providence with Grand Bahama = 20.3%
Index of difference comparing New Providence with Family Islands = 27.7%
Index of difference comparing Grand Bahama with Family Islands = 22.8%

| | *Unemployment and discouraged worker rates: 1986(1)* | | |
	(percentages)		
Unemployment rates	12.2	14.2	9.8
Discouraged worker rates	3.5	5.0	8.1
Totals	15.7	19.2	17.9

Mean incomes for the working population: 1980(2)
($1 Bahamian = $1 US Dollar)

	$6,811	$8,511	$3,623

* The data for industry group and unemployment and discouraged workers are based on a 1986 survey for Abaco, Andros, and Eleuthera, not for all the Family Islands.

Sources: Numbers in parentheses refer to the sources listed below. (1) Department of Statistics (1987); (2) Department of Statistics (1986b).

result of the governmental functions associated with its status as the capital of the Bahamas. The second is the higher proportion of Grand Bahama's labour force employed in the hotel and restaurant industries, a consequence of the development of tourism there. The third is the higher percentage of the Family Islands' workers employed in the primary sector, even though this figure was much lower in 1980 than in 1963.

It is generally believed that unemployment rates are higher in urban areas than in rural locations in most Third World countries. This has also been found to be the situation in most Caribbean countries (Hope, 1986: 16; 60–1). The rationale for this is that in rural areas very few people are unemployed because there is always some work to be found in farming, even if it is not full-time (Cross, 1979: 52). In the Bahamas, this relationship is not so clear. Basic unemployment rates would at first appear to corroborate this principle because the 'official' unemployment rate for the Family Islands in 1986 was significantly lower than those recorded for New Providence and Grand Bahama (Table 11.6). However, when people who have become discouraged from looking for work because they think they cannot find a job are counted, the 'real' unemployment rate is higher in the Family Islands than on New Providence, but lower than on Grand Bahama. In fact, there is not much difference between the three 'real' unemployment rates. Clearly, this is a reflection of the narrowing of the differences in the occupational structures between the two urban islands and the rural Family Islands.

Most studies comparing the incomes of urban and rural workers have determined that the former are more highly paid than the latter (Hope, 1986: 47). This is certainly true in the Bahamas (Table 11.6). In 1980, the highest mean income for workers occurred on Grand Bahama and the lowest was in the Family Islands. In fact, the average income in the Family Islands was only 43 per cent the level on Grand Bahama and 53 per cent of that on New Providence.

As in virtually all Third World countries (Drakakis–Smith, 1987: 65–74), there is a petty-capitalist or informal sector operating in the Bahamian economy. It is, however, more conspicuous in the Family Islands than in either Nassau or Freeport–Lucaya. Although no official statistics are published, a reasonable guess is that it employs less than 5 per cent of the labour force in either Nassau or Freeport–Lucaya, far less than in the cities of most Third World countries. The people employed in this sector in the Bahamas include those who sell fruit and vegetables, artists working as straw vendors, wood carvers and painters, fishermen selling their catches on the docks, Haitians working as day labourers, and those involved in illegal activities, such as prostitutes, criminals, and those engaged in the selling and transporting of narcotic drugs.

Crime

With an increasing share of the labour force of the Family Islands moving out of agriculture and fishing activities, the Bahamas has had to rely more and more on the importation of food to satisfy both its domestic and tourist needs. Currently, more than 80 per cent of its food must be imported (Bahamas Agricultural and Industrial Corporation, 1988: 9). This has caused the price of food items to skyrocket, to the point where they generally cost about 50 per cent more in Nassau and Freeport than they do in nearby Miami. By 1978, a general inflationary surge became apparent, but wages failed to keep up with increasing prices. An epidemic of strikes occurred in the early 1980s as dissatisfaction increased. The ostentatious wealth of tourists and foreign residents, the conspicuous consumption of members of the new black élite class, and inflation caused a general deterioration in the moral climate, as more people turned to a life of crime (Craton, 1986: 299).

By the late 1970s, it was clear that a significant increase in criminal activity had occurred. In 1981, Interpol placed the Bahamas in the top 10 countries of the world for all categories of violent crime and twelfth for burglary. Another source listed the Bahamas second for murder and sixth for rape on a per capita basis (Craton, 1986: 299).

The most corrupting development in the Bahamas during the 1970s and 1980s has been the colossal increase in the trafficking of narcotic drugs, especially cocaine and marijuana. An NBC television programme in September 1983 triggered a new level of awareness as government officials, including the Prime Minister, were accused of complicity in activities that perhaps provided 70 per cent of all cocaine entering the United States. A series of articles followed in the *Miami Herald* that made similar accusations. A picture emerged of a 10-year-old industry that had touched almost all the Bahamian islands. Apparently, given the opportunity, few were able to resist the temptation of the rewards which could be the equivalent of a year's salary for a few hours of work, or for simply looking the other way.

Urban violence and crime have been reported to be at all-time high levels throughout the Caribbean. Virtually all studies have found crime rates to be higher in the cities than in the rural areas. The reason for this is that in rural areas people tend to know one other and usually there is someone at home watching the house and its contents. In cities, there is greater anonymity and both husbands and wives are more likely to be away from the home working, shopping, or attending school. Thus, there is a greater overall opportunity for burglary and robbery in urban areas (Hope, 1986: 51).

Figures for crime in the Bahamas strongly support such reasoning. This is true for crimes against both persons and property. For the 10 year period from 1977 to 1986, there were 697 crimes against persons per 100,000 population in Nassau, whereas the comparable figures for Grand Bahama and the Family Islands were 493 and 103, respectively. When crimes against property are considered, the figures per 10,000 population were 520 on Nassau, 519 on Grand Bahama, and 166 on the

Family Islands. Clearly, crime rates are much lower on the rural Family Islands than they are on the urban islands of New Providence and Grand Bahama. In addition, Nassau has a significantly higher rate of crimes committed against persons than does Freeport–Lucaya, but the rates for crimes against property are almost identical for these two urban areas.

Conclusions

The processes of urbanization in the Bahamas are different from some of those that have taken place elsewhere in the Caribbean. Unlike most of the larger islands, but similar to some of the smaller ones in the eastern Caribbean, the history of urbanization in the Bahamas has been the history of one city, Nassau, until the Freeport–Lucaya complex was initiated in 1955.

Because of its physical environmental characteristics, agriculture never flourished in the Bahamas as it did in most of the rest of the Caribbean, although unsuccessful attempts were made to establish both sugar and cotton plantation systems. The history of the Bahamian islands have been tied more to clandestine activities, such as pirating, privateering, blockade running, and smuggling. Except for the brief periods of prosperity during the American Civil War and the period of prohibition in the United States, the Bahamas was considered a backwater until World War II. As a result, the population growth of Nassau and the rest of the Bahamian islands was slow until the 1940s.

Freeport–Lucaya is the only city in the Caribbean that has been built for the express purpose of promoting both tourism and manufacturing. One of the consequences of its development is that it has siphoned off much of the internal migration in the Bahamas that otherwise probably would have been directed toward Nassau. As a result, Nassau is the only city in the Caribbean whose metropolitan population has not grown at least partly by internal migration since 1960. Clearly, this has been an advantage for this city as its growth has been considerably slower than it would otherwise have been. Because of this, the city has been better able to accommodate its population growth, as is evidenced by the fact that there are almost no squatter settlements on New Providence, besides a few hard-to-find small Haitian settlements in the area surrounding Carmichael Road.

As economic development has progressed in the Bahamas since the 1950s, it is clear that there has been a diminution of the differences between the employment structures of the two urban islands, New Providence and Grand Bahama, and the Family Islands. This has been attributed primarily to the development of tourism in the Family Islands that has drawn many workers away from the primary sector (fishing and agriculture) of their economies. One consequence of this is that it is no longer true that the rural Family Islands have lower 'real' unemployment levels than the urban areas of Nassau and Freeport–Lucaya. However, the incomes of workers on the Family Islands are still much lower than those in Nassau and Freeport.

Except for the Cayman Islands and the United States Virgin Islands, no other Caribbean nation is as dependent upon tourism as is the Bahamas. At least 70 per cent of the legal income (excluding drugs) generated in the Bahamas comes from this industry and it directly and indirectly employs no less than 60 per cent of the Bahamas' labour force. Almost 90 per cent of this industry is concentrated in Nassau and Freeport–Lucaya. As a result, the hotels, casinos, and other facilities that cater to tourists are more prominent in the landscapes of Nassau and Freeport–Lucaya than in most Caribbean cities, perhaps only being exceeded in George Town in the Cayman Islands, and Charlotte Amalie in the United States Virgin Islands.

During the decade of the 1970s, in-migrants from the other Bahamian islands were able to continue moving in large numbers to Freeport–Lucaya partly because of the heavy emigration of many former immigrants, as a consequence of the government's Bahamianization policy. Now that many of the expatriates from other countries have left, it is reasonable to question whether internal migration will continue to be directed primarily to Grand Bahama, or whether it will be directed once again to New Providence.

This depends upon the future development of tourism. Even though the government is encouraging development in the Family Islands, such as a new jet airport on Exuma Island, a new resort on San Salvador Island, and two new casinos and three hotels on Andros Island, most of the development of new facilities is taking place on New Providence. It is most likely that the populations of the majority of the Family Islands will continue the decrease that was initiated during the 1950s and 1960s. The increase of the population of New Providence and Grand Bahama probably will continue, although it is possible that Nassau's population will grow more rapidly than that of Freeport–Lucaya, as a consequence of renewed positive net internal migration to New Providence.

REFERENCES

Albury, P. (1975) *The Story of the Bahamas*, London: Macmillan Caribbean.

Bahamas Agricultural and Industrial Corporation (1988) *Investment Opportunities*, Commonwealth of the Bahamas, Nassau.

Boswell, T.D. (1983) 'In the eye of the storm: the context of Haitian migration to Miami, Florida', *Southeastern Geographer*, **23**: 57–77.

Boswell, T.D. (1986) 'The characteristics of internal migration to and from New Providence Island (Greater Nassau), Bahamas 1960–1070', *Social and Economic Studies*, **35**: 111–50.

Boswell, T.D. and Chibwa, A.K. (1979) 'A comparison of net migration patterns and their spatial correlates in Puerto Rico and the Bahamas during the 1960s', *Geographical Survey*, **8**: 16–29.

Boswell, T.D. and Chibwa, A.K. (1981) *Internal Migration in the Commonwealth of the Bahamas*, Nassau: Clyde–Berren Associates.

Clarke, C.G. (1974) 'Urbanization in the Caribbean', *Geography*, **59**: 223–32.

Craton, M. (1986) *A History of the Bahamas*, Nassau: San Salvador Press.

Cross, M. (1979) *Urbanization and Urban Growth in the Caribbean*, London: Cambridge University Press.

Department of Statistics (1987) '*The Labor Force 1986*', Commonwealth of the Bahama Islands, Nassau.

Department of Statistics (no date) *Report of the 1970 Census of Population*, Commonwealth of the Bahama islands, Nassau.

Department of Statistics (1986a) *Report of the 1980 Census of Population: Demographic and Social Characteristics*, Volume 1, Commonwealth of the Bahama Islands, Nassau.

Department of Statistics (1986b) *Report of the 1980 Census of Population: Economic Activity and Income*, Volume 2, Commonwealth of the Bahama Islands, Nassau.

Department of Statistics (1986c) *Report of the 1980 Census of Population: Migration*, Volume 3, Commonwealth of the Bahama Islands, Nassau.

Department of Statistics (1988) *Statistical Abstract 1986*, Commonwealth of the Bahama Islands, Nassau.

Doran, M.F. and Landis, R.A. (1980) 'Origin and persistence of an inner-city slum in Nassau', *Geographical Review*, **70**: 182–93.

Drakakis–Smith, D. (1987) *The Third World City*, New York: Methuen.

Dupuch, S.P. (1988) *Bahamas Handbook*, Nassau: Etienne Dupuch, Jr. Publications.

Evans, F.C. and Young, R.N. (1976) *The Bahamas*, London: Cambridge University Press.

Goodwin, P.B., Jr (1988) *Latin America: Global Studies*, Guilford, Connecticut: The Dushkin Publishing Group, Inc.

Hope, K.R. (1986) *Urbanization in the Commonwealth Caribbean*, Boulder, Colorado: Westview Press.

Marshall, D.I. (1979) '*The Haitian Problem,' Illegal Migration to the Bahamas*, Institute of Social and Economic Studies, University of the West Indies, Kingston. Jamaica.

Ministry of Housing and National Insurance (1984) *Housing Needs in the Bahamas*, Commonwealth of the Bahamas, Nassau.

Ministry of Tourism (1988a) *Bahamas Tourism Statistics 1987*, Commonwealth of the Bahamas, Nassau.

Ministry of Tourism (1988b) *Exit Survey 1987*, Commonwealth of the Bahamas, Nassau.

Mohl, R.A. (1987) 'Black immigrants: Bahamians in early twentieth-century

Miami', *Florida Historical Quarterly*, (No number volume), January 1987: 271–97.

Population Reference Bureau (1988) *World Population Data Sheet*, Population Reference Bureau, Washington, DC.

Potter, R.B. (1985) *Urbanization and Planning in the Third World*, New York: St Martin's Press.

Registrar General's Department (1965) *Report on the Census of the Bahama Islands Taken 15 November, 1963*, Registrar General's Department, Nassau.

Sealey, N.E. (1982) *Tourism in the Caribbean*, London: Hodder and Stoughton.

Sealey, N.E. (1988) *Human Geography of the Bahamas*, unpublished manuscript, Nassau.

Segal, A.L. (1975) 'Bahamas', in: Segal, A.L. (ed.), *Population Policies in the Caribbean*, Lexington, Massachusetts: D.C. Heath and Company, 103–25.

Whittier, S. (1987) *Bahamas*, Insight Guides Services, Singapore: APA Productions Ltd.

[12]
Puerto Rico and the United States Virgin Islands

Klaus de Albuquerque
and
Jerome McElroy

Introduction

Puerto Rico and the United States Virgin Islands (USVI) are considered together in this chapter because they share a roughly similar economic history and political evolution. Both island groups were 'rescued' from colonial doldrums by the United States primarily for military and political reasons. Puerto Rico was ceded from Spain in the Treaty of Paris (1898) in order to protect access to the Panama Canal (Grusky, 1987: 39–40), while the Virgin Islands were purchased from Denmark for US$25 million in 1917 to preserve American hemispheric hegemony against the perceived threat of a German incursion in World War I (Boyer, 1983: 82–3).

The United States Congress saddled both insular possessions with the same amorphous political identity – the status of unincorporated territory – that precluded their normal evolutionary incorporation as states into the American Federation. After a period of military occupation, relatively brief (1898–1900) in the case of Puerto Rico, but much longer in the USVI (1917–31), civilian rule was established. US citizenship was extended to Puerto Rico in 1917 and to the USVI in 1927, and local voters won the right to elect their own Governor in 1948 and 1968 respectively. Puerto Rico wrote its own constitution and achieved Commonwealth status in 1952, but in the absence of any clear local consensus on future political status, chronic divisions have emerged between assimilationist (statehood), separatist (independence), and status quo (Commonwealth or *estado libre asociado*) factions. In the USVI, the past decade and a half has witnessed several attempts to gain voter approval of a locally written constitution, and a referendum of future political status – which offers Commonwealth status as one of several options – is slated for November 1989 (Leary, 1988).

Although both territories experienced major infrastructure and health improvements during the early years of American rule, the Great Depression spawned accelerated emigration from both island groups to the US mainland (Lopez, 1974; Boyer, 1983). In both cases, the aftermath of the depression generated similar American New Deal 'big push' experiments in state capitalism designed to rebuild the insular economies. These efforts were inspired in each instance by progressive and sympathetic federally appointed governors, Rexford G. Tugwell (1941–46) in Puerto Rico, and Paul M. Pearson (1931–35) in the USVI.

In Puerto Rico, the economic restructuring was based on: (a) an attempted land reform programme designed to encourage the break up of large estates; (b) the start up of new public enterprises in bottling, paper, construction, and leather products: and (c) the institutionalization of an efficient bureaucracy and a network of development instrumentalities (FOMENTO) considered for the time to be 'a remarkable achievement' (Dietz, 1986: 188). Analogously, in the USVI the development effort was under the aegis of the Virgin Islands Corporation (VICORP after 1949) and involved a long-range project to revitalize the sugar industry and diversify the economy into tourism, domestic food production, and non-traditional exports (winter vegetables) for the US market. Both these experiments failed to revitalize the moribund insular economies, and this prompted a new policy direction that stimulated, in each island group, a dramatic post-war programme of socio-economic modernization.

Both island groups followed the same basic development model of industrialization by invitation, attracting mainland capital through tax concessions, cheap labour, access to the US market, and the provision of debt-financed and federally subsidized supportive infrastructure (Miller, 1979; Moscoso and Barton, 1986). Both programmes were led by charismatic local political leaders who dominated their respective development decades: Luis Munoz Marin (1948–65) and Ralph M. Paiewonsky (1961–69). Though their emphasis differed somewhat – labour-intensive manufacturing in Puerto Rico, and heavy industry, tourism and related construction in the USVI – both programmes resulted in rapid increases in the gross territorial product and produced a new kind of prosperity. However, both island groups also experienced continuing decline in agricultural self-sufficiency, increasing incorporation into and satellization by the US economy, and the intensification of cyclical instability (Christopulos, 1974; McElroy and de Albuquerque, 1985). The success of 'Operation Bootstrap', as Puerto Rico's modernization programme was dubbed, was blunted by chronic emigration, double-digit unemployment, and escalating welfare dependence (Weisskoff, 1985). The USVI have likewise been plagued by problems in the post-1970 period: dizzying real estate and food price inflation, racial and ethnic polarities, rising crime, and infrastructure breakdowns (de Albuquerque and McElroy, 1985).

The Large Island–Small Island Case

Despite this shared political history and close socio-economic similarities, for purposes of examining the processes of urbanization, the experiences of Puerto Rico and the USVI must be examined separately because of substantive differences in size, structure, ambience, demographic character, and modernization impacts. To illustrate, although their population densities per square mile are roughly comparable (945 versus 839), Puerto Rico dominates the USVI in sheer size. Puerto Rico is over 26 times larger in area (3,459 square miles versus 132 square miles) and in 1985 had nearly 30 times the population: 3.3 million versus 111 thousand.

In addition, they vary significantly in structure. The USVI constitute an integral island grouping composed of three distinct communities – St Croix (80 square miles, 55,300 population), St Thomas (32 square miles, 52,660 population), and St John (20 square miles, 2,840 population) – each with its own topography and unique response to the pressures of change. On the other hand, Puerto Rico is geologically and socially much more homogeneous since the offshore islands of Culebra and Vieques are negligible in size and peripheral to the mainstream. Puerto Rico, moreover, 'though highly urbanized . . . is quite otherwise' (Weisskoff, 1985: 128), retaining its rural character because of centuries of export monoculture and subsistence farming. In fact, Puerto Ricans are quick to point out that their island is composed of two very distinct worlds – one urban and the other rural, and one has not seen Puerto Rico unless one goes 'en la isla' (out on the island). The USVI, however, share a traditional urban ambience linked to small size, high geographic mobility, and a trade emporium history such that, for example, the name of St Thomas and its capital, Charlotte Amalie, 'are virtually interchangeable in common parlance' (Lewis, 1972: 126)

As a consequence of these different parameters, in Puerto Rico the broad dimensions of urbanization have reflected the familiar Caribbean pattern common to larger islands such as Trinidad, Jamaica, Haiti, and the Dominican Republic. This includes two phases: (1) the rapid urbanization of the primate city (San Juan) induced by large-scale rural–urban migration; (2) followed by extensive suburbanization as the middle-class leapfrogs to the mushrooming affluent metropolitan fringes while poorer rural migrants continue to fill up the commercial core and slum areas (Cross, 1979: 74). On the other hand, the tiny USVI, analogous to the constrained and fragile Lesser Antilles model, accommodated swift economic change primarily by population dispersal in a movement akin to suburbanization. In this way, the process effectively blunted urban–rural distinctions (de Albuquerque and McElroy, 1981). In Puerto Rico, by contrast, though narrowed by modernization, urban–rural differences remain significant in socio-economic content across most measurable dimensions (Daubon and Robinson, 1977: 429).

Urbanization and Development in Puerto Rico

Historical Aspects of Urban Development

The first Spanish settlement was established in Puerto Rico in 1508, but because of a crown policy which severely restricted trade, the colony grew very slowly. By 1765, the island had a population of less than 45,000, a tenth of which lived in San Juan (Wells, 1969). However, between 1765 and 1815 the population almost quintupled to 221,000, as large numbers of immigrants from Spain, the Canary Islands, Haiti and other French colonies in the Caribbean entered Puerto Rico. In 1815, the Spanish Crown instituted by decree (*Cedula de Gracias*) a whole set of liberalizing measures, including tax incentives, land grants, and fewer trade restrictions. The net effect of these measures was to stimulate a new influx of Catholic migrants from the Americas, and to transform the economy from subsistence to commercial agriculture (Mintz, 1956). An island-wide road system was later established to facilitate commercial agriculture and new towns sprang up all over the island. The population grew rapidly, passing 500,000 in 1860 and reaching 953,000 by the time of the first US Census in 1899. This census placed the urban population (a threshold of 1,000 was used to define an urban area) at 14.6 per cent, with over half this population being concentrated in San Juan, Mayaguez, and Ponce (Figure 12.1).

Since 1899, the Puerto Rican population has grown by approximately 1.5 per cent per year, with slightly higher growth in the first four decades than in the last four (Table 12.1), primarily because of emigration in the postwar era.

Out-migration to the United States Mainland

As in most Caribbean societies, the immediate post-war period in Puerto Rico was marked by intense metropolitan emigration. But the sheer volume of this migration dwarfed by contrast the migration from other Caribbean islands. For example, between 1950 and 1972, Puerto Rico lost more people (over 800,000) than any other island (Segal, 1975). The pace of this out-migration was uneven: from a slow take-off between 1940 and 1950 averaging nearly 19,000 persons a year, to an exodus during the peak 1950–60 development decade where nearly a half million people left for the US mainland. Between 1960

Figure 12.1. Consolidated metropolitan statistical area, primary metropolitan statistical areas, metropolitan statistical areas, and selected places in Puerto Rico.

Table 12.1. Population of Puerto Rico by urban–rural residence, 1899–84.

Census year	Total population	% Change[1]	Urban Number	%	Rural Number	%
1899	953,243	–	138,703	14.6	814,540	85.4
1910	1,118,012	17.3	224,620	20.1	893,392	79.9
1920	1,299,809	16.3	283,934	21.8	1,015,875	78.2
1930	1,543,913	18.8	427,221	27.7	1,116,692	72.3
1940	1,869,255	21.1	556,357	30.3	1,302,898	69.7
1950	2,210,703	18.3	894,813	40.5	1,315,890	59.5
1960[2]	2,349,544	6.3	1,039,301	44.2	1,310,243	55.8
1970	2,712,033	15.4	1,575,491	58.1	1,136,542	41.9
1980	3,196,520	17.9	2,134,365	66.8	1,062,155	33.2
1984[3]	3,270,000	2.3	NA		NA	

Sources: 1899–1980: US Bureau of the Census, 1980: Census of Population for Puerto Rico. 1984: US Bureau of the Census, Current Population Report, Series P-26, No. 84–51–c.

Notes: 1. Change from preceding census. 2. In 1960 the definition of urban was expanded to include urbanized areas (densely settled areas that are not identified as places and that have 2,500 or more inhabitants). 3. Estimate, 1 July 1984.

and 1980, out-migration slowed to roughly 15,000 per year, but since 1980, it has accelerated toward the rate of the 1950s.

This migration has had a significant impact on the economy and society of Puerto Rico. By 1970 there were more Puerto Ricans in New York City than in San Juan, and the US mainland population of Puerto

Ricans (by birth and parentage) represented one-third of the total island population (Lopez, 1974). While one might argue that out-migration had the salutary effect of reducing population pressure, as elsewhere in the region, it was selective of young (20–35 years), urban, and relatively more skilled and educated persons (Senior, 1953; Cross, 1979). It also substantially reduced the birth rate, with the greatest declines occurring between 1950 and 1960 when the proportionate loss of young females of child-bearing age was the greatest (de Albuquerque *et al.*, 1976). The sustained out-migration of those in the working-age cohorts also negatively affected the island labour pool. Labour force participation rates (14 years and over) fell from 52 per cent in 1940 to 41 per cent in 1983 (Dietz, 1986), with the greatest decline occurring in the period 1950–60 when the labour force actually shrunk because of massive out-migration.

The Present Rate and Pattern of Urbanization

The changing distribution of the population has followed in the words of two observers 'what one would have expected or predicted from comparative experience in the USA' (Daubon and Robinson, 1975: 429): rapid urbanization until 1960, followed by widespread suburbanization whereby the majority of the urban population came to reside outside the central cities. The pace of urbanization in Puerto Rico, more than twice the overall growth rate, was similar to other large Caribbean island rates between 1950 and 1970 (Hope, 1986). Approximately half this urban growth was due to rural–urban migration.

Decennial changes in the pace of urbanization were quite uneven (Table 12.1). Marginal growth between 1910 and 1920 is attributed partly to the resurgence of sugar with its intense labour demands (Dietz, 1986). The expanding pace between 1920 and 1930 was partly due to the coffee crash when thousands became 'migrants to the cane fields and urban slums' (Christopulos, 1974: 130). The spurt in urban growth between 1940 and 1950 resulted from federal military construction, the creation of new FOMENTO machinery, the centralization of government, consolidation of utilities, and proliferation of public enterprises. Between 1950 and 1970, the urban population almost doubled (Table 12.1), absorbing between 40 and 58 per cent of the total population growth. Within the Caribbean, the rate of urban absorption during the 1950–70 'Operation Bootstrap' period was second only to the Netherland Antilles (Davis, 1969). Rural areas suffered absolute population declines partly because of heavy out-migration to urban areas and partly because many former rural areas, because of urban sprawl, were now redefined as urban.

This large-scale post-war exodus to the cities is particularly striking in the context of massive out-migration to the US mainland and deliberate government efforts to control urbanization. The former factor largely explains the relatively slow growth of the urban population between 1950 and 1960 – only 16 per cent – in contrast to rapid growth in the decades before (61 per cent), and after (52 per cent). The latter refers to the government's rural resettlement, land reform, and factory decentralization policies. By 1965, 363 rural communities had been established involving the relocation of some 65,000 families and 400,000 people, about 15 per cent of the total population (Wells, 1969). These plans were reinforced by a self-help housing scheme based on subsidized building materials, and a committed rural electrification and communication programme.

These planning initiatives, however, were insufficient to withstand the massive incentives and economies of scale the urban areas provided for a rapid industrialization strategy. There was, in addition, a largely federally financed public housing and urban renewal programme that injected $500 million into the cities between 1938 and 1964 alone, and that created some 40,000 new housing units (Wells, 1969). As a consequence, Puerto Rico's urbanization process has been characterized as uncontrolled and chaotic (Villamil, 1976). In many areas the unwanted outcome of planning was the shunting of rural migrants into the decaying cores and shanty towns ringing the main cities (Carnoy, 1970).

Nowhere was growth more intense than in San Juan, exaggerating its dominance over the insular landscape. As early as 1960, the previous decade's population growth had been concentrated in the San Juan metropolitan area, including the city and the five adjoining municipios (the equivalent of counties) of Bayamon, Guaynabo, Catano, Trujillo Alto, and Carolina. The San Juan area grew by 20 per cent between 1960 and 1970, the sprawling suburban fringes accommodating new housing, high-rise hotels, and new factories. By 1970, it contained 35 per cent of the total population and 60 per cent of all urban inhabitants. As the centre of trade, government, and tourism, the city contained roughly 35 per cent of all manufacturing firms and workers, 35 per cent of all direct jobs in commerce, and over 40 per cent of all firms in Puerto Rico (Pico, 1974). The area also produced 47 per cent of island income and contained most of Puerto Rico's massive tourist construction (nearly 10,000 rooms by 1971). Much of the tourism development effort was restricted to the Condado hotel strip and resulted in the so-called 'Miamiazation' of San Juan (Vaughan, 1974: 276).

Several forces were responsible for the exodus from the countryside. Certainly the burgeoning of urban factory and construction jobs was primary, but the possibility of government and professional employment also provided a long-standing attraction (Boswell, 1978). The expanding urban markets for services also created the opportunity for many migrant women to become secondary family income earners (Safa, 1974). Sharp wage differentials of over 2:1 produced a strong pull. Urban access to higher-quality secondary education, universities, and more specialized medical facilities proved an additional motivation (Wells, 1969: 177–8; Carnoy, 1970). Perhaps, however, the most fundamental source of in-migration to urban areas was the impoverishment of the rural periphery. Often rural communities surveyed in the mid-1960s – the heyday of 'Operation Bootstrap' – posted unemployment rates of between 22 and 47 per cent.

Suburbanization and Metropolitanization

The post-war economic restructuring, based on manufacturing and tourism, created a new industrial society. The share of aggregate personal income from wages/salaries rose from 50 to 75 per cent between 1940 and 1970 (Daubon and Robinson, 1975). There were also the expected impacts of greater female participation in the labour force, increasing occupational diffusion as well as major changes in consumption patterns, proportional declines in food purchases and increases in medical, educational and travel expenses.

Together these changes reflect the emergence of an increasingly self-confident and affluent urban middle-class. Their specifically urban concerns – crime protection, improved planning, infrastructure, and education – quickly became national political concerns. Particularly visible evidence of the new middle-class was the American-style flight to the suburbs in the 1960s and early 1970s which compounded the spillover of urban growth beyond traditional borders into adjacent municipios to accommodate pressures from rapid industrialization and tourism development. Although largely a San Juan phenomenon in the early stages, this process of suburban sprawl and metropolitanization became generalized across the island.

Tables 12.2 and 12.3 are suggestive of these trends. For example, between 1960–80 the declining importance of San Juan's central city (the only area of between 250,000 and 499,999 persons in Table 12.2) was more than matched by the increasing significance of the smaller cities and adjacent municipios which sharply expanded their share of the urban population from 34 to 62 per cent. Suburbanization also explains the marked reduction in the size of place of median inhabitant from over 190,000 in 1960 to 92,000 in 1980 (Table 12.2).

Table 12.3 charts the recent growth of Standard Metropolitan Statistical Areas (see definition at the bottom of Table 12.3) and their component municipios. The data trace the rapid expansion of San Juan and the contiguous Caguas SMSA between 1960–70, and the increasing

Table 12.2. Population residing in the urban areas of Puerto Rico by size of place, 1930–80.

	Census year											
	1930		1940		1950		1960		1970		1980	
Size of place	Number	%	Number	%	Number	%	Number	%	Number	%	Number	%
250,000–499,000	–	–	–	–	357,205	39.9	432,377	45.5	452,749	28.9	424,600	22.2
100,000–249,999	114,713	26.8	169,247	29.9	158,436	17.7	114,286	12.0	275,785	17.6	494,661	25.9
50,000–99,999	53,430	12.5	115,558	20.4	62,418	7.0	50,147	5.3	281,668	17.9	235,257	12.3
25,000–49,999	37,060	8.7	–	–	124,155	13.9	60,843	6.4	61,943	3.9	174,704	9.1
10,000–24,999	80,953	19.0	111,423	19.7	95,933	10.7	94,528	9.9	207,884	13.3	272,541	14.2
5,000–9,999	61,076	14.3	86,441	15.3	96,666	10.8	87,746	9.2	143,348	9.1	153,727	8.0
2,500–4,999	79,987	18.7	83,688	14.8			110,658	11.7	145,277	9.3	158,332	8.3
Of median inhabitant	22,366		25,244		71,469		193,749		90,224		92,274	

Source: US Bureau of the Census, 1980 Census of Population for Puerto Rico.

Table 12.3. Population of Puerto Rican Standard Metropolitan Statistical Areas[1] (SMSAs) and their component municipios[2], 1960–80.

SMSAs and their component municipios	1960 Number	1970 Number	1970 % Change	1980 Number	1980 % Change
ARECIBO SMSA[3]	109,856	115,303	11.4	140,608	37.5
Arecibo Central City	28,828	35,484	23.1	48,779	15.0
Outside Central City	81,028	79,819	−1.5	91,829	18.1
Arecibo Municipio	69,879	73,468	5.1	86,766	24.9
Camuy Municipio	19,739	19,922	0.9	24,884	32.2
Hatillo Municipio	20,238	21,913	8.3	28,958	21.9
CAGUAS SMSA[3]	109,651	141,705	29.2	173,961	22.8
Caguas Central City	32,015	63,215	49.4	87,214	38.0
Outside Central City	77,636	78,490	1.1	86,747	10.5
Caguas Municipio	65,098	95,661	59.6	117,959	23.3
Gurabo Municipio	16,603	18,289	10.1	23,574	28.9
San Lorenzo Municipio	27,950	27,755	−0.7	32,428	14.4
MAYAGUEZ SMSA	108,203	116,100	7.3	133,497	15.0
Mayaguez Central City	50,147	68,872	37.3	82,968	7.0
Outside Central City	58,056	47,228	−13.0	50,529	7.0
Anasco Municipio	17,200	19,416	12.9	23,274	19.9
Hormigueros Municipio	7,153	10,827	51.4	14,030	29.6
Mayaguez Municipio	83,850	85,857	2.4	95,193	12.0

PONCE SMSA					
Ponce Central City	191,868	213,984	11.5	253,285	18.4
Outside Central City	114,286	128,233	12.2	161,739	26.1
Juana Diaz Municipio	77,582	85,751	10.5	91,546	6.8
Ponce Municipio	30,043	36,270	20.7	43,505	20.0
Villalba Municipio	145,586	158,981	9.2	189,046	18.9
	16,239	18,733	15.4	20,734	10.7
SAN JUAN SMSA					
San Juan Central City	695,808	936,693	34.6	1,086,376	16.0
Outside Central City	432,377	452,749	4.7	424,600	-1.8
Bayamon Municipio	263,431	483,944	83.7	661,776	26.9
Canovanas Municipio	72,221	156,192	116.6	196,206	25.6
Carolina Municipio	—	—	—	31,880	—
Catano Municipio	40,923	107,643	162.6	165,954	54.2
Guaynabo Municipio	25,208	26,459	5.0	26,243	-0.8
Loiza Municipio	39,718	67,042	40.8	80,742	20.4
San Juan Municipio	28,131	39,062	38.9	20,867	-46.6
Toa Baja Municipio	451,658	463,242	2.6	434,849	-6.1
Trujillo Alto Municipio	19,698	46,384	135.5	98,246	68.7
	18,251	30,669	68.0	51,389	67.6

Source: US Bureau of the Census, 1980 Census of Population for Puerto Rico.

Notes: 1. An SMSA consists of one central city with at least 50,000 persons or contiguous cities with a combined population of at least 50,000. SMSA's typically include some rural populations.
2. Municipios are the equivalent of counties.
3. Became an SMSA in 1980.

importance of Arecibo in the north-west and Ponce in the south between 1970–80. Table 12.3 also suggests that the pattern of suburbanization has varied. Only in the San Juan SMSA did SMSA growth outpace the growth of the central city during both decades. As expected, the most rapid growth spilled over into the areas immediately adjacent to San Juan City: Toa Baja, Bayamon, Guaynabo, Trujillo Alto and Carolina, as well as Caguas and Gurabo in the Caguas SMSA to the immediate south.

In all SMSAs, except Ponce, the growth of urban areas outside the central city accelerated over the two decades. In the case of every SMSA, similar to the San Juan experience, the municipios registering the greatest growth rates between 1970–80 were again those just adjacent to the central cities: Camuy and Hatillo in Arecibo, Gurabo in Caguas, Hormigueros and Anasco in Mayaguez, and Juana Diaz in Ponce. The uniqueness of Ponce is due to the fact that in terms of its internal ecological structure it resembles the traditional Latin American or Spanish city dominated by the plaza and cathedral (Schwirian and Rico-Velasco, 1971).

Since 1980, the overall rate of population growth and the intensity of suburbanization has decreased considerably. For example, between 1980–84 the population has risen only at an average annual rate of 0.6 per cent. Of the four Metropolitan Statistical Areas (100,000 or more population with one urban area 50,000 or more) established by the US Census in 1983, only the Mayaguez MSA grew faster than both the average metropolitan and non-metropolitan growth rate (see Table 12.4). The MSAs of Ponce in the south and Arecibo and Aguadilla in the north-west grew much more slowly than the overall population. The evidence from Table 12.4 suggests that the San Juan-Caguas metro-politan area still dominates as the destination for the majority of the internal migrants.

Much of this marked slow down in both overall population growth and urbanization can be attributed to the recession-ridden post-1980 economy, weakened by downturns in petroleum, derivative products and tourism with unemployment approaching one-fourth of the workforce, and, above all, accelerating mainland emigration climbing towards the historic highs of the 1950s (Dietz, 1986: 285). Clearly, however, the data confirm that Puerto Rico has become a metropolitan island. According to Table 12.4, by 1984, 2.7 million or roughly 80 per cent of the approximately 3.3 million inhabitants resided in areas defined as metropolitan.

Table 12.4. Estimates of the population of Puerto Rican metropolitan areas, 1980–84.

Metropolitan areas (MSAs, CMSAs, and PMSAs)[1]	1 April 1980 (Census)[2]	1 July 1982	1 July 1984	% Change (1980–84)
Aguadilla MSA	152,793	155,400	155,000	1.8
Arecibo MSA	160,336	162,700	163,300	1.8
Mayaguez MSA	200,464	209,400	209,800	4.5
Ponce MSA	232,551	236,300	234,500	1.6
San Juan-Caguas CMSA	1,775,260	1,812,400	1,816,300	2.3
Caguas PMSA	265,854	272,700	275,300	3.6
San Juan PMSA	1,509,406	1,539,800	1,541,000	2.1
Metropolitan	2,521,404	2,576,500	2,579,300	2.3
Non-metropolitan	675,116	688,900	691,100	2.4

Source: US Bureau of the Census, Current Population Report, Series P-26, No. 84–51–C.

Notes: 1. In 1983 the US Census Bureau introduced three new metropolitan designations to replace SMSA. A Metropolitan Statistical Area (MSA) is an area that has at least one city with 50,000 or more population or contains an urbanized area of 50,000 or more with a total metro population of 100,000 or more. An MSA can be one county (municipio) or a group of counties. A Consolidated Metropolitan Statistical Area (CMSA) contains a contiguous metropolitan area of 1 million or more population and contains a qualifying Primary Metropolitan Statistical Area (PMSA) within it. A country or group of counties which form a metropolitan complex and is so recognized locally may constitute a PMSA.
2. Adjusted to include new component municipios.

Socio-economic Correlates of Urban Development

Table 12.5 documents the socio-economic changes associated with the post-war transformation of the economy. These trends reveal the predictable contours of modernization. For Puerto Rico as a whole, and both rural and urban areas, these include steady decreases in fertility (child–woman ratio) especially after 1960, the familiar fall in the sex ratio associated with emigration, and substantial reductions in average family size – from 5.1 to 3.7 persons per household – plus a marked narrowing of urban–rural differences in household size. They also include progressive increases in the median age, education levels, school enrolment, family income, and female labour force participation rates, all of which tended to rise faster in the rural areas and in the urban fringe than in the central cities.

Four additional trends deserve mention. First, across nearly all dimensions, urban–rural differences narrowed between 1950 and 1980. This has been observed previously by others (Daubon and Robinson, 1975; Stinner *et al.*, 1975; Cross, 1979), and is certainly consonant

Table 12.5. Socio-economic indicators for the Puerto Rican population by residence, 1950–80.

Indicator	Puerto Rico				Rural areas			
	1950	1960	1970	1980	1950	1960	1970	1980
Median age	18.4	18.9	21.6	24.6	16.5	16.7	19.1	22.5
Sex ratio[1]	101.0	98.0	96.2	94.9	107.4	102.9	101.3	101.0
Child–woman ratio[2]	780	664	481	412	929	793	579	471
Persons per household	5.07	4.79	4.23	3.66	5.46	5.19	4.61	3.95
% Living in diff. house 5 yrs ago	NA	38.9	44.3	29.1	NA	31.8	35.8	25.8
Median school yrs completed (25 yrs+)	3.9	4.6	6.8	9.4	3.4	3.6	4.5	6.7
% Aged 16–17 enrolled in school	38.4	47.1	74.2	76.3	29.4	38.2	56.8	70.0
Median family income (US$)[3]	378	1,082	2,584	5,348	275	752	1,633	3.886
% Families below poverty level	NA	NA	59.6	58.0	NA	NA	78.4	73.8
% Females 14+ in labour force[4]	21.3	20.0	22.9	29.1	16.5	13.3	16.3	23.1
% Employed in manufacturing	16.5	17.1	20.6	19.7	14.8	14.8	22.6	25.9
% Unemployed	2.4	5.8	5.6	15.2	1.6	5.5	7.1	19.4

Sources: US Bureau of the Census, 1950–80 Censuses of Population for Puerto Rico.

Notes: 1. Number of males per 100 females.
2. The number of children aged 0–4 divided by the number of women aged 15–44 and multiplied by 1,000. The child–woman ratio is an indirect measure of fertility.
3. For families and unrelated individuals.
4. Data for 1980 are for females 16 years and older.

with the post-war pattern of intensifying suburbanization/metropolitanization. Second, since 1960, the highest concentrations of manufacturing employment were in rural and urban fringe areas. This certainly explains the high percentage of women working in those areas. Third, between 1970 and 1980, the importance of manufacturing employment declined in all but the rural areas. This may partly explain the slowdown in industrialization and the increases in unemployment and families below the poverty level for all urban areas. Finally, the sharp decline in residential mobility after 1970 (per cent living in a

	All urban areas				Urban areas — Central cities				Urban fringe		
1950	1960	1970	1980	1950	1960	1970	1980	1950	1960	1970	1980
21.2	22.2	23.4	25.6	NA	22.7	24.6	27.1	NA	20.4	22.5	24.7
92.3	92.1	92.7	92.1	NA	92.4	91.9	89.2	NA	96.1	94.3	94.5
609	531	420	385	NA	509	380	357	NA	602	440	393
4.58	4.36	3.99	3.53	NA	4.32	3.84	3.32	NA	4.67	4.22	3.72
NA	47.7	50.3	30.7	NA	49.9	50.5	31.4	NA	52.2	57.6	29.9
5.3	6.5	8.8	11.0	NA	7.2	9.1	11.7	NA	7.0	10.4	11.0
51.8	59.8	79.4	79.8	NA	59.7	81.5	80.5	NA	55.0	80.1	79.8
617	1,595	3,338	6,238	NA	1,762	3,283	6,306	NA	2,042	4,622	6,781
NA	NA	47.7	50.7	NA	NA	45.7	47.8	NA	NA	38.0	49.4
26.6	26.8	25.8	31.7	NA	27.1	27.7	32.0	NA	26.9	27.8	32.3
19.4	19.2	19.8	17.6	NA	16.6	16.6	15.6	NA	21.8	23.7	17.0
3.5	6.1	4.7	13.6	NA	NA	NA	13.4	NA	NA	NA	12.9

different house five years ago) may presage the general deceleration of suburbanization and the gradual stabilizing of a metropolitan insular population. It is interesting to note that the greatest decline in residential mobility occurred in the urban fringe areas – precisely the area that has witnessed the greatest growth between 1950 and 1980.

Table 12.5 also presents the basis for examining the rural–urban continuum, the contrasting behaviour between large and small urban centres, and the differences between metropolitan areas. In the first instance, the presence of a rural–urban continuum is quite evident. In contrast to rural areas, San Juan, at the urban end of the continuum, recorded a substantially higher median age, greater residential mobility, and higher levels of educational attainment, school enrolment, family income and female labour force participation. San Juan also predictably recorded lower levels of fertility, persons per household, manufacturing employment, unemployment and poverty.

Table 12.5. *continued*

	Urban areas							
	Places of 10,000 or more				2,500–9,999			
Indicator	1950	1960	1970	1980	1950	1960	1970	1980
Median age	NA	22.2	23.2	25.4	NA	21.8	21.8	23.9
Sex ratio[1]	NA	90.5	90.9	91.7	NA	89.9	94.3	94.8
Child–woman ratio[2]	NA	544	449	404	NA	553	479	451
Persons per household	NA	4.28	3.93	3.54	NA	4.38	4.15	3.68
% Living in diff. house 5 years ago	NA	45.2	46.2	31.7	NA	39.5	43.3	30.1
Median school yrs completed (25 yrs+)	NA	5.1	7.7	10.0	NA	5.3	7.3	9.3
% Aged 16–17 enrolled in school	NA	58.6	77.6	80.4·	NA	63.4	74.8	76.7
Median family income (US$)[3]	NA	1,237	2,521	5,128	NA	1,138	2,713	4,882
% Families below poverty level	NA	NA	57.8	57.8	NA	NA	58.7	61.6
% Females 14+ in labour force[4]	NA	27.3	24.8	29.5	NA	25.5	25.8	30.2
% Employed in manuf.	NA	24.6	22.2	21.2	NA	22.5	26.1	26.3
% Unemployed	NA	NA	NA	14.9	NA	NA	NA	17.0

Sources: US Bureau of the Census, 1950–80 Censuses of Population for Puerto Rico.

Notes: 1. Number of males per 100 females.
2. The number of children aged 0–4 divided by the number of women aged 15–44 and multiplied by 1,000. The child–woman ratio is an indirect measure of fertility.
3. For families and unrelated individuals.
4. Data for 1980 are for females 16 years and older.

In the second instance, a careful reading of the differences between small and large urban areas in Table 12.5 reveals an overall pattern of urban or metropolitan diffusion from larger to smaller urbanized areas. Along this spectrum, the San Juan SMSA typifies the polar case representing the most distinctly urban area in the Puerto Rican landscape: high income, educational attainment and mobility, low fertility, small households, and so on. At the other end, are the small urban areas (2,500 to 10,000 population) with characteristics opposite to San Juan, and most closely parallel to rural areas. In fact, the small towns appear to be significantly more rural than urban with respect to the selected socio-economic indicators included in Table 12.5.

				SMSAs							
Mayaguez				Ponce				San Juan			
1950	1960	1970	1980	1950	1960	1970	1980	1950	1960	1970	1980
20.2	22.1	23.6	25.7	19.9	18.8	21.3	22.7	21.4	21.4	24.0	26.5
95.4	95.1	95.6	94.6	94.9	93.9	93.9	94.5	96.1	94.9	93.5	91.2
654	513	402	360	750	695	497	466	610	533	394	360
4.64	4.23	3.82	3.47	4.63	4.63	4.30	3.87	4.71	4.47	3.97	3.45
NA	41.4	46.1	33.4	NA	42.5	41.7	29.8	NA	50.9	52.2	30.0
4.2	5.0	7.8	9.1	4.3	5.0	8.3	9.4	9.4	7.1	10.1	12.1
43.0	52.6	76.0	79.3	46.3	52.2	79.5	73.5	47.1	56.8	79.9	82.3
438	1,062	3,074	5,656	465	1,173	3,272	4,987	795	2,026	4,595	7.118
NA	NA	55.2	53.4	NA	NA	54.2	61.8	NA	NA	40.5	44.7
35.2	22.7	25.7	33.5	19.6	19.8	21.2	26.2	25.6	27.2	27.8	33.1
34.3	25.1	27.9	29.1	21.5	23.5	25.3	21.0	11.8	15.7	15.2	11.8
4.6	6.4	4.7	13.8	9.3	6.9	5.1	18.3	8.6	5.7	4.5	11.5

Finally, with respect to differences between the three SMSAs, San Juan again represents the most metropolitan area, with Mayaguez somewhere in between, while Ponce, with its higher fertility, larger household size, lower median income and residential mobility, and higher unemployment and poverty rates, resembles more closely the small urban areas.

Urbanization and Development in the United States Virgin Islands

The USVI typify those Caribbean islands like Bermuda, the Caymans, New Providence (Bahamas), and St Maarten that are distinguished by their small size and fragile ecology, and which have experienced strong development thrusts particularly in the post-war decades. Two systemic processes generally define the contemporary history of such islands:

economic restructuring and the accompanying intensifying urbaniza-
tion/suburbanization, and a migration reversal that witnesses the transition from an emigrant to an immigrant society.

The first process identifies the deliberate strategy of export
substitution whereby former primary producers are transformed into
economies based on international services (tourism, off-shore banking,
etc.) and export manufacturing. The second signifies a migration
reversal whereby former labour-exporting countries become labour
importers. This so-called 'migration transition' takes place when the
rapid growth imperatives of tourism, manufacturing, and related
construction outpace the insular labour supply and result in noticeable
immigration and return migration (McElroy and de Albuquerque, 1988).

In addition, there are two other aspects that especially distinguish
the modernization process in these mini-states from the larger islands
like Puerto Rico. First, the perennial dominance of the major coastal city
as the primary export entrepôt in the colonial network of trade is
exaggerated in small islands because their compact nature and often
steep topography confine most population growth to relatively flat
areas surrounding the capital city. As a result, short distances separate
town and country, and, the difference between the two is often more
spatial and categorical than real in socio-economic terms. In other
words, small islands historically have retained an urban ambience that is
constitutive of an insular society (Demas, 1965).

Second, whereas larger islands have responded to post-war
modernization with intense rural–urban migration and the increasing
urbanization of primate cities, in the mini-states development has
unleashed a reverse movement – a sprawling demand for settlements
and commercial facilities up steep rural hillsides and down into shoreline
niches formerly untouched because of the constraints of topography and
the agrarian economy. In some cases, growth has resulted in stressful
population–land ratios and has noticeably altered the 'natural genius of
the place' (McElroy, Potter and Towle, 1989).

Historical Aspects of Urban Development

The USVI is considered a classic example of this widespread
phenomenon of post-war movement to the rural areas (really suburban
areas, since few places on a small island have really 'rural' attributes), a
shift that accelerated after the take-off of the tourism, manufacturing,
and construction boom in the 1960s. This island group, located some 40
miles east of Puerto Rico, consists of nearly 70 volcanic islets and cays.
The three most important are St Croix, St Thomas, and St John (Figure
12.2). The two smaller islands of St Thomas and St. John share a similar

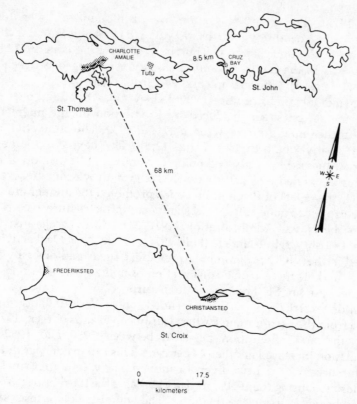

Figure 12.2.   Urban areas in the US Virgin Islands.

rugged mountainous topograhy. St Thomas, dominated by the capital of Charlotte Amalie, is the political, commercial, and tourist centre, whereas nearby St John is primarily a preserve of the US National Park Service. Some 40 miles to the south, St Croix, the agricultural and industrial centre because of its flatter terrain, contains the sister cities of Christiansted and Frederiksted (Figure 12.2).

The Early Period

Population growth in the islands has closely paralleled long-period economic cycles. During the heyday of sugar between 1773 and 1835, the population grew more than 50 per cent. From 1835 to 1917, however, the population declined by 40 per cent as a result of cumulative changes and misfortunes: natural disasters, emancipation, the decline in sugar profitability in St Croix, and the advent of steamships, which greatly reduced St Thomas's importance as an entrepôt

(Lewis, 1972). Persistent emigration was compounded by natural decreases (excess deaths over births) due to high rates of infant and child mortality. At the time of the US purchase of the islands in 1917, the economy was in the doldrums and unemployment ranged between 30 and 40 per cent (de Albuquerque and McElroy, 1985).

Mainland job opportunities provided by US affiliation, plus the negative impact on sugar produced by Prohibition on the mainland, fostered further emigration between 1917 and 1930. The population fell again by nearly one-fifth (see Table 12.6). The next two decades, however, witnessed the early beginning of a migration transition as the population expanded over 20 per cent. This growth was due to several factors: (1) the repeal of Prohibition which promoted the immigration of many Puerto Rican cane cutters; (2) significant infrastructure expansion begun in the Naval Administration (1917–31) which accelerated the inflow of British Virgin Islanders (Hill, 1971); (3) the New Deal activism embodied in the VICO programme to revitalize sugar and diversify the economy; and (4) the wartime construction of military installations – a submarine base in St Thomas and an airport in St Croix – when immigration restrictions were suspended and West Indians were recruited from the surrounding Eastern Caribbean islands (Green, 1972).

Growth and immigration persisted between 1950 and 1960 as the population increased another 20 per cent. This expansion was due to the early success of a new diversification strategy into tourism and light industry. During the 1950s, the USVI became the third fastest growing Caribbean tourism destination. The number of cruise ship calls increased from 15 to 126, and air arrivals rose ten-fold (McElroy and Tinsley, 1982: 29). The number of hotel facilities grew from 11 in 1946 to 84 by 1962 (Lewis, 1972: 124). By 1960, there were 52 new firms enjoying tax exemptions based on the 1949 Industrial Incentives Act modelled after FOMENTO's 1947 legislation in Puerto Rico.

The Development Decade and After

The 1960s proved to be a watershed for the necessary and inevitable modernization. Under the pro-business leadership of Governor Paiewonsky, the population more than doubled in response to the 'astonishing explosion in economic prosperity that took place within less than a decade' (Lewis, 1972: 122). Over 60 per cent of this population growth was due to the massive immigration of West Indian construction and service workers and, to a lesser extent, US mainland professionals and entrepreneurs (de Albuquerque and McElroy, 1982). They were attracted by a post-Castro tourism boom, the establishment of oil and alumina heavy industry complexes on St Croix, and related

Table 12.6. Total population of the United States Virgin Islands by island, 1890–1985.

Year	Virgin Islands Number	Virgin Islands % Change	St Croix Number	St Croix % Change	St John Number	St John % Change	St Thomas Number	St Thomas % Change
1890	32,786	0.1	19,783	7.3	984	−1.0	12,019	−16.5
1901	30,527	−6.9	18,590	−6.0	925	−6.0	11,012	−8.4
1911	27,086	−12.7	15,467	−16.8	941	1.7	10,678	−3.0
1917	26,051	−3.8	14,901	−3.7	959	1.9	10,191	−4.6
1930	22,012	−18.3	11,413	−23.4	765	−20.2	9,834	−3.5
1940	24,889	11.6	12,902	13.0	722	−5.6	11,265	14.6
1950	26,665	6.7	12,103	−6.2	749	3.7	13,813	22.6
1960	32,099	20.4	14,973	23.7	925	23.5	16,201	17.3
1970	75,151	134.1	35,942	140.0	1,924	108.0	37,285	130.1
1980	96,569	28.5	49,725	38.3	2,472	28.5	44,372	19.0
1981	98,300	1.8	50,800	2.2	2,480	0.3	45,020	1.5
1982	101,500	3.3	52,200	3.0	2,490	0.4	46,710	3.8
1983	103,700	2.2	53,800	2.9	2,590	4.0	47,310	1.3
1984	107,500	3.7	55,000	2.2	2,680	3.5	49,820	5.3
1985	110,800	3.1	55,300	0.5	2,840	6.0	52,660	5.7

Sources: 1. 1835–1980 from US Bureau of the Census, 1980 Population for the Virgin Islands of the United States.
2. 1981–85, US Virgin Islands Economic Indicators, Office of Policy Planning and Research, VI Department of Commerce, 1986.

infrastructure and housing construction. Between 1965–70, immigration averaged 4,000 annually, and augmented the insular population and labour force by 10–15 per cent per year.

It was a decade of truly unprecedented change. There were manifold increases in all indices of economic performance. The value of new construction rose ten-fold. Tax revenues increased seven-fold and public employment soared. Per capita income rose four-fold. The labour force tripled, the number of hotel rooms increased 2.5 times, and the stock of housing doubled. By 1970, the number of annual cruise ship calls exceeded 500, the number of tourists (hotel and cruise combined) approached one million, and total visitor spending reached 100 million per year (McElroy, 1975). While unemployment fell virtually to zero, the cost of living rose 25–30 per cent above that of the mainland.

The tourism bonanza was due to a variety of fortuitous factors. The internal advantages included: the unique Danish heritage of the towns, an excellent deepwater harbour (Charlotte Amalie) for cruise ships, duty-free status for low-cost bargains on liquor and European luxuries, and the privileges for US visitors associated with territorial status: special gift item/liquor customs exemptions, and the absence of language, currency, and passport barriers. The external advantages included rising US affluence and vacation demand, the availability of jet travel to the islands (1962), and the American embargo of Cuba.

The 1970s witnessed a sharp reduction in economic growth and increased immigration restrictions. The islands were buffeted by several US-induced recessions and severe inflationary pressures from OPEC's impact on transportation costs. New construction fell off drastically. Tourism problems were exacerbated by crowding, utility breakdowns, and rising crime. Unemployment reached double-digit levels and fiscal deficits matched by US. Congressional bailouts became routine. Since the deep 1981–82 recession, however, population growth has regained momentum, spurting above 3 per cent annually (see Table 12.6). This expansion is fuelled mainly by the in-migration of mainlanders on the heels of a renewed tourism/finance mini-boom sparked in part by political instability in other resort destinations and regions.

Urbanization–Suburbanization

The impact of the development decade is probably most visible in the striking redistribution of the population since 1960. For over 100 years (1855–1960), more than half the territory's inhabitants resided in the three main towns (see Table 12.7). The historical dominance of these towns structured the urban character of island life. According to US Census data, the urban–rural ratio, which had averaged close to 60/40

Table 12.7. Total population for towns and rural areas in the United States Virgin Islands by island, 1835–80.

Island/Area	Census year										
	1835	1855	1880	1901	1917	1930	1940	1950	1960	1970	1980
Virgin Islands	43,178	37,137	33,763	30,527	26,051	22,021	24,889	26,665	32,099	75,151	96,569
Urban	19,194	19,378	20,183	17,768	15,465	13,501	14,296	15,581	18,017	29,862	37,730
Rural	23,984	17,759	13,580	12,759	10,586	8,511	10,593	11,084	14,082	45,289	58,839
St Croix	26,081	22,862	18,430	18,590	14,901	11,413	12,902	12,103	14,973	35,942[1]	49,725
Christiansted	5,806	5,260	4,939	5,483	4,574	3,767	4,495	4,112	5,137	3,020	2,904
Frederiksted	2,317	2,957	3,480	3,745	3,144	2,698	2,498	1,961	2,177	1,531	1,046
Rural	18,558	14,645	10,011	9,362	7,183	4,948	8,407	7,991	9,836	28,759	40,310
St Thomas	14,022	12,560	14,389	11,012	10,191	9,834	11,265	13,813	16,201	37,285[1]	44,372[1]
Charlotte Amalie	11,071	11,161	11,764	8,540	7,747	7,036	9,801	11,469	12,880	15,977[2]	19,304[2]
Rural	2,951	1,399	2,625	2,472	2,444	2,798	1,464	2,344	3,321	14,862	16,057
St John	2,475	1,715	944	925	959	765	722	749	925	1,924	2,472
Rural	2,475	1,715	944	925	959	765	722	749	925	1,924	2,472

Sources: 1. US Bureau of the Census, 1917–80 Censuses of Population for the Virgin Islands of the United States.
2. McElroy and de Albuquerque (1981).

Notes: 1. Population of towns and rural areas do not add up to total island population because peri-urban areas and new urban areas were not included.
2. These are adjusted figures. Census estimates for Charlotte Amalie (with the town's boundaries being very narrowly defined) in 1970 and 1980 were 12,220 and 11,671 respectively.

between 1917 and 1960, dramatically reversed itself to a 40/60 rural imbalance between 1960 and 1970.

Even when a more liberal definition of urban is used – that is, less restrictive than the US Census minimum of 2,500 people – to include all the traditionally recognized urban areas like Cruz Bay in St John, the same urban-to-rural reversal is observed between 1960 and 1970 (McElroy and de Albuquerque, 1981). According to the adjusted data in Table 12.8, the urban–rural ratio, which averaged 66/34 between 1917 and 1960, abruptly changed direction after 1960, becoming 40/60 by 1970.

This rapid dispersal to the countryside represented a widespread pattern of suburbanization (in a small island not continental sense) as residential settlements in the USVI adjusted to the enormous changes unleashed by a population doubling. The process, while analogous to the familiar North American pattern, was different in that few 'suburbs' were typical in the North American sense, most homes being built by individual families and not developers. But like the North American pattern, the lower-income immigrants (West Indian) were crowded into the dense and noisy towns while affluent residents fled to the suburbs (de Albuquerque and McElroy, 1982). So extensive was this flight away from the towns that between 1960 and 1980 all three towns (if the narrow census boundaries are used for Charlotte Amalie) experienced declines.

Size and topography also played a role in the spatial assimilation of the 'country' bound population. This is evident from examining the different expressions of ruralization (suburbanization) in St Thomas and St Croix. For example, according to the adjusted data in Table 12.8, between 1960 and 1970 the urban population of St Thomas declined nearly 20 percentage points. In St Croix the drop was nearly 33 points. The greater suburbanization in St Croix is obviously due in part to its larger size, flatter topography, and hence cheaper real estate and construction costs since both islands had virtually the same population increase (21,000) over the decade.

In addition, the geographic character of suburbanization followed the familiar diffusion pattern found in Puerto Rico and the mainland. This involved the initial incorporation of urban fringe areas, and then a spilling into adjacent zones in a kind of metropolitan sprawl. For example, those districts that grew most rapidly in St Thomas were the two adjacent to Charlotte Amalie. In St Croix, the most populous new communities were those that ring the towns of Christiansted and Frederiksted. The other growth areas were located between these two, thereby forming one continuous narrow strip of urban settlement linking the two main towns (McElroy and de Albuquerque, 1981). These trends, in conjunction with the most recent data contained in

Table 12.8. Population distribution for urban and rural areas in the United States Virgin Islands by island, 1917–80[1]

| | Census data | | | | | | Adjusted data[3] | | | | | |
| | St Thomas | | St Croix | | St John[2] | | St Thomas | | St Croix | | St John | |
Year	% Urban	% Rural	% Urban	% Rural	% Urban	% Rural	% Urban	% Rural	% Urban	% Rural	% Urban	% Rural
1917	76.0	24.0	51.8	48.2	0.0	100.0	76.0	24.0	51.8	48.2	80.0	20.0
1930	71.5	28.5	56.6	43.4	0.0	100.0	71.5	28.5	56.6	43.4	72.9	27.1
1940	87.0	13.0	34.8	65.2	0.0	100.0	87.0	13.0	54.2	45.8	80.2	19.8
1950	83.0	17.0	34.0	66.0	0.0	100.0	83.0	17.0	50.2	49.8	78.0	22.0
1960	79.5	20.5	34.3	65.7	0.0	100.0	79.5	20.5	48.8	51.2	92.9	7.1
1970	42.9	57.1	10.2	89.8	0.0	100.0	60.1	39.9	15.6	84.4	96.2	3.8
1980	63.8	25.2	18.9	81.1	0.0	100.0	–	–	–	–	–	–

Sources: US Bureau of the Census, 1917–80 Censuses of Population for the Virgin Islands of the United States.

Notes: 1. Urban includes Charlotte Amalie in St Thomas and Christiansted and Frederiksted in St Croix. After 1930 Frederiksted is counted as rural because its population fell below 2,500, the US Census Bureau's threshold for urban classification. In 1980, Tutu in St Thomas was classified as urban.
2. There is no urban area on St John which has 2,500 inhabitants or more.
3. The adjusted data, which include all traditionally recognized island urban areas, assume that the numerical threshold of 2,500 does not adequately capture an urban milieu in an insular micro-state.

Table 12.8, suggest that the overall pattern of suburbanization is intensifying.

The flight out of the towns was fostered by a variety of factors. The first was the rising affluence derived from the economic boom. The second was the increased preference for detached housing coupled with the desire to escape the noise and bustle of the towns whose central business districts had become particularly crowded with shopping tourists. The third involved a deliberate government low-income housing island-wide dispersal strategy, and the sponsoring of a federally financed road-building programme. The fourth was the off-island demand for vacation and retirement homes in the secluded hillsides and beach fronts. Finally, there evolved a supportive network of banking–realty institutions that facilitated the financing of mortgages and the purchase of imported consumer durables and automobiles.

While suburban settlement has allowed the Virgin Islands to absorb massive population growth since 1960, overall densities have risen sharply. In 1985, St Thomas surpassed Barbados to post the highest population density (1,646 persons per square mile) in the Caribbean (de Albuquerque and McElroy, 1987); and these figures exclude the heavy daily influx of air and cruise ship visitors. Increasingly in the territory, such densities are associated with environmental erosion because of continuous development pressure up the hillsides, the disappearance of permanent streams, and the irreversible alteration of the coastline and local topography for tourism and related construction (Towle, 1985). These visible and unwanted spillovers will eventually damage the long-term viability of the tourism base.

Socio-economic Correlates of Urban Development

Table 12.9 assembles data on several selected indices of socio-economic change for the 1950–80 period. These reveal several expected trends. First, in most cases, the indices move in directions predicted by the modernization thesis. Second, by and large, urban–rural differences are minimal except where extraneous factors are operative. Had the data been based on figures adjusted to account for traditional urban areas, the discrepancies would become even less significant. Third, where differences do exist, they tend to have diminished over time.

To illustrate, between 1950–80 there have been marked increases in median school years completed, school enrolment, median family income, female labour force participation, and the proportion of the labour force in professional and technical occupations. Most of these increases took place during the development decade. The slight dip in manufacturing employment between 1970 and 1980 is partly due to the instability in the international oil industry, as well as reflective of

Table 12.9. Selected socio-economic indicators for the United States Virgin Islands population, 1950–80.

Indicator	1950			1960			1970			1980		
	Total	Urban	Rural	Total	Urban	Rural	Total	Urban	Rural	Total	Urban	Rural
Median age	22.0	21.3	23.0	22.7	20.0	21.7	23.0	24.0	22.7	22.5	21.3	23.3
Sex ratio[1]	96.2	86.7	111.3	98.5	90.8	109.3	97.5	96.8	100.4	91.7	88.2	94.1
Child–woman ratio[2]	565	536	644	797	762	849	560	548	564	415	428	406
Persons per household	3.3	3.4	3.3	3.6	3.7	3.6	3.4	3.3	3.5	3.4	3.4	3.4
% Living in diff. house 5 yrs ago	NA	NA	NA	NA	NA	NA	56.2	46.6	59.4	39.8	38.1	40.8
Median school years[3] completed (25 yrs +)	6.2	6.5	5.7	7.3	7.5	7.0	9.5	8.2	10.1	12.0	10.3	12.2
% Aged 16–17 enrolled in school	60.5	67.5	50.8	59.6	65.2	51.6	72.7	75.0	71.9	81.2	80.5	81.7
Median family income[4]	460	503	421	1,621	1,686	1,525	6,612	5,461	7,059	11,090	9,334	12,406
% Females 14+ in labour force[5]	32.9	35.3	29.0	39.2	43.7	32.8	50.0	53.5	48.8	54.5	54.9	54.3
% Employed in manuf.	5.6	5.1	6.2	8.0	6.4	10.1	9.1	4.9	10.5	8.8	3.8	11.9
% in professional and technical occup.[6]	7.3	8.0	6.3	8.3	8.1	8.6	11.4	9.6	12.0	13.3	10.3	15.2
% Unemployed	3.2	4.0	2.1	3.4	4.0	2.6	4.0	4.0	4.0	6.2	6.4	6.1
% Born outside the Virgin Islands	26.4	22.9	31.4	36.6	33.2	41.0	53.5	50.3	54.5	49.7	47.0	57.4

Sources: US Bureau of the Census, 1950–80 Population Censuses for the Virgin Islands of the United States.

Notes: 1. Number of males per 100 females.
2. The number of children 0–4 divided by the number of women aged 15–44 and multiplied by 100.
   The child–woman ratio is an indirect measure of fertility.
3. For persons 14 years and older in 1960.
4. For persons in 1950.
5. For females 16 years or more in 1970 and 1980.
6. For 1980 includes professional specialty occupations and technologists and technicians.

the dominating importance today of tourism and public sector employment in the insular economy.

Another cluster of variables demonstrates the sizeable influence of heavy immigration, most notably the substantial rise in fertility (child–woman ratio) during the 1960s (a remarkable 40 per cent), the doubling of the proportion of persons born outside the USVI (54 per cent in 1970), and the increasing proportion of persons of working age (15–64) in the population.

Across most socio-economic dimensions, urban–rural (really suburban) differences have narrowed. This was the case for unemployment rates, increases in proportion foreign born, female labour force participation and school enrolment, and decreases in fertility, median age, and residential mobility. In other instances, significant urban–rural differences emerged or were reversed after 1970. For example, by 1980, rural areas clearly contained more residents in high-income families who were foreign born, in professional and technical jobs, and who possessed high educational and low fertility levels. These data tend to describe the likely effects of the suburbanization process, as the more affluent residents (and mainland retirees) leap-frogged after 1960 from the towns to the suburbs.

Conclusion

The post-war patterns of urbanization–suburbanization in Puerto Rico and the USVI represent, in broad brush, classic case studies of large and small Caribbean islands responding to the pressures of modernization. Both these US dependencies experienced generally the same contours of political development and economic transformation. In both cases, restructuring followed the same capital-by-incentive, export-led model of growth, with substantial infrastructural and income support from the US federal treasury. In both cases, domestic agriculture was virtually destroyed, dependence on the local and federal government increased rapidly, and the scarred landscape became a visible reminder of the sprawling over-urbanization that accompanied development, despite the availability of planning machinery (Lewis, 1972: 142).

There were clear differences, however. What distinguished Puerto Rico was: (1) emigration to the metropole in classic Caribbean style; (2) extensive rural–urban migration; (3) the associated build-up of traditional urban centres; (4) followed by increasing suburbanization into adjacent areas. What characterized the Virgin Islands was: (1) the traditional urban ambience; (2) the concentrated pace of growth; (3) the migration reversal; and (4) the early accommodation of these intense development thrusts through a sharp residential exodus to what were previously rural areas, but which became, for all intents and purposes, suburbs.

Likewise, some of the major consequences of modernization for the two insular societies were different. In Puerto Rico, these included chronic unemployment, expanded welfarism, and the acceleration of mainland emigration. In the Virgin Islands, the aftermath included intense crowding, inter-group tensions, dizzying real-estate speculation, multiple job-holding to keep up with inflation, and a legacy of catch-up planning and environmental restoration. The most likely future directions for urbanization processes in these two US affiliated Caribbean islands suggest trends similar to the past but at more modest levels. Any significant alteration in political status, however, like opting for statehood or independence, could alter this course in the future.

REFERENCES

Boswell, T. (1978) 'Internal migration in Puerto Rico prior to economic development', *Social and Economic Studies*, 27 (4), 434–63.

Boyer, W. (1983) *America's Virgin Islands: A History of Human Rights and Wrongs*, Durham, North Carolina: Carolina Academic Press.

Carnoy, M. (1970) 'The quality of education examination performance and urban–rural income differences in Puerto Rico', *Comparative Education Review*, 14 (3), 335–49.

Christopulos, D. (1974) 'Puerto Rico in the twentieth century: a historical survey', 123–163, in: Lopez, A. and Petras, J. (eds) *Puerto Rico and Puerto Ricans: Studies in History and Society*, New York: John Wiley and Sons.

Cross, M. (1979) *Urbanization and Urban Growth in the Caribbean*, London: Cambridge University Press.

Daubon, R. and Robinson, W. (1975) 'Changes in consumption patterns during economic development: Puerto Rico, 1940–1970', *Social and Economic Studies*, 24 (4), 420–32.

de Albuquerque, K., Mader, P. and Stinner, W. (1976) 'Modernization, delayed marriage, and fertility in Puerto Rico: 1950 to 1970', *Social and Economic Studies*, 25 (1), 55–65.

de Albuquerque, K. and McElroy, J. (1981) 'Residential patterns in United States Virgin Islands, 1917–1976', *South Atlantic Urban Studies*, 5: 287–303.

—— (1982) 'West Indian migration to the US Virgin Islands', *International Migration Review*, 16 (1), 61–101.

—— (1985) 'Race and ethnicity in the US Virgin Islands', *Ethnic Groups*, 6, 41–96.

—— (1987) 'Economic and demographic transformation of the US Virgin Islands, 1917–1987'. Paper presented to the Midwest Association of Latin Americanists, DePaul University, November.

Davis, K. (1969): *World Urbanization 1950–1970 Volume 1*. Institute for International Studies, University of California, Berkeley.

Demas, W. (1965) *The Economics of Development in Small Countries with Special Reference to the Caribbean*, Montreal: McGill University.

Dietz, J. (1986) *Economic History of Puerto Rico: Institutional Change and Capitalist Development*, Princeton, New Jersey: Princeton University Press.

Green, J.W. (1972) 'The British West Indian alien labor problem in the Virgin Islands', *Caribbean Studies*, **12** (1), 56–75.

Grusky, S. (1987) 'The changing role of the US Military in Puerto Rico', *Social and Economic Studies*, **36** (3), 37–76.

Hill, V. (1971) *Rise to Recognition: An Account of Virgin Islanders from Slavery to Self-Government*, St Thomas: St Thomas Graphics.

Hope, K.R. (1986) *Economic Development in the Caribbean*, New York: Praeger.

Leary, P. (1988) 'Political status and political status options: a brief introduction', St Thomas, VI, University of the Virgin Islands, Bureau of Public Administration.

Lewis, G. (1972) *The Virgin Islands: A Caribbean Lilliput*, Evanston, Illinois: Northwestern University Press.

Lopez, A. (1974) 'The Puerto Rican diaspora: a survey', 316–46, in: Lopez, A. and Petras, J. (eds) *Puerto Rico and Puerto Ricans: Studies in History and Society*, New York: John Wiley and Sons.

McElroy, J. (1975) *The Virgin Islands Economy*, St Thomas: VI Planning Office.

McElroy, J. and de Albuquerque, K. (1981) 'Residential patterns in the United States Virgin Islands, 1917–1970', *South Atlantic Urban Studies*, **5**: 287–303.

McElroy, J. and de Albuquerque, K. (1985) 'Federal perceptions and reality', *The Review of Regional Studies*, **14** (3), 47–55.

—— (1988) 'The migration transition in small northern and eastern Caribbean states', *International Migration Review*, **22** (3), 30–58.

McElroy, J., Potter, B. and Towle, E. (1989) 'Challenges for sustainable development in small Caribbean islands', in: Beller, W. (ed.) *Sustainable Development and Environmental Management of Small Islands*, New York: Praeger (forthcoming).

McElroy, J. and Tinsley, J. (1982) 'United States Virgin Islands', 23–65, in: Seward, S. and Spinrad, B. (eds) *Tourism in the Caribbean: The Economic Impact*, Ottawa: International Development Research Centre.

Miller, R. (1979) *The Economy of the Virgin Islands*, Washington, DC: Department of Interior, Office of Territorial Affairs.

Mintz, Sidney (1956) 'Canamelar', 314–417, in: Steward, J.H. *et al.* (eds) *The People of Puerto Rico*, Urbana: University of Illinois Press.

Moscoso, T. and Barton, H. (1986) 'Commonwealth and the economics of development', 49–52 in: Falk, P. (ed.) *The Political Status of Puerto Rico*, Lexington, Massachusetts: Lexington Books.

Pico, R. (1974) *The Geography of Puerto Rico*, Chicago: Aldine.

Safa, H. (1974) *The Urban Poor of Puerto Rico*, New York: Holt, Rinehart and Winston.

Schwirian, K. and Rico-Velasco, J. (1971) 'The residential distribution of status groups in Puerto Rico's metropolitan areas', *Demography*, **8**, 81–90.

Segal, A. (1975) *Population Policies in the Caribbean*, Lexington, Massachusetts: D.C. Heath.

Senior, C. (1953) 'Migration and Puerto Rico's population problem', *Annals of the American Academy of Political Science*, 285: 130–36.

Stinner, W., de Albuquerque, K. and Mader, P. (1975) 'Metropolitan dominance and fertility change in Puerto Rico: 1950–1970', *Social and Economic Studies*, 24 (4), 433–44.

Towle, E.L. (1985) 'The island microcosm', 589–749, in: Clark, J.R. (ed.) *Coastal Resources Management: Development Case Studies*, Washington, DC: National Park Service.

US Bureau of the Census *1950–1980 Censuses of Population for Puerto Rico*. Washington, DC: GPO.

—— *1917–1980 Censuses of Population for the Virgin Islands of the United States*, Washington, DC: GPO.

—— (1984) *Current Population Report*, Series P-26, No. 84–51-C, Washington, DC: GPO.

Vaughan, M.K. (1974) 'Tourism in Puerto Rico', 271–95, in: Lopez, A. and Petras, J. (eds) *Puerto Rico and Puerto Ricans: Studies in History and Society*, New York: John Wiley and Sons.

Villamil, J. (1976) 'Urban planning in Puerto Rico', 42–51, in: Antonini, G. (ed.) *Urban and Regional Planning in the Caribbean*, Gainesville, Florida: UNICA.

Virgin Islands Department of Commerce (1986) *US Virgin Islands Economic Indicators*, St Thomas: Office of Policy Planning and Research.

Weisskoff, R. (1985) *Factories and Foodstamps: The Puerto Rican Model of Development*, Baltimore: Johns Hopkins University Press.

Wells, (1969) *The Modernization of Puerto Rico*, Cambridge, Massachusetts: Harvard University Press.

[13]
Caribbean Urban Development and Planning: Conclusions

Robert B. Potter

The chapters in this volume demonstrate the importance of urbanization within the Caribbean. Notwithstanding the fundamental role played by agriculture in the region, towns and cities have been pivotal to its history. During the colonial–mercantile period urban places acted as centres of commercialization, accumulation and control. Since 1945, although urban areas have become the preferred locus for new developments in manufacturing and tourism, towns and cities have grown demographically at a pace which has far exceeded that at which employment opportunities have been created. It is by virtue of restricted production capabilities that Caribbean urban development can be regarded as quite different from that experienced by the developed world during the eighteenth and nineteenth centuries. On the other hand, with regard to both individual and collective consumption, there are signs of similarity between Caribbean and Western towns and cities. In the present volume, for instance, Kingston is described as a symbol of urban sophistication and modernity, representing a transplanted European town which has of late been reconstructed along American lines. It is the juxtaposition of the processes of divergence and convergence as discussed in the opening chapter that is setting the scene for distinctive patterns of Caribbean urban development in the late twentieth century (Armstrong and McGee, 1985).

The majority of contributors to this volume stress the importance of dependency. Both by virtue of their histories and their size, the nations of the Caribbean have not been in the past, and are by no means today, the masters of their own destinies. It is clearly necessary to think of different types of dependency, ranging from the socialist dependency of Cuba as described in this volume, to the more conventional capitalist dependency of the member states of the Eastern Caribbean. At the global scale, the states of 'development' and 'underdevelopment' exist as corollaries. The same is true within Third World nations where urban and rural are organically linked.

In considering in detail the process of urban change and development in the Caribbean region, a number of other commonalities emerge. The principal similarity is, of course, the occurrence of urbanization in advance of industrial development. Owing to the over-inflated labour markets existing in such countries, people have endeavoured to create their own jobs. This has given rise to the evolution of the low capital, high labour, small-scale activities of the informal sector (Santos, 1979). Several of the authors contributing to the essays in this volume agree that programmes of industrialization by invitation have not been an unqualified success. At best they have resulted in economic growth rather than genuine economic progress, while at worst they have provided too few jobs.

Dependent urbanization has also been associated with the over-concentration of activities and population into a limited portion of the national territory, normally the coastal belt. One contributor notes that some 66 per cent of all settlement in Dominica is coastal. Such an unequal structure not only involves the distribution of population, but more so the provision of services in both the public and private domains. Complex and sustained urban–rural flows serve to maintain these sharp spatial polarities. This appears to be particularly the case in the small islands such as those of the Eastern Caribbean and Barbados, where it is possible for people to live in the rural areas and commute to work in town. But even in certain of the larger islands, extensive axial belts over which large volumes of daily movement occur can be recognized, as in Jamaica. In this regard, several of the principal features of dependent urbanization identified in Figure 1.3 have been vindicated by the accounts contained in this volume, although size of territory is obviously a crucial mediating variable. The other type of migration has been that which has seen nationals leaving the country altogether, and in Guyana, Jamaica and the Eastern Caribbean, the emigration of professional groups and an associated brain drain seem to be giving considerable grounds for concern.

Another general feature is the neglect of agricultural production for domestic consumption. Agriculture as an activity is generally held in low regard, with little effort being made to provide for the basic needs of the local population. It is frequently maintained that the education system has served to reinforce these fundamentally anti-rural and pro-urban perspectives. The rise of tourism, which might conceivably have led to the amelioration of this problem, has apparently exacerbated it by pulling in huge quantities of imported foods to satiate the desires of visitors for the kinds of foods they eat at home.

Recent developments appear to be replacing old forms of dependency with new but nonetheless virulent ones. Much of the recent urbanization chronicled in the chapters of this book has been tourism-led, as for example in the cases of the Netherlands Antilles and Bahamas. It has led to what has been described as the 'Miamiazation' of San Juan in Puerto Rico. A recent book examined tourism and its impact on small developing countries judged it to be an 'ambiguous alternative' (Britton and Clark, 1987). As well as the reasons cited in relation to the depression of agriculture, several authors argue that tourism brings few benefits for the majority of the population owing to the normally high levels of foreign ownership of plant and low tourist multipliers. This is closely related to the fact that tourist complexes are frequently developed in the existing capital city regions, and this is especially so in small territories. Thereby, such changes often seemingly serve to bolster existing spatial and social divides.

A further important point that emerges from the chapters is the tendency towards suburbanization that has occurred within Caribbean territories since the late 1960s and early 1970s. Thus, several commentators talk of the distinction between urban and suburban as currently being more salient than that between urban and rural (for example, Puerto Rico, Barbados). A limited form of polarization reversal (Richardson, 1980) appears to be characterizing at least some of the islands, such as Puerto Rico. This appears mainly to have taken the form of spread within the metropolitan region. Thus, 'concentrated deconcentration' is occurring rather than genuine decentralization and intra-regional convergence. There is some evidence that affluent middle-class groups are moving out of the city toward the suburbs in a sectoral manner rather as in North American cities (Hoyt, 1939). This sort of development, which characterizes many Latin American cities (Amato, 1970; Griffin and Ford, 1980; Lowder, 1986; Morris, 1976) can be witnessed in Port of Spain, San Juan, Nassau and elsewhere. But in other respects, the morphology of Caribbean towns and cities fits poorly with Western models and norms and strong elements of the colonial imprint can be seen to remain.

Rising land prices, often affected by tourism and by speculative land holding, is an issue affecting a large number of islands and has certainly been instrumental in the French West Indies, Puerto Rico, the Virgin Islands and Grenadines. The demand for urban housing has far exceeded the ability and willingness of governments to supply dwellings of a suitable type, leading to problems of housing quality, shanty towns and squatter developments. It is facts such as these that have resulted in more than one of the writers in this volume referring to 'uncontrolled urbanization' in the Caribbean region.

This leads to a discussion of broad areas of agreement among the contributors concerning the role, status and achievements of planning in the Caribbean. The first point concerns national economic development planning which in most circumstances seems to have taken a basically top-down and centre outward philosophy as its starting point. In this connection, despite experiments in Guyana, Grenada and Jamaica with socialist paths to development, Cuba appears to be the only country that has taken decisive action to promote genuine deconcentration and decentralization. As the chapter on Cuba exemplifies, efforts to reduce Havana's supremacy and to integrate town and country have been witnessed by an emphasis on the prime role of agriculture, rural new towns and the clustering of population around well-distributed health and educational facilities. In this connection, the use of classical central place ideas in the promotion of more equitable systems of national settlement distribution has clearly been of significance. This is true in the case of both Cuba and Barbados, for instance. The fact that the approach has had some success under the socialist formulation of Cuba acts as a corroboration of the long-standing assertion that the normative foundations of central place theory are based on an implied system of state control of the process of distribution (Potter, 1982).

A general point of agreement appears to be that despite Caribbean countries developing systems of physical development or spatial land use planning in the post-war period, there is an apparent lack of concern for spatial issues within the region among those with real executive power. Closely connected to this is the assertion by a number of contributors that physical planning is weak and has assumed a subordinate status relative to other types of planning in Caribbean countries. Thus, in connection with planning in Jamaica and Trinidad as well as elsewhere, it is suggested that the aims of physical planning have been poorly linked to the macro-objectives of national development plans. Others stress what they see as the fundamental issue of power, arguing that planners in the Caribbean have little real authority in relation to their political masters, so that patronage and influence deflect attention from what really needs to be done. Thus, what ostensibly are well-considered and well-thought-out plans on paper, remain just that – paper plans that are never in any real danger of being implemented.

The understaffing of town and country planning offices is a further area of concern in the region, as is the fact that until recently, so many planners were trained overseas (Potter, 1985). Collectively, the essays in the present book emphasize how small countries such as those of the Eastern Caribbean are in just as much need of highly qualified planning officers as their larger counterparts. In planning as in development as a whole, the small countries of the Caribbean suffer from marked diseconomies of scale. Hudson (1984) has suggested that Caribbean countries need to create a team of peripatetic planners, while at the macro-level, there is the need for economic and political integration to increase local effective demand and market size.

Systems of patronage seem also to be vital in relation to planning for the provision of housing in Caribbean urban areas. This is well exemplified by the accounts on Guyana and Jamaica presented in this book. Until quite recently, housing seems to have been another area where the nations of the Caribbean have been slow to learn from the mistakes of others. Thus, government after government has invested large public sums in a few expensive and essentially symbolic schemes, often consisting of high-rise blocks which are not affordable to the poor, and which may well be culturally inappropriate, thereby leading to alienation and classic oppressive housing conditions. The writers on the French West Indies and the Eastern Caribbean in the present volume stress this. It has only quite recently come to be fully appreciated that the state must spend more time helping the poor to help themselves through systems of aided self-help and upgrading, as is shown now to be starting in Barbados (see also Potter, 1989b).

In conclusion, post-war urbanization and development in the Caribbean stress the conceptual efficacy and appropriateness of the dependency model of development, rather than models of dualism (Rostow, 1960; Hirschman, 1958) which are associated with top-down systems of change. As noted in Potter (1989a), it was a Chicago-trained economist, Andre Frank, who did much to promote a global perspective to development studies. His principal ideas were outlined in *Capitalism and Underdevelopment in Latin America* (Frank, 1969) where he argued that the condition of South American and West Indian countries was not the outcome of a failure to develop, but a reflection of the manner of their incorporation into the international system of capitalism. Thus, development and underdevelopment are linked states, not a dichotomy which is to be overcome by doing the technically 'correct' thing. In the Caribbean, the local variant of dependency is the 'plantation economy', which has come to be associated with a state that Beckford (1972) has characterized as *persistent poverty*. Surplus value has been extracted from peasant farmers, field workers and the like, and successively moved up the economic chain via processes of unequal exchange and terms of trade. This explains why from the fifteenth century onward, the expansion of capitalism has been synonymous with colonialism and underdevelopment, and Caribbean urban places became points of administrative control and commercial nodes for the transhipment of social surplus product to Europe. Spatially and socially polarized patterns of dependent urbanization have resulted.

Such outcomes can be judged only in political terms. It is, of course, virtually impossible for small dependent countries like those of the

Caribbean to cut themselves off from the economic mainstream. But it can be posited that if genuine processes of development and change are to be fostered in the region, the basic or everyday needs of the population at large must be stressed. In so doing, the social welfare of the rural periphery must be accorded a high priority, so as to raise the overall quality of life (Potter, 1989a). The need is for integrated urban–rural programmes of development, that is, programmes which consider carefully the balances established between rural and urban, large and small, production- and consumption-oriented, indigenous and exogenous imperatives. Above all, perhaps, in considering Caribbean urban development and planning, it must be appreciated that social criteria are as important as pure economic circumstances.

REFERENCES

Armstrong, W. and McGee, T.G. (1985) *Theatres of Accumulation: Studies in Asian and Latin American Urbanization,* London: Methuen.

Amato, P. (1970) 'Elitism and settlement patterns in the Latin American city', *Journal of the American Institute of Planners,* **36**, 96–105.

Beckford, G. (1972) *Persistent Poverty: Underdevelopment in Plantation Economies of the Third World,* New York: Oxford University Press.

Britton, S. and Clark, W.C. (1987) *Ambiguous Alternative: Tourism in Small Underdeveloped Countries,* Fiji: University of the South Pacific Press.

Frank, A.G. (1969) *Capitalism and Underdevelopment in Latin America,* New York: Monthly Review Press.

Griffin, E. and Ford, L. (1980) 'A model of Latin American city structure', *Geographical Review,* **70**, 397–422.

Hirschman, A.O. (1958): *The Strategy of Economic Development,* New Haven, Connecticut: Yale University Press.

Hudson, B. (1984) 'Human resources for physical planning in Caribbean territories'. Paper presented to the Regional Conference of Physical Planners, Mona: University of the West Indies, Jamaica.

Hoyt, H. (1939) *The Structure and Growth of Residential Neighbourhoods in American Cities,* Washington, DC: Federal Housing Association.

Lowder, S. (1986) *Inside Third World Cities,* London: Croom Helm.

Morris, A. (1976) 'Urban growth patterns in Latin America with illustrations from Caracas', *Urban Studies,* **15**, 299–312.

Potter, R.B. (1982) *The Urban Retailing System,* Aldershot: Gower Press.

Potter, R.B. (1985) *Urbanization and Planning in the Third World: Spatial Perceptions and Public Participation,* London: Croom Helm and New York: St Martin's.

Potter, R.B. (1989a) 'Rural–urban interaction in Barbados and the Southern Caribbean: patterns and processes of dependent development in small countries', ch. 9, in: Potter, R.B. and Unwin, T. (eds), *The Geography of Urban–Rural Interaction in Developing Countries,* London and New York: Routledge.

Potter, R.B. (1989b) 'Urban housing in Barbados, West Indies', *Geographical Journal*, 155, 82–94.

Richardson, H.W. (1980) 'Polarization reversal in developing countries'. *Papers of the Regional Science Association*, 45, 67–85.

Rostow, W.W. (1960) *The Stages of Economic Growth: A Non-Communist Manifesto*, London: Cambridge University Press.

Santos, M. (1979) *The Shared Space: The Two Circuits of the Urban Economy in Underdeveloped Countries*, London: Methuen.

Index

323